THE IRWIN SERIES IN ECONOMICS

CONSULTING EDITOR

LLOYD G. REYNOLDS
YALE UNIVERSITY

BOOKS IN THE IRWIN SERIES IN ECONOMICS

ECONOMICS: AN ANALYTICAL APPROACH

DEDICATION

This book is respectfully dedicated to all the members of the Departments of Economics and Industrial Management of Purdue University and to the continued growth and professional attainment of the community of friendly scholars which they represent and of which the authors are privileged to be a part.

ECONOMICS: AN ANALYTICAL APPROACH

BY

RALPH K. DAVIDSON Ph.D.

VERNON L. SMITH Ph.D.

JAY W. WILEY Ph.D.

ALL OF THE ECONOMICS DEPARTMENT
PURDUE UNIVERSITY

1962 · Revised Edition

RICHARD D. IRWIN, INC.

HOMEWOOD, ILLINOIS

PREFACE

The current revision of this textbook was made with the thought in mind that the authors would accomplish three things: They would rectify as much as possible any errors of fact or logic which appeared in the first edition of the book. They would add certain materials which various users of the text have suggested to them as important matters for inclusion in *Economics: An Analytical Approach.* They would bring up to date the tables and other data which refer to the current scene.

With these purposes in mind, the text has become a trifle longer than the original text. Added material included the appendix to Chapter 4, on stock versus flow factors involved in price determination for durable goods, a fuller description of monopoly, monopolistic competition, and oligopoly, an additional production function for a batch process, derivation of an industry supply curve, and a short discussion of the consequences of technological change in agriculture. All this was provided by Professor Smith. Professor Wiley introduced a brief analysis of the current balance of payments problem of the United States and related simple economic growth models to the problems of economic development. Professor Davidson added a summary discussion of national income statistics and wrote an entire new chapter on money, income, and employment in which the analysis of changes in money supply and its consequences for real income in an economy helped throw light on the controversial topic of cost-push inflation. The new chapter includes a model and its development which was influenced by a paper by George Horwich and V. L. Smith, "A Reconsideration of Aggregate General Equilibrium Theory." The original paper was produced at the Purdue University School of Industrial Management during the year 1959.

A major reorganization of the order in which materials in the book are presented also was undertaken. Chapters 16 to 22 of the first edition have become Chapters 7 to 13 in the revised edition. Similarly, Chapters 7 to 15 are now Chapters 14 to 18 and 20 to 23, with a new Chapter 19 added.

The authors wish to thank the many friendly correspondents who have suggested changes and additions to the text. We are especially grateful to Gerald Cummings for his careful criticism of many parts of the first edition and his thoughtful suggestions for changes which might be made. These economists have been the inspiration for many of the changes which were actually made. However, the authors hold only themselves to blame for the corrections in content which did not appear and for any errors in presentation which do appear.

RALPH K. DAVIDSON
VERNON L. SMITH
JAY W. WILEY

West Lafayette, Indiana
January, 1962

CONTENTS

LIST OF ILLUSTRATIONS

xiv · LIST OF ILLUSTRATIONS

LIST OF TABLES

Chapter 1

INTRODUCTION

1.1. *Human Wants and the Scarcity of Goods*

The study of economic science has as its starting point the observation that there is a fundamental inequality between people's wants and the material goods available for the satisfaction of these wants. Although differing degrees of acquisitiveness have been exhibited in different civilizations, it appears indisputable that human wants can be regarded as insatiable. At no time in our own society has our economic system had sufficient resources to produce all the goods that would be needed to satisfy everyone. Wants, W, have been and remain greater than the quantity of goods, Q, available for the satisfaction of these wants. This basic empirical law of economics can be expressed mathematically in terms of the simple inequality, $W > Q$. Furthermore, due to the seemingly infinite expansibility of W, there is no expectation that Q will ever approach equality with W.

The "law of scarcity," $W > Q$, is the most fundamental and universal in economics. The immediate consequence of this law is that man has to devise means by which his society is to determine how and in what amounts its scarce resources are to be allocated among the variety of possible want-satisfying goods which can be produced. One means of obtaining a solution to this choice problem is through a free *pricing system*. Under this type of economic organization prices are used to establish a system of priorities for the determination of what and how much shall be produced and how the resulting products are to be distributed. This book will be devoted to a study of this type of economic organization. In the course of this study it is well not to lose sight of the fact that the law of scarcity is the motivating principle from which all economic activity arises. Without scarcity there would be no allocation problem, no need for a pricing system, and no need for the economic institutions that have arisen in connection with the pricing system. Indeed, there would be no need for the study of eco-

1

nomics, for economic phenomena would not exist under such hypothetical conditions.

As man has struggled with the problem of scarcity in his efforts to better himself and the society of which he is a member, he has developed a complex, highly interrelated social organization. That aspect of social organization which is known as the *economic system* is concerned with the management of the scarce goods of society in a manner designed to bring about maximum material welfare. Just what "maximum welfare" is is impossible to define without taking into account and accepting the goals which a certain economy has. For instance, maximum welfare may be thought of as the achievement of maximum material production; the highest efficiency in the employment of resources; superior allocation of resources among competing alternative uses; equity in the distribution of income; or stability in economic society which avoids the changes in production, employment, and prices of the cycle of prosperity and depression or of rising or falling prices. It may include security for all in the certainty that there will continue to be a market for their efforts and the products they turn out with those efforts, and a degree of growth in productive capacity. In a democratic society, all of these would be measured in terms of the aspirations of the people as a whole.

Not only is it difficult to define the goal of maximization, but the aspects of that goal, as we have outlined them, are, to a certain extent, inconsistent with each other. Within the economic system, choices must be made among alternatives. Does society want security? Does it want growth? Does it want efficiency? Equity in distribution of income? Effective allocation of resources? Economics involves the making of choices. Within the economic system decisions are being made continuously which determine the extent to which the economy is being organized to achieve a portion of each of the alternative goals.

An important part of the organization of the economic system in working toward the achievement of broad socioeconomic objectives is its role as a communication machine, that is as a generator of data. These data include prices, costs, wage payments, interest rates, and the like, which are vital to decision making in the business firm, and by individuals, agencies of government, and other units within the economic system. Most of the consumption decisions of individuals and the production decisions of firms must be based in part upon knowledge of prices and costs. In our introduction to economic analysis we shall study some of the forces and factors which determine the values of these variables.

We shall also be concerned with the decision problems of the individual business. One of our major concerns will be to show how technical data and economic data must be combined to reach production decisions. As a generator of economic data, the economic system helps provide the information which, combined with technical data, is a basis for production decisions. In turn, the results of the actions taken by business firms react upon the economic system and change such economic variables as prices, incomes, and other economic data generated by the economy.

We should point out that not all of the decisions which affect the functioning of the economic system are made on the basis of prices. In fact, the underlying framework for economic decisions is established in a different fashion. The very beliefs which we express when we indicate that we "must" have new automobiles, variety in food, comfortable homes, and all of the other paraphernalia of life are made by us in terms of the culture in which we live and the institutions which we uphold. The requirements of the economy may also be dictated by authority, the consequence of political decisions, such as the decision to have protective tariffs against low-cost imports or to maintain "free" public schools. The operations of the economic system are made possible because we accept rules—rules of social behavior and rules of political law. Without them the entire process of exchange, which is fundamental to economic organization, would be impossible.

However, economics as a separate branch of social science does not attempt to explain the full social process. It accepts the social framework within which the economic system exists. We view economics as *a study of the manner in which, and the institutions through which, an economic system, and the individuals composing it, effect an allocation of scarce means to alternative competitive ends.* Included in this view of economics is the problem of enforced idleness of men and machines, that is, their allocation between producing and undesired unemployment, and we will spend a considerable amount of time analyzing the determination of the general level of income and employment. From this point of view the determination of the ends is not strictly an economic problem. The desired ends are presumably selected by the people or the government, and, as we all know, the selection often is not made on the basis of scientific analysis, and there may be wide disagreement concerning the desirability of certain goals, such as stable prices, or high employment. However, there is widespread agreement concerning the economic analysis which is used to analyze the cost of achieving any certain goal. Irrespective of the economist's opinion concerning the goal, the economic analysis itself is the same; there is not one economic analysis for free traders, another for those supporting tariffs, or one economic analysis for the AFL-CIO and another for the National Association of Manufacturers. There is one economic analysis for all.

1.2. Illustrations of Economic Problems

It is not our purpose to collect or classify various definitions of economics, and perhaps the best way to acquaint the student with what economics is all about is through a few illustrations of economic problems. For the economy as a whole, how is the nation's output of steel, for example, to be allocated among all the competing uses of steel, such as automobiles, ships, aircraft, refrigerators, buildings, rockets, and so forth? At any one time there are limited quantities of steel available, and some means must be used to allocate this scarce resource, steel, among competing ends. How is the nation's available productive land to be allocated among competing uses to which it may be put, such as producing timber, wheat, corn, grass, or to be used as building sites, public parks, roads, air terminals, and so forth? For the economy as a whole these are economic problems which need to be solved in order that resources may be used as efficiently as possible.

An individual consumer is also faced with an economic problem. How is he to allocate the expenditure of his income (scarce means) among the alternative goods and services (alternative ends) that he may desire to satisfy his material wants? How is the individual to allocate his time (a scarce means) between acquiring an income and enjoying leisure? How is the student to allocate his scarce time among the alternative ends, such as sleeping, eating, studying, leisure, and various pursuits of pleasure?

Businesses face extremely complex allocation problems. For example, how is a business firm to allocate its limited financial resources to different possible products that might be produced and among different techniques of production that might be employed?

In the area of engineering, the engineer, whether he is concerned with production or design, is rarely confronted with a wholly engineering problem, that is, a problem concerned wholly with the analysis of physical systems independently of the problem's economic setting. Thus the civil or structures engineer has a very clear engineering objective in the design of a bridge—to design the bridge so that it does not fail under traffic and wind loads. But there are thousands of possible ways of achieving this objective, using different designs, materials, and methods of construction, each involving a different total cost. The task of the bridge builder is not only to achieve the engineering objective of building a bridge that will not fail, but to do it at least cost— which is an economic problem.

1.3.   The Law of Scarcity and Specialization

One of the consequences of the law of scarcity is that we attempt to find ways to circumvent it. The principal means of doing this is by specialization and exchange. Each of us is a specialist, producing certain goods and services and exchanging the product for the production of others. By specialization, rather than self-sufficiency, we greatly increase our total production. The advantages of specialization may be summarized as follows:

1. Each party to a system of specialization may turn to the task for which it is best suited. One area of land is used for cattle grazing, another for cotton cultivation. One country turns out, for international trade, the products of heavy industry, another light manufactures, another raw material. One individual works as a typist, another as an engineer, another as a farmer. This generalization does not hold true universally. Some of us are square pegs in round holes. Some of us become Jacks-of-all-trades. However, the general tendency to follow the most productive lines of endeavor holds valid.

2. As we specialize, we learn to do well those things in which we have much practice. There is acquired learning and dexterity, which also adds to productivity. This is as true for a nation, from which comes the most efficient production of certain products (e.g., watches from Switzerland), as it is for an individual.

3. By specialization, we make possible the employment of machinery and the combination of resources in the most suitable relationship with each other for the turning out of products efficiently. It is hard to conceive of a large industrial plant which produces everything. Even the requirement for flexibility and adaptability for changing from one product line to another forces the technical decisions as to the manner of production to be made in a fashion which is inconsistent with the most efficient production of any one article from a plant.

Specialization, however, requires exchange. We cannot specialize in production if we are unable to dispose of the surplus we turn out beyond our own needs, that is, to exchange our surplus for the products which others have produced and which we require but do not produce ourselves. Consequently a system of prices prevails, a means for measuring the alternatives which are open to us as purchasers and as producers. The study of the pricing system is one of the principal areas in economic analysis. The study of the determinants of price, demand and supply, will occupy us for some time.

1.4. Diminishing Utility and Diminishing Returns

When we speak of the insatiability of human wants we do not mean that each individual in society wants an unlimited quantity of any one thing. Instead, it is the multiplicity of human wants to which we refer. In fact, our enjoyment of additional units of any good diminishes as we possess more and more of it. The term "utility" is used to indicate the power of a good to satisfy wants. The utilization of additional units of a good gives additional utility or else we would not use them, but the added utility becomes smaller and smaller. We can recognize this rather specifically with food; for any one food our appetites become satisfied rather easily (with the possible exception of salted peanuts). The same holds true for each of our other possessions. How many television sets do you want to have? Or automobiles? Or suits of clothes? How many golf balls do you carry with you in your golf bag? The additional utility derived from the additional unit you possess becomes smaller and smaller.

Consequently, among a number of alternatives, each individual will hold a stock of goods which is such that he does not believe that he can gain in satisfaction by exchanging them for a different combination of goods. And as he possesses more and more of any one good, the added or *marginal utility* derived from the last unit acquired of that good becomes less and less, so that, in order to acquire a desired product which he does not have at the moment, he would give up a fair amount of the good held in abundance. If, however, the initial good were in scarce supply for the individual, he would only give up a smaller amount of it than in the other case in order to acquire a unit of the desired second good.

Note that total utility does not necessarily decline; it is only marginal utility which declines. This law may have exceptions under special circumstances, such as for habit-forming products, the items in a rare collection, and similar circumstances. Furthermore, although the principle may be true for some forms of society and some cultures, it is not known that it is valid in other and different systems.

The law of diminishing returns is a natural law, analogous to the laws of thermodynamics in natural science. It has universal applicability for any economic system. It was, in effect, stated by Aesop when he said, "Two heads are better than one," but "Too many cooks spoil the broth."

A formal statement of the law of diminishing returns would be as follows: "If one or more factors of production is held constant and additional amounts of the other factors of production are applied with the fixed factors, beyond a certain point the addition to total product will become smaller and smaller."[1] This law depends upon the fact that all economic production involves the combination of different resources, or factors of production, in turning out the goods being produced. Labor works with tools on land. Labor does not operate alone. It also assumes that there are no changes in the state of the arts during the period of increasing applications of variable resources to fixed resources. As the increases in application of the variable resources are made, there is an increase in the additions to output, up to a point. Beyond that point, the point of diminishing returns, additions to output decrease.

The variable resources may be labor and machinery, working on a fixed land area, as in farming production or in the production of a country. The variables may be raw materials and labor in a fixed-size plant. They may be size of plant, labor inputs, and raw material applications with a unitary concept for management. In any event, for any combination of productive effort in economic life, there must, at some point, be changes in the proportions among the inputs, and hence there will be diminishing returns.

The problems associated with decision making by the units within the economic system depend, then, on the universality of scarcity and the multiplicity of wants. They stem from the variety of exchanges which must take place in any economy. They depend upon the existence of diminishing utility and diminishing returns. Rational conduct involves making the choices of action which lead most efficiently toward chosen goals. The economist can point out what the choices of conduct may be and how they are arrived at. He does not as an economist choose the goals. Goals are chosen in terms of social values, but methods for reaching those goals are selected partly in terms of values as well. We shall assume that we understand and accept the values of our society wherever we indicate a preferable plan of action. These values are implicit, in the economic system, in the acceptance of the role of the consumer as final arbiter of what is to be produced and in the freedom of the owners of productive services to choose among alternative employ-

---

[1] See Chapter 10 for another statement of this law and for its application to production by a firm.

ments for their services as they see fit. With such assumptions in mind, we shall assume that the price system is the director of production and the awarder of shares of product. Before our attention is turned to the analytical procedures we employ for describing how actions are carried out and what alternative methods for reaching goals involve, it is necessary that we explain what economic method involves and what may be the particular peculiarities of methodology which appear in this book.

1.5. Economic Method

There are two distinct subjects of inquiry in the scientific study of economics. One is concerned with economics as an *explanatory science*, the other with economics as a *policy-making science*. In its explanatory function, economics is concerned with the economic behavior of individuals, groups, and institutions and the effect of this behavior on the economy at large. For example, an economist might spend years studying the behavior of buyers and sellers in the stock market in an attempt to understand the workings of that market and its effect on the ability of businesses to raise capital funds for purposes of expanding production. Or, one might study the ups and downs in business activity with the idea of obtaining a better understanding and explanation of the causes of unemployment. Such studies might be and sometimes are carried out purely as a matter of scientific interest without regard to their immediate usefulness, just as a physicist might study the intensity of cosmic radiation from outer space in the hope of providing some explanation of the origin and meaning of this puzzling natural phenomena.

As a policy-making science economics is concerned with rules or policies for best action given the objectives of the individual, or group, involved. Thus, for example, an economist specializing in such matters might prescribe the best course of action for a paint manufacturer who wants to minimize the cost of meeting his expected sales requirements. Or, an economist might be called upon by the federal government to prescribe various ways in which government action can prevent excessive unemployment. In such situations the economic scientist takes as given the objectives which the individual or institution wishes to achieve (provided, it should be added, that such objectives are not in some sense contradictory or inconsistent). He then proceeds to analyze the problem and to try to formulate a policy or set of alternative policies which will best achieve these stated objectives.

In economic science, just as in the physical sciences, men exhibit a strange human passion of wanting to understand and to comprehend as fully as possible the phenomena which are the subject of their professional studies. This passion leads inevitably to the construction of theories or "models" as they are often called. Since economics is in considerable measure a quantitative science concerned with the movement of measurable variables such as prices, production, consumption, expenditures, interest rates, and so forth, many economic models are mathematical models, being expressed either in terms of graphs or in terms of mathematical symbols. Consequently, when an economist studies the ups and downs of business activity he inevitably is led to construct a model or perhaps several alternative models of the cyclical behavior of business activity. He does this in order to try to obtain a deeper understanding of the underlying forces causing these ups and downs, and the manner in which these forces are interdependent. Similarly, when the economist addresses himself to the problem of production planning in, say, a paint factory, he first tries to construct a mathematical model of the problem that sets forth the various production alternatives which are achievable, and the consequences of various courses of action. Only then does he try to construct and analyze the implications of a "best" course of action.

In this book we will have occasion to use both graphical and mathematical tools of analysis. The major mathematical tool with which the student is expected to be or become familiar is the concept of a function. In mathematics if a variable y depends upon or is a function of another variable x, we express this dependency by writing $y = f(x)$, meaning literally that given x, y is determined. In economics this concept arises in the form of *behavior functions* which express the relationship among two or more variables implied by the behavior of an individual, or a group of individuals. Thus, in studying "demand" we will have occasion to assert that the behavior of buyers is such as to cause the number of units of any commodity (an article possessing utility), which they will buy, to depend upon the price which prevails in the market for that commodity. This implies that a behavior function exists which relates quantity purchased, y, to price, p, that is, $y = D(p)$ meaning "quantity is a function (the D function) of price." D is used instead of f for the functional notation to remind us that the function represents an hypothesis about demand behavior. Similarly, when we come to study fluctuations in business activity we will have occasion to introduce, among other things, a relationship between the amount of money that a community will spend on consumption goods, C, and the amount of the community's total income receipts after taxes, Y_d (disposable income). This consumption behavior function is written $C = C(Y_d)$, meaning that consumption expenditures are a function of, or depend upon, income receipts. Throughout this book when a variable such as p or Y_d is written in parentheses, as in these examples, it is to be understood that a functional relation is implied between the indicated variables. Sometimes a variable may be considered to be a function of more than one other variable; for example y may depend upon the variables x_1, x_2, x_3, and so forth, in which case $y = f(x_1, x_2, x_3 \ . \ . \ .)$ expresses this multidimensional behavior relationship.

As will be seen in the course of this introduction to economic analysis, it is extremely important for the student to learn very early to "think functionally" about economic problems, that is to think in terms of the existence of certain fundamental behavior relationships among the variables of particular problems.

Although it is important in the study of economics to construct models of the behavior of the economic system and components of the economy, it is perhaps equally important not to become so fascinated by model building that one loses sight of the behavior responses which the model is intended to simulate or represent. Behavior equations, which are the building blocks of economic models, should be firmly founded upon the facts of observational experience. For this reason, whenever a behavior function is introduced in this book, some attempt is made to relate this function to observational experience—either to personal (subjective) experience, as in the case of demand, or to actual physical data as when production problems are analyzed. No economic model can be any more valid than the assumptions which underlie it.

It should be borne in mind by the student that an economic model and reality are two different things. Nevertheless, models, properly conceived and used, help us to understand the relationships among the principal variables of economic life and consequently to comprehend the phenomena which are basic to the operation of the economic system.

Chapter 2   THE NATURE OF DEMAND

In the opening chapter we indicated the central importance of the existence of human wants and the scarcity of the means of satisfying those wants, in giving rise to the necessity for economizing on the use of our resources. We simply do not have enough resources to produce all the goods and services that people would like to have. Some way must be found of deciding which of the human wants will be satisfied and which wants will go unsatisfied. In the course of human history, various methods of allocating goods and services have been utilized—force, custom, status, prices. In this, and the following four chapters we will consider various aspects of the allocation of scarce means among alternative uses through a pricing system. We will show how prices in a competitive economy serve as regulatory devices for rationing means to alternative ends. A study of the determination of prices of individual economic goods is a part of what we call microeconomics.

Our first task is to express the hazy and indistinct idea of "wants" in a form which is more usable for scientific analysis. This is accomplished in this chapter through the introduction of a precise, quantitative concept of demand. In Chapter 3 we will introduce the concept of supply and then examine the determination of the price of a good as the result of the interaction of the forces of supply and demand.

2.1. Individual Demand

Fundamental to the study of that part of economics which attempts to explain the formation of prices is the idea of the insatiability of human wants. But wants by themselves are not enough to explain the varying degrees of eagerness to buy which individuals exhibit toward various goods. We observe that our eagerness to buy varies from one good to another, and for the same good the eagerness to buy apparently differs among individuals. However, the idea of "eagerness to buy" is a rather hazy one and does not appear to be sufficiently precise for the purposes of the economist.

11

It would appear that the quantity of a particular good that an individual consumer will purchase depends upon many things, but, in general, the list can be reduced to four major items, namely (1) the price of the good; (2) "tastes," or the intensity of the desire for the good; (3) the income of the consumer; and (4) the prices of other commodities available to the consumer.

In general we can say that the quantity of a particular good purchased by an individual varies inversely with the price of the good, directly with "tastes" and income and either directly or inversely with the prices of other goods, depending upon the exact relationship between the good in question and other goods available to the consumer. For example, if the good considered is butter, then we would expect the quantity of butter purchased to vary directly with the price of margarine, since the higher the price of margarine the less margarine and the more butter would an individual be likely to buy. On the other hand if pretzels are consumed only with beer, then the quantity of pretzels purchased would vary inversely with the price of beer, since the higher the price of beer the less beer and therefore the less pretzels would be purchased.

2.2. *Individual Demand Defined*

The first item above—the price of the good—is deemed such an important influence over the quantity of the good purchased, that "demand" is customarily defined by the economist as a schedule of all the various amounts of a good that a consumer will buy at a corresponding schedule of prices per period of time. Thus "demand," as a rigorous formulation of "eagerness to buy," is defined as a relationship between quantity and price.

An example of a demand schedule is given in Table 2–1. The hypothetical demand schedule given there says that if the price of a good, y, in dollars, p, were $11, the consumer would not purchase any of the good in question, $y = 0$. If the price, p, were $10, the consumer would buy two units per week ($y = 2$); if the price were $9, he would purchase four units per week, etc.

A demand schedule can be plotted in a price-quantity plane and the resulting line is called a demand curve. The demand curve in Figure 2–1 is based on the data in Table 2–1, with price on the vertical axis and quantity on the horizontal axis. Although price is taken as the independent variable, it is customary in economics to plot it on the vertical axis.

Generally demand curves slope downward to the right, as the de-

TABLE 2–1

A HYPOTHETICAL DEMAND SCHEDULE

Price, in Dollars	Quantity, in Physical Units per Week
p	y
11	0
10	2
9	4
8	6
7	8
6	10
5	12
4	14
3	16
2	18
1	20
0	22

mand curve shown in Figure 2–1. The relationship between price and quantity embodied in the shape of the demand curve has been formalized in the "law of demand," which asserts that quantity and price are

FIGURE 2–1

A HYPOTHETICAL DEMAND CURVE

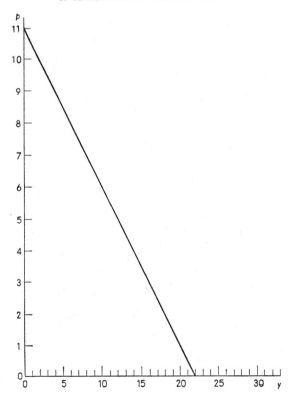

inversely related. That is, other things being equal (held constant), the greater the price of a good the smaller the quantity purchased. The law of demand, when applied to the demand of an individual consumer, can be based on introspection or observation, with the condition other things equal carefully followed, or it can be logically deduced from the assumptions that consumers attempt to maximize their satisfaction from a given income, that income to the consumer is limited, and that as additional units of a particular good are acquired by the consumer in some given time period, the additional satisfaction obtained by the consumer from these units declines. However, we shall not pursue the pure theory of consumer behavior, as it is called, any farther; we shall take the law of demand as based on experience.

2.3. A Shift in Demand

Using the definition of demand given above in Section 2.2, it is clear that the demand relationship may change because of a change in tastes, income, or the prices of other goods. Such a change in demand will cause a shift in the entire relationship between price and quantity. If a shift in one of the factors brings about an increase in demand, we mean that the consumer will purchase a larger quantity of the good at each possible price after the shift than before the shift. In the same manner, a decrease in demand means that the consumer will purchase a smaller quantity at each price in the schedule after the shift than before.

Let us consider butter for a moment. Margarine is a substitute for butter, however perfect or imperfect, and the demand for butter is influenced by the price of margarine. If the price of margarine increases, the demand for butter increases, other things equal. Such a shift in demand is seen in Figure 2–2A. On the other hand, if the price of margarine falls, the demand for butter will fall, as in Figure 2–2B.

FIGURE 2–2A	FIGURE 2–2B
INCREASE IN DEMAND FOR BUTTER	DECREASE IN DEMAND FOR BUTTER

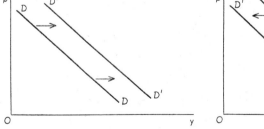
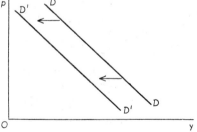

2.4. The Demand Function

In terms of the very compact, shorthand language of mathematics we can state the general demand relationship in the following form:

$$(2.1) \quad y_1 = f(p_1, p_2, p_3, \ldots ; I, T).$$

Equation (2.1) says that the demand of the consumer for good number one is a function of its own price (p_1), the prices of other goods (p_2, p_3, and so forth), the consumer's income (I), and his tastes (T). For example, the number of pounds of beef sold per year (y_1) depends upon the price of beef (p_1), the price of pork (p_2), the price of chickens (p_3), and so forth.

From the demand function, as it is called, we can see that the so-called "law of demand" is a hypothesis concerning the relationship between y_1 and p_1, assuming p_2, p_3, . . . I, and T remain constant. Specifically the law of demand says that $\partial y_1/\partial p_1 < 0$[1] for a very small change in p_1.

In its earliest form, the demand function was written simply as:

$$(2.2) \quad y_1 = D(p_1).$$

This says simply that the quantity demanded of a good is a function of its price and takes all other factors as given and unchanged. For some problems this may be a useful simplification. For example, the hypothetical demand schedule in Table 2–1 is derived from such a demand function, i.e., we used:

$$(2.3) \quad y_1 = a - bp_1,$$

in which a and b are constants. The linear form of the function was chosen as a matter of convenience. Demand functions can also be nonlinear.

The weakness of such a formulation for many economic studies is apparent; it does not take explicit account of the prices of other goods. For example a change in the price of pork would certainly influence the quantity of beef purchased, but if Equation (2.3) represented the demand for beef, the change in the price of pork would necessitate a change in the value of the constant a. The value of the constant a, therefore, would be partially determined by the influence of the prices of many other goods, but for some purposes we would like to separate out the influence of changes in the prices of other goods—a change in the

---

[1] The partial derivative $\dfrac{\partial y_1}{\partial p_1}$ is the rate at which y_1 changes with respect to incremental changes in p_1 while all other variables are held constant.

price of pork, for example, on the demand for beef. The demand function was reformulated to rectify this weakness and was written as we presented it in Equation (2.1). A linear demand function of this kind is often used for empirical demand studies and is written as:

$$(2.4) \quad y_1 = a + bp_1 + cp_2 + \ldots + np_n.$$

The object of applied demand analysis is to estimate the values of the constants in the equation and thus to be in a position to make predictions concerning what will happen when prices change.

2.5. Total Demand and Individual Demand

Normally, in any particular market, the total demand for a good is much greater than the demand for that good on the part of any one individual. The total demand for a good is compounded of all the individual demands for the good. If we add together all the individual demand schedules in a particular market, we have a market demand schedule for the particular good considered. Suppose we have a market containing six individual buyers, individuals A, B, C, D, E, and F, in Table 2–2, with their individual demand schedules. In order to find the market demand schedule, we add together what each individual desires to buy at each of the series of prices. For example, at the price of $8 per unit, individual A desires to purchase 6 units; B, 3 units; C, 1 unit; D, 0 units; E, 5 units; and F, 0 units, for a total demand of 15 units at the $8 price. If this is done for each price, the result is the market demand schedule—the columns headed p_1 and y_1 make up the market demand schedule in Table 2–2.

The behavior of individuals A, B, C, and D, in Table 2–2 conforms

TABLE 2–2

A MARKET DEMAND SCHEDULE

Price in Dollars	Quantity Demanded by Individuals in Physical Units						Market Demand in Physical Units per Week
p_1	A	B	C	D	E	F	y_1
11	0	0	0	0	5	1	6
10	2	1	0	0	5	1	9
9	4	2	0	0	5	1	12
8	6	3	1	0	5	0	15
7	8	4	2	0	5	0	19
6	10	5	3	0	5	0	23
5	12	6	4	7	5	0	34
4	14	7	7	10	5	0	43
3	16	8	8	13	5	0	50
2	18	9	10	16	5	0	58
1	20	10	13	19	5	0	67
0	22	11	18	25	5	0	81

to the law of demand—at higher prices they purchase smaller quantities of the good, but they differ as to the price at which they will begin buying and the quantities they buy. Notice, however, the behavior of individuals E and F. Within the price range considered, individual E purchases the same number of units of the good. Undoubtedly he uses the good for one specific purpose and he buys just the necessary amount, if he buys at all. The action of F appears to be contrary to the general law of demand, within the price range considered. Such behavior as F's is generally explained on the basis of an exception to the law, called conspicuous consumption. He purchases the good at high prices, but not at low prices, as an indicator of his economic status. Some might want to call this behavior snob appeal. Generally, however, the market consists primarily of individuals like A, B, C, and D, rather than F, so that the market demand schedule does follow the law of demand.

FIGURE 2–3

DERIVATION OF A MARKET DEMAND CURVE

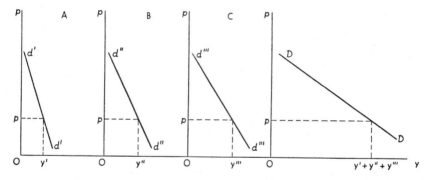

The derivation of the market demand curve from the individual demand curves is accomplished by a process of horizontal addition. In Figure 2–3 we have three individuals, A, B, and C, with the demand curves $d'd'$, $d''d''$, and $d'''d'''$, respectively. At the price p, A demands the quantity y'; B, y''; and C, y'''. If we add these together, at the price p, the market demand is $y' + y'' + y'''$. If we do this for all the prices in the range considered we derive the market demand curve DD seen in Figure 2–3.

2.6. Elasticity of Demand

The "law of demand" places only the general condition on demand curves that they be downward sloping to the right—most buyers purchase larger quantities at lower prices. Within this condition demand curves may have widely varying characteristics, as we have seen above.

The concept of price elasticity of demand is used to classify demand curves according to certain important characteristics. If we look at the demand schedules in Table 2–2, we notice that there is considerable difference in the response of the various buyers to price changes. This variation in response to price changes is indicated by the price elasticity of demand. In the same manner, market demand curves for different markets exhibit different responses to price changes. The coefficient of elasticity, E, of a demand curve at the point (y,p) is defined as:

$$(2.5) \quad E(y,p) = \frac{\% \text{ change in } y}{\% \text{ change in } p} = \frac{\dfrac{dy}{y}}{\dfrac{dp}{p}} = \frac{p}{y} \cdot \frac{dy}{dp}.$$

We define elasticity in this way rather than $(E = dy/dp)$ so that we can obtain a characterization of demand which is dimensionless, i.e., independent of units of measurement. This allows the comparison of the demands for entirely different products, and products whose quantities and prices are measured in different physical and monetary units. Since demand curves are almost invariably negatively sloping, E is negative. Note that the coefficient E is not, in general, a constant but varies with the values of y and p at different points along the demand curve.

With the aid of the coefficient of price elasticity of demand, we can classify the responses to price changes into five different patterns; at the point considered, the demand curve may be perfectly elastic, relatively elastic, of unit elasticity, relatively inelastic, and perfectly inelastic.

1. With a perfectly elastic demand, the buyers are willing to purchase, at a given price, any quantity of the particular good offered, but they will purchase nothing at any higher price. Therefore, an infinitesimal percentage change in p will lead to an infinite percentage change in y. Thus $E = -\infty$. For example, the demand curves for gold and price supported crops can be viewed as perfectly elastic at the maintained price. The U.S. Treasury stands ready to buy all the gold offered to it at the fixed price of \$35 an ounce. This has the effect of creating an unlimited demand at the fixed price. The treasury will buy zero gold at any price greater than \$35 an ounce.

2. If a demand curve is relatively elastic at the point considered, a small percentage change in p causes a more than proportionate percentage change in y. In this case $-\infty < E < -1$. For example, consider the demand for a good that has close substitutes such as a particular brand of gasoline. If the price per gallon of a particular brand of gaso-

line is increased above the prices of equally well-known gasolines, with the same octane rating, it is easy for the customers to shift to the substitutes.

3. There may be cases where a small percentage change in p causes an equal percentage change in y. Then $E = -1$, and we have unitary elastic demand. Such a demand curve has the general shape of a rectangular hyperbola.

4. If a small percentage change in p causes a less than proportionate percentage change in y, the demand curve is relatively inelastic at the point considered. Thus $-1 < E < 0$. It is commonly believed that the demand for products such as salt, tobacco, liquor, and such agricultural products as wheat is relatively inelastic—over a wide range.

5. Finally, there is the case where a small percentage change in p causes no percentage change in y—perfectly inelastic demand. Therefore $E = 0$.

The responsiveness of buyers to price changes, which economists indicate with the elasticity of demand, depends, to an important degree, upon the period of time considered. Generally, it is held that the demand for a particular commodity is more elastic the longer the time period. For example, the market demand in Table 2–2 would be more elastic if the time period were changed from a week to a year. This increase in elasticity of demand with time depends upon such factors as habits of buyers, buyer knowledge of the price changes, and durability of the good in question.

People are generally creatures of habit and it takes time for them to change their habits to take advantage of changes in relative prices. For example if we are beefeaters and the price of pork falls relatively to beef, it takes some time to adjust our habits and consume relatively more pork. Also, knowledge of price changes is not known immediately by all buyers of a good. As the price cut becomes more widely known, more buyers will switch to the cheaper good, and thus the demand is relatively more elastic in the longer time period. If the good in question is relatively durable, buyers may respond to price cuts only after some time, when the good needs to be replaced. For example, suppose that the price of electricity fell very markedly in comparison with oil, when used for home heating. Immediately, perhaps, only buyers building new homes at that time would switch from oil heaters to electricity. But in a longer period of time, oil furnaces would need replacement and these buyers, at that time, might switch from oil to electricity. Thus the demand would be more elastic in the longer period.

2.7. Geometric Interpretation of Elasticity

Thus far we have discussed price elasticity of demand at a point on a demand curve but for many applications of the concept economists desire to consider elasticity over a small range of the demand curve—arc elasticity. The definition of arc elasticity is basically the same as for point elasticity:

$$(2.6) \quad E(\text{arc}) = \frac{\% \text{ change in } y}{\% \text{ change in } p} = \frac{p}{y} \cdot \frac{\Delta y}{\Delta p} .$$

Let us consider the response to the price change shown in Figure 2–4, where the quantity demanded increases from OA to OH as the price

FIGURE 2–4

ARC ELASTICITY OF DEMAND

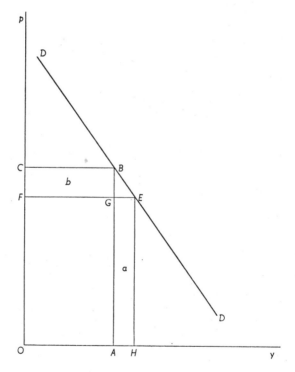

falls from OC to OF. There are various ways of calculating the arc elasticity of the demand curve DD over the arc BE, but we shall use the method that makes the most economic sense, in that we can interpret elasticity in terms of areas in the diagram and the areas also can be related to expenditures. First we need to find price times the change in quantity $(p\Delta y)$. This is seen to be the area *AHEG* in Figure 2–4 because we take p to be *OF*, which equals *AG*, and the change in the quantity demanded is *AH*. Next we need to find the quantity times the change in price $(y\Delta p)$. In terms of the diagram in Figure 2–4 this is the area *FGBC*, since the quantity is taken to be *OA* which equals *FG* and the change in price is *CF*. Therefore the arc elasticity is the ratio of the areas labeled a and b, and as the change in price is negative, the arc elasticity is negative.

If $a > b$, the demand curve is relatively elastic in the range considered; if $a = b$, the demand curve has unit elasticity in the range, and if $a < b$, the demand curve is relatively inelastic in the range.

2.8. *Elasticity of Demand and Expenditures*

It will be evident that the relative elasticity of demand for a product is not only of abstract interest to the economist but of practical interest to the individual firm as a seller of a product and to industry groups and government agencies for policy purposes.

If the demand curve *DD* in Figure 2–4 is taken to be the market demand curve for a particular product, then the area *OABC* represents the total expenditure by the buyers (total receipts of sellers) on the product, i.e., price times quantity, *OC* times *OA*. After the price is reduced to *OF*, total expenditure for the product is equal to the area *OHEF*. Since the area *OAGF* is common to both total expenditures, the change in the total expenditure for the product caused by the price change is equal to the area *AHEG* minus the area *FGBC*, or the area a minus the area b, in Figure 2–4. Thus if $a > b$, total expenditures on the product will increase as the result of a price cut, but if $a = b$ there will be no change in total expenditures, and if $a < b$, a price cut will reduce total expenditures.

The relationship between the price elasticity of demand and changes in expenditures as the result of a price change should be evident. The condition for a relatively elastic demand in the relevant range is precisely the condition for an increase in total expenditures after a price cut. Likewise, we can connect unit elasticity with no change in total expenditures and relatively inelastic demand with a decrease in expenditures as the result of a price cut.

APPENDIX TO CHAPTER 2

Let us assume that all the factors in the demand function in Equation (2.1) are held constant except the price of the good considered. Then we can write the demand function as:

$$(2.7) \quad y = D(p),$$

where y equals the quantity, and p the price of the good.

Price elasticity of demand was defined to be:

$$(2.5) \quad E(y,p) = \frac{p}{y} \cdot \frac{dy}{dp}.$$

Let us now investigate the relationship between elasticity of demand and total expenditures of buyers (revenue of sellers). We have

$$(2.8) \quad R = py,$$

where R is the total expenditures.

Then

$$(2.9) \quad \frac{dR}{dp} = y + p\frac{dy}{dp},$$

but $dy/dp = Ey/p$ [from (2.5)], therefore

$$(2.10) \quad \frac{dR}{dp} = y + p\left(\frac{Ey}{p}\right) = y(1 + E).$$

This shows how the rate of change in total money expenditure for y (seller's receipts) depends upon E.

The relationship between E and changes in R, brought about by changes in p is as follows:

1. Perfectly elastic demand: $E = -\infty$; $dR/dp = -\infty$.
2. Relatively elastic demand: $-\infty < E < -1$, therefore $dR/dp = y(1 + E) < 0$. An increase in price lowers total expenditure or a decrease in price increases total expenditure.
3. Unitary elastic demand: $E = -1$, therefore $dR/dp = y(1 + E) = 0$. An increase (or decrease) in price causes no change in total expenditure.
4. Relatively inelastic demand: $-1 < E < 0$, therefore $dR/dp = y(1 + E) > 0$. An increase in price causes an increase in total expenditure and a decrease in price lowers total expenditure.
5. Perfectly inelastic demand: $E = 0$, therefore $dR/dp = y(1 + E) = y$. An increase in price causes an increase in total expenditure equal to the fixed amount demanded times the increase in price. Similarly, a decrease in price causes a decrease in total expenditure equal to the fixed amount demanded times the decrease in price.

QUESTIONS AND EXERCISES

1. Given the following demand schedule:

Price per Unit in Cents	Quantity of Units
90	400
80	500
70	600
60	700
50	800
40	900
30	1000
20	1100
10	1200

a) Determine on the basis of total spending in what portion of the above schedule demand is elastic, if at all; in what portion unitary elasticity exists, if at all; and in what portion the demand is inelastic, if at all.

b) Now, considering that the demand function for the data above can be expressed as

$$p + \frac{y}{10} = 130,$$

find the elasticity at prices of 60, 65, and 70 cents per unit.

2. Suppose we have the demand function:

$$y_1 = \frac{500}{p_1 + 5} - 10.$$

a) Construct the demand schedule for the above function.

b) Over what price range will the demand be relatively elastic? Relatively inelastic? At what price will the demand have unit elasticity?

c) For what ranges of values for y_1 and p_1 can this equation represent a demand function?

3. Suppose we have the demand function:

$$y_1 = a - bp_1 + cp_2,$$

where p_1 is the price of y_1, p_2 the price of another good, y_2, and a, b, and c are positive constants; $a = 34$, $b = \frac{1}{2}$ and $c = 3$.

a) If we take $p_2 = 2$, construct a demand curve representing the function.

b) At what price is the demand curve of unit elasticity?

c) If p_2 changes from 2 to 4, does the demand for y_1 increase or decrease? At what price is this new demand curve of unit elasticity?

d) What happens to the elasticity of demand at a given price, when p_2 increases? decreases?

e) How would you show a change of taste by the buyers?

4. Suppose we have the demand function:

$$y = ap^{-m}.$$

a) What is the price elasticity for all values of p?

b) Interpret your results for m greater than, equal to, or less than 1.

5. Suppose Congress passes a law requiring the federal highway department to spend one billion dollars per year for ready mixed concrete to build highways and bridges. If p is the price of concrete per ton, and y is the number of tons of concrete that would be purchased by the federal government, write the exact equation representing the government's demand for concrete. Draw a graph of this demand curve. What is the elasticity of this demand curve? Would you expect this to be the typical equation form for most demand curves? Why or why not?

6. Suppose Congress passes a law requiring the federal government to spend one billion dollars per year for sand and cement to make concrete for highways and bridges. Let p_c be the price of cement per ton and p_s the price of

sand per ton, y_c the tons of cement purchased, and y_s the tons of sand purchased under this law.

a) Assuming that concrete for these uses is mixed using three parts sand to one part cement, write equations representing the government's demand for sand and for cement.

b) If the price of sand is regarded a constant, show that the government's demand for cement is relatively inelastic throughout its entire range.

7. Consider the linear demand function $y = a - bp$, where $a > 0$, $b > 0$. Prove the following statements and illustrate graphically: If

$$a)\ p = \frac{a}{b},\ \text{then}\ E = -\infty$$

$$b)\ \frac{a}{b} > p \geq \frac{a}{2b},\ \text{then}\ -\infty < E \leq -1$$

$$c)\ \frac{a}{2b} > p \geq 0,\ \text{then}\ -1 < E < 0$$

Chapter 3 : SUPPLY AND COMPETITIVE PRICE

A discussion of supply parallels in many ways the discussion of demand. In Chapter 2 we introduced the concept of demand as a rigorous formulation of the notion of "eagerness to buy" based on the fundamental idea of human wants. In this chapter the concept of supply is presented as a more precise formulation of the notion of "willingness to sell." After the concept of supply is examined, we will turn to the determination of competitive price, that is, the determination of the prices of products in competitive markets.

3.1. *Supply Schedule of an Individual Seller*

In a private enterprise economy, one of the most pervasive incentives inducing the production and sale of goods is the expectation of profits. There are very many factors that affect the expectations of profits by an individual seller; therefore, the quantity of a particular good that an individual seller will be willing to sell depends upon many variables. Some of the more important appear to be the prices of the various factors of production used in its production; the available productive capacity; the availability of necessary factors of production; the prices of by-products of the particular good, if any; the techniques of production; the weather; and the price of the good itself.

The relationship between the quantity of a good supplied and its price is deemed of such importance that "supply" is customarily defined in economics as a schedule of all the various amounts of a good that a seller or supplier will sell, at a corresponding schedule of prices, per period of time. Thus, we see that the concept of a supply schedule parallels that of a demand schedule. "Supply," in economics, is also defined as a relationship between quantity and price.

For many purposes of analysis it is useful to divide the analysis of supply into supply in the short run and supply in the long run, with the short run defined as a period during which productive capacity cannot be expanded. Supply in the short run can be expressed in the following form:

$$(3.1) \quad y_1 = f(p_1, w_1, w_2, \ldots, w_n; K)$$

with p_1 being the price of the particular good considered and w_1, w_2, . . . , w_n the prices of the various factors of production used in the production of y_1. K is the limit of the fixed productive capacity in the short run.

Supply in the long run can be expressed as follows:

$$(3.2) \quad y_1 = g(p_1, p_2, \ldots, p_n; w_1, w_2, \ldots, w_n; A)$$

with p_1 being the price of the good considered and p_2, . . . , p_n being the prices of other goods that might be supplied, the w's the prices of the factors of production used in producing the goods, and the A representing the state of the arts—technological knowledge.

Equation (3.1) says that in the short run the supplier decides whether or not to supply the particular good, and if he does decide to supply the good, the quantity he supplies depends upon the price of the good, and the prices of the resources he uses in production, with an upper limit imposed by the fixed productive capacity.

In the long run, however, suppliers are not restricted to continue producing and supplying what they have in the past, but can shift their activities into various alternatives. Whether or not a supplier does shift into some other line of activity depends, to a large degree, upon the relative profitability of the alternatives open to him, which, in turn, depends upon the price of the good considered and the prices of the factors used in its production. Thus in the long run the supply of any single good depends upon, or is some function of, its own price, the prices of other goods, the prices of factors of production, and the state of the arts, as in Equation (3.2).

If we take all the w's in Equation (3.1) as given and unchanged during the relevant period, the supply function reduces to a relationship between quantity and the price of the good. Unlike the demand function, as the price of the good increases, the quantity supplied also increases. A hypothetical supply schedule is shown in Table 3–1. At a higher price the supplier will employ more factors and use his capacity more intensively, and thus supply a larger quantity of the good.

3.2. Individual Supply and Total Supply

Just as a demand schedule can be shown graphically as a demand curve, a supply schedule can be plotted on a graph, with price on the

TABLE 3–1

A HYPOTHETICAL SUPPLY SCHEDULE

Price in Dollars	Quantity in Physical Units per Week
p	y
8	30
7	28
6	25
5	20
4	14
3	7
2	0
1	0

vertical axis and quantity on the horizontal axis and the points con-nected to form a supply curve. The supply curve, SS, in Figure 3–1 is based on the supply schedule in Table 3–1.

A market supply schedule, the schedule relating the total quantity that suppliers are willing to put on the market at a series of prices, is the summation of all the individual supply schedules. In the same way, the market supply curve is the result of adding together all the individ-

FIGURE 3–1

A HYPOTHETICAL SUPPLY CURVE

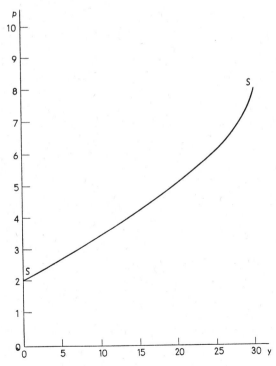

ual supply curves in the market. Suppose we have a market with three suppliers who have the supply curves $s's'$, $s''s''$, and $s'''s'''$ in Figure 3–2. The market supply curve, SS, is found by adding up what each of

FIGURE 3–2

DERIVATION OF A MARKET SUPPLY CURVE

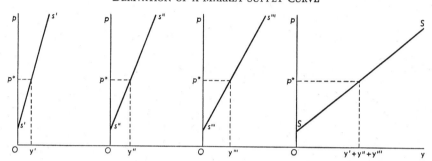

the individual suppliers are willing to supply at each of the prices. Thus, at the price p^* the market supply is equal to $y' + y'' + y'''$.

3.3. Elasticity of Supply

In measuring the responsiveness of supply to a change in price, the concept of elasticity is used in the same manner as it was used in connection with demand. The elasticity of supply is a measure of the ease or difficulty of expanding output in response to an increase of price or of reducing output in response to a reduction of price. For a supply curve, the coefficient of elasticity, E, is defined exactly the same as it was for demand—at the point (y,p), the coefficient of elasticity is defined as:

$$(3.3) \quad E(y,p) = \frac{\%\text{ change in } y}{\%\text{ change in } p} = \frac{p}{y} \cdot \frac{dy}{dp}.$$

Since supply curves are almost invariably rising with an increase in price, the elasticity coefficient of supply is normally positive.

Using the coefficient of elasticity as a guide, the responses of suppliers to price changes can be classified into five general patterns: perfectly elastic, relatively elastic, unitary elastic, relatively inelastic, and perfectly inelastic supply.

1. With perfectly elastic supply, at the point considered, an infinitesimal change in price will lead to an infinite change in the quantity supplied. Thus $E = \infty$. A perfectly elastic supply implies that the suppliers are willing to supply all the market wants at a given price, but will supply nothing at a slightly lower price.

2. If the supply curve is relatively elastic at the point considered, a

small percentage change in the price causes a more than proportionate percentage change in the quantity supplied. Therefore $\infty > E > 1$.

3. If a small percentage change in the price results in an equal percentage change in the quantity supplied, the supply curve is of unitary elasticity at the point considered. Thus $E = 1$.

4. Then there are cases where a small percentage change in the price causes a less than proportionate percentage change in the quantity supplied. The supply curve is relatively inelastic at the point considered and $1 > E > 0$.

5. Finally, we have the situation where a small percentage change in the price of the good causes no change in the quantity supplied. The supply curve is perfectly inelastic at the point considered, and $E = 0$.

Since the elasticity of supply measures the difficulty of expanding output, in response to a price increase, or of reducing output in response to a price reduction, it will be different whether one is considering a short-run or a long-run response. Capacity can be increased in the long run, and since it is usually easier to expand output with increased capacity, the supply curve normally will be more elastic in the long run than in the short run as the limits of short-run capacity are reached. Supply, in both the short and long run, depends on cost. If output can be expanded with relatively little increase in cost, the supply curve will be relatively elastic, but if output can only be expanded with relatively large increases in cost, the supply curve will be relatively inelastic.

3.4. Equilibrium of Supply and Demand

Let us now combine our concepts of supply and demand and see how the price of a good is determined in a perfectly competitive market. The concept of a perfectly competitive market is an idealization which is never fully achieved in any actual market for a commodity. The concept, as an idealization, is similar in some respect to that of a perfect gas. No gas behaves literally in accordance with the perfect gas law, but many gases are fair approximations to a perfect gas in the ordinary ranges of temperature and pressure.

A perfectly competitive market is usually defined as a relatively large group of independent buyers and sellers actively dealing in a more or less homogeneous good, with no buyer or seller, acting alone, able to influence noticeably the market price. The buyers and sellers are assumed to have a knowledge of the prices at which transactions are taking place, and all buyers and sellers are willing to deal with each other. Of course, some individuals may act as both a buyer and a seller. Perfect competition is approached in actual markets in varying degrees.

A few, such as the agricultural commodity markets in Chicago and Kansas City, the New York stock exchange, and the market for foreign exchange (the "money market" where dollars, francs, pound sterling, etc., are bought and sold), are approximated to a considerable degree by the ideal of perfect competition.

Given a competitive market, we can say that the price of a good will tend to a level which equates the total quantity demanded of the good with the total quantity supplied. This is the equilibrium price. Suppose in a particular market for some good, that *DD* is the demand curve and *SS* the supply curve as shown in Figure 3–3. With the given

FIGURE 3–3

THE EQUILIBRIUM PRICE

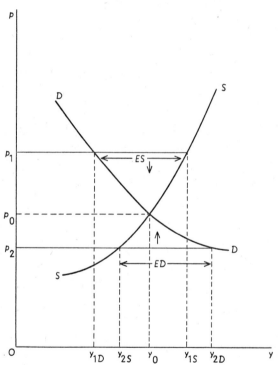

demand and supply curves, the equilibrium price, in Figure 3–3, is p_0, with the total quantity demanded and supplied per period of time equal at y_0.

If the price is not at the equilibrium point, will it tend to move to equilibrium or will it remain above or below the equilibrium level? Suppose the price in the market is above the equilibrium level, say at p_1 dollars per unit, in Figure 3–3. At this price the suppliers in the market are willing to supply y_{1S} units per period, but the buyers in the market only desire to purchase y_{1D} units per period. There is an excess supply of $y_{1S} - y_{1D}$ units per period, designated as ES in Figure 3–3. The excess supply will generate pressure to reduce prices, since the sellers can dispose of their unsold surpluses only at lower prices. The competition between sellers to dispose of their surplus stocks will cause any price above p_0 to fall. As the price falls toward the equilibrium level, the excess supply will gradually diminish, partly because at lower prices suppliers will put a smaller quantity on the market and partly because at lower prices the buyers will take a larger quantity of the good off the market.

Similarly, if the price is below the equilibrium level, say at p_2, in Figure 3–3, there is an excess demand for the product, equal to $y_{2D} - y_{2S}$ units per period, ED in the figure. In this situation more is being demanded than is being supplied to the market, and some potential buyers are unable to purchase the good at the current price, but are willing to pay a higher price. These would-be buyers raise their bids in an effort to obtain the product. Thus the competition between buyers tends to increase the price under conditions of excess demand.

In the situation shown in Figure 3–3, the price p_0 is a stable equilibrium price in the sense that any deviation of price from p_0 generates forces tending to restore the price to p_0. If we write $y = D(p)$ for the demand function and $y = S(p)$ for the supply function, our condition for equilibrium is that

$$(3.4) \quad y = D(p) = S(p),$$

which is satisfied when $p = p_0$, and the quantity demanded and supplied are equal, $y_D = y_S = y_0$.

The equilibrating mechanism of a competitive market can also be described from an output point of view. Let us assume that Figure 3–4 represents some market with the demand curve DD and the supply curve SS. Under these conditions the equilibrium price is p_0 and equilibrium output is y_0. If the quantity supplied to the market is $y_1 < y_0$, then the price at which the buyers in the market will purchase this quantity is p_{1D}, i.e., the market will just be cleared at the price p_{1D}, but this price is greater than p_{1S}, the minimum price necessary to induce the suppliers to put the quantity y_1 on the market. Hence, the suppliers will make profits over and above the "normal" profits necessary to keep them in operation, and the extra profits will induce the suppliers to expand and supply a greater quantity of the good. As the increased quantity appears on the market, the market-clearing price will fall, and therefore extra profits will fall. This process will continue until the expanding supply on the market has brought the price down to p_o and extra profits for the last unit of production, y_o, have been reduced to zero. At this level of output the incentive to expand will be gone.

Similarly, if output were $y_2 > y_o$, the market-clearing price p_{2D} is

FIGURE 3–4

EQUILIBRIUM OUTPUT

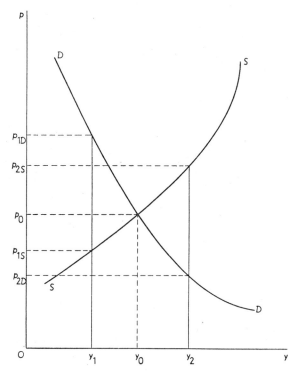

less than the minimum price p_{2S} necessary to induce the suppliers to put the quantity y_2 on the market. Thus some suppliers will make losses, and output will decline by the withdrawal of suppliers and/or the re-stricting of output until the losses are eliminated.

3.5. An Analogy from Mechanics

The supply and demand equilibrium represents an equilibrium of economic forces. On the one side we have human desires backed with willingness to pay money for the goods, and the lower the price, the greater is the quantity the buyers will take. But on the production side, it is costly to produce goods, and the greater the rate of output of an industry, the more intensively it must bid scarce resources—labor, capital, materials—away from other industries; this leads to rising unit costs in a competitive market. The selling price of a good continues to rise or to fall until these forces are in equilibrium.

An analogy with mechanics may help to clarify the idea of economic equilibrium. Suppose a mass is acted upon by a force, F, which is inversely proportional to the velocity, v, of the mass, that is

$$(3.5) \quad F = \frac{\alpha}{v}.$$

As the mass is accelerated to higher velocities, the applied force diminishes. Suppose further that air friction sets up a resistance force, R, which is proportional to velocity, that is

$$(3.6) \quad R = \beta v.$$

Then the equilibrium rate of travel of the mass is given by the condition that

$$(3.7) \quad R = F, \text{ that is } \beta v = \frac{\alpha}{v},$$

FIGURE 3–5

EQUILIBRIUM VELOCITY

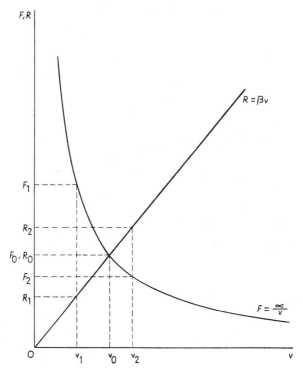

from which we deduce that in equilibrium the velocity of the mass will be constant at

$$(3.8) \quad v_0 = \sqrt{\frac{\alpha}{\beta}},$$

where v_0 is the equilibrium velocity and α and β are constants. The situation is illustrated in Figure 3–5.

The system is in equilibrium only when $v = v_0$. If, initially, the mass is given a velocity $v_1 < v_0$, then the motive force

$$(3.9) \quad F_1 = \frac{\alpha}{v_1} > R_1 = \beta v_1,$$

the resistance force, and the velocity of the mass is increased.

If however, the mass is given a velocity $v_2 > v_0$, then

$$(3.10) \quad F_2 = \frac{\alpha}{v_2} < R_2 = \beta v_2,$$

and motion of the mass is retarded. Note that velocity is quite analogous to y, the rate of production and sales. Both are rates per unit of time. In economics, rates are often referred to as flows. For example, production, sales, and consumption involve flows of goods over time.

3.6. Price as a Rationing Device

We are now in a much clearer position to see how prices serve as rationing devices, and how the pricing system generally serves as an allocating mechanism for regulating the composition and flow of economic goods.

Consider a competitive market in equilibrium, illustrated in Figure 3–6. The price that prevails in the market is p_0, and this price performs two economic functions.

1. It rations the flow of the good y among buyers in such a way that only the more eager buyers that stand behind the demand curve above p_0 are satisfied. Buyers whose wants or purchasing power are not sufficient to buy at the price p_0, or above, are rationed out of the market and thus are not allocated any of the good y.

2. The price p_0 also serves to ration out of the market any and all suppliers who cannot produce efficiently enough to meet all costs of production and make "normal" profits at a selling price of p_0. It also rations out those techniques and methods of production which cannot be supported except at a price greater than p_0.

In a private enterprise economy price thus serves to allocate goods among buyers and production among producers.

FIGURE 3–6

PRICE AS A RATIONING DEVICE

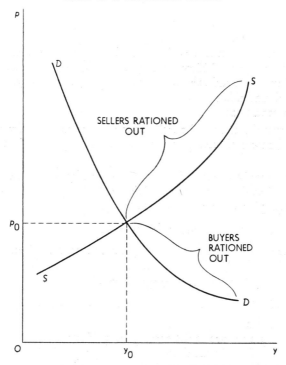

QUESTIONS AND EXERCISES

1. After a severe snow storm a large city is temporarily isolated from the rest of the world. Draw a supply curve for replacement links in tire chains, with a time interval consisting of the day immediately following the storm.

2. Find the equilibrium price in the following situation: $y_1 = 1$ is the supply function for a piece of real estate. The demand function for that piece of real estate is given by:

$$y_1 = 10 - .01p_1 .$$

Why is the supply function for a particular piece of real estate written in the form used above? What is its elasticity?

3. Suppose the demand for a good is given by:

$$y_d = 140 - \tfrac{1}{2}p$$

while the supply of the good is given by:

$$y_s = p - 40$$

a) Determine the equilibrium price and quantity of the good exchanged.

b) If the market price were 90 at any time, what would be the excess demand at that price?

c) If market price were 150, what would be the excess supply?

d) Suppose sellers in expectation of receiving a price of $140, place 100 units on the market. What is the market clearing price for these 100 units? By how much does demand price exceed or fall short of the expected supply price? How would you expect suppliers to react?

4. In what situations could one say that price was determined by:
   a) demand conditions,
   b) supply conditions?

5. Since the quantity of a good purchased is equal to the quantity sold in every transaction, how can price be determined by the equality of supply and demand?

6. Construct a supply schedule for the following supply function, for integral prices from 0 to 40. Graph the schedule.
   a) Is the supply schedule relatively inelastic?

$$y_{1s} = \tfrac{1}{10}p_1^2 - 10 .$$

   b) Find the equilibrium price if the demand function is given as

$$y_{1d} = \frac{1200}{p_1 + 10} - 10 .$$

   c) If the price in the market happened to be 30, would there be an excess supply or demand? How much?

   d) What would happen to the excess supply (demand) at the price 30 if the constant (1200) in the demand function increased to 2187.5?

   e) What would be the new equilibrium price and sales?

7. Derive the form of the supply curve with unit elasticity, constant elasticity.

Chapter 4

APPLICATIONS OF SUPPLY
AND DEMAND ANALYSIS

Sufficient tools of analysis have now been developed for us to understand the circumstances under which price changes may occur. In the last chapter we learned that in a competitive market price tends to the level at which the quantity of a good supplied is equal to the quantity demanded. In this chapter we will first examine what happens to the price when there is an increase in demand. Next we will analyze the repercussions arising from shifts of the supply function. We will then apply our supply and demand analysis to various problems, such as price support programs, crop reduction programs, taxes and subsidies, and business decisions.

4.1. An Increase in Demand

Let us first analyze the effect on the equilibrium price of some good of an increase in the demand for that good. In Chapter 2 we stated the general demand relationship as:

$$(2.1) \quad y_1 = f(p_2, p_2, p_3, \ldots, p_n; I; T).$$

An increase in the demand for a product, y_1, may result from a change in the tastes of consumers (T), a change in their incomes (I), or a change in the prices of other goods $(p_2, p_3, \ldots, p_n)$. If we have given the demand curve, DD, and the short-run supply curve, S_sS_s, in Figure 4–1, our supply and demand analysis tells us that the equilibrium price is p_0, at which level the quantity demanded and the quantity supplied are equal at y_0. As a result of an increase in demand, suppose that the demand curve shifts to $D'D'$. We see that this increase in demand will raise the equilibrium price of the product.

Under the new demand conditions, the old equilibrium price gives rise to an excess demand, which, as we saw in Section 3.4, causes price to increase. How much the price will increase depends upon the period of time we consider and the mobility of the factors of production, or inputs, into the industry in question. In the short run the price of the good will tend to rise to a level which is higher than its long-run position. In the short run the output of the firms in the industry can only be increased by employing their fixed facilities more intensively. Output

FIGURE 4–1

REPERCUSSIONS OF AN INCREASE IN DEMAND

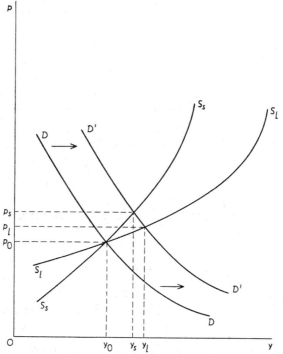

expands along the short-run supply curve until short-run equilibrium is reached, in the situation shown in Figure 4–1, at a price of p_s with the quantity supplied and demanded equal to y_s.

At the short-run equilibrium price, p_s, however, it will pay firms in the industry to expand their capacity. In the long run, supply is more elastic, as new firms and less mobile resources are attracted into the industry in response to the higher price of the product and greater profits for the firms. In Figure 4–1, the long-run supply curve is given as $S_L S_L$. Given the opportunity to reorganize their productive efforts, we see, from the long-run supply curve, that the firms would be willing to supply a quantity greater than y_s at the price p_s. However, as the industry expands capacity and output, the increased output can only be taken off the market at a reduced price. Assuming no other changes, the final long-run equilibrium is reached when the price falls from p_s to p_L and the quantity supplied and demanded are equal at y_L. Notice that in the final equilibrium position, both the price and the quantity are greater than in the initial position. The increase in price, of course, results from having a long-run supply curve with a positive slope, that is, the industry will only supply a greater quantity in the long run at a higher price. If the long-run supply curve had been constant, the price would have fallen back to the original level, after its short-run increase. And, if the long-run supply curve had a negative slope, the long-run equilibrium price would have fallen, after the initial short-run rise following the increase in demand. A reduction in demand, of course, will be just the reverse of the above analysis, and we leave it as an exercise for the student.

4.2. A Shift in Supply

Since price in a competitive market is determined by the interaction of demand and supply forces, a shift in supply will also cause a change in the competitive price. If there is a change in the supply function—either the short-run or the long-run supply function—say a decrease in

FIGURE 4–2

EFFECT ON PRICE OF A DECREASE IN SUPPLY

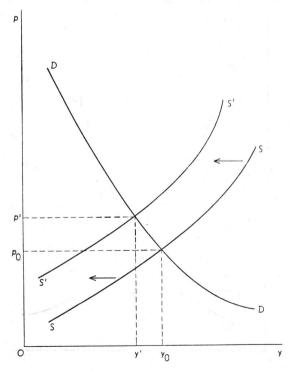

supply because of an increase in the price of a factor, perhaps wages, or an increase in supply because of technological improvements, this will cause the price to rise or fall.

An increase in the price of a factor used in the production of a particular good will, other things equal, bring about a decrease in the supply of the good. Since costs will have increased, the suppliers producing the good will have to receive higher prices in order to cover their costs. The effect of such an increase in, say, wages is a shift of the supply curve to the left; that is, less will be supplied to the market at any price. For example, suppose we have a market with the demand curve, *DD,* and the supply curve, *SS,* shown in Figure 4–2. The equilibrium price and quantity are p_0 and y_0. Next let us assume that the wages of labor used in the production of the good, y, are increased. As a result, the supply curve shifts to the left, to *S'S'*. The equilibrium price rises to p' and the quantity sold falls to y'. Thus, as a result of a decrease in supply the equilibrium price is pushed up and, with demand unchanged, the quantity sold falls.

If a new technique of production is introduced making it possible

FIGURE 4–3

EFFECT ON PRICE OF A TECHNOLOGICAL IMPROVEMENT

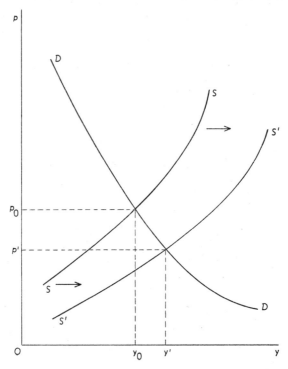

to produce any given level of output at a lower cost, all the firms will in time be forced to adopt the new technique, since the firms that initially introduce the innovation will be able to undersell those firms that do not. Suppose that an innovation is introduced into an industry represented by the supply curve *SS*, in Figure 4–3, with the demand curve *DD*. Before the innovation influences the supply function, the equilibrium price and quantity are p_0 and y_0. As a result of the new technology the supply curve shifts to $S'S'$. With the new supply function, given an unchanged demand function, the equilibrium price will fall to p' and quantity supplied and demanded increases to y'. We note that, other things equal, an increase in supply causes a fall in the equilibrium price and an increase in the quantity of the good bought and sold.

The elasticity of demand, in the relevant range, is clearly of more than passing interest to the industry affected by a change in technology. We saw above that a technological improvement will result in a lower price for the product. We also recall, from Section 2.8, that the change in total expenditure for a good, caused by a price cut, depends upon the coefficient of arc elasticity of the demand curve. If the demand curve is relatively inelastic (elastic) in the relevant range, then increases in supply tend to reduce (increase) the total money receipts per unit of time of the suppliers.

In agriculture, much of the pressure for price supports arose because of declines in farm income. These declines could have been caused by a rapid rate of technological improvement in agriculture if the demand for agricultural products had been relatively inelastic.

4.3. Application of Supply and Demand to Problem of Price Supports

Governmental price supports have been used extensively in the area of agriculture and the purchase of silver. Congress, by a series of acts, has required the Treasury to bid for silver at a price which has been increased from 50 cents an ounce in 1934 to 90.5 cents an ounce in 1946.

Let us apply our supply and demand analysis to the general problem of price supports. Suppose the government is committed by law to buy a sufficient quantity of corn to prevent the price of corn from falling below p^* dollars per bushel in Figure 4–4, which represents the corn market, and that p^* is determined by some legal formula based upon the prices farmers have to pay for the things they buy. Then if the equilibrium market price p_0 is greater than the support price, the law will not affect the price of corn or the allocation of resources. In Figure

4–4, after putting the support price at p^*, the effective demand curve changes from DD, the free market demand, to $DD'D''$ with the segment $D'D''$ representing the effect of the fixed support price. That is, at p^* the government stands ready to buy unlimited quantities of corn.

Suppose, however, that the support price p^* is higher than the equilibrium market price, p_0, as it is in Figure 4–5, where DD repre-

FIGURE 4–4

INEFFECTIVENESS OF A SUPPORT PRICE LESS THAN MARKET PRICE

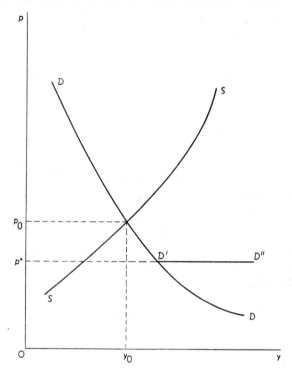

sents the free market demand, SS the supply curve of corn and $D'D''$ the price support demand curve. In the market, shown in Figure 4–5, the equilibrium price and quantity under free market conditions is p_0 and y_0. With the introduction of a supported price, higher than the equilibrium price, the effective demand curve becomes $DD'D''$. At the support price of p^*, the buyers in the market only desire to purchase the quantity y^* but the suppliers are willing to supply a greater quantity, y'. Hence, if the government is to maintain the support price p^*, it must be ready and willing to purchase the excess supply $y' - y^*$ to prevent competition from driving the price below p^*. Note that after the institution of price supports, the quantity taken by the market falls from y_0 to y^*.

FIGURE 4–5

AN "EFFECTIVE" PRICE SUPPORT

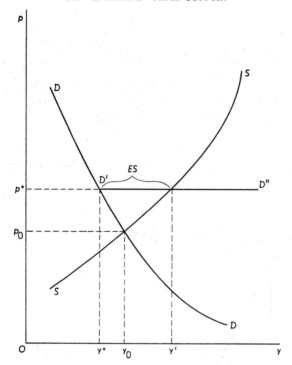

A support price above equilibrium discourages some buyers who would have been willing to buy at p_0.

If the government does not want to accumulate the excess supply at the rate $y' - y^*$ per period of time indefinitely, a crop restriction program may be introduced in connection with the price support program, as has been done in the areas of tobacco, wheat, and corn. In terms of Figure 4–5, output needs to be restricted to the level y^* if the aim is to maintain the market price at the level of p^*. In the United States, this has been attempted, not too successfully, by means of acreage allotments. Note that again the result, as far as the consumers are concerned, is a smaller quantity of the good at a higher price.

If the aim of the price supports or the crop restriction program is to increase the income of producers without having the government acquire large stocks, then it would appear to make more sense when applied to goods with a relatively inelastic demand and supply, in the relevant range, than when applied to goods with a relatively elastic demand and supply. If we recall our analysis in Section 2.8, it is easy to see that a crop restriction program will only increase the income of the producers if the demand curve for the particular controlled good is relatively inelastic, in the range considered. In the price support program, if the demand curve is relatively elastic and the support price is higher than the free market price, the resulting reduction in the quantity of the good purchased by buyers in the market will be proportionately greater than the increase in price—leaving a greater quantity for the government to take off the market and put into storage. We leave it to the student to work out the relationship between the elasticity of supply and quantities stored under a support program.

4.4. Taxes and Subsidies

Supply and demand analysis gives an insight into many past price changes and expected price changes, including those influenced by taxes

FIGURE 4–6

EFFECT OF A TAX OR SUBSIDY

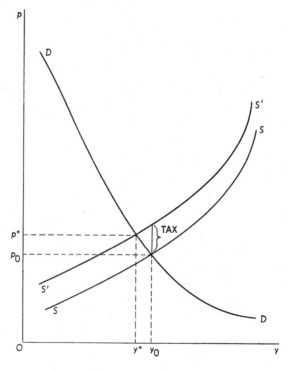

or subsidies. Suppose the government passes a law levying a tax per unit of output on the production of some particular product, say copper. Other things equal, the supply curve will shift to the left, from SS to $S'S'$ in Figure 4–6. Remember, the supply curve provides the quantities suppliers are willing to put on the market at a series of prices. With the introduction of the tax per unit, the suppliers will require this much more per unit if they are to continue to secure normal profits. Therefore, the vertical distance between SS and $S'S'$, in Figure 4–6, is equal to the tax.

Each producer will see the tax as an increase in his costs. The quantity that he formerly was willing to supply at a given price, would be supplied after the tax if the new price exceeded the old by the amount of the tax. Given the demand curve, DD, the equilibrium price before the tax is p_0 and the quantity bought and sold in the market is y_0. After levying the tax, the market price rises to p^* and the quantity sold falls to y^*. Note that the market price does not, in this case, rise by the full amount of the tax. In this situation, as pictured in Figure 4–6, the suppliers sell a smaller quantity and receive a lower net price, and the buyers purchase a smaller quantity and pay a higher price, than before the tax was put into effect. Thus we can say the buyers pay part of the tax and the suppliers pay part of the tax.

The above analysis assumed that the demand for the product remains unchanged, but this assumption may not be completely correct. Earlier we pointed out that the demand for any commodity was a function, not only of its own price, but of the prices of other goods. The change in the price of copper, in our example, may shift the demand curve for copper substitutes, and their prices may consequently change, which in turn may shift the demand curve for copper. For a simple first approximation, these secondary shifts may be ignored. The net effect on the price of the commodity taxed and the quantity sold, however, will depend upon the relation between the price of the article taxed and the prices of its substitutes.

A per-unit subsidy granted by the government on the production of some commodity will shift the supply curve of the commodity to the right, other things equal. For example, during World War II, the U.S. government used a subsidy on copper to induce an increase in the output of copper without raising the market price, which was controlled. With the use of a subsidy, the government induced a larger output at the given controlled price. In Figure 4–6, assume that the original supply curve of copper is $S'S'$ and the introduction of a per-unit subsidy shifts the supply curve to SS. Consequently, other things unchanged, the price will fall and the quantity taken off the market will increase. Again this is a first approximation, because demand has been assumed to remain constant, whereas the final position will depend upon the interrelationships among the various commodities.

4.5. Applications to Business Decisions

Suppose an engineer is working for a company that is contemplating a large plant construction project. In addition to being called upon to help on the construction and design plans, he is asked to express his views on the question of when this construction project should be initiated. The project will require quite large amounts of aluminum. It is not an urgent project, and could be postponed for as long as six years without endangering the firm's competitive market position.

He argues for a four-year postponement of the project based on the following reasoning: He has been following the research reports in the engineering journals on the use of solar energy and atomic power for the generation of electric power. From recent reports there is strong evidence to suggest that a very cheap method of generating electric power, either from solar energy or atomic power, will obtain wide commercial application within the next three or four years. Since this will tend to increase the supply of any product which requires large amounts of electric power in its production, he argues that there is a good chance that the market price of aluminum will fall, perhaps considerably, in the near future. Since the project in question requires a great deal of aluminum, he maintains that its postponement may well provide a considerable saving in construction cost.

Or, to take another example, suppose the project requires a great deal of concrete. He knows that the country is engaged in a widespread highway construction program. This highway building program—federal and state—means that the demand for concrete will rise sharply and remain high for many years. Consequently, he argues that the company should begin its construction project as soon as possible, and immediately negotiate, at the current price, a contract for the future delivery of the needed concrete.

Or, suppose you are a consultant working for a firm that is designing a new high-school building that is expected to last fifty years. A question arises as to the type of heating to install in the building, and an important determinant for the school board is the expected annual cost of heating. You are asked to express your opinion. You favor heating by electricity on the following grounds: You have been following the relationship between supply and demand for heating oils, gas, and coal and you expect the price of these fuels to rise because of increased demands and increases in costs of operation in the industries. On the other hand, from your reading of research reports you expect the price of electric power to remain constant or fall as the result of new technologies that seem likely to appear in the area of generating electric power by means of solar energy or atomic power. You reason that the result of the expected price movements will be to make electric power the cheapest source of power for heating over the life of the building.

These examples and the problems considered in the previous sections serve to illustrate how a knowledge of market forces and familiarity with general economics can be of direct interest to the general citizen in aiding his understanding of policy problems and can be of direct interest to engineers and others engaged in planning. It also shows how technical knowledge can be useful in practical economic analysis.

APPENDIX TO CHAPTER 4

APPLICATION OF SUPPLY AND DEMAND TO PRICING OF DURABLE GOODS

In recent years[1] an important extension of the supply and demand theory has been made to the pricing of durable goods. There are two kinds of durable goods—consumer durables such as refrigerators, automobiles, and television sets, and producers durable equipment such as trucks, punch presses, and steam boilers. The analysis of competitive markets for these kinds of goods is complicated by the fact that we do not consume them as fast as they are purchased. They are consumed only over relatively long periods of use.

The price analysis of durable goods requires a fundamental distinction to be made between the demand for such goods as a *stock* or asset to "hold" in use, and the demand for newly produced units of such goods as a *flow*. Suppose as a concrete example we consider the market for trucks. Then there exist two kinds of demand conditions for trucks, a demand for a certain total stock of trucks to be used in performing the daily hauling tasks of the trucking industry, and a demand for new trucks to replace that portion of the total stock of trucks that is wearing out each year. Thus, in Figure 4–7A, *DD* represents the aggregate stock demand for trucks. It is a schedule of the various quantities of trucks industry will desire to maintain in use at a corresponding schedule of prices for trucks. For simplicity we will ignore the problem of pricing trucks of different ages and express price in terms of new vehicles. The stock demand curve *DD* slopes down to the right, since the lower is the price of trucks the greater is the number of trucks, X, which businesses will want to maintain in use. In Figure 4–7B, *dd* represents the annual flow demand for new replacement trucks. The flow demand curve *dd* slopes down to the right because the lower the price of trucks, the more intensively and carelessly will trucks be used with the result that they will wear out faster and increase the replacement rate, x.

The curves *DD* and *dd* represent the stock-flow conditions of demand for trucks. We must also develop a characterization of the supply side of the market. The supply of trucks as a stock or asset at any time is determined by the past history of production and replacement of trucks, and for that instant in time is a

[1] See R. W. Clower, "The Dynamics of Investment," *American Economic Review*, March, 1954, pp. 64–81.

constant equal to the number of trucks physically in existence. Hence the stock supply curve is perfectly inelastic, as indicated by SS in Figure 4–7A. On the other hand, the flow supply curve will represent the various quantities of new trucks that truck manufacturers will desire to produce *per year* as a function of the going price for new trucks. The flow supply curve will therefore be a production response curve exactly like the other supply curves we have been discussing. Such a supply curve representing the annual flow of newly produced trucks into the market is indicated by ss in Figure 4–7B. In summary, the full conditions of supply and demand for a durable good such as trucks is represented by DD, SS, dd and ss in Figure 4–7A and B.

FIGURE 4–7

RELATIONSHIP OF STOCKS AND FLOWS

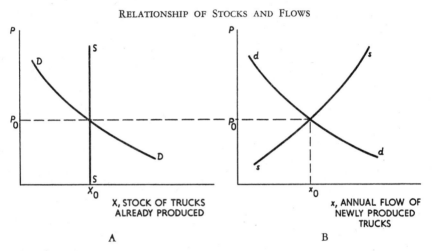

X, STOCK OF TRUCKS ALREADY PRODUCED

A

x, ANNUAL FLOW OF NEWLY PRODUCED TRUCKS

B

Now, if such a market is competitive it will be in full long-run equilibrium at a price p_0 such that the stock demand, DD, is equal to stock supply in existence, SS, and such that the replacement demand rate, dd, is equal to the supply of new trucks being produced, ss. The equilibrium is shown in Figure 4–7A and B, with the using industries satisfied to hold the stock X_0 at the price p_0, and with the replacement rate just equal to the production rate of new trucks, x_0, at that price.

In order to see how the system responds to a change in conditions, suppose a highway expansion and improvement program causes a sudden increase in the demand for trucks from DD to $D'D'$. It is likely also that dd would increase, but let us suppose that all the behavior functions except DD remain as they were before. The effect of the increase in stock demand is shown in Figure 4–8A and B. Since, in the short run, it is not possible appreciably to increase the existing stock of trucks, the effect of the increase in demand to $D'D'$ is to increase the price of trucks to p_0' as trucking firms bid competitively against each other to try to get more trucks. At the temporary equilibrium p_0', truck manufacturers are able to make more profits on the production of new trucks. Specifically, they find it profitable to increase their production of trucks from x_0 to x_s' along the flow supply curve, ss, as shown in Figure 4–8B. With new trucks more expensive, trucking firms now try to make their existing fleets last longer, with more thorough maintenance and servicing. The higher investment cost of trucks means that it pays to spend more on upkeep. This causes a temporary reduction in the replacement rate of trucks from x_0 to x_d'. With the production rate of new trucks increased to x_s', and the replacement rate of old trucks decreased to x_d', it is clear that there is a surplus of $x_s' - x_d'$ new trucks coming into the market per year. This excess flow supply of new trucks into the market causes the existing stock of trucks to increase at the rate $\dfrac{dX}{dt} = x_s' - x_d'$. The competition of sellers to market these new trucks causes price to fall from the p_0' level along the line AB in Figure 4–8A. As price falls, the excess flow supply

FIGURE 4–8

RESTORATION OF EQUILIBRIUM, STOCK AND FLOW

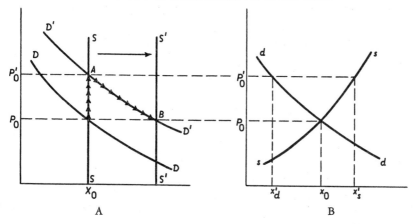

A   B

of new trucks also decreases, but as long as there is any excess of current production over current replacement, the existing stock of trucks must increase. It will continue to increase until it reaches $S'S'$, and price falls back to p_0. At this price the system is again in equilibrium with the replacement rate equal to the production rate at x_0'.

QUESTIONS AND EXERCISES

1. With a diagram similar to that in Figure 4–1, analyze the short- and long-run responses of the cotton piece goods industry (which we take to be competitive) to the introduction of a major technological improvement. Now assume that the industry experiences a decrease in demand. Trace the short- and long-run responses.

2. Find the equilibrium price in a butter market with the following demand-supply functions, where y_1, y_2, p_1 and p_2 represent the quantities and prices of butter and margarine respectively, and p_2 is taken to be 50:

$$y_{1d} = 60 - 2p_1 + p_2 ,$$
$$y_{1s} = 40 + 3p_1 - 2p_2 .$$

a) Suppose the price of margarine (p_2) falls to 40 as the result of a fall in the cost of production of margarine. What happens to the equilibrium price and quantity sold of butter?

b) Suppose that the butter industry introduces an advertising campaign which shifts the demand for butter to

$$y_{1d} = 80 - 1.5p + p_2 .$$

Find the new equilibrium price and quantity sold of butter (assume p_2 remains at 40).

c) Consumers have become more and more concerned about saturated fats. How would you expect this concern to affect the demand for butter?

3. Assume that pretzels are consumed only with beer. If a tax is introduced on beer, what would you expect to happen to the quantity of pretzels consumed? To the price of pretzels?

4. Assume that there is a substantial increase in the price of steel. Trace through the probable impact of such a price increase on the consumption of petroleum products, glass, and rubber.

5. In some market, demand and supply conditions are given as:

$$y_{1d} = 100 - 2p_1 ,$$
$$y_{1s} = 3p_1 - 20 .$$

Now a tax of 5 per unit is levied by the government.

a) Does the total amount paid per unit by the buyers change? If it does change, in what direction and by how much does it change?

b) What happens to the receipts per unit of the sellers? The quantity sold? To total receipts?

c) Who "pays" the tax? How would you alter the condition of demand and/or supply so as to have the buyers pay all the tax? The sellers?

d) Assume, instead, that the government had paid a subsidy of 2 per unit. What is the new equilibrium price paid by the buyers and quantity purchased? How does this new equilibrium price compare to the price in the no-tax, no-subsidy case? Who receives the subsidy?

6. In some cities the rents of some housing units are controlled. Analyze the effect of such control on the construction of new buildings. Trace through the consequences of the removal of rent control.

7. Suppose the demand function $y_{1d} = 120 - 2p_1$ represents the relationship between quantity in any "year" and the price at which the market will just be cleared. Suppose the supply function $y_{1s} = 1.5p_1 - 15$ represents the relationship between price in any "year" and the quantity of the good, y_{1s}, which will be supplied the *following* "year." (Note these are special supply and demand curves.)

a) Suppose in "year" 1 production equal to 80 units is placed on the market. What will the price be in Year 1? What will production be in Year 2? Price in Year 2? Find the prices and quantities for "years" 3, 4, and 5. What is the equilibrium price and quantity?

b) Suppose now the demand function shifts to $y_{1d} = 90 - 1.5p_1$, with the supply function unchanged. If 60 units are placed on the market in "year" 1, what will the price be in Year 1? Trace the prices and quantities for the next four "years." What is the equilibrium price and quantity? Will they be attained? (Remember the demand function in this problem states the relationship between quantity in any "year" and the price at which the market will just be cleared. The supply function represents the relationship between price in any "year" and the quantity of the good which will be supplied the *following* "year."

c) Suppose the demand function now shifts to $y_{1d} = 60 - p_1$. If 32 units are placed on the market in "year" 1, what will be the market clearing price in Year 1? Find the prices and quantities for the next five years. What happens to price and quantity in successive "years"? How many "years" are required for the market to reach equilibrium?

d) Compare the price elasticities of supply and demand, at the equilibrium price, in the above three cases. Is there any relationship between the elasticities and the behavior of price and quantity over time?

8. In this chapter it has been argued that price tends to fall when there is excess supply, and rise when there is excess demand. Suppose we make the specific hypothesis that price falls or rises at a *rate* in a direct *proportion* to excess supply or demand, that is, $\frac{dp}{dt} = \beta(x_d - x_s)$, where x_d is demand at p, x_s is supply at p, and $\beta > 0$. Beginning with some initial price p_0, at time $t_0 = 0$, what will be the path of p as a function of time, $p(t)$, if $x_d = a - bp$, and $x_s = A + Bp$, where a, b, A and B are all positive?

9. Starting with the initial stock-flow equilibrium in Figure 4–7, analyze the equilibrating adjustments that would follow a decrease in *DD*.

10. Reconstruct the stock-flow analysis of Figures 4–7 and 4–8, assuming that the replacement demand is proportional to the existing stock, that is $x_d = kX$. In other words, a constant fraction, k, of the stock of machines wears out per unit of time independently of age.

Chapter 5

SUPPLY AND DEMAND FOR INPUTS—PRODUCTIVE SERVICES

In Chapter 1 it was pointed out that the economic process involves specialization in production by firms, which produce a variety of goods that are exchanged, in the market, for each other. In subsequent chapters the analysis of the pricing of products was developed by indicating the factors which make up demand and supply for products. The price of a product was determined by the interaction of all of the factors which went into the determination of demand, on the one hand, and supply, on the other hand. Several of the special problems associated with price determination were then presented, and the determination of equilibrium price under the conditions involved was analyzed. Attention must now be turned to the determination of the prices which the firms must pay for the productive services used in the process of creating products.

5.1. Productive Services, or Factors of Production

Factors of production consist of the services of property, services which are used in the productive process. Thus, *labor* is a factor of production derived from the human body. Labor involves the *flow* of effort, both physical and mental, which persons contribute to the production of goods. The productive service, labor, is paid *wages*. The use of *land* involves the flow of the productive service of land. For this service the economist speaks of the price which must be paid as *rent*. Note that it is the service of land which is being used in the productive process. The land, itself, is not used up; as a bit of geographical space, it is still there. If irreplaceable resources are taken from the land, a royalty may be paid for the using up of this aspect of land's productivity. Services of houses, machines, and other material equipment are factors of production derived from the form of property which yield them. The payment for the use of this specialized equipment, called *capital*, is also rent. The capital itself is assumed to be replaced, by depreciation expenditure and maintenance cost, as will be indicated more fully in later chapters. Rent then is a payment for a *flow* of services from the existing *stock* of capital. This payment is often stated as a percentage of the value of the stock of capital involved, in which case the price of the flow of services from capital is called *interest*. Money capital merely represents spending power which can be assigned to the creation of real capital, the buildings, machines, and other equipment referred to above. In order to persuade the owners of money capital to devote that purchasing power to the creation of real capital, the holders of money will be paid, and that payment is also stated as a percentage, or interest. Thus we can say that the factors of production are the services of labor, land, and capital, and the payments accorded to them are wages, rent, and interest.

5.2. Determination of the Prices of Productive Services

The "equilibrium price" of productive services bought and sold in a competitive market is determined by the now familiar principle of clearing the market. The equilibrium price is that price at which the quantity of the service which its owners are willing to offer is equal to the quantity of the service which its employers—buyers—are willing to take. We can construct demand and supply schedules, showing the relation between hypothetical prices and the quantities of the service supplied and demanded at the prices, and then find the equilibrium price and quantity, in the same manner as for products. It should be noted that in Figure 5–1, "Equilibrium Price for a Productive Service," the quantity measurement on the horizontal axis is identified by the symbol x, whereas in the figures used for illustrating the pricing of products the

FIGURE 5–1

EQUILIBRIUM PRICE FOR A PRODUCTIVE SERVICE

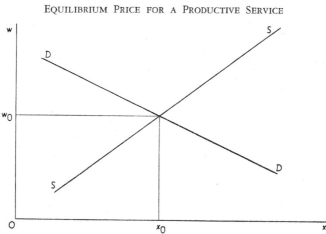

quantity of the product was identified with y. The different notations are used to distinguish between inputs, x, and outputs, y.

In Figure 5–1, the equilibrium price for a productive service, w_0, is that price at which the market for the service is cleared, in that the quantity demanded is the number of units of the service, x_0, and the quantity supplied is the same number of units, x_0, at that price.

Although it is quite correct to indicate that the prices of productive services are determined by the interrelationships among demand and supply for those services, in different markets at different times, in order to give an adequate explanation for a particular price for a particular service, it is necessary to inquire into the factors which determine the demand and the supply in each case.

5.3. Demand for Productive Services

A more extended explanation of the demand for productive services will have to be postponed until the theory of production is developed in subsequent chapters (Chapters 18 to 22). There are, however, a few propositions concerning the demand for productive services or factors of production that can be examined with the tools of demand and supply analysis. These propositions will be presented in connection with the demand for the service, *labor,* but they *apply equally well to the other productive services,* with the exception that the demand for the other productive services is often translated from a demand for the service itself, a flow, into a demand for the stock of goods from which that flow of services originates.

The demand for labor is a derived demand. Firms hire labor because with its aid they can produce or acquire some other commodity which consumers demand. Productive services are demanded because they are used in producing commodities and services which firms believe consumers wish to buy. Because of the fact that the demand for the service is a derived demand, there are four general propositions concerning that demand which can be enunciated at this point, in terms of the demand and supply tools.

1. The first proposition follows from the fact that the demand for labor is derived. It is that an expected change in the demand for a product will cause a change in the demand for the services used to produce the product. For example, the expected rise in the demand for superhighways causes a rise in the demand for civil engineers. The employers may be right or wrong in their expectations, but it is their opinion and not the accuracy of that opinion which determines the demand for the services of civil engineers. Similarly, the expectation that more contracts

will be let by the government for basic research in physics causes the managers of research laboratories to increase their demand for physicists. This proposition may be illustrated graphically by Figure 5–2. An increase in the demand for the product, Figure 5–2A, causes an increase in the demand for the service, Figure 5–2B.

FIGURE 5–2

EFFECT OF THE INCREASE IN THE DEMAND FOR A PRODUCT ON THE
DEMAND FOR SERVICES

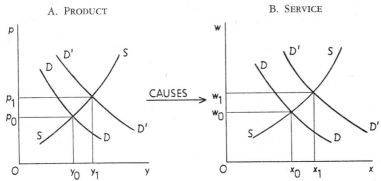

2. The second of these propositions might be called the importance of being unimportant, for the smaller the part played by a productive service in the production of a commodity, the more inelastic is the demand for it likely to be. For example, the wages of labor employed in the operation of shovels used in digging the excavation for a building is a very small part of the total cost of the building. As a consequence, a rather considerable increase in the wages of such labor would have little effect on total costs of construction of the building and therefore would have little effect on the employment of that labor. In fact, in the building industry, there exists a condition where the provider of each component believes that his price is such a small part of the total price of the building that he may very well increase his price without greatly affecting cost for the entire project. However, when each party to the entire project increases his charge, the cost of the entire building increases very noticeably. On the other hand, no seller of any component in the total building believes that a decrease in his charges will have any noticeable effect on the cost of the entire building and therefore will in no way influence the level of demand for buildings; consequently, each is unwilling to lower price.

Under the assumption of this proposition, large increases in price for a service cause small decreases in supply of the product and therefore cause only a small decrease in the quantity sold. Hence, there is only a small decrease in the employment of that service. The demand for the service is relatively inelastic. Figure 5–3 illustrates this relationship. The change in the price of the service, from w_0 to w_1 in Figure 5–3B results in a relatively small decrease in supply from SS to $S'S'$ and, since

FIGURE 5–3

EFFECT OF CHANGE IN PRICE OF A SERVICE ON THE SUPPLY OF A PRODUCT

A. PRODUCT   B. SERVICE

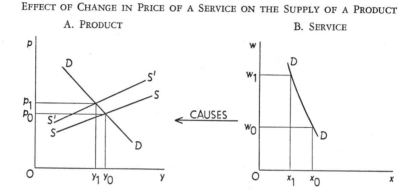

the service is assumed to play a very small part in production, therefore a small decrease in quantity of product taken from y_0 to y_1 in Figure 5–3A. The effect is that the quantity of the service employed as a result of the increase in its price is reduced only slightly, from x_0 to x_1, Figure 5–3B.

3. The next proposition states that the elasticity of demand for the product affects, in the same direction, the elasticity of demand for the services used in producing the product. For example, the demand for a certain brand of an article will be very elastic if there are other brands of very similar products also on the market. As a consequence, a union with a collective bargaining contract with one firm in an industry but not with others will not be able to press its wage demands very far for fear of the impact on price of the product and the loss of employment for labor at that company. The union sees for itself the necessity of getting acceptance at all firms in the industry and of presenting a unified wage demand to all of the firms if it wishes to protect, to some extent, employment for union members when there is a wage increase. Figure 5–4, A and B, illustrates this relationship. An increase in the price of the productive service from w_0 to w_1 results in a shift in the supply curve for the product from SS to $S'S'$ and a decrease in sales from y_0 to y_1. The consequence is a reduction in employment of the productive service from x_0 to x_1.

4. In addition, the elasticity of demand for a productive service will be determined partly by factors of substitution. If there is a close substitute for the service in the making of products, the demand for the service will be relatively elastic. For this reason, labor unions attempt to eliminate competition from a close substitute for union members' labor—the labor of men not members of the union. This can be done in

FIGURE 5–4

ELASTIC DEMAND FOR PRODUCT AND FOR SERVICE USED IN PRODUCTION OF IT

A. PRODUCTS   B. SERVICES

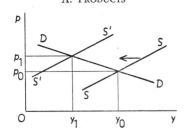
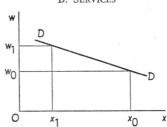

two ways. One of these ways is to make the union members so superior to nonunion men that employers will not consider using nonunion labor. It is no longer a close substitute. This can be accomplished by means of a training program and apprenticeship period for new union members and by maintaining work discipline over the union members. The other method of eliminating the competition of the close substitute is to deny it access to the labor market.

The elasticity of demand for the resource, labor, shows how much a change in the wage (the price of labor) affects the amount of employment. There are three steps connecting supply and demand for the product with the demand for a productive service, or factor of production. The wage affects the supply curve of the product (other things being equal), the supply curve of the product affects the output of the product, and the output of the product affects the amount of employment. Symbolically we could write

$$\left(\begin{array}{c} w' \\ \uparrow \\ w \end{array}\right) \longrightarrow \left(\begin{array}{c} SS \\ \downarrow \\ S'S' \end{array}\right) \longrightarrow \left(\begin{array}{c} y \\ \downarrow \\ y' \end{array}\right) \longrightarrow \left(\begin{array}{c} x \\ \downarrow \\ x' \end{array}\right).$$

(implies)
(or causes)

which reads "an increase in wages implies or causes a reduction in supply, a reduction in supply implies reduced output, and reduced output implies a reduction in the quantity of labor demanded."

5.4. Supply of Productive Services

The important elements in an analysis of the supply of the factors of production are the position of the supply curve, the ease with which the supply can change, and the elasticity of supply. The position of the supply for any factor of production depends upon its relative scarcity compared with the other factors of production with which it must be combined in a productive use. For example, in some countries of the world labor is relatively plentiful while the services of land and capital are relatively scarce. As a consequence, the supply of labor available will, in general, be great, and wages will be low. Capital and land will, on the other hand, command relatively high prices. In such countries, skilled labor may also be scarce, so that it commands high wages, relative to unskilled labor.

In the United States, the plentiful supply of land and capital have made it possible for real wages to be so high that a large proportion of the work force has been able to afford education sufficient to make it into skilled labor, or managerial and professional labor. In consequence, unskilled labor (e.g., domestic servants) is relatively more scarce than it is elsewhere, and unskilled and semiskilled laborers enjoy a wage scale that has no comparison in history. In fact, the most rapid rise in real wages in the United States, during the twentieth century, has occurred for the unskilled and semiskilled labor groups. The position of their supply curves has moved steadily to the left.

The ease with which the supply of a resource can change is largely a function of time. In the short run, it may be impossible to acquire a very great addition to the supply of a particular productive service. However, over time, the supply might change rather considerably. The changes in the entire schedule of supply for a service are functions of the underlying relationships referred to above with respect to the position of supply.

An analysis of supply for factors of production will be made by considering the factor of production, labor, and then turning to the other factors of production to determine in what major respects the conditions of supply for those factors differs from the supply of labor. The supply of labor means the relationship between the price of labor and the quantity of labor offered for sale at each hypothetical price. Labor is generally measured by hours of work. The total quantity of any given type of labor offered to employers then depends upon two factors. These are the number of hours each worker is willing to work and the number of workers. The number of workers is related to the size of the population, to the cultural requirements of the society with respect to the persons who may work—for instance, women and children—and to the age and sex distribution within the population. The number of hours each is willing to work is partially an institutionalized pattern of acceptance of working time. In addition it depends upon the aspirations of the workers. One of the things a worker may do is take leisure. If his aspirations are for a higher income and living standard he may deny himself leisure, in spite of the wage he receives. He is eager to make progress, with the income he may earn, toward his goal. On the other hand, many workers have no desire to change their status and, once they have earned enough wages to take care of their needs, they will refuse to work more hours. If wages are high, the number of hours of work may be very few. Figure 5–5 illustrates the backward-bending supply curve for labor

FIGURE 5–5

THE BACKWARD-BENDING SUPPLY CURVE FOR LABOR

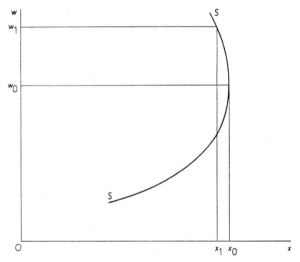

when there is competition between work and leisure, and high wages make leisure possible rather than induce the laborer to more effort. The total income of the laborer, $w_0 \cdot x_0$ is smaller than the total income, $w_1 \cdot x_1$, even though the hours of employment at x_1 are fewer than at x_0. Leisure is one of the things that the worker can afford when his wage is high. The number of workers in the market, however, may include enough individuals who will work additional hours at high wages to offset the effect of the backward-bending supply curve for some of the laborers so that the total supply schedule will slope upward to the right.

5.5. The Elasticity of Supply of Labor

If the number of hours to be worked by each individual is fixed by custom or contract, the elasticity of supply of labor will depend almost entirely on the mobility of labor into the occupation in question and out of other occupations. If there is high mobility, the supply will be relatively elastic (Figure 5–6A). On the other hand, if mobility of labor is

FIGURE 5–6

ELASTICITY OF SUPPLY OF LABOR

A. ELASTIC SUPPLY   B. INELASTIC SUPPLY

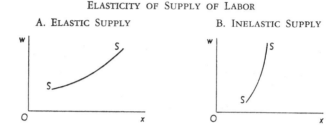

low, the supply will tend to be inelastic, Figure 5–6B. Mobility of labor is partly a function of time. In the short run, it may be impossible for many laborers to change to a different job. In the long run, however, the changes may be accomplished.

5.6. The Principle of Equal Advantage

In a free economy, any individual is allowed to put the resources which he owns to any use he thinks fit, provided he does not thereby violate the property rights of others. This apportionment of the resources is governed by a principle called the principle of equal advantage: "If the owners of any resources think that they can be put to better advantage in some other use than the one in which they are employed, these resources will be transferred from the less advantageous to the more advantageous use."[1] We might say, simply, that just as liquids run downhill seeking their own level, so productive services run uphill, seeking the best possible return. And, just as the effect of the flow of liquids tends to be to create a uniform level, so the movement of productive resources among uses tends to result in their receiving everywhere the same rate of return. If there were no friction reducing mobility, if there were perfect knowledge on the part of all the possessors of productive services, and if there were no nonmonetary considerations as part of income, the prices of productive services would be the same everywhere and in all uses.

[1] Kenneth Boulding, *Economic Analysis* (3rd. ed.; New York: Harper & Bros., 1955), p. 169.

Actually, of course, there are *nonmonetary considerations* which frequently play an important part in the allocation of factors of production among uses. Consequently, when equilibrium is reached, advantages are equal in all employments, but money payments may not be equal. That is, nonmonetary advantages of A plus monetary advantages of A equal nonmonetary advantages of B plus monetary advantages of B, for any A or B. The movement toward equilibrium is illustrated by Figure 5–7. In Market A, the equilibrium wage had been w_0 and the

FIGURE 5–7

THE PRINCIPLE OF EQUAL ADVANTAGE

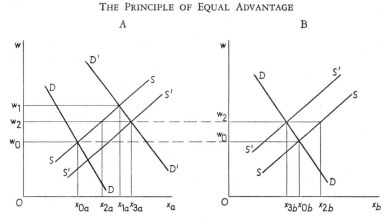

volume of employment x_{0a}. The equilibrium wage and volume of employment in Market B had been w_0 and x_{0b}, respectively, as well. There was no tendency for labor to move from one market to the other, if the combination of monetary and nonmonetary considerations was included in the measurement of w. However, the increase in the demand for labor in Market A had the effect of changing the wage to w_1 and calling forth more hours of labor from the workers in Market A.

The elasticity of supply of labor in Market A determined the extent of the wage increase which was necessary to restore temporary equilibrium in that market. For instance, had the supply of labor been perfectly elastic there would have been no increase in wages of any sort in Market A. As a consequence of the increase in wages in Market A, however, disequilibrium came into existence between the two markets, since wages were lower in Market B than in Market A as a consequence of the changed demand in Market A. To the extent that labor was mobile and able to move between the two markets, labor would shift from Market B to Market A, increasing wages in Market B and depressing wages in Market A until there was no longer any motive for change when wages became the same in both markets. At final equilibrium wages in both markets would have become w_2, and the quantity of hours of labor employed in each market would be x_{3a} and x_{3b}, the transfer of $x_{2b} - x_{3b}$ hours of labor from Market B to Market A having accomplished the restoration of equilibrium.

Similarly, if the wage w_1 in Market A represented monetary plus nonmonetary factors while in Market B there were no nonmonetary factors, the equilibrium wage would represent a situation equivalent to that represented in Figure 5–7, with the exception that the equilibrium wage in Market A, w_2, would include nonmonetary advantages while the equilibrium wage in Market B, also w_2, would not include nonmonetary advantages. If one assumes that there is mobility of labor among different employments, one may say that the difference in wages be tween the two markets places a monetary valuation on the differences in the nonmonetary advantages between the two markets. For example, if a physician will accept employment in research work for $10,000 a year when he could have earned $50,000 a year in private practice, the nonmonetary advantage of the research employment as compared with private practice would, for him, be $50,000 — $10,000 or $40,000.

Nonmonetary advantages are sometimes referred to by the term *psychic income* in order to represent that they do have a value as income. Some possible sources of psychic income would be prestige, a sense of dedication, the pleasantness of surroundings, and the enjoyment derived from doing work one wants to do. Other advantages are frequently labeled nonmonetary advantages, but this type of label involves misunderstanding of the nature of the appeal one employment has over another. For instance, if the opportunities for advancement are greater in one employment than another, other things being equal, one would expect labor to move to the employment with the greatest opportunity. But in terms of life chances, the two employments would presumably have equal total income if knowledge and mobility were present. Another factor, which is really a monetary one, is security. If a person is certain of employment for fifty-two weeks a year, year in and year out, he may be willing to work for a lower hourly or weekly wage than one who is certain of only sporadic employment. The price of the insecurity associated with the latter employment would be measured as being the higher wages that would be paid in that task than in some other, more secure one.

5.7. Impediments to the Mobility of Productive Services

It is not necessary that the holder of each unit of a productive service be able to move it from one employment to another for there to be mobility. For example, in Figure 5–7, only the amount of labor, $x_2 - x_3$, need be moved from Market B to Market A for equilibrium between the two markets to be restored. The requirement is that enough units of a factor of production be mobile to allow the principle of equal advantage to effect an equilibrium. Therefore, some impediments may exist to perfect mobility without destroying the validity of mobility as an equalizer. Whenever the immobility of resources is such that equality of payment is not the equilibrium condition, there must be true impediments to movement among alternative employments.

For labor, we might classify immobility between kinds of employment and between geographical areas. Immobility between different kinds of employment is observable whenever wage rates vary in an area according to the type of employment by more than enough to be accounted for by nonmonetary advantages. From a short-run point of view, such immobility exists because of *ignorance,* the specific types of *skills required,* or *artificial restrictions.* People may not know of the higher wages being paid in other employment and hence may not move from the lower-paying employment to the higher. They may not possess the training and skills required to occupy jobs that pay better wages than they are receiving and, in the short run at least, they are unable to receive the schooling and the training necessary to perform different tasks. Once a person has been trained for a certain type of employment, he cannot change over to another which requires extensive training without going through that training. Many professional men today earn less in their employments than, let us say, engineers earn in theirs. Nevertheless, it is too late for them to change, even though they might possess the inherent capacity to become engineers. Furthermore, artificial restrictions may create unsurmountable impediments to mobility. These restrictions include the licensing requirements for many professions, the admission requirements of unions, and the impositions exercised against minority groups.

In the long run, the artificial impediments to mobility may be maintained; individuals may not be able to afford the training period required to prepare themselves for remunerative occupations; and ignorance may not disappear. In addition, the *inherent capacity* to handle certain employment is involved. Not all of us possess the skill of a Roger Maris as a hitter in baseball. Very few of us have the brains of an Einstein; many of us could not handle the task of the managing officers of large corporations, where a combination of judgment and daring along with acquired knowledge is needed. Wage differences will persist as long as people have different capabilities.

Geographic immobility stems from ignorance, social inertia, and artificial restrictions. Although we suspect that farther fields are greener, we may not be wholly aware of it. Consequently, we do not move to the areas of the world where rewards for the services we can offer are greater. An important factor in this is risk. Since we do not know of the actual conditions which exist for our services elsewhere, we request that we receive a payment for taking the risk of committing ourselves to the changed location. Consequently, even though we know that some productive services similar to our own are being paid for handsomely elsewhere, we do not know that we will receive such payment if we venture out, and we ask for compensation just for moving greater than the difference between the payments in the two areas.

Social inertia may be an important factor in the maintenance of a differential between wage payments in two communities. We enjoy our native hills and valleys; we have friends and acquaintances where we are; our families are contented with life as it is. Who is to deny us the judgment we make that we have the "good life" at present? In this respect, social inertia is closely related to the nonmonetary advantages referred to earlier. The difference is that social inertia works in both directions. It isn't that we all want to live in beautiful California (or Florida) and thus cause wages to be depressed there. Instead, we actually enjoy our homes wherever they may be.

One more aspect of social inertia should be mentioned. Frequently, mobility is possessed by those who do not need it, the socially enfranchised. There will be groups in the society who do not possess social status. Frequently the lack of social status is associated with the lack of economic position and is accompanied by the lack of mobility, geographically and among occupations. Studies have shown, for instance, that individuals who do not complete high school have less mobility, even within their group, than individuals with more education than they.

Artificial restrictions on geographic mobility include the nonacceptance of minority groups in certain areas of the country and limitations on migration. Immigration laws of nations prevent the movement of people from low-income countries to high-income countries. What immigration is allowed is generally assigned on a selective basis. Persons of certain skills may be welcome as immigrants into underdeveloped countries. Similarly, during the days of mercantilism, people with special skills who were thought to enrich a country were frequently denied the right to emigrate from their countries.

The principle of equal advantage applies to property services as well as to labor. There are certain distinctions in the application of this principle to property services which should be pointed out. In the first place, the service of land is specifically immobile geographically. There is only so much land, and it is all located. As a consequence, when land is desired, since it cannot be moved and cannot be added to or destroyed, the price which will be paid for it depends upon its demand for different uses, and not upon any elasticity with respect to supply. A corner location in the center of the shopping district of a large city may command a very high rent, with the user who places the highest price upon it being the one to acquire the use of the site. If there is a movement for retailing to move to the outskirts of the city, the landowner cannot pick up his land and move too. He must accept the shift in demand without being able to adjust for it.

The same is, to a certain extent, true for specialized capital. In the short run, it may be irreplaceable, the time within which additional specialized capital can be produced being longer than the time interval in question, and the time it takes for the capital to wear out being long also. In such a case, specialized capital receives a payment based on fixed supply, just like the payment for the use of land. It receives economic rent.

In the long run, there may be changes in the supply of fixed capital; additions to the stock may occur, or the old stock may wear out. In this event, the determination of the price for the capital will be the determination of the price of liquid, uncommitted capital. The principle of equal advantage would determine that capital would be paid the same everywhere, except for any restrictions on its mobility which might exist. These restrictions would include the artificial restrictions authorized by law, such as patent rights, and restrictions imposed by social practice, such as the nonacceptance by most persons of certain antisocial uses for capital. Munitions makers were supposed to have done very well for themselves, during the nineteenth century, because there were few who would enter the field and because they frequently had control over processes and products by invention.

The risk factor is very important in determining the different rates of return which liquid capital will receive. Generally, the higher the risk which is assumed to exist, the higher will the requested return have to be before capital will be assigned to a specific use. One of the sources of geographic differences in interest rates lies in the risks associated with making an investment in a region where there is little control over the investment or where laws and customs are unfamiliar.

5.8. Opportunity Costs and the Least-Cost Combination

If any productive service would be assigned to the use for which it receives the highest return, it would follow that in order to command the use of the service in one employment it would have to be paid as much as it could earn in any other employment. It would have to receive as much as would be offered it by any opportunity for other use. This payment, then, is *opportunity cost.* In a price sense, it is the price of any other opportunity for employment. In a real sense, the cost of any product is the products which could have been produced with the same productive services used in employment where the advantage to it is equal to the advantage the services enjoy in the chosen employment.

A schedule of alternative employments for productive services, to measure opportunity cost accurately, would have to be based upon the most effective combination of the services being employed for a specific productive purpose. If the most effective combination were not employed, other users of the productive services involved would be in a position to bargain for those services and pay enough to command them for themselves. Consequently, each employer of a combination of productive services would endeavor to use a *least-cost combination* of them to insure for himself that they would not be bargained away to some other employment. If there can be a variety of combinations of resources employed, and there is one combination which is a least-cost combination, then there is possible substitution of one resource for another. And the *principle of substitution* would indicate that one resource will be substituted for another wherever substitution results in the lowering of costs.

In Section 5.4 it was pointed out that productive services are used in combination with each other and that the relatively scarce service will have the greatest relative demand, and hence price. It should be added that as one productive service becomes less costly, it will be substituted for the other services to some extent, thus decreasing the demand for the other services. The more plentiful productive service will be substituted for the more scarce and expensive productive services. Thus, we find that we tend to economize on the employment of the scarce services, while, at the same time, in terms of all uses, the scarce services become scarcer and more expensive as the plentiful services increase in supply.

An increase in population will cause wages in an area to fall, other things being equal, and the prices of land and capital to become higher. Consequently, a region of large labor supply would have its lowest costs, relative to the rest of the world, in labor-intensive industries, that is, in industries where labor can be substituted for the other factors of production. The same applies to the land-intensive industries in countries where labor and capital are relatively scarce and to capital-intensive industries in countries where labor and land are relatively scarce. In Chapter 22 the implications of this for international trade are developed. Within a country, specialization in production will exist according to the relative plentifulness of the productive resources employed in the industries for which location advantages occur. As a consequence, if the plentiful labor of one region cannot move to regions of scarce labor, due to factors creating geographic immobility, the products which it helps to make can be sold on an interregional basis, thereby increasing the demand for the products in the making of which the labor is employed and increasing the derived demand for the labor.

5.9. Production Possibility Curves

Since the prices of productive services can be stated as opportunity costs, the things which these services help to produce, in one employment, have a cost which is equal to the things which could have been produced with those services in another employment. The relationships among the alternative products which could be produced with given resources are production possibilities. If the decision is made in an economy to produce a certain amount of one thing, it is necessary that productive services be released from other employment for the desired quantity of the one thing to be produced.

These decisions, which direct production, are made by means of prices in a free enterprise economy. Price allocates resources to certain uses and away from others. In a planned society, the decision on the uses for productive services may be made by a planning agency. In either case, the real costs of the things produced are the things not produced. The cost of military supremacy is the consumers' goods an economy might have had but for the expenditures on war, or it is the cost of factories and machines which might have added to the future output of the country but for the using up of the productive services on military equipment.

For the economy as a whole then, the opportunity cost concept expresses the concept of the alternatives open to the society. For a two-commodity model, this relationship is shown graphically, in Figure 5–8, in which the line $y_1'M\ M'y_2'$ represents maximum output for the economy of any combinations of the products y_1 and y_2. All resources could be used to produce only product y_1, in which case total output would be y_1' of y_1 and none of y_2, or, conversely, only y_2 might be produced, with maximum output at y_2' of y_2 and none of y_1. Also, some of each product might be produced. The possible production, at point M, would be y_1'' of y_1 and y_2'' of y_2. Production of y_2 could be increased only at the expense of some of the production of y_1 which would have to be foregone.

FIGURE 5-8

A PRODUCTION POSSIBILITY CURVE

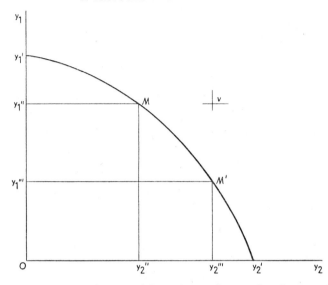

For example, it would be possible to have the production combination y_1''' of y_1 and y_2''' of y_2 represented at the point on the production possibility curve, M'. But it is not possible to reach the point V, which would indicate a production of y_1'' of y_1 and y_2''' of y_2. The opportunity cost of employing resources to produce one product is the amount of other products which must be foregone in order for that production to take place. Because the combination of resources required for most efficient production of y_1 is different from the combination of resources required for most efficient production of y_2, and resources are not perfect substitutes, as either extreme is approached, the production possibility curve, concave to the origin, indicates the relatively small gain in production which would exist if all resources were shifted only to one product. Equilibrium would exist in the products and services markets when the ratio of the quantity of y_1 that would have to be surrendered to the quantity of y_2 that would be gained, for any point on the production possibility curve would be the inverse of the prices of the two products.

QUESTIONS AND EXERCISES

Indicate, where needed, what assumptions you use in answering the following questions:

1. Indicate how different the demand functions for labor may be in
    a) A firm producing hand-made boots.
    b) A firm engaged in plastering walls of buildings.

2. Will the operation of the principle of equal advantage make the wages of all workers equal? Explain your answer.

3. Suppose the social prestige of the physicist increases very much. Do you think this will affect the income of physicists? Explain.

4. In England, after World War II, there was a shortage of miners in the coal mines. Some said wages of miners should be increased to obtain more labor, but others said wages should *not* be increased, rather more and better goods should be put in the shops. Explain the conditions necessary for (*a*) the first point of view to be correct, (*b*) the second point of view.

5. A tax is levied on improved real estate in one of two adjoining cities but not in the other. Show short- and long-run effects of this tax on rentals and on construction activity in the two cities.

6. In a two-commodity model, a production possibility function for the commodities y_1 and y_2 might be written

$$(y_1 + 6)^2 + y_2^2 = 100$$

for positive values of y_1 and y_2. If production of y_1 is increased from 0 to 2, what consequences does this have for production of y_2? If production of y_1 is increased from 2 to 4, what consequences does this have for production of y_2? Explain why such a relationship as shown in this model might exist.

7. Given the production possibility function of the above question, what would be the ratio between the prices of y_2 and y_1 at equilibrium if production were to be 6 of y_2 and 2 of y_1?

8. If it is hoped that distortion in income distribution is to be lessened, suggest means for doing this which take advantage of the market price mechanism.

9. Suppose that in two different markets for the same resource the demand and supply functions have been:

$$y_{1d} = 20 - \tfrac{1}{2}p; \, y_{1s} = p - 1$$
$$y_{2d} = 30 - p; \, y_{2s} = 2p - 12 \,.$$

Subsequently, demand in market one changes to $y_{1d} = 29 - 1/2 \, p$. What changes must take place in supply schedules to restore equilibrium between the two markets, if slopes of the supply function do not change?

Chapter 6

GENERAL EQUILIBRIUM: ADJUSTMENTS IN A COMPETITIVE ECONOMY

Now that we have seen what is meant by an equilibrium in each of the markets—the market for products and the market for productive services—we shall bring the two together and consider the interrelationships which exist between the two. Opportunity costs may indicate the cost of possessing one product instead of another, but they do not indicate why one product is preferred to another or what may be the adjustment mechanism for change from the production of a certain ratio of quantities among products to a different ratio. In this chapter it will be shown how changes in demand—shifts from one product to another—and in supply, work themselves out in a money-using competitive economy.

The analysis will begin by assuming that both markets are in equilibrium. Although this assumption would not be descriptive of the actual world, which is always in a process of change, it is a very useful analytical device for isolating the effects of changes on the economy. Departures from equilibrium and the consequent adjustments in the economy which bring about a new equilibrium position will be described, using three different examples. In the first example, we shall trace through the effects and adjustments brought about by a shift in consumer preferences which leads to a shift in demand between two products, and the adjustments in production, in the productive services market, and in other products which will be necessary to re-create a condition of general equilibrium. The example chosen will be a shift of consumer preference from canned vegetables to frozen vegetables. Second, a shift in the supply schedules of products, based on changes in the technique of production, will be considered. The example in this case will be a shift in the supply curve for agricultural products as a result of technological changes in agricultural production. The third example will refer to a shift originating in the productive services market because of a change in preference on the part of labor. In this example the adjustments examined will be brought about by persons deciding to transfer out of agriculture and into manufacturing industry. The changes will be treated in a step-by-step fashion to bring out the interrelationships which exist, but such changes would, if they were real, be occurring simultaneously in both the products and productive services markets.

6.1. The Circular Flow of Economic Life

In Figure 6–1 a diagram of a circular flow economy is presented.[1] The economy is divided into two sectors, one, on the left-hand side of the diagram for firms, and the other, on the opposite side of the diagram, for households. It is assumed that all production is undertaken by firms, and all productive services originate in households. It is further assumed that there is no unemployment of any factors of production which are seeking employment at prevailing prices. Finally, it is assumed that all money received by households as the price for the employment of the productive services which they provide is spent by the households on consumers' goods; the supply of money is constant; no money is withdrawn from spending for saving, for tax payments, or to purchase imports; and no money comes to firms from any other source than the consumption spending of households. It is quite clear that this is a very simple model of an economic system. Yet the assumptions are such that the basic relationships which exist in economic life, and which are to be outlined in the chosen hypothetical adjustment relationships, are not seriously disturbed by the employment of these simplifying assumptions.

The supply and demand diagrams on the right side of the figure, belonging to households, represent the various productive services, ranging from x_1, x_2, x_3, x_4 to x_n. As a result of the forces of supply and demand, the equilibrium prices for the various productive services are shown in each diagram with the accompanying equilibrium quantities of services. The line across the top of the diagram represents a two-way flow, a flow of productive services from the owners of the services, the households, to the firms where the productive services are used in the production of the various products y_1 to y_n. In the reverse direction the line represents a flow of money income received by the owners of the productive services ($x_1, \ldots, x_n$) and paid by the business firms. The total income an individual receives, in this simple flow

---

[1] The circular flow diagram used is adapted from one developed by E. T. Weiler in his book, *The Economic System* (New York: Macmillan Co., 1952), p. 191. A large part of what follows in this chapter is based on the material in Chapter 10 of Professor Weiler's book, and is used with permission of the publisher.

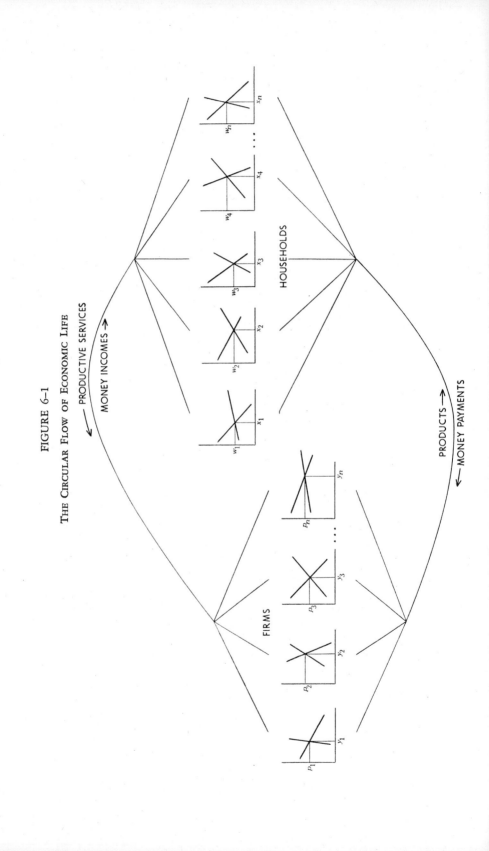

FIGURE 6–1

THE CIRCULAR FLOW OF ECONOMIC LIFE

model, depends on the quantity of services he sells and the prices at which he sells them.

In turn, the owners of the productive services use their incomes to purchase the goods (products) produced by the business firms (products $y_1, \ldots, y_n$). Therefore the line on the bottom of the page also represents a two-way flow. It represents, first, a flow of products from the business community to the owners of the productive services and secondly, a flow in the reverse direction of money payments from the resource owners to the business firms to pay for the products they have received from the business firms. In turn, the business firms that receive the money payments will then be in a position to hire additional productive services for further production.

Thus the underlying flows of productive services and products proceeds as follows: Households supply various quantities of the different types of productive services ($x_1, \ldots, x_n$). These productive services flow to businesses. They are divided and allocated among groups of businesses, or industries, and among the businesses comprising these groups. The allocation is accomplished by the allocation effect of prices paid to the services, so that, in terms of the principle of equal advantage, each productive service is paid as much as it could earn in any other employment, taking into account the nonmonetary advantages and disadvantages of different employments. The demand for each productive service is derived from the demand for the products in the production of which it is employed. The combination of productive services used for each article produced is dependent upon the least-cost combination of them, in a competitive economy.

Since it is the demand for the products, by households, combined with the supply conditions established by the supply of the factors of production and their availability among employments, that determines what is produced, it also determines the products' flow to the households from which the demand originates. The households are divided among occupational groups and holders of different kinds of productive services. Those with the productive services in greatest demand, and with the greatest quantities of such productive services, have the greatest ability to influence the direction of production, and the distribution of products to themselves.

If the economy is in what is called static equilibrium (i.e., no changes taking place in any of the variables), the flows of money payments would be the same, period after period, and the flow of products would also remain the same, period after period. The same amount would be spent for a given amount of clothing, and the same amount would be spent for a given amount of new television sets. In the same manner, the same amount would be spent period after period for engineers' services, for mechanics' services, for the services of land, and for the services of capital. That is, prices, quantities, and incomes would remain the same, period after period, and the economy would be characterized by endless repetition in the process of production and consumption.

6.2. Effects of a Change in the Demand for Products

In order to illustrate the effects of a change in the demand for products on the entire circuit flow system, a hypothetical example will be developed. Suppose that the demand for canned vegetables declines, and the demand for frozen vegetables increases. For purposes of exposition, each of the expected developments will be discussed separately; however, it should be remembered, as emphasized above, that the changes take place approximately simultaneously in all markets.

1. *Sales Response.* As a result of the increased demand for frozen vegetables, the quantities sold and/or the prices paid for frozen vegetables would rise. As a result of the decline in the demand for canned vegetables, the quantities sold and/or prices paid for canned vegetables would decline. How much of the change would be in quantity and how much in price would depend on the willingness of producers in both industries to permit changes in their inventories.

2. *Production Responses.* Canned-food producers, seeing changes in their prices and/or sales, would tend to reduce their outputs. They would do this by releasing workers, by buying less vegetables and fewer cans, and by failing to replace equipment as it wears out. Some firms would also drop out of the canned-vegetable business altogether. Meanwhile, the frozen-food producers would tend to increase their outputs. This would be particularly likely to occur if frozen-food prices were to rise so that it would be profitable to increase their outputs. Those producers already in the industry would tend to increase their purchases of productive resources—workers, raw materials, machinery, and vegetables—and new producers would be attracted into the industry by the prospect of higher than normal profits. Productive services would tend to be diverted from the canned-food industry into the frozen-food industry.

3. *Induced Changes in Productive Service Demands.* Simultaneously with the diversion of productive services from the canned-food industry into the frozen-food industry, there would be a change in the structure of productive service demands. Some types of productive serv-

ices might be used in both industries, and in this case the impact on the producers of vegetables might be canceled out by sales to the frozen-food industry instead of the canned-vegetable industry. However, the switch from canned foods to frozen foods would increase the demand for paper cartons used to hold the frozen foods and at the same time reduce the demand for tin cans. This would bring with it a change in the demand for productive services, increasing the demand for the services used in the production of paper and reducing the demand for services used in the production of tin plate.

The resulting change in the structure of productive service demands would cause changes in the relative prices of productive services. (If productive service prices were inflexible, sectional unemployment would appear in some occupations and worker shortages would appear in others.) Two other types of changes would therefore occur. (*a*) Producers generally would tend to adapt their combinations of productive services to the changed set of productive service prices. In order to do this they would tend, so far as possible, to choose those combinations which would use more lower-priced productive services—the ones being released by the canned-food and tin plate industries and not being absorbed by the frozen-food and paper industries—and less higher-priced productive services. (*b*) Productive service suppliers would tend to shift their services out of occupations or uses marked by lower prices or unemployment into uses marked by higher prices or employment opportunities. Thus, the operation of the principle of equal advantage would tend to create a new balance among the set of productive service prices.

Both of these changes would occur simultaneously with the diversion of productive services in the products market from canned-vegetable production to frozen-vegetable production. In the end, part of the changes in the structure of productive service demands would work itself out through the shifting of productive services from one occupation or use to another and part through the rationing effect of relative price changes.

4. *Cost Changes.* To the extent that changes in the relative prices of productive services occur, the per-unit costs of production of products would also change. The per-unit cost of producing canned vegetables and tin plate would tend to decline as would the cost of production of other products using resources released by the canned-food and tin plate industries. The per-unit cost of producing frozen vegetables, paper cartons, and other products using the same type of productive services would tend to rise. Such changes would tend to lower the prices of canned vegetables and raise the prices of frozen vegetables.

5. *Shifts in Product Demands.* The changes in the relative prices of products would typically cause households to revise their purchase plans, and demand curves would shift with the changes in the prices of other goods. Typically, households would tend to restrict their purchases of the products that had increased in price (frozen vegetables) and expand their purchases of products that had fallen in price (canned vegetables). Moreover, the decrease in the purchase of canned vegetables would be less marked than would have been the case if relative prices had not shifted in response to the change in consumer tastes. Thus the changes in product prices and productive services prices act as rationing devices, diverting households from those products produced with the relatively scarce resources and turning them to the products produced by the more abundant resources.

6. *Adjustment Processes Are Continued.* However, the process does not end at this point. The adjustment processes which we have been describing would cause changes in the interhousehold distribution of money income. Owners of services used in the production of canned vegetables and tin plate would receive less income. The owners of factors used in the production of frozen vegetables and paper would receive more income. However, for the owners of resources used in both the canned- and frozen-food industries, where the increase in demand from the one industry exactly offsets the decrease in demand of the other industry, there is a net change in demand of zero. Those persons' incomes would remain unchanged. The owners of productive services who received an increased income would buy more goods, and those individuals who received less income would buy fewer goods. The increased buying of the one group need not be for the same products which were formerly purchased by the individuals who suffered the income decline. Thus, in the economy as a whole, there would be a secondary shift in consumer demand as a result of the adjustment process set in motion by the original shift in consumer demand. These changes would, in turn, necessitate further adjustments, gradually diminishing in strength until the economy reached a new equilibrium or until a new disturbing force set in motion the adjustment process once more. For these reasons, we say that prices and production in the economy *tend* to move toward equilibrium. In a dynamic world of continuous change they *never reach* equilibrium.

6.3. *Effects of a Change in Supply Schedules for Products*

Another source of disequilibrium which sets in force the movements toward a new equilibrium is the change in supply conditions for products stemming from changes in technology. Let us suppose that an improved technology is introduced into agriculture, effectively shifting the supply curve of agricultural products to the right. The economy may be assumed to have been in a position of equilibrium when producers in agriculture introduce new techniques that enable them to lower the costs of production and consequently shift the supply curve for agricultural products to the right.

1. *Price and Output Response.* As a result of the introduction of the new technology, which would lower the per-unit cost of production, profits would be above normal at the original price. The increased profits would tend to result in the expansion of output by the existing producers. At the existing demand, the resulting increased quantity would only be taken off the market at a reduced price, and the price would continue to fall and output would continue to expand until profits in the industry were once more at a normal level for the producers employing the new technology.

2. *Consumer Real Income Would Be Affected.* As a result of the decline in the prices of agricultural products, consumers would be able to buy greater quantities at the lower prices. If we assume that the demand for agricultural products, in the relevant range, is relatively inelastic, the price decrease will bring with it a decrease in total expenditures on agricultural products. If consumer incomes were at the original level, consumers would then be able to increase their purchases of nonagricultural products, which would appear as an increase in demand for the products of the producers of nonagricultural goods.

3. *Changes in Productive Service Demands and Their Responses.* The introduction of the technological change in agriculture would reduce the demand for some productive services and increase the demand for other services. The reduction in the demand for some services would more than offset the increase in the demand for other services since the technological change, which economizes on resource use, releases resources from agricultural employment, and the demand for agricultural products is sufficiently inelastic that the released resources are not all called back to provide an expanded volume of products. The resulting change in the structure of productive service demands would cause changes in relative prices of productive services. If productive service prices were inflexible, or if the released resources were immobile, sectional unemployment would exist in agriculture and worker shortages would appear in the nonagricultural sectors of the economy. Similarly, if some producers in agriculture were unable to use the new technology and did not leave agriculture, they would be earning subnormal profits,

since they would be forced to accept lower prices for their output while they would, at the same time, be using a relatively inefficient high-cost method of production. In the end, part of the change in the structure of productive service demands would be worked out through the shifting of productive services from one employment to another under the pressure of price and income changes, and part of the change would come through the rationing effect of price changes.

4. *Cost Changes and Interproduct Substitution.* Additional changes in the structure of the economy would occur in the same manner as outlined above for the consequences of a shift in consumer demand coming from a change in tastes. The adjustment process itself would bring about changes in incomes, demands, and costs, and the process of adjusting to changing prices would continue in a diminishing sequence until the economy reached a new equilibrium point with the new technology fully incorporated into the industrial system. The change in technology would have made possible an increase in production with the existing resources and consequently would have made possible a higher average standard of living. However, the functioning of the adjustment process would not necessarily result in all incomes rising, or even remaining the same as before the change; it is also probable that the incomes of some resource owners would fall.

6.4. Effects of the Decisions of Resource Owners to Change Employment

If, with the economy in equilibrium, some workers decide to change employment for reasons not associated with the wage price scale ("How can they keep them down on the farm after they've seen Paree?"), this would affect the working of a competitive economy. A brief step-by-step analysis would demonstrate the stream of consequences of this source of change, with all changes occurring more or less simultaneously.

1. *Productive Service Price Responses.* If prices were flexible, the wage rates of agricultural workers would rise, and the wage rates of industrial workers would fall as a consequence of the transfer of workers from agriculture to manufacturing industry. Agricultural labor would be scarce, and industrial workers would be looking for jobs.

2. *Induced Changes in Technique.* The change in the relative prices of productive services would, over a period of time, cause producers to adopt those combinations of productive services which would use less of agricultural labor and more of industrial labor. Agricultural

producers, for example, would be induced to use more machinery and less labor.

3. *Product Cost and Price Changes.* Because productive services are not perfect substitutes for each other, products containing relatively large amounts of agricultural labor would rise in price, and products containing relatively large amounts of industrial labor would fall in price. The changes in the relative prices of products would cause households to purchase less agricultural output and more industrial output. In this manner, prices, acting as rationing devices, would cause households to adapt their income-apportioning decisions as consumers to their occupational decisions as suppliers of productive services.

4. *An Expanding Series of Readjustments Would Ensue.* The change in the relative prices of productive services would cause changes in the distribution of income. Some families would get more income than before and some would get less. These changes in income, in turn, would result in changes in the structure of product demands. The changes in product demands would in turn cause additional changes in productive service demands, which would in turn cause further occupational shifting and further changes in demand, in a continuous series of changes as the economy tended toward a new equilibrium.

6.5. Summary

In a competitive private enterprise economy two sets of fundamental decisions will determine the final outcome of the adjustment process. These two sets of decisions are (1) the product demand decisions of consumers (households) and (2) the occupational and property use decisions of households as owners of productive services. We can think of prices and money payments in a competitive money-using economy as a means by which households, acting as consumers, tell the economic system what products they want. They are also a means by which households, acting as suppliers of productive services, inform the economic system concerning their work preferences and the natural limitations which exist on the supply of productive services. Prices and money payments are the means used by the participants in the economic process to solve the central problem of allocating resources to satisfy competing ends.

We can view the interrelationships which exist in the economy as a system of simultaneous equations, the solution of which gives us the equilibrium price and quantity for each product and productive service. A change in any of the equations making up the system will, in general, result in a different solution for the set of equations. In effect, in the analysis developed in this chapter, we have shown the consequences for equilibrium which come from the alteration of a few of the equations, initially, and, finally, as a result, the alterations and changes in the equilibrium values of the variables of the system.

QUESTIONS AND EXERCISES

1. It is impossible to trace all of the interrelationships of prices that exist in a general equilibrium pattern, but show the effect of the acceptance of oleo margarine on:

   a) The price of butter.

   b) The supply of cotton cloth (assume cotton seed oil is used in producing margarine).

   c) Cigarettes.

   d) The rent for sheep grazing lands in Nevada.

2. Some agricultural economists have argued that the various forms of government assistance to agriculture do not, in the long run, aid the farmers' incomes but all of the government assistance ends up as part of land owners' incomes because of higher rents. Discuss.

3. Discuss the proposition that maintenance of income to farmers is essential for the maintenance of prosperity in the remainder of the economy. Is this not so for engineers? School teachers? Laborers?

4. A community is enlarged by the establishment of a new industrial firm employing several thousand workers. Show the short- and long-run effects on the economic position of:

   a) Laborers already in the town.

   b) Other employers of industrial labor already in the town.

   c) Retail and wholesale merchants.

   d) Landowners.

5. Suppose a shift to demand for imported articles of merchandise results in a foreign demand increase for U.S. made computers, machine tools, and metal toys. Trace out the impact of this change on such industries as steel, coal, cotton textile, and so forth. Include both direct and indirect effects on prices, production, and resource employment in your analysis.

6. Suppose the government abolishes its gold and silver purchase program. Discuss the resulting effect on the gold, silver, coal, copper and iron mining industries, the steel and electrical industries, and the automobile industry.

Chapter 7

THE ORGANIZATION OF MODERN BUSINESS

Our initial discussion of the economic structure of society was devoted to the determinates of demand and supply. From that analysis we moved on to demonstrate the interaction of prices in society as they determine the allocation of resources and the distribution of products among recipients. In this fashion we were able to construct a general equilibrium system for an economy.

We now direct our attention to the economic relationships which help to determine activity within the individual firms in an economy. The analysis of Chapters 7–13 will be devoted to what is called in economics the "theory of the firm." As we explore this area of economic analysis we should keep in mind the impact which outside events and changing economic relationships in the rest of the economy has on the economic behavior of the firm which now becomes the subject of analysis.

7.1. Advantages of the Business Corporation

The most important form of business organization in the United States today is the corporation, for although only about 500,000 of the 4,000,000 businesses in the country are incorporated, corporations produce about one half of national income. In mining, manufacturing, transportation, communication, power production, trade, and finance, corporations are responsible for nearly 100 per cent of the business being done in these areas. It is apparent that analysis of the legal framework of the American business firm should be directed at the corporation in order to discover what it is that makes this form of business so significant and also what contribution the corporation has made to modern industry.

Separate Existence. The corporation is a legal entity, a person. It is created or incorporated under law and is empowered to enter into contracts in its own name, to sue and be sued, and to survive independently of the interest or lives of the original incorporators or of any owners. This separate existence for the corporation is the unique characteristic which distinguishes it from either of two other business forms, the sole proprietorship and the partnership.[1]

In a free enterprise society the individual acquires a bundle of rights to private property. When the individual operates as a business, he is relatively free to do as he likes in order to make a profit, but he is also responsible to the utmost for what he does. The proprietorship is an unincorporated enterprise, in that it has not been recognized by the state as a separate corporate body from its owner. As a consequence, any obligations of the business are obligations of the individual in whose name the business is being carried on. Its debts are the owner's debts. The business cannot be sued separately but instead the owner is sued. This places severe limits on the capacity of the firm to enter into obligations, to acquire capital, and to survive for a long period of time. The capacity of the owner is the capacity of the business. Although that owner may borrow funds, he is in a final sense limited in his acquisition of capital for the firm by his own financial strength. When the owner dies, the business dies, and unpaid obligations fall due. The owner's estate must pay these claims, so that the business is quite likely to be liquidated in order to settle the claims on the owner. This limitation of ownership obviously restricts the capacity of the firm to attain size and to enter into long-run projects.

The partnership, in general, differs from the proprietorship only in that there is more than one owner, more than one individual's financial capacity involved, and more than one person who is in a position to obligate the business and all of the owners for actions he has undertaken in the name of the firm. As with the proprietorship, there is unlimited liability on the owners for all of the claims against the business. Also, when any partner desires to withdraw from the firm, or when any partner dies, the firm itself ceases to exist. This is the case because of the fact that the business of the concern is carried on in the names of the partners and not in the name of the business itself. Although there may be more flexibility in acquiring owner capital when there are many partners than for the firm with only one proprietor, the limit on capacity to attain size through capital investment and the limit on duration of existence for the partnership is very much the same as for the sole proprietorship.

As a consequence of these limitations, the unincorporated enter-

[1] The *co-operative* is a special form which, like the corporation, is a legal entity created by the state. It differs from the corporation in that for the co-operative there is ordinarily one vote per shareholder rather than per share and the earnings are divided up in accordance with patronage rather than number of shares held. In the United States the principal area where co-operatives are found is agricultural marketing.

prise tends to exist in areas of business where the talents of the owners are the chief stock in trade, where capital requirements are small, and where liability for large sums is not likely to exist. Most farming enterprises are unincorporated. The same may be said for organizations in the professions, in service industries, and in some parts of retail trade.

Duration of Existence. Let us contrast these limitations on the economic potential of the proprietorship and the partnership with the advantages which accrue to the corporation, which we have mentioned only briefly above. A legal definition of the corporation would specify that it is an association of individuals, known as stockholders, sanctioned by government and empowered by charter, through a board of directors and under a corporate name, to act as one person in the conduct of a specified business. It should be noted that the corporation is granted a charter to conduct specified business. Ordinarily the charter is given by the state for a specific period of time, but it is subject to renewal as long as the laws of the issuing state are complied with. As a consequence, the corporation may have perpetual life. The incorporated firm is therefore in a position to undertake long-range ventures. It can acquire fixed capital which will recover its investment only over a period of many years without there being fear that the firm will, in the meantime, have to be dissolved because of a change in ownership.

Ease of Acquiring Capital. Another important advantage for the corporation, which is derived from its legal existence as a person, is the power which it possesses to issue shares of ownership, called stock, to many persons. None of the owners need fear that the remainder of his personal estate may be jeopardized by some action of the corporation or its agents. Through the sale of stock, the corporation can acquire large sums of liquid capital or other property rights. In addition, since the owners of the shares of stock do not pledge themselves to cover the obligations of the corporation, the firm can acquire additional funds through borrowing without the owners fearing financial liability for themselves.

In addition, since the creditors of the company have no claim against the owners for other than the value of stock for which the owners have subscribed, there is no legal limit on the power of the owners of stock to transfer their holdings to others. The transferability of ownership makes possible for each owner a liquidity for his investment that exists separately from the uses to which the firm puts its capital. The existence of organized security exchanges and of investment dealers arises out of the limited liability and consequent transferability of ownership of shares in corporations.

As a consequence, then, of the possible continuous existence of the corporation, of the limited liability of the stockholders, and of the transferability of ownership, the corporation is in a position to assemble the relatively small savings of thousands of individuals for large investment projects. This has made possible the achievements of modern industrial organization, which usually depends for its economic effectiveness on a size beyond the capacity of any one or small group of investors to provide. In fact, modern collective capitalism would be impossible without the development of the corporate form of business organization, or something much like it.

Management and Size. A further advantage which may accrue to the corporation as an accompaniment of size is its power to employ the very best managers money can buy. For, just as the baseball team of a small town cannot afford to hire a Casey Stengel as manager or a Roger Maris as a player, so the small concern cannot attract the highest-priced managerial talent. As a consequence, the corporation is in a position, once having acquired a large capital structure, of employing management and technical talent, of investing in research and development, and of making improvements in processes and products which are in an absolute sense very costly but in relation to the unit of product or the dollar of investment very inexpensive. The result has been that large corporations tend to be the most successful economic enterprises. Small businesses may feel that they are placed at an increasing disadvantage as compared with the corporate giants. Nevertheless, as long as the directors and managers are embued with a progressive and competitive spirit, economic progress is perhaps more likely to result from the presence of the corporate form than from the small-scale business organizations to which the proprietorship and the partnership are limited.

On the other hand, some economists, notably the late Joseph A. Schumpeter of Harvard University, have argued that the limited liability provision is contrary to the spirit of capitalism. They have argued that the full risks as well as rewards of business should fall upon the shoulders of the owners, who are responsible for the actions of a business. When the risk is borne in part by others—notably bondholders, and banks—there is less of a deterrent to business incompetence. The costs of business errors are borne in part by individuals or groups who are not responsible for those errors.

7.2. Implicit Costs and Profits

The corporation may be a legal entity, but it is not a final consumer. Everything it owns in turn belongs to someone else. The rights to the possessions, or assets, of the corporation are conveyed in the form of property rights assigned in the contracts with stockholders, bond-holders, and holders of other claims against the firm. Similarly, in the giant, impersonal corporation, the management of the firm does not receive its reward as a reward for ownership. There are many owners, but there are few managers. An examination of the stream of incomes and expenditures for the corporation make it possible to interpret ac-curately the meaning of costs. Costs are the payments for the use of resources, either real money payments or implicit ones. In the corpora-tion the stockholder receives a dividend or ownership of undivided prof-its to compensate him for his investment. The bondholder and the lender on short-term account receive interest. If the payments made for the use of capital are not sufficiently great to be equivalent to what capital earns elsewhere, no further investment in that firm would take place. A normal rate of return on investment is, then, a cost—the cost of obtaining capital. The proprietor may speak of the entire income he receives from his business as profit. It must, however, just as surely include the cost of the use of his own capital as the corporation gross income should, and as the interest paid for borrowed capital represents. This cost is the opportunity cost of using capital funds in one enterprise rather than placing it elsewhere.

The manager is hired by the corporation. He receives salary and bonus as a wage of management. The sum he receives must be enough to attract him to this employment rather than to some other one. Simi-larly, the owner-manager of a proprietorship should consider part of his gross income as being a wage of management, the opportunity cost of having him associate himself with his own firm rather than work for someone else. His gross income is not all profit. It includes the cost of labor of management as well as the cost of the owner's own capital in-vestment. The same could be said for the payment of rent for using one's own land.

After all money costs as well as implicit costs have been accounted for, any difference which remains is profit, either positive or negative. Profit is not a payment for the use of capital and it is not a payment for managerial labor. In the absence of monopoly, profit is a reward some receive for the successful bearing of uncertainties. The party to the or-ganization who meets the uncertainties is the one who has assumed the guarantee of payment to the other resource owners involved in the en-terprise. He is the business enterpriser. In the small proprietorship it is easy to identify this party as the owner who commits his own labor and capital and also hires other labor and capital for the conduct of a business on the basis of his own forecasts of the immediate future in the industry in which he operates. In the corporation, the receipt of profits would accrue also to the owners, the common stockholders, for it is they who, in the last analysis, have made the guarantees and the pledges to others. They may have delegated responsibility for control to others; they may have assigned the burden of the risks of the business to other parties, such as the bondholders and the banks mentioned above; but the residual burden lies with the stockholders. They make large profits or suffer losses in that dividends may be low or nonexistent.

Tax law has been set up to levy taxes against "profits" of corporations, based partly on the assumption that the government is recovering a claim against the original extension of the right to incorporate, and partly based on grounds which may have no logical justification in economics. Under tax law, certain accounting procedures are required for identifying taxable income. These procedures do not allow for the separation of implicit economic costs from economic profits in determining taxable income. This is not to say that the difference does not, in economic analysis, exist. In fact, the definition of excess profits in tax law corresponds fairly closely with the economic definition of profits.

7.3. Types of Corporation Securities

Stocks. One of the advantages which have accrued to the corporation is the power granted to it by its charter and in accordance with its bylaws to issue a variety of different sorts of securities, designed to attract capital from investors who have varying motives and desires when they make their investments. The principal division between types of corporate securities is between *stocks* and *bonds. Stocks* are evidences of ownership. Owners assume the risks associated with the operation of a business enterprise. The owners receive the rewards, if any, in the form of profits and bear the burden of losses, if there be such. The position of the owner, the stockholder, is residual, both with respect to income and with respect to ownership and distribution of assets if the company is dissolved. Since there may be no limit on the size which earnings may reach and on the appreciation in the value of assets, investors in stocks will be persons who are interested in the chance of large earnings and will take the risk of having no earnings and of having all or part of the value of their investments wiped out. In addition, if investors believe that there may be general price inflation in the country, they are more likely to wish to own stocks, for which inflated values of assets and sales may reflect in inflated values of securities and of earnings, than to own bonds, which represent debt of the companies which issue them. Furthermore, ownership of stock may give voting power and control in a company.

Classes of Stock. The classes of stock are divided into *common stock* and *preferred stock*. *Preferred stock* has a prior ownership claim on the assets and income of a company, after all creditors' claims have been met. Since the claim of the preferred stockholders must be met prior to any claims by common stockholders, the size of that claim is fixed. Preferred stock receives a fixed dividend. That dividend must be met before the other stockholders are paid anything. Preferred stock also has a fixed claim on assets, an amount established by the par value of the stock, which must be paid to the preferred stockholders if the company should be dissolved, prior to the residue being divided among the common stockholders.

The preferred position of this stock gives rise to the further classification of preferred stock in accordance with the extent to which this preference may be exercised. *Noncumulative* preferred stock is stock which loses its right to a dividend for a particular period if the directors of the company decide that no dividend should be paid for that time. It must receive a dividend if common stock is to receive a dividend, but there need not be any dividend for either class of security. *Cumulative* preferred stock must receive all back dividends owed to it for periods in which dividend payments were not made before any payment can be made to the common stockholders. This stock is most nearly similar to bonds, in that the payment of a share of the income of the company must be made if there is to be any payment to the other stockholders.

Participating preferred stock is entitled to share in extra profits with common stockholders when dividends to common stockholders go beyond a certain rate. The formula for participation is stated in the contract under which the stock is issued. Investors in securities who like to eat their cake and have it will desire participating preferred stock when they fear that inflation will increase the money value of the company's earnings and wipe out the purchasing power of the fixed dividend payment. At the same time, the participating preferred stockholder desires prior treatment to the common stockholder if earnings are low.

A fourth category of preferred stock which is sometimes issued is *convertible* preferred. This type of stock may be converted into other securities in a manner and at a time specified in the contract agreement for the stock. It is designed to attract the money of the conservative investor, just as participating preferred stock is.

Common stock, if there is also preferred stock for a company, is the final claimant to corporate earnings and assets. Because common stock is placed in this relatively inferior position, it is usually assigned the voting power of the company, with no vote being given to the preferred stockholders. However, in some corporations there are two or more classes of common stock. Some classes of common stock will have voting power and others will not. Generally, when this is the case, the voting stock will be retained by the insiders, the promoters, and others who wish to retain control of the company, and the nonvoting stock will be sold to the general investing public. The possession of voting power in the large corporations may not be as important as it seems, as will be indicated in the next section, 7.4. One exception to this general rule on voting power is quite often provided for in the bylaws of the corporations. This is a provision that all stockholders, preferred and both voting and nonvoting common, have voting rights on possible dissolution of the company or major change in corporate structure, such as the changes which would accompany merger with another firm.

Preferred stock must have a par value assigned to it which represents the amount of asset value which the preferred stockholder can hope to receive if the company is dissolved. Common stock needs no par value since the claim on assets is residual. Frequently "no-par" common stock is issued, or the par value may be only nominal. "Par" originally referred to the price at which stock was presumed to have sold when the stock was issued.

Bonds. Bonds do not represent ownership at all. Instead they are evidences of debt. The bondholders are creditors of the company. As such, they must receive regular interest payments, and amortization schedules for bonds must be met, or the company will be in default. Bonds merely represent the subdivisions of a large loan. A trustee holds a contract, called a *bond indenture,* which authorizes him to represent the interests of the bondholders in the event of default. Various legal procedures may be followed for recovering these creditors their claims.

Bonds are divided into types according to the collateral which is pledged to protect the interests of the bondholders. *Mortgage bonds* have as the collateral pledged to protect them mortgages on all or a part of the company's property. The quality of a mortgage bond depends on the quality of the real property mortgaged and on the ability of the borrower to meet his required payments. *Collateral trust* bonds have securities of other corporations owned by the issuing company put up as security to back the issuance of the bonds. Collateral trust bonds may be of high quality or inferior quality, also depending on the quality of the collateral. *Equipment bonds* carry collateral in the form of the pledge of certain equipment, such as the rolling stock of a railroad. All of these classes of bonds have prior claim to the general assets and gross earnings of a company before the stockholders may receive anything. In addition, they have the special pledge of the collateral which protects them. Consequently, if the collateral is of good quality, the holders of such bonds are in a superior position to other general creditors of the firm and may as a consequence have been willing to purchase such bonds with payment of only a low rate of interest.

Another class of bonds which occupies a special place in the category of securities is the *income* or *debenture bond.* This type of security has a prior claim on future earnings of the company but it has no prior rights to the corporation's assets. In effect, the income bond shades into stock in the type of risk associated with its ownership.

7.4. Separation of Ownership from Management

Mention was made in Section 7.1 of the possibility of separating ownership from management in the large corporation. The voting stockholders are the owners, but ordinarily they vote only for the directors of the company. The directors, in turn, determine broad company policy and select the officers who actually run the company. As a consequence, the owners feel far removed from the acts of management of the corporation and in no way responsible for the things which their agents, the managers, do. This remoteness of owners from management is emphasized by the size of the company and by the tendency for the managers to hold only a very small share of the outstanding stock of the company. For instance, at the 1957 annual meeting of the stockholders of the Standard Oil Company of New Jersey, 305,134 shareholders, holding 166,177,358 shares of stock, were represented. The Standard Oil Company of New Jersey is proud of the way the company is run and believes its annual stockholders' meetings are as democratic as is possible, given the size of the company. There were, however, almost 100,-000 shareholders, who owned 30,000,000 shares of stock, not represented at the meeting. In addition, of the shareholders represented, a great majority were not present in person at that meeting. Instead, they had assiged voting rights, or *proxies,* to someone else who voted for them. In another example, the entire board of directors and principal officers of the American Telephone and Telegraph Company own less than 1 per cent of the stock of that company. Indeed, since the assets of the company exceed $4 billion, those officers and directors would have to be very heavy investors in the company if they were to own a majority of the stock.

The diffusion of ownership of the large corporation and the use of voting rights assigned by stockholders to insiders in the company help to create a separate group, the management group, which represents interests not exactly the same as the interests of the owners of the company. The use of the holding company furthers this separation of ownership from control. In the holding company, the company holds stock, presumably enough to possess control, in one or more subsidiary companies. Other stockholders in the subsidiary companies find that their voting rights have negligible importance.

The management group can then represent, in the manner in which it conducts the affairs of the company, all of the diverse interests brought together in the corporation: the stockholders, the creditors, the employees, the customers, and the social community. In many cases, the consequence is no doubt that the company is managed in a manner to forward the over-all interests of society. There remains, nevertheless, the possibility that a company management, being in effect answerable to no one, could conduct affairs of the concern in a fashion injurious not only to the owners but to society as well. The corporate form, in breeding the giant collective organization, the modern large corporation, has changed the nature of contemporary capitalism and created a number of social and political problems, which continue to be the subject of public inquiry today.

7.5. The Financial Statements of Corporations

The two most important financial statements which businessmen employ are the balance sheet and the profit and loss or income statement. Both are important sources of data and tools of analysis for management when the over-all position of the firm is examined. Both are taken from the books of the corporation which are maintained by double entry bookkeeping. They are summary statements. These statements are based on the fact that everything the firm owns, it in turn owes to someone else. The business firm is not a final consumer, although its owners and creditors may be. Consequently, every time something is added to the firm's possessions, there is also an addition to the firm's obligations to others; every time there is a deduction from what the firm possesses there must also be a deduction from what it owes to others, the creditors or the owners.

The Balance Sheet. The most commonly seen of these statements is the balance sheet. It is a report of the various assets or items of value owned by the firm and of the claims held against these assets. These assets and claims are not normally itemized in detail, but are grouped together in convenient aggregations. The balance sheet shows these aggregates as of a moment of time. It represents a *stock* as opposed to a *flow* description of the firm's position. A single balance sheet can tell us nothing about the course of the business over time (such as profits per year), but only about the *state* of the business at a given moment of time.

Since the balance sheet is concerned with stocks, it represents fundamentally a report on the sources of the money capital available to the firm, and the uses to which this money has been put. The money capital available to a firm must come from one of the following sources: (1) original capital contributed by owners, (2) the accumulation over time of business income not distributed to owners (retained earnings), and (3) borrowed capital, either short-term or long-term. These invested dollars are embodied in property of various forms which are listed on the balance sheet as assets.

The basic formula in the balance sheet is *Assets = Liabilities + Net Worth*. An examination of the imaginary comparative balance sheet which follows illustrates this formula. It shows the state of the business at the close of the years, 1961 and 1962. A description of the various items on the balance sheet follows:

(1) *Current assets* are normally considered by the accountant to be those which are expected to be converted into cash within the course of a year. They represent assets which are, relatively speaking, near to money or equivalent to money. Thus, current assets include cash, U.S. government securities; accounts receivable, i.e., bills that customers owe the company; and inventories of raw materials, goods in process, and finished goods. Cash, U.S. government securities, and accounts receivable are often called "quick assets" because they are already in the form of cash or can be converted into cash very quickly. The valuation placed on each of these assets by the accountants is very easy to determine. Ordinarily, U.S. government securities are held as a temporary investment of otherwise liquid funds, for some planned use in the near future or as a sinking fund for the eventual replacement of fixed assets as they become obsolete or worn out. Accounts receivable are carried at book value, often less an amount which might be separately stated as a reserve for bad debts.

Some judgment must be used in valuing inventories. Many companies use original cost or replacement cost of inventories, whichever is lower, in establishing a value figure for inventories. Whatever method of valuation is used, the federal government requires that accountants hold to one method of valuation, inasmuch as the method chosen affects profit figures and hence corporation income taxes.

(2) *Fixed assets* represent the firm's estimate of the value of the physical property, such as plant and equipment, owned by the firm as of the date for which the balance sheet applies. They consist of things which are not expected to be converted into money within a year. In the ordinary manufacturing firm, fixed assets bulk large in total assets, since most of the available money capital in such firms is embodied in stocks of physical capital goods.

The plant and equipment category states the original value or cost of the fixed assets owned by the firm, while the "reserve" for depreciation category represents an estimate of the total accumulated decline in the value of these fixed assets resulting from use since their original installation. It should be noted that this "reserve" for depreciation is simply a bookkeeping allowance for wear and tear and obsolescence of plant and equipment. It is not of itself a reserve of cash or of anything else. The sum of money representing the allowance involved is not necessarily set aside as a pool of funds. It may be paid out to stockholders, invested in equipment, held as cash or sinking fund bonds, or anything else. As will be pointed out in more detail below, that sum merely represets the part of the gross earnings of the company which represent the capital consumption allowance of this firm.

All depreciation methods are, in a strict economic sense, arbitrary. What is known is that a firm has certain receipts each year from current sales and has certain out-of-pocket costs, for raw materials, labor, and other current inputs during the year. The difference between these current receipts and current costs represents a sum which can be divided in any arbitrary manner between profits for the year and an amount to be allocated to the depreciation of fixed capital inputs for their services in production during that year.

To illustrate this point, suppose a firm buys $10,000 worth of equipment which, as it turns out, is used for five years after which time the equipment is no longer economical to use and is discarded. Over the five-year period the firm has $5,000 worth of receipts annually over and above the direct costs of raw materials, labor, supplies, and similar recurring expenditures. It is arbitrary whether the $10,000 worth of equipment is depreciated at a constant rate of $2,000 per year, leaving $3,000 per year of profits, or $15,000 for the five years, or whether the equipment is depreciated in two years, at $5,000 per year. The profits would be nil for the first two years but would be $5,000 for each of the remaining three years and would be, in total, $15,000. Consequently, it follows that if depreciation is too rapid, profits are understated at first and overstated later on but end up at the same total figure for the entire period.

THE IOTA NU BETA CORPORATION

COMPARATIVE BALANCE SHEET

December 31, 1961–1962

ASSETS	1962	1961
(1) Current Assets		
Cash in bank and on hand	$ 450,500	$ 500,000
U.S. government securities	1,150,000	1,500,000
Accounts receivable	672,000	500,000
Inventories	6,250,000	6,000,000
	$ 8,522,500	$ 8,500,000
(2) Fixed Assets		
Plant and equipment	$33,250,000	$30,000,000
Less "reserve" for depreciation	11,000,000	8,000,000
	$22,250,000	$22,000,000
(3) Intangible Assets		
Goodwill, patents, trade-marks, and other intangibles	$ 500,000	$ 500,000
Total Assets	$31,272,500	$31,000,000

LIABILITIES	1962	1961
(4) Current Liabilities		
Notes and accounts payable	$ 1,325,000	$ 1,500,000
Accrued salaries, wages, etc.	2,150,000	2,000,000
Accrued taxes	525,000	500,000
(5) Long-Term Liabilities	4,000,000	4,000,000
NET WORTH		
Preferred stock, 7%	5,000,000	5,000,000
Common stock	10,000,000	10,000,000
Surplus	8,272,500	8,000,000
Total Liabilities and Net Worth	$31,272,500	$31,000,000

There is no unambiguous way to allocate to a current period costs which have not been incurred during that time for goods which are used up in production during that period. Aside from tax considerations, the only reason that firms need be concerned about depreciation accounting is that it is desirable to provide a routine means of spreading the cost of a capital good over the life of that good. If this is done, then when the machine must be replaced there will have been recognition of the fact that it has been slowly used up, and there will have been opportunity to make provision for the new purchase so that the full burden of the purchase will not have to fall entirely on the operating period in which the purchase is made.

(3) *Intangible assets,* goodwill, patents, trade-marks, and other intangibles represent an estimate of the value to the company of its patents, its name, and other intangibles. These are assets, just as Items (1) and (2) are because they increase the earning ability of the firm. Their valuation would be the present discounted value of all the additions to earnings which they will contribute over the life of the firm. The next chapter describes the method used for determining the present value of a future stream of income. In effect, what is involved is the translation of a future flow of income into a present stock of value.

The liability and net worth side of the balance sheet shows the distribution of claims against the assets of the company. It should be noted that there is no attachment of any specific liability or net worth item to any specific asset. The claims are general ones, representing the amounts which each of the claimants would receive if the firm were dissolved and present asset values were recovered.

(4) *Current liabilities* represent claims on the assets of a company which are expected to be payable within one year. Notes and accounts payable refer to the amounts the business owes on short-term loans, and for goods bought from other businesses. Accrued salaries, wages, etc. represent the amount owed to employees and others who have rendered services in production. Accrued taxes refers to the amount owed to the government for taxes. Current liabilities also represent the amount of short-term credit which has been extended either voluntarily or involuntarily to the firm and is a source of money capital for investment in property.

The difference between current assets and current liabilities is called "working capital,"[2] for it is from this difference that the firm

[2] "Working capital" sometimes has a vaguer, but important, meaning. It may refer to the amount of money a new firm has to carry it from the time it starts in business until it is operating normally. About one half of business failures come from lack of working capital in this sense of the term.

acquires the funds with which to finance expansion and to pay its expenses. The current assets must be used first to pay the current liabilities, the remainder is put to work. Sometimes the term "current ratio" or "working capital ratio" is used to identify the ratio of current assets to current liabilities as a test of the liquidity of a company.

(5) *Long-term liabilities* represent long-term debt, such as bonds which the firm has outstanding as of a given date. It is the bondholders' claim on the assets of the company.

(6) The *net worth* part of the balance sheet represents the owners' or stockholders' claims on the assets of the business. They are the final claimants to the corporation's assets. Net worth is the sum of the stated value of the corporation's stock plus surplus. This stated value is the total par value, if there be such, of the stock outstanding. If there is "no-par" stock, that stock is assigned a nominal value on the balance sheet of the corporation. The "book value" of preferred stock is the same as the stated value, or total par value outstanding. The book value of common stock is its stated value plus the surplus. The stated value and the book value of the stock bear no necessary relationship to the market value of the stock, which may fluctuate from hour to hour. "Surplus" is an unfortunate word. This item is really a residual one. Any time that total assets increase without an accompanying increase in liabilities, for instance when profits are retained by the company or when the value of any asset is restated at a different figure, the net worth item must rise. Similarly, a decrease in valuation of assets, such as is accomplished by depreciation expense, would cause the net worth item to decrease. This is accomplished by adjusting the size of surplus.

If we remember the basic balance sheet formula, *Assets = Liabilities + Net Worth,* we become aware of another important point which the net worth sector of the balance sheet reveals. This is simply that, as an offset to assets, the larger the net worth is, the smaller the liabilities must be. The ratio between liabilities and net worth is a partial indicator of the long-run solvency of the firm. If asset values shrink to become less than liabilities, the firm is insolvent. The greater the proportion of net worth to assets, the less likely it is that this calamity will befall the firm. Also, as gross income shrinks, the greater the net worth which does not *have to* be paid an income at definite times, the less likely it is that the firm will become in default on its liabilities.

Hence, of three ways of raising funds for acquiring assets, through the creation of debt, through the issuance of stock, and through reinvesting of earnings, the first is most risky from a long-time point of view. The second may be undesirable from the point of view of stockholders who do not wish to lose control of a company through the sale of additional stock. Consequently, expansion through the reinvestment of earnings becomes the soundest method of expansion, from the viewpoint of a present stockholder.

However, if assets earn, on the average, more than liability holders are paid in interest, the difference belongs to the stockholders and would swell the size of earnings. For example, with $1,000,000 of assets, which earn $100,000 from operations, if $900,000 of liabilities, at 5 per cent interest, must be paid, only $45,000 of the $100,000 is used up in interest payments. The remaining $55,000 represents the returns for the $100,000 of net worth, a rate of 55 per cent. The temptation to pyramid earnings in this fashion tends in the direction of a very thin equity, or small net worth/liability ratio. The need for security of investment, on the other hand, tends toward a large net worth/liability ratio.

It should be pointed out that assets are important to a company only because they determine the *flow* of net earnings which the company can obtain. Indeed, the firm can be thought of as continually transforming assets into earnings through production and sale. For example, fixed assets are transformed through production into inventories of final goods; cash assets are converted by the purchase of labor and raw materials, and through the process of production, into inventories of final goods; and, finally, inventories of final goods are transformed into earnings through market sale. This is a continual process. The balance sheet gives us observations on this process at a particular instant of time.

The Income Statement. The income or "profit and loss" statement shows the flow of income over time, usually a year, and it is thus an important source of data and a tool of economic analysis. This statement is a flow description of the firm's position as it is engaged in transforming assets, through the processes of production and sale, into earnings.

Specifically, the income statement is concerned with the flows of receipts, expenses, and earnings. The receipts of the firm come primarily from the sale of goods produced by the firm, while the deductions from receipts consist of manufacturing or production expenses, selling and administrative costs, interest on debt, various taxes, and dividends to stockholders. In its simplest form the statement reports the income from sales, the expenses to be charged against those sales, and the profit remaining after the expenses have been deducted from the income receipts. An imaginary corporation income statement is given next.

THE IOTA NU BETA CORPORATION

INCOME STATEMENT

From January 1, 1962 to December 31, 1962

Sales of products and services to customers....................			$50,000,000
Deduct: Depreciation of plant and equipment....	$ 3,000,000		
Materials purchased..................	24,000,000		
Other operating costs, expenses, and charges...........................	20,000,000		
Add: Beginning inventory.................	6,000,000		
	$53,000,000		
Deduct: Closing inventory....................	6,250,000		
Equals: Cost of goods and services sold...........	$46,750,000	46,750,000	
Income from operations......................................		$ 3,250,000	
Less: Fixed interest charges and local taxes..................		300,000	
Net earnings before income taxes.............................		$ 2,950,000	
Less: Corporation income taxes............................		1,327,500	
Net earnings after taxes.......................................		$ 1,622,500	
Less: Dividends on preferred stock........................		350,000	
Net earnings of common stockholders.........................		$ 1,272,500	
Less: Dividends paid on common stock.....................		1,000,000	
Additions to surplus, or reinvested earnings...................		$ 272,500	

An explanation of the various items in the income statement follows:

1. This is a *statement of flows,* shown in convenient aggregates, which reports the following: (*a*) the company's income from sales in 1962, (*b*) the total expenses charged against these sales, and (*c*) net earnings remaining after the expenses have been deducted. It should be observed that *expenses do not necessarily become expenditures* during the same accounting period. Inspection of the balance sheet for the firm will show that the accrued salaries, wages, taxes, and the like, carried from 1961 into 1962 amounted to $2,500,000 and the same items carried into 1963 totaled $2,675,000. There were expenses during the accounting period of 1962, but the expenditures were not made at the same time and to the same amount. A comparison of the balance sheet with the income statement will show to what extent expenses for one accounting period are carried over to become expenditures in another accounting period.

If we look at the right-hand column of figures in the income statement, we will observe that sales were $50,000,000, and the cost of goods and services sold totaled $46,750,000, leaving $3,250,000 as income from operations. However, the accrued salaries and wages figure in the comparative balance sheet increased by $150,000, showing an addition to current liabilities, which will have to be met in the near future. In the meantime, notes and accounts payable decreased by $175,-

000, indicating again that the figure on the income statement for operating costs, expenses, and charges does not represent the sum of actual expenditure in this category.

Out of the income from operations is deducted $300,000 in fixed interest charges and local taxes. Again, it is possible that not all of the local tax liability has been met, since the balance sheet for the end of 1962 shows an increase in the accrued-taxes figure of $25,000 over what it was at the close of the year 1961.

Income taxes of $1,327,500 were deducted, leaving net earnings after taxes equal to $1,622,500. Dividends of $350,000 were paid to the preferred stockholders, leaving a residue of $1,272,500 for the common stockholders. This residue was divided between $1,000,000 of dividends for the common stockholders and $272,500 left for reinvestment in the expansion of the company. The $272,500 of surplus increases the book value of the common stock. It represents the decision of the board of directors to require that the common stockholders save part of their earnings, in reinvestment in the company.

2. The firm accumulated *inventory* during the year's operation; thus all of the operating costs could not be charged against the goods actually sold, as some of the costs were attributable to goods to be sold in the future. In order to reach a valid figure for cost of goods sold, an adjustment had to be made for the change in inventory. Instead of subtracting the change in inventories directly, the accountant accomplished this in two steps, first adding in the beginning inventory and then deducting the closing inventory. This procedure would have taken care of the case if the inventory at the close had been less than the inventory at the beginning.

3. *Depreciation* represents an estimate of the total accumulated decline in the value of fixed assets resulting from their use. Depreciation also represents an expense and not an expenditure. When and if the used-up fixed assets are replaced depends on a number of other contingencies. However, since depreciation is taken as a deduction from the net sales of the company, the figure, cost of goods sold, does not represent actual cash outlays. It is possible for a company to sell at a loss and yet end up with more cash than it started out. Just as the United States had negative private investment in 1933 and 1943,[3] so the company could be eating up its assets if depreciation is not offset by investment in other assets by the company. The comparative balance sheet illustrates that depreciation increase by $3,000,000, as shown on the income statement, but that total asset values did not decline but actually

[3] See Chapter 16, Appendix, Table 16–5.

increased by the $272,500 of surplus as well as being maintained by the expenditure on other assets of an amount equivalent to the depreciation for that period.

Although the plant and equipment is being used up all the time, the depreciation methods used to show this are essentially arbitrary. The value of equipment declines as the result of age and use. In recognition of this the accountant depreciates the value of these fixed items by some arbitrary formula. Among the various depreciation methods are these:

a) *Straight-line depreciation* is one of the most widely used methods. The depreciation is allocated evenly over all the years of the estimated life of the asset. If p = purchase price, s = salvage value, d = depreciation per year, and y = years, $d = \dfrac{p-s}{y}$ and undepreciated asset life in value after n years would be $p - \dfrac{(p-s)n}{y}$.

FIGURE 7–1

STRAIGHT-LINE DEPRECIATION

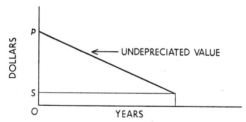

b) Under the *service-unit method* of depreciation, the purchase price of the asset minus salvage value is allocated equally over all the estimated service units of the asset. The annual depreciation charge will

FIGURE 7–2

SERVICE-UNIT DEPRECIATION

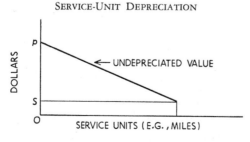

then depend upon the use of the asset during the year. Over the business cycle, this method of depreciation will increase the depreciation charge in years of high activity and reduce the depreciation in years of low activity, thus tending to stabilize taxable income, in comparison with the straight-line method.

c) The 1954 Federal Income Tax amendments also allow a depreciation rate equal to *double the straight-line rate,* applied to the declining book value of an asset for showing depreciation.[4] Note that the whole value will never be completely charged off, but this is rectified if the salvage value happens to match the balance. Undepreciated value after *n* years would be $p\left(1 - \dfrac{2}{y}\right)^n$. For example, if *p* is 100, *s* is 10, *y* is 20 years, when *n* is also 20 years, undepreciated value would be $12.15. By the straight-line method undepreciated value would equal salvage value at the end of twenty years. Also, after ten years, unde-

FIGURE 7–3

DOUBLE STRAIGHT-LINE DEPRECIATION

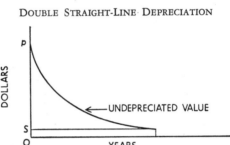

preciated value under the double the straight-line rate would be $34.87, and for the simple straight-line rate it would be $55.00.

Different methods of depreciation result in different apparent distributions of earnings over time and therefore result in a different pattern of corporation income taxes over time. Naturally, a businessman prefers a method of depreciation that will make his income average out more steadily over time—so as to keep his taxes as low as possible. A company could pay more taxes on a certain total income over a period of years if its annual income varied widely from year to year than if its income were the same every year. This, however, is of importance to the small firm rather than to the large firm, as the corporation normal

---

[4] The straight-line rate expressed as a percentage is the amount charged off in any year, $\dfrac{y}{p-s}$, divided by the net investment in the asset, $p-s$. Therefore, double the straight-line rate would be $2\dfrac{\frac{p-s}{y}}{p-s} = \dfrac{2}{y}$.

income tax is 30 per cent on the first $25,000 income and 52 per cent on all income over $25,000. Thus, the average income tax rate approaches 52 per cent asymptotically.

The Relationship between the Profit and Loss Statement and the Balance Sheet. The balance sheet indicates an instantaneous financial picture at a particular point in time. The income statement indicates the flow of sales, costs, and earnings over a particular accounting period, usually one year—the period of time between successive balance sheets. The change in the net worth between the beginning of the accounting period and the end—seen by the comparative balance sheet for December 31, 1961 and December 31, 1962—is also seen in the surplus shown at the end of the income statement—the reinvested earnings.

Similarly, there has already been pointed out the relationship between the figures shown in the income statement and the changed size of the figures on the comparative balance sheet for the items inventories, reserve for depreciation, accrued salaries and wages, and accrued taxes. The income statement does not, however, show what changes take place in other asset items or in other liabilities whenever such changes are not revealed as being the direct result of the income flow for the current period. In the comparative balance sheet shown on page 93, changes in cash in bank and on hand, minus $500, in U.S. government securities, minus $350,000, and in "reserve" for depreciation, plus $3,000,000 help to account for, along with the increase in surplus, the increases which have occurred for accounts receivable, of $172,000, and in plant and equipment, of $3,250,000, as well as the increase in inventories of $250,000 which was shown in the income statement. The changes which have occurred for these assets, as well as the changes which have taken place within the liabilities and net worth sections, represent the fact that the balance sheet merely shows a cross section of the position of the business as of an instant of time.

It is as if the balance sheet were one frame, drawn from a reel of film used for moving pictures. The balance sheet for the close of a period differs from that for the start of the period by the action which has taken place during the period. The income statement, or profit and loss statement, shows how some of the items have changed. It depicts that action which is reflected in the profits or losses for the firm. In the moving picture of our simile, the hero moves across stage, carrying on actions which help to unfold the plot. This is depicted in the income or flow statement. At the same time, stagehands are altering the scenery. This is not shown in the income statement, but it does show up in the changed position of the items in the balance sheet, with respect to each other. The income statement shows only the alteration in the total balance sheet figures, as well as some of the changes, but not all of them, which affect the total and the internal composition.

However, the conversion of any arbitrary income stream into a capital value is not shown in either the balance sheet or the income statement. What method is used for valuing income-producing assets rather than a statement of what income they have produced during one accounting period still needs to be examined.

QUESTIONS AND EXERCISES

1. Draw up a chart in which you compare the corporation, the general partnership, and the sole proprietorship with respect to:
   a) Transferability of ownership.
   b) Longevity of organization.
   c) Liability of owners.
   d) Ease of formation.
   e) Sources of capital.
   f) Relationship between management and ownership.
2. Contrast the order of priority of claim on the earnings and assets, the expected rate of return, and the voice in management of the company of bonds, preferred stock, and common stock.
3. Discuss the sources of money capital to the corporation and relate these sources to the balance sheet.
4. Construct a balance sheet and compute net worth and surplus for a hypothetical firm with the following characteristics:

Cash	11,000	Inventories	20,000
Accounts Receivable	34,000	Plant and machinery	25,000
Automobiles (4)	10,000	Capital stock	15,000
Notes payable	25,000	Bonds (it owns)	41,000
U.S. government bonds	$10,000		

5. Income statement for the firm in 4 above shows that each automobile was driven 50,000 miles with a life of 150,000 miles, and was new at the time of the first balance sheet; cost of goods sold included a final inventory figure of $25,000; earnings included $3,000 net which was not distributed to stockholders. From these income statement items, show adjustments in the balance sheet for the end of the period (Q. 4 balance was at the start of the period). What items on the balance sheet might change during the operating period and yet not be reflected in the income statement?
6. Under what conditions would a firm have negative working capital? Is this a source of capital for long-term investment?

THE INTEREST RATE IN
ECONOMIC CALCULATIONS:
INCOME STREAMS AND
CAPITAL VALUES

Chapter
8

On several occasions in past chapters, we have pointed to the importance of distinguishing between stocks and flows in various aspects of economic analysis. A business enterprise can be thought of as a collection of assets—stocks of goods possessing economic value—which are transformed into a stream of earnings through the processes of production and sale. Fixed assets such as buildings and machinery; cash assets used to purchase labor, electric power, and so forth; and finally, inventories of raw materials, parts, and semifinished products are all transformed through the process of production into inventories of finished products. These finished products are then converted into a stream of money earnings through market sale. Some of these categories of cost, such as labor, may involve weekly or monthly outlays; others, such as raw materials, may involve semiannual outlays for replenishing inventory stocks, while buildings and durable machinery may involve large investment outlays many years apart. A basic problem in business planning is to place these various categories of cost, showing different time patterns, on a basis allowing them to be combined or compared.

In this chapter our objective is to show that the interest rate provides a means of converting *any arbitrary income stream* (dollars per unit time) into an *equivalent capital value* (dollars); or conversely, any arbitrary capital value into an equivalent income stream. Thus the interest rate will be seen to provide a link between value flows (income) and value stocks (assets). This type of analysis is important, for businesses are continually faced with problems of comparing alternatives, one of which involves an income or outgo stream and the other a capital value or investment outlay. For example, should a firm invest $50,000 in a machine, with a life of ten years, to perform a particular operation automatically, or pay two men a total of $8,000 per year to perform the operation by hand? Before a decision can be reached it is necessary to have a means of comparing a $50,000 lump-sum outlay with an $8.000 annual outlay.

8.1. Compound Interest

Suppose the sum of $100 is invested at a compound rate of interest of 3 per cent per year. If the interest is added each year, then at the end of the first year the original investment will have grown to the value $100 + (0.03) \, 100 = \$100(1 + 0.03) = \$103$. Similarly, the amount at the end of the second year is equal to the amount at the end of the first year plus the interest on this amount or $103 + (0.03)\$103 = \$103(1 + 0.03) = \$100(1 + 0.03)^2$. After three years the amount is $100(1.03)^3$ and so forth for as many years as the original sum is allowed to accumulate interest. After n years the amount would be $100(1.03)^n$. In general, if v_0 dollars are invested at a compound rate of $100i$ per cent per year, then the amount after n years, V_n, is given by

$$(8.1) \quad V_n = v_0(1 + i)^n .$$

A graph of Equation (8.1) is shown in Figure 8–1 for $v_0 = \$100$, and $i = 0.03$. Note that the sum V_n grows at an increasing (geometric) rate with the number of years, n.

FIGURE 8–1

GRAPH OF WHAT THE SUM OF $100 AMOUNTS TO AFTER
n YEARS AT 3 PER CENT INTEREST COMPOUNDED
ANNUALLY

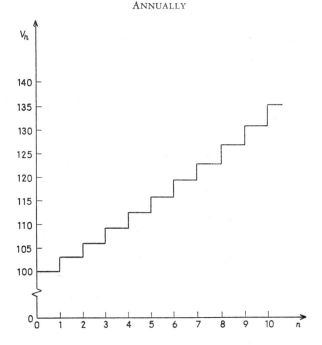

Consider next the effect of adding interest not once each year, but twice each year. Then at 3 per cent per year, 1.5 per cent is added at the end of the first six months of every year, and 1.5 per cent is added at the end of the last six months of every year. What the original sum of $100 will amount to at the end of any year or any six months interest period is given in the following table:

Year	1		2		...
Interest period	1	2	3	4	...
What $100 amounts to at indicated time	$100(1.015)	$100(1.015)²	$100(1.015)³	$100(1.015)⁴	...

At the end of n years, if interest of $100i$ per cent is added twice each year, then a sum v_0 will amount to V_n as given by the expression

$$(8.2) \quad V_n = v_0\left(1 + \frac{i}{2}\right)^{2n},$$

where n may take on the values $\frac{1}{2}, 1, \frac{3}{2}, 2, \frac{5}{2}, \ldots$.

As a generalization of Equation (8.2), if interest is added θ times per year instead of twice each year, then after n years the expression for V_n becomes

$$(8.3) \quad V_n = v_0\left(1 + \frac{i}{\theta}\right)^{\theta n},$$

where n may assume any value which is an integral multiple of $1/\theta$.

8.2. Application of Compound Interest to Simple Decision Problems

There are many examples of choices faced by individuals and businesses, which involve a comparison of lump-sum incomes at two different points of time. One such example is as follows: An individual has $2,000 which he can invest in a savings account at $3\frac{1}{2}$ per cent compounded annually. His intention is to use this money at some time to purchase a new automobile. Let us suppose he is considering only two alternatives. One is to purchase an automobile now. The second is to purchase an automobile after five years. If he postpones the purchase for five years, and in the meantime places the $2,000 in a savings account, then at the end of the period his $2,000 will have grown to a larger sum. At $3\frac{1}{2}$ per cent compounded annually, $2,000 will, after five years, amount to a sum which can be computed from Formula (8.1). This sum will be $V_5 = \$2,000(1 + 0.035)^5$, which is approximately $2,370. The computation can be made by consulting compound interest tables, or a close approximation can be obtained by slide rule computation.

The question facing our individual is now clear. He has a choice between a $2,000 automobile today and a $2,370 automobile five years from today. His choice will depend upon how urgent is his desire for an automobile, the risks that he may run in postponing the satisfaction of his wants (disability or death may occur before the five years is up), and perhaps many other factors. But however complex the subjective nature of the decision, the choice cannot be made rationally without knowledge of the value that $2,000 can attain after five years, and this value depends upon the rate of interest. The higher the rate of interest, the greater is V_5 and therefore the greater is the payment or reward for waiting.

Another example of the application of compound interest concepts to a decision problem arises in the business of timber development. To make this problem very simple suppose it takes exactly fifty years to grow a $2 pine sapling into a tree worth $100 for lumber-cutting purposes. If a timber company has to pay a 6 per cent rate of interest to raise money in the capital markets for long-term investment, does it pay the company to invest in saplings to grow timber? The problem in making such a decision is that the cost or outlay involved occurs at one point of time while the income involved occurs at a much later point in time. Before a decision can be reached as to whether the investment pays, outlay and income must be computed for the same point in time. In this example the cost to the company of growing trees which mature in fifty years is not only the $2 outlay for saplings now, but also the interest cost on the $2 over a fifty-year period. At a 6 per cent rate of interest, $2 will, after fifty years, amount to $V_{50} = \$2(1 + 0.06)^{50}$ or about $37. Therefore, the cost of a tree including interest on the invested capital is $37. Since the value of the tree is $100, a decision can readily be made in favor of planting saplings. This illustration ignores certain costs, such as upkeep on the trees during the growing period and insurance against loss, which should be taken into account in any actual decision problem.

It should be noted in the last example that the calculations are the same *independently of whether or not the company actually does borrow money and pay out the indicated interest.* Even where a firm uses its own capital, the effect of interest should be allowed to exert its influence on the decision, for the firm always has the alternative opportunities of investing its capital in saplings or lending it out in the capital markets at interest. Whether money is actually borrowed for the venture or not, there is a real interest cost in tying up capital in the venture.

8.3. Capital Values and Income Streams

Suppose the sum of v_n dollars is due n years from now. Given the rate of interest, i, compounded annually, we can determine V_0, the sum to invest now, which will produce v_n at the end of n years. This problem is simply the reverse of the previous problem in which we wanted to determine how much a given sum would amount to after n years. If Formula (8.1) is applied to the present problem, then $v_n = V_0(1+i)^n$. Therefore, solving for V_0 gives

$$(8.4) \quad V_0 = v_n(1+i)^{-n}.$$

V_0 is called the *present value* or the *discounted value* of the sum v_n due n years hence. Equation (8.4) is the general formula for the present

FIGURE 8–2

PRESENT VALUE OR DISCOUNTED VALUE OF $100 DUE IN
n YEARS, AT 3 PER CENT INTEREST

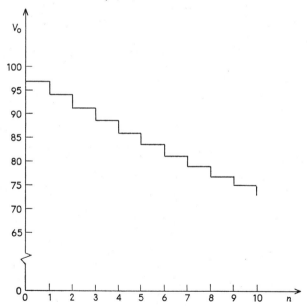

value of a sum due in n years. A graph of this equation for $v_n = \$100$, and $i = 0.03$ is shown in Figure 8–2.

The notion of the present value of a future sum can be extended to that of finding the present value of an entire series of sums to become available at different points of time in the future. Let us suppose that a piece of property, such as a building, a share of stock, a machine, or a piece of land, is expected to yield a net income of v_1 dollars, at the end of one year. The following year it is expected to yield an income of v_2 dollars, and so forth for n successive years. The present value of the income stream of $v_1, v_2, \ldots v_n$ dollars is called the *capital value* of the piece of property which yields the income. The present value of this stream of income will be the present value of the first year's income, $v_1(1+i)^{-1}$, plus the present value of the second year's income, $v_2(1+i)^{-2}$, and so forth up to the present value of the nth year's income, $v_n(1+i)^{-n}$. If we denote this capital value by $V(n)$, then the expression for $V(n)$ can be written:

$$(8.5) \quad V(n) = \frac{v_1}{1+i} + \frac{v_2}{(1+i)^2} + \cdots + \frac{v_n}{(1+i)^n} = \sum_{k=1}^{n} v_k(1+i)^{-k}.$$

There is a different, but very instructive, way to look at this rather illusive and strange concept of the present value of a series of income or cost payments. The present value of a series of payments due in the future may be viewed as that sum of money which, if available now and if invested at the rate of interest i, would just barely allow sums equal in amount to all of the payments in question to be withdrawn, so that the amount left in the fund would be exactly zero after the last withdrawal. For example, suppose three payments are due in the future: a payment of v_1 dollars at the end of the first year, v_2 dollars at the end of the second year, and v_3 dollars at the end of the third year. The present value of these three payments is a sum, $V(3)$, such that when invested at the interest rate i, and the amounts v_1, v_2 and v_3 are withdrawn at the end of each of three consecutive years, there will be zero dollars in the "account" at the end of the third year. The total of all additions to and subtractions from this hypothetical account must be zero. At the beginning of year one $V(3)$ is put into the fund. At the end of year one the first year's interest on this amount, $iV(3)$ will be added to the fund and the first withdrawal, v_1, will be made. This leaves $V(3) + iV(3) - v_1 = (1+i)V(3) - v_1$ still in the fund. At the end of year two the interest on this remaining sum will be added and the second withdrawal of v_2 dollars will be made, leaving $(1+i)^2 V(3) - (1+i)v_1 - v_2$ in the fund. At the end of year three, interest on this last remaining sum will be added and the last withdrawal of v_3 dollars will be made leaving finally $(1+i)^3 V(3) - (1+i)^2 v_1 - (1+i)v_2 - v_3$. But this last sum must be equal to zero by definition of $V(3)$ as the present value of the payments v_1, v_2 and v_3. Hence,

$$(1+i)^3 V(3) - (1+i)^2 v_1 - (1+i)v_2 - v_3 = 0.$$

Dividing through by $(1 + i)^3$, gives

$$V(3) - \frac{v_1}{1 + i} - \frac{v_2}{(1 + i)^2} - \frac{v_3}{(1 + i)^3} = 0$$

or $\quad V(3) = \dfrac{v_1}{1 + i} + \dfrac{v_2}{(1 + i)^2} + \dfrac{v_3}{(1 + i)^3}$,

which is simply the formula of Equation (8.5) for the case $n = 3$. In general $V(n)$ in Equation (8.5) is that sum of money which if allowed to accumulate interest at the rate i, will permit the amounts $v_1, v_2, \ldots v_n$ to be withdrawn and leave zero dollars in the fund at the end of the nth year. This is the *meaning* of the statement that $V(n)$ is the *present value* of the stream of payments $v_1, v_2, \ldots v_n$.

If the income stream in Equation (8.5) is constant from year to year, say v dollars per year, then $v = v_1 = v_2 = \ldots = v_n$, and $V(n)$ becomes:

$$(8.6) \quad V(n) = \frac{v}{1 + i} + \frac{v}{(1 + i)^2} + \ldots + \frac{v}{(1 + i)^n} = \sum_{k=1}^{n} v(1 + i)^{-k} =$$

$$v \sum_{k=1}^{n} (1 + i)^{-k} \cdot$$

It should be noted that Equation (8.6) involves a simple geometric progression with constant ratio $(1 + i)^{-1}$. It happens that such a progression can be summed to give, in general, a simple closed expression as follows:[1]

$$(8.7) \quad V(n) = v \sum_{k=1}^{n} (1 + i)^{-k} = \frac{v}{i} [1 - (1 + i)^{-n}] .$$

When n becomes very large this expression takes on a particularly simple form. This can be seen by finding the limit, V, of $V(n)$ as n approaches infinity, that is,

$$(8.8) \quad V = \lim_{n \to \infty} V(n) = \lim_{n \to \infty} \frac{v}{i} [1 - (1 + i)^{-n}] = \frac{v}{i} \cdot$$

Equation (8.8) says that the present value of an income stream of v dollars per year extending indefinitely into the future, at a rate of in-

---

[1] The derivation proceeds by first writing out the sums for $(1 + i)V(n)$ and for $V(n)$:

$$(1 + i)V(n) = v[1 + (1 + i)^{-1} + (1 + i)^{-2} + \ldots + (1 + i)^{-(n-1)}]$$
$$V(n) = v[(1 + i)^{-1} + (1 + i)^{-2} + \ldots + (1 + i)^{-(n-1)} + (1 + i)^{-n}] \cdot$$

Subtracting the second sum from the first gives:

$$(1 + i)V(n) - V(n) = v[1 - (1 + i)^{-n}] .$$

Solving for $V(n)$ we have

$$V(n) = \frac{v}{i} [1 - (1 + i)^{-n}] \cdot$$

terest i, is given by the ratio v/i. Or, if the sum V is invested at the rate i, an annual income of $v = iV$ dollars can be earned indefinitely into the future.

8.4. Capital Values and Income Streams Applied to Decision Problems

A few simple examples will serve to illustrate how Equations (8.4) through (8.8) can be used as an aid in solving certain kinds of business decision problems involving the comparison of costs and incomes at different points of time or with different patterns over time.

Consider first the application of the present value equation in (8.4) to the tree investment example in Section 8.2. In that example we compared the $100 maturity value of the tree with what the cost of a sapling would amount to after fifty years at 6 per cent interest. In problems such as this it does not make any substantive difference which particular point of time is chosen, in terms of which all values are to be expressed. What is important is that all the outlays and revenues be evaluated with respect to the *same* point of time. That point of time can be at the end of the investment period, at the beginning of the period, or at any intervening time. In the tree example we could as well apply Equation (8.4) to the maturity value of the tree, and compare this with the cost of a sapling. If this is done we get $V_0 = \$100(1 + 0.06)^{-50}$, or about $5.40, for the present value of a tree worth $100 after fifty years. This sum is greater than $2, the present cost of a sapling that will grow into a tree in fifty years. In this case we are using the beginning of the investment period as the point of reference in terms of which the relevant values are to be expressed. In Section 8.2 the point of reference was the end of the investment period. For purposes of decision making it is immaterial which point of reference is used. However, as a matter of customary practice such problems are usually solved by expressing all sums in terms of their present value, that is, the point of reference is usually chosen to be the beginning of the investment period, or simply "now."

As an illustration of the problem of determining the capital value of a piece of productive property, suppose a machine is expected to earn a net income of $10,000 at the end of its first year of operation, $5,000 at the end of its second year of operation, and $2,000 at the end of its third year. Also at the end of the third year, the machine will have a realizable junk value of $1,000. In other words the owner of this machine will realize three income payments, each one year apart, from the ownership of this property. The third payment will total $3,000 and will consist of the machine's income plus its junk value. In Equation (8.5) we thus have $v_1 = \$10,000$, $v_2 = \$5,000$, and $v_3 = \$3,000$. If the appropriate discount rate or interest is 5 per cent, then the capital value of this machine, $V(3)$ is

$$V(3) = \frac{\$10,000}{1.05} + \frac{\$5,000}{(1.05)^2} + \frac{\$3,000}{(1.05)^3} = \$9,500 + \$4,550 + \$2,600,$$

or about $16,650. One would have to pay less than this amount for the machine in order to earn a return above straight interest of 5 per cent on the invested capital.

A bond pays an income of $5 per year, starting one year hence for the next ten years. At the end of the ten-year period the bond has a maturity value of $100. If an investor requires at least 4 per cent compounded annually on an asset before he will buy it, what is the maximum price he would be willing to pay for this bond? The maximum price such an investor would be willing to pay is the present value of the income stream which the bond yields. The income afforded by the bond is $5 at the end of each of ten years plus $100 at the end of the tenth year. Using both Equations (8.7) and (8.4), the present value of all these payments is

$$V = \frac{\$5.00}{0.04}\,[1 - (1.04)^{-10}] + \frac{\$100}{(1.04)^{10}} = \$40.50 + \$67.50,$$

or about $108. The present value of the $5.00 income stream is about $40.50, while the present value of the $100 maturity is about $67.50.

Two methods of producing an item can be used by a firm. One method requires the purchase of a $50,000 machine. Assume that the machine lasts seven years and requires no maintenance or operating expenses. Another method is to hire two men at $4,000 each to produce the item by hand. At an interest rate of 6 per cent, which process is the most economical? The machine method requires a $50,000 outlay now for seven years of production service, while the hand method requires an annual outlay over time. To put the costs of the two methods on a comparable basis we ask, "What sum of money invested now in an imaginary fund, at a 6 per cent rate of interest will allow $8,000 per year to be withdrawn from the fund and make the fund become zero at the end of seven years?" In other words we want that sum of money which at 6 per cent interest will allow the purchase of just exactly seven years of production service by the hand production method. This sum is simply the present value of $8,000 per year for seven years and is comparable with the $50,000 machine cost which purchases seven years of production service by the machine method. The present value of $8,000 per year for seven years is given by Equation (8.7), that is,

$$V(7) = \frac{\$8,000}{0.06} [1 - (1.06)^{-7}],$$ or about $44,600. The hand produc-

tion method is seen to involve a lower cost than the machine method, taking into account interest cost in the comparison.

The last problem could be solved in a different but completely equivalent way. Instead of finding the present value of a seven-year income stream of $8,000 per year and comparing with the lump-sum cost of the machine, we could turn the problem around and ask, "What constant annual income stream of seven years' duration is equivalent to $50,000?" In other words we want that constant series of annual payments which will pay off a loan of $50,000 at 6 per cent interest in exactly seven years. (But remember the necessity for the computation is not dictated by an actual loan having been made.) Such a constant income stream can be obtained by solving for v in equation (8.7), and letting $V(n) = \$50,000$, $n = 7$, $i = 0.06$. That is,

$$v = \frac{iV(n)}{1 - (1 + i)^{-n}} = \frac{(0.06)(\$50,000)}{1 - (1.06)^{-7}},$$

or approximately $8,950. This is the annual cost of tying up $50,000 of capital in the machine for seven years, and is higher than the annual outlay for labor to do the same job by hand.

8.5. The Problem of Optimal Timber Cutting

In the timber-cutting example discussed in Sections 8.2 and 8.4 it was assumed that it takes exactly fifty years to produce a tree suitable for lumber purposes. A more realistic view is to assume that trees grow according to a biological law, and can be harvested at any time depending upon the owner's decision. Under these circumstances the question arises, "What is the best or optimal harvesting time for trees?" Suppose it is assumed that there is no upkeep on trees during their growing period. Let the number of usable board feet of lumber in a tree depend upon the age of the tree in years at the time of cutting. This growth function will be written symbolically as $f(n)$. Figure 8–3 shows a graph of this function for the case in which $f(n) = 200\sqrt{n} - 600$. According to this growth function, a tree does not contain any usable board feet of lumber until it reaches an age of nine years. For n between zero and nine years, $f(n) = 200\sqrt{n} - 600$ is negative and therefore does not represent the tree's real development. Actually $f(n) = 0$ for

$0 \leq n \leq 9$, which states mathematically, that the tree produces no usable lumber up to nine years of age. It is for $n > 9$ that the tree grows according to the law $f(n) = 200\sqrt{n} - 600$.

If the "price" of one board foot of uncut and uncured lumber is p, then the value of a tree of age n at the time n is given by the product

FIGURE 8–3

THE GROWTH CURVE FOR A TREE

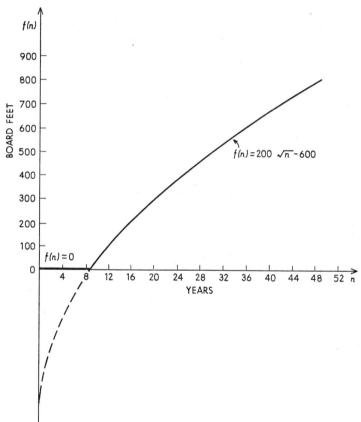

$pf(n)$. That is, the total value of a tree is the value of one board foot times the number of board feet in the tree. Now, the quantity $pf(n)$ is a sum of money which is realizable after n years from planting a sapling now. If we want to find the present value $R(n)$ of a sapling as a function of the number of years it is allowed to grow, it is necessary to apply Formula (8.4) to the sum $pf(n)$ due n years from now. At a rate of interest i, the expression for $R(n)$ becomes

$$(8.9) \quad R(n) = (1 + i)^{-n} pf(n) .$$

As an example of the form of $R(n)$, suppose $p = \$0.20$, $i = 0.04$, and $f(n) = 200\sqrt{n} - 600$. Then Equation (8.9) takes the form

$$R(n) = (1.04)^{-n}(0.20)(200\sqrt{n} - 600) = (1.04)^{-n}(40\sqrt{n} - 120) .$$

This function is shown graphically in Figure 8–4. It is seen from this graph that the present value of a sapling reaches a maximum at an age $n_0 = 30$. On the basis of a 4 per cent rate of discount, and a timber

FIGURE 8–4

PRESENT VALUE OF A TREE AS A FUNCTION OF AGE

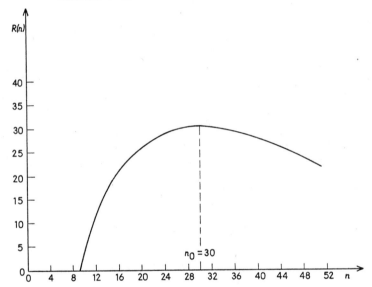

value of twenty cents per board foot, the best time to cut a tree is at an age of approximately thirty years. The present value of the tree at this age is about $31. As is evident from the relatively flat peak reached by the curve, the cutting age is not very critical. Cutting anywhere between twenty-six and thirty-four years will not influence the revenue from the venture by very much. On the other hand, revenue would be considerably reduced by cutting after only fifteen years of growth, or if the tree is allowed to attain an age of fifty years.

From the above analysis, the present value of a sapling to a company which follows an optimal harvesting program is $31. To arrive at an answer to the question as to whether it pays to plant saplings at all, this sum must be compared with all the relevant costs associated with tree growing. If these costs are all investment costs, that is, costs incurred at the beginning of the growing period, then it is only necessary to compare such costs directly with the $31 present value of a tree. Thus, if the only cost is a $2 initial outlay per sapling then the present value of net profit is $29 per tree. If certain costs, such as upkeep, are incurred over time, then they may influence the optimal harvest time. The manner in which such costs must be introduced explicitly into the analysis is illustrated in the Appendix to this chapter.

It should be pointed out that in this illustration, prices, costs, and interest rates were taken as given. These parameters may have certain known values at the time a sapling is planted, but there is no guarantee that they will remain constant over a long period. For example, the price of lumber may be expected to rise, in which case one should not use the present price of trees in Equation (8.9), but rather the price that is expected to prevail at the time of cutting. There are more advanced methods of analysis which can be brought to bear on the more difficult problem of deciding upon the optimal harvest time under conditions of uncertainty as to the values that the parameters of the problem may assume in the future. It will suffice in the present introductory treatment to merely call atention to the existence of such problems.

APPENDIX ON CONTINUOUS DISCOUNTING

8.A.1.   The Concept of a Continuous Rate of Interest

A great deal of the literature in economics on the subject of capital and interest theory makes use of the notion of continuously compounded interest. This concept is derived by investigating the consequences of letting θ, the number of times per year that interest is added, in Formula (8.3), become indefinitely large.

First, it should be observed, that the base of natural logarithms, denoted by the letter e, is defined by the limit

$$ e = \operatorname*{Lim}_{m \to \infty} \left(1 + \frac{1}{m}\right)^m . $$

The manner in which e is introduced when interest is compounded continuously can be shown by rewriting Equation (8.3) as follows:

$$ V_n = V_0 \left(1 + \frac{i}{\theta}\right)^{\theta n} = V_0 \left\{ \left(1 + \frac{i}{\theta}\right)^{\frac{\theta}{i}} \right\}^{in} = V_0 \left\{ \left(1 + \frac{1}{m}\right)^{m} \right\}^{in} , $$

where $\theta = im$. The limit of this expression, as $m \to \infty$ and therefore $\theta \to \infty$ can be written

$$ V = \operatorname*{Lim}_{m \to \infty} V_n = \operatorname*{Lim}_{m \to \infty} V_0 \left\{ \left(1 + \frac{1}{m}\right)^{m} \right\}^{in} = V_0 e^{in} . $$

It is customary to use the variable t, rather than n, for time, and to use r, rather than i, for the interest rate parameter in continuous discount equations. With this change of notation, the expression

$$(8.A.1) \quad V_t = v_0 e^{rt}$$

gives the amount that the sum v_0 will become after t years at a continuous rate of interest r. Equation (8.A.1) is the continuous version of the annual and semiannual discount formulas in (8.1) and (8.2).

The result contained in (8.A.1) is of great value in setting up many problems involving interest, because of the simplicity that it introduces into the calculating problem. At the same time the continuous formula, by proper choice of r, can be made to approximate the annual or semiannual formulas very closely. In actual practice, of course, interest is almost always compounded annually or semiannually, but (8.A.1) can be used as an approximation to practice with a great gain in computational efficiency.

The present value, V_0, of a sum, v_t, due at time t, at a continuous rate of discount is

$$(8.A.2) \quad V_0 = v_t e^{-rt} .$$

This formula is the continuous counterpart of Equation (8.4) for annual compounding.

Suppose a piece of property is expected to yield an income which varies with time. Let $v(t)$ be the function relating the income of the property with time. Suppose further that this income is expected to accrue to the owner of the property for a period of T years. The amount of income received during an interval of time dt, at time t, is given by $v(t)dt$. The present value of this increment of income is

$$dV = v(t)e^{-rt}dt .$$

Therefore, the integral of this expression from 0 to T represents the present value of the income stream $v(t)$ extending T years into the future. That is,

$$(8.A.3) \quad V = \int_0^T v(t)e^{-rt}dt .$$

If the income stream happens to be constant with respect to time, say $v(t) = v$, then the capital value of the income stream is

$$(8.A.4) \quad V = \int_0^T ve^{-rt}dt = v\int_0^T e^{-rt}dt = \frac{v}{r}(1 - e^{-rT}) ,$$

where $(1 - e^{-rt})/r$ is the discount factor which converts the uniform flow of income, v, into its equivalent capital value, V. Equations (8.A.3) and (8.A.4) are the continuous analogues of Equations (8.5) and (8.6) for annual compounding.

8.A.2. Application to Timber-Cutting Problem

Making use of the continuous discounting formulas developed above, we can now obtain a more complete solution to the timber-cutting problem discussed in Section 8.5.

Measuring time continuously, suppose $f(t)$ represents a tree's growth as a function of its age t. If p is the price of a board foot of uncut timber, and r is the continuous rate of discount, then the value of a tree, $R(t)$, at time t is

$$(8.A.5) \quad R(t) = pf(t)e^{-rt} .$$

Since $R(t)$ is a continuous function of t, the maximum value of (8.A.5) can be found by setting the derivative of $R(t)$ equal to zero. That is,

$$(8.A.6) \quad \frac{dR}{dt} = p[-rf(t)e^{-rt} + f'(t)e^{-rt}] = 0 ,$$

which can be rearranged to give

$$(8.A.7) \quad \frac{f'(t)}{f(t)} = r .$$

Equation (8.A.7), when solved for t, gives the optimal cutting age of a tree. This equation can be given a very simple interpretation. The ratio $f'(t)/f(t)$ is simply the *percentage rate* of growth of a tree—the rate of growth at time t divided by the size of a tree at time t gives its percentage rate of growth at t. Hence, at time t Equation (8.A.7) says that the best time to cut a tree is when the percentage rate at which it is growing is just equal to the (percentage) rate of interest.

As a special case suppose $f(t) = 200\sqrt{t}$, and $r = 0.04$. Then

$$f'(t) = \frac{100}{\sqrt{t}} ,$$

and

$$\frac{f'(t)}{f(t)} = \frac{\dfrac{100}{\sqrt{t}}}{200\sqrt{t}} = r .$$

Hence,

$$t = \frac{1}{2r} = \frac{1}{2(0.04)} = 12.5 \text{ years} .$$

Equation (8.A.5) ignores any costs that might be incurred in timber production. If the initial cost of a sapling is k dollars, and the upkeep and insurance on timber is approximately constant at C dollars per year, then $N(t)$, the *net* present value of a tree as a function of its age is

$$(8.A.8) \quad N(t) = R(t) - C\int_0^t e^{-et}dt - k$$

$$= pf(t)e^{-rt} - \frac{C}{r}(1 - e^{-rt}) - k$$

$$= \left(pf(t) + \frac{C}{r}\right)e^{-rt} - \frac{C}{r} - k .$$

The function $N(t)$ is maximized when

$$(8.A.9) \quad \frac{dN}{dt} = pf'(t)e^{-rt} - r\left(pf(t) + \frac{C}{r}\right)e^{-rt} = 0 ,$$

or when

$$(8.A.10) \quad pf'(t) = rpf(t) + C .$$

In words, the term $pf'(t)$ is the (incremental) addition to revenue, at time t, of allowing a tree to grow for an additional year. $rpf(t)$ is the additional interest cost of allowing the realizable value of the tree to remain unrealized for an additional year. C of course is simply the added cost of another year's upkeep and insurance on a tree. Hence, (8.A.10) says that when the additional revenue created by another year's growth equals the additional outlay necessitated by the year's growth, it is time to cut the tree.

QUESTIONS AND EXERCISES

1. Wartime savings bonds were sold to the general public for $18.75 and paid $25 at maturity 10 years later. Assuming annual compounding of interest, what rate of interest was paid on these bonds?

2. A bond yields an income of $6 per year and has 5 years to go before maturity, at which time it has a value of $100. What is the highest price an investor should pay for this bond if he requires a 5 per cent rate of return on an investment.

3. Machine Number 1 costs $20,000, lasts 10 years, requires maintenance and repair outlays of $800 per year over its life, and has no salvage value at the end of its life. Machine Number 2 costs $27,000, lasts 10 years, requires no maintenance and has a salvage value of $1,000 at the end of its life. If these two machines produce the same quantity and type of output, which is the better investment at a 5 per cent rate of discount? Note: $(1.05)^{10} = 1.63$ and $(1.05)^{-10} = 0.614$.

4. Suppose it takes 50 years to grow a tree that will be worth $500 when mature. The care and upkeep on the tree in its growing period is $1 per year. If a sapling costs $5, and the interest rate is 6 per cent, what is the present value of the net profit to be realized from investing in saplings. Note: $(1.06)^{-50} = 0.054$, $(1.06)^{50} = 18.52$.

5. An automatic machine costs $80,000. Assume that the machine requires no maintenance expenses and will last 10 years. The machine produces the same output that two men could produce at a wage cost of $10,000 per year. How would you determine which method is best at an interest rate of 4 per cent?

6. A fully automatic machine costs $70,000 and will last 10 years. Maintenance expenditures of $1,000 per year will be required for the machine. The same output can be produced by two men each year. If it is believed that the workers can be hired for $8,000 per year for each of the first 5 years but can be hired only for $10,000 per year for the remaining 5 years, should the machine be purchased at a market rate of interest of 4 per cent?

7. Find the continuously compounded rate of interest, r, that will cause any sum to grow to the same amount that it would have become in the same period of

time if interest were compounded at the annual rate i. r in this case is the continuous equivalent of i. Show that when i is small, r and i are approximately equal.

8. A firm needs to construct a new warehouse. A $10,000 building has an estimated life of 10 years, while a building costing $20,000 is expected to last 40 years. If the two buildings provide the same service, and require the same operating expenses, which building would you recommend at a 5 per cent cost of capital? If the rate of interest were 8 per cent?

9. A bending fixture that will save $.06 operating cost per unit of product can be built for $600. Maintenance on the fixture is $30 per year. If 3,500 units are made per year, how long will it take the fixture to pay for itself if money earns 6 per cent? If interest is 10 per cent? 15 per cent?

Chapter 9

SURVEY OF THE ELEMENTARY
THEORY OF THE FIRM

In this and in subsequent chapters we will be concerned with the theory of the firm as it relates to the production decision problems of the business enterprise. The theory of the firm is concerned with two interdependent decisions: What rate of output is it best to produce? What is the best method or technique for producing that rate of output? In this area of economic analysis the study of engineering and of economics blends one into the other. Neither the economist nor the engineer can afford to ignore what the other has to say.

9.1. The Production Function

The theory of the firm is founded upon the hypothesis of a functional relationship between the quantity of output of a firm or a process and the quantities of the various inputs which can be employed in the production of that output. A direct correspondence is expected to exist between the quantity of output which a productive organism can produce and the quantities of all the various agents of production that are employed in the process. A distinction is made between the variable inputs such as labor, power, fuel, raw materials, etc., and the so-called fixed inputs such as individual items of plant and equipment. Variable inputs are characterized by the fact that their consumption in the production process can be *directly* associated with individual units of output. For example, 2.5 man-hours may be used in the production of a casting. Fixed inputs are capital goods whose contribution to production *cannot* be allocated in an unambiguous way to individual units of output.

For analytical purposes it is convenient to distinguish between long-range and short-range planning. The *long-range* production plans of a firm involve decisions as to how much of the various fixed inputs to employ, while the *short-range* plans of a firm involve decisions as to how much of the different variable inputs to employ. These short-

and long-range decisions are behind the distinction between short- and long-run supply curves discussed in Chapters 3 and 4.

We shall begin by considering the simplest case of production in which there is only one variable input to the process. Then, given the quantity and characteristics of the fixed input or inputs that are employed, we can associate various quantities of the variable input with corresponding quantities of output. If y is the quantity of output per unit time and x is the quantity of the variable input per unit time, then we have the production function or input-output function:

$$(9.1) \quad y = f(x).$$

The first derivative of (9.1), which may be written dy/dx or df/dx, is called the *marginal productivity* (*MP*) of x in the production of y. It is the rate of change of output with respect to incremental changes in the variable input. The general principle called the *law of diminishing returns* governs the shape of (9.1). According to this principle, if certain inputs to a process are held fixed, and the quantity of one of the inputs is increased, the marginal productivity of that input must eventually decline. Mathematically, this empirical law states that there must exist some quantity of input beyond which the function has a negative second derivative.

The top of Figure 9–1 shows a graph exhibiting the general shape of the two-variable production function. Up to the point $x = \bar{x}$ the function is convex from below, indicating that marginal productivity is increasing (that is, the second derivative of the function is positive). Beyond the point $x = \bar{x}$ the function is concave from below, meaning that marginal productivity is decreasing (that is, the second derivative of the function is negative).

It should be noted very carefully that there is a distinction between marginal productivity and what is called average productivity. *Average productivity* (*AP*) is simply the ratio of the output to the variable input, y/x; for example, output per man-hour would be the average productivity of labor in a process using labor. At the point P in Figure 9–1, marginal productivity is given by the slope of a line tangent to the curve at that point. Average productivity, on the other hand, is given geometrically by the slope of a line connecting the origin with the point P. At the bottom of Figure 9–1 is shown graphically the manner in which marginal productivity and average productivity each varies with the rate of input. It is seen that marginal productivity reaches a maximum at Q, average productivity reaches a maximum at R, and marginal productivity becomes zero at S.

FIGURE 9–1

THEORETICAL PRODUCTION FUNCTION

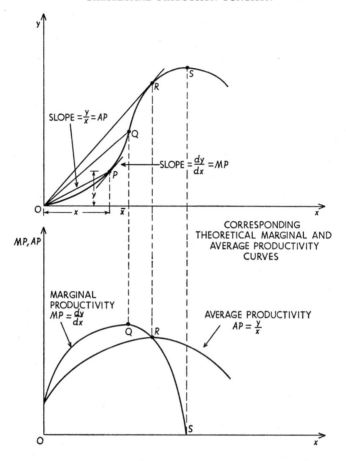

9.2. An Application of the Two-Variable Production Function

A very simple process of production which illustrates the general form of the production function is that pertaining to the conversion of electrical into mechanical energy, or of mechanical into electrical energy.

The conversion of electrical energy into mechanical energy requires two major inputs—the fixed input, electric motor, and the variable input, electrical energy. (The conversion of mechanical into electrical energy requires alternator input, and mechanical energy input.) There are other variable inputs such as maintenance and oil but let us assume that these are negligible relative to the electrical energy input. From the performance curves of an electric motor (or alternator) one can derive a production function of the form (9.1), since the fixed input is specified once the motor (or alternator) is chosen.

Table 9–1 is extracted from the performance characteristics of a 5 hp 220 volt induction motor. The instantaneous variable input is measured in kilowatts while output is measured in horsepower. The production function or input-output relation for this motor is shown

TABLE 9–1

RELATION OF OUTPUT TO INPUT—AN ELECTRIC MOTOR

Kilowatts—Electrical Energy Consumed	Horsepower—Output
.75	0.5
1.05	1
1.32	1.5
1.70	2
2.52	3
3.39	4
5.33	6
7.00	7.5
11.12	9.7

graphically at the top of Figure 9–2, while the average and marginal productivity curves are shown at the bottom of Figure 9–2. Table 9–2, Columns 3 and 4, illustrate the computation of average and marginal productivity.

It is clear from the graph in Figure 9–2 that the phenomena of diminishing returns begin to occur at an input of about 1.05 kilowatts. Beyond this point, larger and larger quantities of electrical energy input are required to produce successive increments of horsepower output. It is a familiar fact to the engineer that as the load on such equipment increases, the energy loss, due to internal resistance, eventually rises very rapidly. This principle is a completely general one. As the load (output level) rises on a plant producing, say, automobiles, it becomes progressively more difficult to increase output. When speaking of this phenomena in regard to energy-transforming equipment such as motors, transformers, boilers, and turbines, the engineer talks in terms of efficiency. The efficiency (energy output divided by energy input) rises to a peak and then declines.

It may be instructive to point out that the engineer's concept of efficiency is parallel to the economist's concept of average productivity, and that the two become *identical* in the case of energy transformation processes since input and output can be measured in the same units for such processes (this is due simply to the basic equivalence of all forms of energy). In our electric motor example the average produc-

FIGURE 9–2

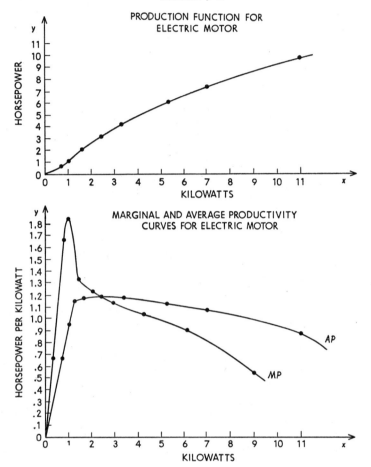

tivity curve becomes an efficiency curve if we measure both input and output in kilowatts (horsepower is converted to kilowatts when multiplied by .746). In most productive processes, however, the two concepts are merely analogues and are not identical.

9.3. The Short-Run Cost Function

The manner in which the cost of operating a plant or a process varies with the level of output can be directly related to the two-variable production function. Suppose we let w be the price or unit cost of the variable input, and F be the cost of fixed inputs which has been allocated (by some arbitrary rule) to the successive time periods with respect to which the variable input and output rates are measured. In the example of a motor, these fixed costs include depreciation and in-

TABLE 9–2
SHORT-RUN PRODUCTION—COST RELATIONSHIPS FOR AN ELECTRIC MOTOR

(1) Kilowatts Input, x	(2) Horsepower Output, y	(3) Average Productivity y/x	(4) Marginal Productivity $\frac{\Delta y}{\Delta x} \cong \frac{dy}{dx}$	(5) Total Fixed Cost F	(6) Total Variable Cost $C-F = wx = wg(y)$	(7) Total Cost C	(8) Average Total Cost $ATC = \frac{C}{y}$	(9) Average Variable Cost $AVC = \frac{C-F}{y}$	(10) Marginal Cost $MC = \frac{dC}{dy}$
0	0			.03	0	.03	∞		
0.75	0.5	0.67	0.67	.03	.038	.068	.136	.076	.076
1.05	1.0	0.95	1.67	.03	.053	.083	.083	.053	.030
1.32	1.5	1.14	1.85	.03	.066	.096	.064	.044	.026
1.70	2.0	1.18	1.32	.03	.085	.115	.058	.042	.038
2.52	3.0	1.19	1.22	.03	.126	.156	.052	.042	.041
3.39	4.0	1.18	1.15	.03	.170	.200	.050	.042	.044
5.33	6.0	1.12	1.03	.03	.266	.296	.049	.044	.048
7.00	7.5	1.07	0.90	.03	.350	.380	.051	.047	.056
11.12	9.7	0.87	0.53	.03	.557	.587	.061	.057	.094

terest on the investment in the motor, and would continue even if the motor were not used. Then the total cost per unit time, C, of the fixed and variable inputs is

$$(9.2) \quad C = wx + F .$$

From the production function (9.1) we can associate a unique rate of output, y, with each rate of input x. Thus (9.1) will have an inverse:

$$(9.3) \quad x = f^{-1}(y) = g(y) ,$$

which can be substituted in (9.2) to give

$$(9.4) \quad C = wg(y) + F .$$

This expression relates cost to output instead of input and has the form shown in Figure 9–3.

The variable component of total cost, $wg(y)$ is usually called *total variable cost* (*TVC*). Total cost divided by output is *average total cost* (*ATC*), variable cost divided by output is *average variable cost* (*AVC*), fixed cost divided by output is *average fixed cost* (*AFC*), while dC/dy, the rate of change in total cost with respect to changes in the level of output, is *marginal cost* (*MC*) or incremental cost. We shall have occasion to refer many times to these various derived concepts of cost.

In comparing the graph of the production function in Figure 9–1 with the cost function in Figure 9–3, it will be seen that the "S shape"

FIGURE 9–3

A TOTAL COST FUNCTION

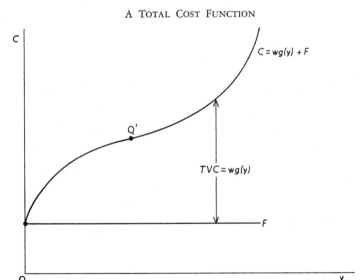

of the cost curve comes directly from the "S shape" of the production function. The point of inflection on the production function, Q in Figure 9–1, corresponds to the point of inflection Q' on the cost curve in Figure 9–3. Therefore, since marginal productivity is a maximum at Q (refer to Figure 9–1), and marginal cost is a minimum at Q', it follows that marginal productivity is maximum at the same level of output that marginal cost is a minimum. A similar statement holds for average productivity and average variable cost. That is, since $AP = y/x$, and $AVC = wx/y$, then $AP = w/AVC$. It follows that the output at which average variable cost is minimum is also the output for which average productivity is a maximum.

9.4. An Application of the Short-Run Cost Function

Our previous example of a simple production function can be used to derive a total cost curve for the conversion of electrical into mechanical energy. If fixed cost F is \$0.03 per hour, and the unit cost, w, of electricity is \$0.05 per kilowatt-hour, then total cost can be derived as shown in Table 9–2, Column 7, page 125. Average total cost, average variable cost, and marginal cost are computed in Columns 8, 9 and 10, and are shown graphically in Figure 9–4. ATC is determined by dividing the entries in Column 7 by those in Column 2, while AVC is obtained by dividing Column 6 by Column 2. The computation

FIGURE 9–4

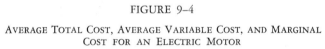

AVERAGE TOTAL COST, AVERAGE VARIABLE COST, AND MARGINAL COST FOR AN ELECTRIC MOTOR

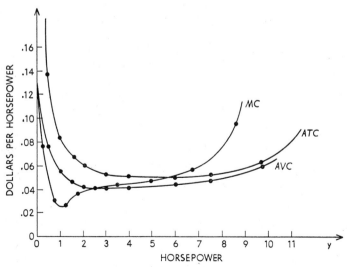

of *MC* is best illustrated by an example. If output is increased from 1 to 1.5 (Column 2), this increases total cost by $0.013 = $0.096 — $0.083 (Column 7). Since marginal cost is the rate at which cost changes with respect to changes in output, *MC* is $\dfrac{.096 - .083}{1.5 - 1.0} =$ $0.026 (Column 10).

9.5. Competitive Market Structure and the Firm's Demand Curve

Before a solution can be obtained to the problem of determining the most profitable rate of output for a firm, it is necessary to discuss the demand curve faced by the individual enterprise. The concept of the demand for a commodity has already been developed, but the demand for the product of an individual firm is somewhat more complicated in that it depends not only upon the total demand for the product of the industry but also upon the competitive character of the industry and the manner in which total demand is distributed among the individual firms in the industry.

Economists distinguish several forms of market competition depending upon the homogeneity of the product and the number of firms in the industry. The broad market categories which are found useful for analytical purposes can be listed as follows:

1. Pure competition
2. Monopolistic competition
3. Oligopoly
4. Pure monopoly

Under *pure competition* the product is homogeneous, that is, alike for all buyers and sellers, and the demand for the product of the individual firm is perfectly elastic. The individual firm can sell all that it can feasibly produce at the market price without itself having any significant effect on that price. Most agricultural products such as wheat, corn, soybeans, and cotton are sold in markets which come very near to this theoretical concept of pure competition. The individual farmer can sell all he can produce at the market price without having any influence over that price. Market price is fixed by the general conditions of supply and demand where supply is affected by what producers as a whole do but not by what any one producer does.

Monopolistic competition is also characterized by a large number of producers, but the product is differentiated among the various producers. That is, each producer, though he sells a product which is in the same competitive group as those of his competitors, produces a slightly different product. Indeed, each producer will attempt through quality changes, design changes, service, and/or advertising to differentiate his product in the consumer's mind. The product need not in fact be different. All that is required is that consumers have reasons to prefer the product of one firm to that of another. Under this situation each firm will face a downward-sloping demand curve. Because of the differentiation in his product, the individual producer is able to exercise some control over price. He can even charge a somewhat higher price than his competitors if he wishes, since there will be some customers who, because they prefer his product, will be willing to pay the higher price rather than shift to a competitor's substitute. However, control over price is limited, since if it is too high, even those customers with strong preferences for the product of one firm will be induced to shift over to purchasing the lower-priced close substitutes of its competitors. Canned fruits and vegetables, whisky, clothing, and perhaps some college textbooks are examples of products sold under conditions approaching that of monopolistic competition. Of course, no real market will fit perfectly into any theoretical model, but this is not necessary in order that the model be useful.

Oligopoly is characterized by the existence of a number of producers few enough so that no firm can afford to consider a change in business policy without taking into account the possible reaction of his rivals. For example, in the steel industry, no single firm can afford to assume that if its price is lowered, the other firms in the industry will not also lower their prices. No supermarket in a city can afford to assume that, if it stays open one extra hour a day, or gives out trading stamps, this action will not be followed by a similar reaction on the part of its rivals. Oligopoly markets are characterized by *rivalry* among the individual firms in the industry. In contrast, under pure competition there is no rivalry among producers because the fortunes of one firm are not affected in the least by the policies of one or even several other firms. Under oligopoly where numbers are few, the fortunes of each are sometimes vitally affected by the policies of a rival. Such industries are often plagued by periodic price wars, advertising wars, additive wars as in the oil industry, or stamp wars.

Pure monopoly is perhaps the rarest of all forms of market structure. Pure monopoly is a situation in which there is only one firm producing a product that has no close substitutes. A hotel in a small isolated town or a public utility such as the gas, water, or electrical company of a city are examples. Complete monopoly is rare for the reason that most products have close enough substitutes to give any would-be monopolist a tough job of controlling his market price. In the above examples, if there are motels or rooming houses in a town with a single hotel, then there are severe limits to the power of the local hotel manager to control room rates. Similarly, the gas company must compete with the coal producers (the coal industry, by the way, is highly competitive, with thousands of producers), and the producers of bottled gas. Even the water company may have limits to its monopoly power in that if prices are too high, people drill their own wells.

Of these four forms of market competition, three of them—pure competition, monopolistic competition, and pure monopoly—are alike in that they assume that the individual demand curve faced by the firm is independent of the price and other policies of competing or potentially competing firms. Oligopoly stands apart in that it takes explicit account of the fact that where there are only a few firms in an industry, say two, ten, or twenty, the position of each firm's demand curve depends upon the individual policies of the other firms in the industry.

The analysis to follow will be restricted to market situations which come under the heading of pure competition, monopolistic competition, oligopoly or pure monopoly.

9.6. *The Optimal Rate of Output*

Under conditions of pure competition, price to the individual firm becomes a constant, and the firm's total revenue, R, in dollars per unit time, is simply:

$$(9.5) \quad R = py \ ,$$

where p is the fixed market price of the product and y is the quantity of product produced and sold by the firm per unit time.

Profit per unit time, π, is given by

$$(9.6) \quad \pi = R - C = py - C \ .$$

To make π a maximum it is necessary to adjust y to a level at which any small variation in y will cause no change in profit; that is, we seek that value of y for which

$$(9.7) \quad \frac{d\pi}{dy} = \frac{dR}{dy} - \frac{dC}{dy} = p - \frac{dC}{dy} = 0 \ .$$

dR/dy is called *marginal revenue* (the slope of the total revenue curve) and is equal to p if and only if p is independent of y. Hence, the condition for maximum profit is that marginal cost equals price in the special case of pure competition, and marginal cost equals marginal revenue in the general case in which p is not independent of y.

Total revenue, total cost, and profit as functions of output are shown graphically at the top of Figure 9–5 for the case of pure competition, while the graph at the bottom of Figure 9–5 shows the corresponding marginal revenue (MR), marginal cost (MC), average variable cost (AVC), and average total cost (ATC) curves.

FIGURE 9–5

THE RELATIONSHIP OF PROFITS TO COST AND REVENUE—PURE COMPETITION

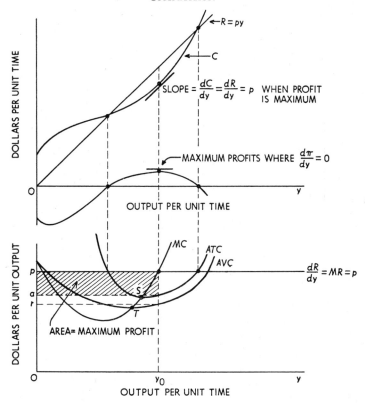

When the firm cannot sell an unlimited quantity of output at a fixed price, as is the case for most manufacturing establishments, it is necessary to introduce a demand function. The firm, in order to sell a larger quantity, must decrease its selling price. That is, the quantity which the firm can sell is a decreasing function of price, or, stated differently, the price which the firm is able to get is a decreasing function of the quantity placed on the market,

$$(9.8) \quad p = D(y), \frac{dp}{dy} < 0 .$$

It follows that total revenue is now given by

$$(9.9) \quad R = R(y) = yD(y) \,.$$

In this case the condition for maximum profit is that derived in Equation (9.7), except that marginal revenue is no longer constant and equal to price.

The total revenue, total cost, and profit curves for the monopoly or monopolistically competitive firm are shown at the top of Figure 9–6, while the graph at the bottom of Figure 9–6 shows the corresponding marginal revenue, marginal cost, and average total cost curves. These are the same as for pure competition in Figure 9–5 ex-

FIGURE 9–6

THE RELATIONSHIP OF PROFITS TO COST AND REVENUE— MONOPOLY OR MONOPOLISTIC COMPETITION

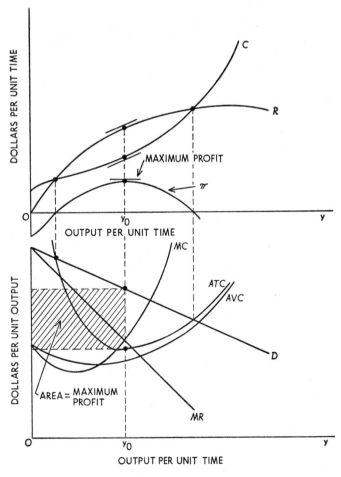

cept that the total revenue curve increases at a decreasing rate with quantity sold, and therefore the marginal revenue curve declines with quantity sold. These results are due to the assumption that the firm cannot sell additional quantities of product without lowering price to attract additional buyers.

Observe carefully in Figures 9–5 and 9–6 that the total profit curve, or the difference between total revenue and total cost, is greatest at the same rate of output at which the marginal cost and marginal revenue curves intersect.

9.7. Most Profitable Output Not the Most "Efficient"

It has been shown that the engineer's concept of efficiency is very similar to average productivity and that the two concepts are identical when the theory of production is applied to energy transformation processes. It has also been shown that average variable cost is at a minimum when average productivity is at a maximum. Therefore, the point T in Figure 9–5, corresponds to the point of maximum average productivity or "efficiency." But this is *not the point of maximum profitability*. Maximization of profits does not in general imply operating at the point of maximum "efficiency" in the engineering sense. The most profitable rate of output will be greater than the most "efficient" rate of output.

9.8. The Economist's Concept of Long-Run Total Cost, and Normal Profit

For purposes of analyzing the long-run response of firms and industries to changes in demand or costs of production, it is important to be aware of the fact that there are costs associated with the production of a commodity which are not readily measurable. These are the so-called implicit costs discussed in Chapter 7 and are associated with the fact that unless an industry is sufficiently profitable relative to other industries to make it attractive for firms to remain in the industry, there will be a long-run tendency for firms to leave the industry and go into the production of alternative products. This is simply an application of the principal of equal advantage. A certain minimum profit must be earned by the firms in an industry in order to hold resources in that industry. These minimum profits are called *normal profits*. If profits are below normal, there is a long-run tendency for investment in the industry to be withdrawn and placed in other industries. If profits are above normal, there is a long-run tendency for the industry to attract new firms and for investment in the industry to expand.

Normal profits are, therefore, part of the social costs of producing a commodity, since if these costs are not met, the production of the commodity shrinks, either until profits become normal again or until the industry passes out of existence. For this reason the economist includes normal profits in addition to interest and depreciation costs in the total cost and average total cost curves. In Figures 9–5 and 9–6 the *ATC* curves would include normal profits. In Figure 9–5 this means that, at the output y_0, the firm in question is earning a *pure profit* over and above normal profit. Since a is the average total cost, including normal profits, of producing y_0 units of output, this pure profit is given by $(p-a)y_0$. In Figure 9–5 pure profits are made as long as price is above the point at which *ATC* is a minimum. If price is equal to minimum *ATC*, a normal profit is earned, while if price is below minimum *ATC* a less-than-normal profit is made, providing an inducement for firms to leave the industry in the long run.

For the purely competitive firm shown in Figure 9–5, the indicated pure profits will attract new firms into the industry. As these new firms enter, invest in new facilities, and begin production, total industry output will rise and price will fall. As price falls, the pure profits of our representative firm will decline. New firms will continue to enter until the industry is just normally profitable, which occurs when the price line in Figure 9–5 has fallen to the level represented by S, the minimum point on the *ATC* curve. The minimum point of *ATC* is of special significance for economic efficiency. The average total cost of producing any particular output can be thought of as a measure of the resources— raw materials, labor, capital, management, etc.—that must be consumed per unit production of the given product. Production at minimum *ATC* is economically efficient in the sense that the product is being produced with the smallest consumption of resources per unit of output. In this special sense, pure competition implies economic efficiency. Note, however, that the economist's concept of efficiency, so defined, is not the same as the engineer's concept discussed above.

9.9. Monopoly and Pure Competition Contrasted

In the case of monopoly it is not possible, by definition, for new firms to be attracted into the monopolized industry, though this may be typically the process whereby temporary monopoly power is broken. Under circumstances of persistent monopoly there can be no tendency in the long-run for profits to be normal. If the monopoly happens to be a profitable one, the situation might appear as in Figure 9–6. Since normal profits are included in the *ATC* curve, such a monopolist earns a pure profit above normal which is given by the rectangular shaded area. Note, however, that if the monopolist's demand curve is below *ATC* for all outputs, then he makes subnormal profits.

Since firms are not free to enter the monopolized industry, it follows that there is no long-run tendency for price to equal minimum *ATC* under monopoly. Hence, monopoly is less efficient than pure competition, since production under monopoly does not tend to a level where the least amount of resources are consumed per unit of output.

9.10. Long-Run Tendencies in Monopolistic Competition

As indicated in our earlier discussion the only difference between pure competition and monopolistic competition is that in the former the product is homogeneous, while in the latter, the product is differentiated from one firm to another. Each firm, through product differentiation, attempts to make its demand curve less elastic, thereby allowing more control over price. Thus, in Figure 9–7 the representative firm under monopolistic competition might face a demand curve (and average revenue curve) given by DD. The profit maximizing price is P, with output y_0. Under the assumed condition a pure profit, $(P - a)y_0$, is obtained by the firm. Since there is free entry in a monopolistically

FIGURE 9–7

LONG-RUN EQUILIBRIUM UNDER MONOPOLISTIC COMPETITION

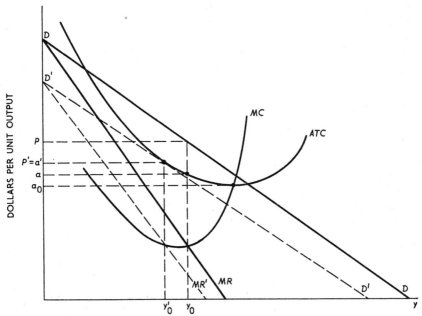

competitive industry, this pure profit enjoyed by the typical firm attracts new firms into the industry. These new firms must advertise and promote their new products, and bid competitively against the existing firms in an attempt to obtain some of their customers. As some of these customers shift to the products of the new firms, the demand curves of the old firms fall, and their profits decline. As profits in the industry decline, this tends to slow the rate of entry of new firms. However, new firms will tend to continue entering the industry until the demand curve of the representative firm has fallen to $D'D'$ as shown in Figure 9–7. Price will now be $P' = a'$, output y_0', and pure profits $(P' - a')y_0' = 0$. The industry will now be in long-run equilibrium. In this process we assumed that costs did not change as the adjustment took place— only the demand curve changed. More commonly one would expect existing firms to counter the competition of new firms by increased advertising and promotion in an attempt to arrest the declining demand. The expenses of such promotional activities would cause ATC to rise so that in long-run equilibrium ATC might rise to meet the declining demand curve. Whatever may be the combination of declining demand and rising cost that reduces pure profit, the end result is a tendency toward a long-run equilibrium characterized by tangency between the demand curve $(D'D')$ and the ATC curve as shown in Figure 9–7.

Unlike pure competition, the long-run equilibrium is at an average cost of production, a', which is above the minimum point, a_0, of ATC. In this sense monopolistic competition is less efficient than pure competition. But such a comparison is not really valid, since consumers in a monopolistically competitive industry get a diversity of differentiated products from which to choose in return for the higher price they must pay.

9.11. One Theory of Oligopoly

There are many theoretical models of oligopolistically competitive industries. Each of these models contributes to an understanding of some aspect of the complicated competitive structure which characterizes the automobile, tobacco, steel, and other such industries composed of a relatively few firms.

One such theory is based upon the so-called "Kinked Oligopoly Demand Curve." The argument of this theory proceeds somewhat as follows. Consider an industry with only a few firms—so few that any given firm cannot afford to ignore the individual reactions of his competitors whenever the given firm changes his price policy. Suppose the price structure in this industry has been stable for some period of time without any price wars. We choose a typical firm in this industry and find that he is currently charging a price P for his product. Now, given that there are so few firms in this industry, what might our firm think about the sales consequences of a deviation in the price he charges for his product? In different words, what does our firm think about the individual demand curve it faces? It would seem reasonable for our firm to assume that if its price is raised, other firms will find it to their advantage to leave their prices unchanged thereby attracting some of our

FIGURE 9–8

THE KINKED OLIGOPOLY DEMAND CURVE

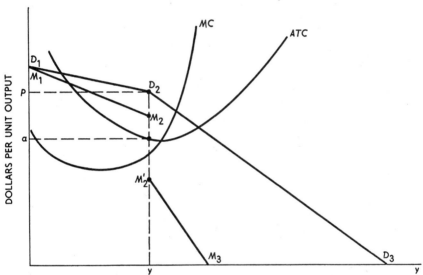

firm's customers. As customers shift away from our firm, sales will fall off rather rapidly. Hence, for price increases above P, our firm may expect to face a fairly elastic demand curve such as D_1D_2 in Figure 9–8. On the other hand, if our firm should lower its price below P, it would be highly unrealistic to assume that its competitors are going to hold their prices unchanged as customers shift to the now cheaper product of our firm. The conservative assumption is to suppose that other firms will follow our firm's price reduction. As a consequence our firm will attract relatively little additional buying strength, and sales will rise only modestly. This implies that the demand curve is comparatively inelastic below the historically ruling price P, as indicated by D_2D_3 in Figure 9–8.

The result of this analysis is that our firm's expectations or beliefs about its market situation is equivalent to the hypothesis that it faces a demand curve such as $D_1D_2D_3$ in Figure 9–8 with a "kink" in it at the price P. By drawing in the firm's marginal revenue, and cost curves we can deduce some implications of these assumptions. Note first that the firm's marginal revenue curve contains a discontinuity at the output y_0. That is, the marginal revenue curve corresponding to D_1D_2 is M_1M_2 while that corresponding to D_2D_3 is $M_2'M_3$. At output y_0 associated with price P, marginal revenue falls abruptly from M_2 to M_2'. If MC passes through this gap in the marginal revenue curve, then the firm's profit maximizing price and output are P and y_0. (Note that marginal cost = marginal revenue is no longer a condition for profit maximization. Our condition now is $M_2 \geqq MC \geqq M_2'$.) It follows that cost can change over a reasonably wide range without altering the firm's profit maximizing price-output policy. Within the framework of elementary firm theory, this provides a rationalization for the fact that price is often stable over considerable periods of time in oligopolistic industries. Though such price stability can be due to collusive agreements among firms, it can just as easily be due to each firm's fear of injuring himself by any alteration of price. The very experience of a severe price war is often sufficient to instill in each firm the kind of fears which form the assumptions underlying our kinked demand curve.

9.12. Summary

The elementary theory of the firm is concerned with the determination of the most profitable short-run (given fixed inputs or "plant") rate of output. This requires knowledge of two kinds of information: (1) the relationship between price and sales (the demand curve), and (2) the relationship between cost and output (the cost curve). In the special case of a simple process of production with only one variable input, the cost curve can be obtained if we have knowledge of the production function and the price of the variable input. Ultimately, then, the best short-run rate of output requires knowledge of (1) the demand curve, (2) the production function, and (3) the price of the variable input. Of these three kinds of information it is the price of the variable input (or inputs) which the typical firm knows with the greatest certainty and accuracy. Though the average firm does not have precise knowledge of its production function, or functions, it nevertheless usually has a wealth of technological knowledge concerning its particular production problems.

By far the most uncertain and least accurate information possessed by the typical firm is that concerning its demand curve. It is demand which is one of the major concerns and headaches of management and of the market analysis department.

This chapter has attempted to develop the theoretical scheme which shows the relationship between these various kinds of information, and the manner in which they must be blended together in rational firm decision making. Only the barest of elements has been considered, but even at this stage the role of technological data should be clear. Its primary concern is with matters which in one way or another have to do with the production function, and the production function is only one of several interdependent ingredients in business planning.

QUESTIONS AND EXERCISES

1. Draw a typical total cost function such as that in Figure 9–3. Directly under it, using the same scale for y, draw MC, ATC, AVC, and AFC relating each of these curves to the slopes of appropriate lines drawn on the graph of the total cost curve. (Hint: Proceed by analogy with Figure 9–1.)

2. In the absence of government regulation, are there any limits imposed upon the ability of a monopolist to charge any price he pleases? Discuss.

3. Suppose all U.S. copper production were controlled by a single firm. Would this be a case of pure monopoly? From your knowledge of the determinates of the demand for such a commodity, discuss the extent of the monopoly power of this copper producer.

4. A steam-generating power plant using natural gas for fuel operates with an over-all plant efficiency, e, given by

$$e = 1.2 \cdot 10^5 x - 0.6 \cdot 10^{10} x^2,$$

where x is the input of natural gas to the plant measured in energy units (e.g. B.T.U.'s or kilowatts) per hour. Derive the production function and the average productivity and marginal productivity functions for this plant.

5. Suppose the production function for electricity in a coal operated power plant is given by

$$y = 10^{a-b/x}, \ a, b > 0,$$

where y is output in kilowatt-hours and x is the input of coal which might be measured in energy units or tons per unit time.

   $a)$ Verify that this equation has the general properties of a production function.

   $b)$ Derive the average productivity and marginal productivity functions for this production function.

   $c)$ If w is the price of coal and F is the fixed cost of operating a plant, derive the total, marginal, and average cost functions for a coal-operated plant.

   $d)$ If p is the fixed selling price of electricity, state the condition for determining that rate of output which will maximize profits (or minimize losses).

6. Given the short-run cost function of a firm,

$$C = y^3 - 5y^2 + 10y + 50,$$

where C is the total cost per day in dollars and y is the number of units of output per day:

a) Calculate for outputs from 0 through 8 the total cost, average total cost, average variable cost, and marginal cost of a day's production. Tabulate this data.

NOTE: 1. The last term in the cost function above represents the fixed cost.

2. Calculate marginal cost for precise output units of 0 through 8 working from the cost function.

b) Plot total cost on one graph.

c) Plot average total cost, average variable cost, and marginal cost on a second graph.

7. Assume the firm above is in an industry characterized by perfect competition and the market price, p, for the product is $58.

a) How many units per day should the firm produce to maximize profit?

b) What will be the daily profit (above the normal profit needed to keep owners' capital in firm) at the most profitable output rate?

c) In the long run, is the situation likely to continue? *Why or why not?*

8. Now assume the firm is in an industry characterized by monopolistic competition and has a demand function represented by

$$p = -3.125y + 66.25.$$

a) How many units per day should the firm produce to maximize profits?

b) What will be the daily profit (above the normal profit needed to keep owners' capital in firm) at the most profitable output rate?

c) Calculate and plot on the same graph as average total cost, average variable cost, and marginal cost, the above demand function and the marginal revenue function.

9. Could it pay for a monopolist to incur advertising and product promotional expenses? An individual firm in pure competition? Monopolistic competition? Oligopoly?

10. Draw total revenue and total cost curves for the oligopolistic firm in Figure 9–8. From the resulting curves verify that the condition $M_2 \geqq MC \geqq M_2'$ holds for maximum profit at output y_0.

THE THEORY OF COST

AND PRODUCTION

When there is only one variable input to a process, as in the case treated in the previous chapter, the decision as to how much input to employ to produce any given output becomes a trivial problem; given the type of fixed inputs being used, and the state of technical knowledge [in other words, given the function $f(x)$], there is one rate of variable input associated with each rate of output. But as soon as we broaden the analysis to more complicated processes requiring two or more variable inputs, we find that there may be many input combinations, which, from a technical point of view, can be used to produce each possible output. The theory of cost and production is concerned with the general problem of choosing a least-cost input combination. In the example of the electric motor discussed previously, if the quantity of capital input (motor size) is allowed to become a decision variable, then there will be two variable inputs to the process, and we have a problem of determining the least-cost input combination.

10.1. *The Three-Variable Production Function*

Consider a process of production requiring two inputs. Let x_1 and x_2 be the respective quantities of the two inputs and y be the quantity of output. Then the production function can be written

$$(10.1) \quad y = f(x_1, x_2) .$$

This function provides a complete catalogue or quantitative description of the various quantities of the two inputs which can be employed to produce y. Strictly speaking we should think of (10.1) as providing us with the largest output, y, which can be produced by given x_1 and x_2. There are some production decisions which can be made on purely technical grounds without any knowledge of costs whatsoever. These decisions can be called *engineering decisions* as opposed to *economic decisions*. Thus, if a modification of the manner in which a process is performed allows the same output to be produced, and permits the quantity of at least one input to be reduced without requiring an increase in the quantity of any other input, then a decision in favor of the modification can be made on engineering grounds alone without any knowledge of input prices. An action which saves on one input without altering any other requirement of a process will lower cost regardless of the price of that input.

The production function in (10.1) presupposes all such engineering decisions to have been made. In constructing this function all methods, techniques, or processes which require more of one input and not less of any other input are rejected. Once all such engineering decisions have been made, we are left with the best engineering technology. But with this technology we are still left with a large number of input possibilities which have the characteristic that output cannot be maintained at a given level when one input is reduced, unless we increase some other input. The choice among these remaining input combinations is an *economic decision* in the sense that the decision requires knowledge of input prices.

Briefly stated, economic decisions require knowledge of input prices and best engineering technology. Engineering decisions are concerned with best engineering technology and require technical knowledge of physical processes.

10.2. Characteristics of the Three-Variable Production Function

The production function as defined in the previous section will, in general, be expected to exhibit the following characteristics:

1. If either input is held constant while the other is increased (decreased), output will increase (decrease). Mathematically, this is equivalent to stating that $\partial f/\partial x_1 > 0$ and $\partial f/\partial x_2 > 0$. The partial derivatives $\partial f/\partial x_1$ and $\partial f/\partial x_2$ are called the *marginal productivities* (MP_1 and MP_2) respectively of x_1 and x_2 in the production of y. In words, the marginal productivity of input Number 1 is the rate at which output changes with respect to changes in the quantity of input Number 1 used, the quantity of input Number 2 being held constant.

2. If output is held constant, a decrease (increase) in one input will require an increase (decrease) in the other input. Mathematically $\partial x_2/\partial x_1 < 0$. The partial derivative $\partial x_2/\partial x_1$ is the *marginal rate of substitution* between x_1 and x_2.

3. If y is held constant, the marginal rate at which x_1 substitutes for x_2 increases as x_1 increases. Mathematically,

$$\frac{\partial}{\partial x_1}\left(\frac{\partial x_2}{\partial x_1}\right) = \frac{\partial^2 x_2}{\partial x^2_1} > 0 ,$$

and we say that the production function is *convex* to the origin in the plane of x_1 and x_2.

10.3. The Iso-Product Contour Map

These characteristics of the typical production function can be summarized with an iso-product map. An *iso-product contour* (constant output curve) is a curve connecting all those combinations of x_1 and x_2 that are required to produce a specified quantity of output. An iso-product map is simply a family of such curves, each curve corresponding to a different level of output. Such a map is shown in Figure 10–1 for output levels of 10, 20, 30 and 40 units respectively.

FIGURE 10–1

AN ISO-PRODUCT CONTOUR MAP

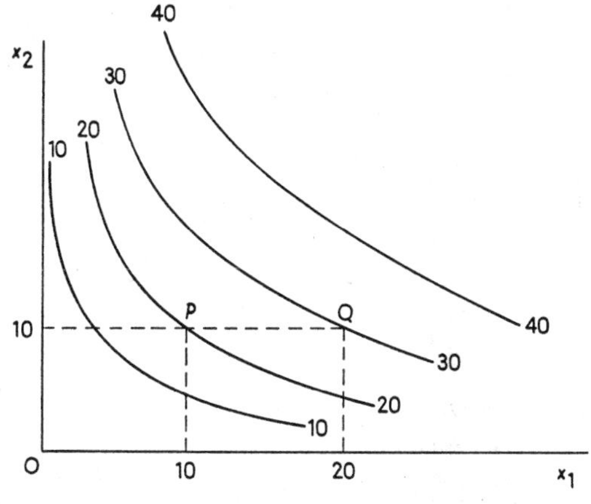

It can be readily verified that the production function mapped in Figure 10–1 satisfies the three conditions listed previously. If the amount of x_2 is kept constant at 10 units, and x_1 increased from 10 to 20 units, corresponding to a movement from Point P to Q, it is seen that output rises from 20 units to 30. Condition (2) is satisfied since the iso-product contours slope downward to the right, and condition (3) is satisfied since the contours are convex as viewed from the origin.

10.4. Perfect Substitutes

There are many processes in which two (or more) inputs are perfect substitutes in the production of an item. For some purposes, for example, it might not make any difference to prospective buyers whether a certain kind of pipe is made out of plastic or fiber. If pipe made of either material is completely satisfactory, then the two materials are perfect substitutes in the manufacture of this pipe.

Suppose in this case that the manufacture of pipe of a given diameter requires 2 pounds of fiber material per foot if fiber is used or 3 pounds of plastic material per foot if plastic is used. When x_1 pounds of fiber input are used to make pipe, the output of fiber pipe in feet is $x_1/2$. If x_2 pounds of plastic input are used to make pipe, then $x_2/3$ feet of plastic pipe can be produced. Now, if the two kinds of pipe are completely interchangeable, they can be considered the same product and can be added to get the total output, y, of the process. Therefore, in this case the production function can be written in the especially simple form

$$(10.2) \quad y = \frac{x_1}{2} + \frac{x_2}{3}.$$

The iso-product contours for this process are straight lines and are shown in Figure 10–2. Note also that the marginal rate of substitution

FIGURE 10–2

ISO-PRODUCT CONTOURS—PERFECT SUBSTITUTES

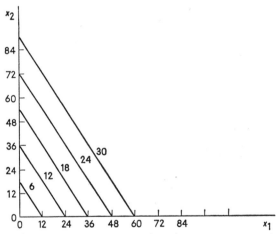

between x_2 and x_1 is constant, i.e. $\partial x_2/\partial x_1 = 3/2$, and 1.5 pounds of plastic substitute for 1 pound of fiber for all levels of output and all input combinations.

10.5. Limitational Inputs

In some processes certain inputs may be uniquely determined by the rate of output. If a specified quantity of product is to be produced, then a certain unique quantity of each input must be used. Excesses of any one input contribute nothing to production, while shortages of any one input limit the output that can be produced. Thus, to dig a trench by hand, one man must be combined with one spade, and one man cannot produce any more with two spades than with one.

An example of a process employing limitational inputs might be the production of insulated copper wire. The production of a given sized wire might require 0.2 ounce of rubber per foot and 0.4 ounce of copper per foot. If x_1 is the number of ounces of rubber required, x_2 is the number of ounces of copper required, and y is the output of rubber-covered copper wire, in feet, then the following equation set describes the input-output characteristics of the process:

$$(10.3) \quad \begin{cases} x_1 = 0.2y \\ x_2 = 0.4y \end{cases}.$$

The ratio x_2/x_1 is

$$(10.4) \quad x_2/x_1 = 2 ,$$

which is the ratio at which the inputs must be combined. The iso-product map for this process is shown in Figure 10–3. The slope of the

FIGURE 10–3

ISO-PRODUCT CONTOURS—LIMITATIONAL INPUTS

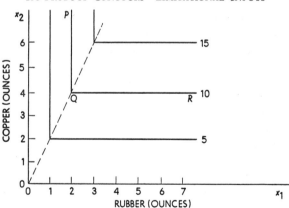

dotted line represents the ratio at which the two inputs must be combined. If 10 units of output are to be produced, no less than 2 ounces of rubber and 4 ounces of copper are required. If more than 2 ounces of rubber is available, and only 4 ounces of copper are available, no more than 10 feet of wire can be produced. Hence, the line segment $\overline{QR}$ is the portion of the iso-product contour corresponding to excesses of rubber input when output is 10. If more than 4 ounces of copper is available when only 2 ounces of rubber are available, then again no more than 10 units can be produced. The line segment $\overline{PQ}$ corresponds to the excesses of copper input when output is 10. The complete iso-product contour for $y = 10$ is PQR, showing no substitution between x_1 and x_2.

10.6. *Limited Substitution*

Our analysis has considered three cases of input substitution. Figure 10–1 shows a process in which the inputs are imperfect substitutes for each other, and, since the iso-product contours are asymptotic to the two axes, the inputs can be substituted for each other without limit. Figure 10–2 shows the contours for a process with perfect substitution, and Figure 10–3 for a process with no substitution.

A final example that occurs frequently in production processes is that of limited substitution. In many, perhaps most, processes certain inputs can be substituted for each other but not without limit. The larger the pipe used to transport water, oil, or gas, the smaller the pumping capacity required, and vice versa. Pipe size and pumping horsepower are substitutes in the transmission of gas and fluids, but they are not substitutes without limit. It would be impossible to use pipe so large that no pumps would be needed, and impossible to install so much pump capacity that no pipe would be required. Two iso-product contours for such a limited substitution process appear in Figure 10–4. Note that it is not possible to produce 1,000 units of output with less than 20 units of input Number 1, nor with less than 40 units of input

FIGURE 10–4

ISO-PRODUCT CONTOURS—LIMITED SUBSTITUTION

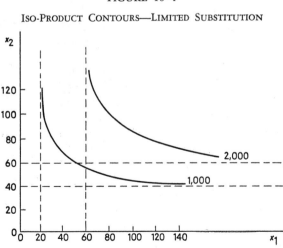

Number 2. Furthermore, if only 20 units of input Number 1 were used it would require an unlimited amount of input Number 2 to produce 1,000 units. Similarly the production of 1,000 units of product with only 40 units of input Number 2 would require unlimited quantities of input Number 1.

10.7. Diminishing Returns and Returns to Scale

The understanding of the concept of diminishing returns, introduced in the previous chapter, can now be deepened through illustration by means of the iso-product map.

Consider a process employing only two inputs with iso-product contours shown in Figure 10–5. Suppose that we hold one input constant (a key condition underlying the law of diminishing returns), say $x_2 = 12$, and inquire as to how output changes as the other input is allowed to vary. From Figure 10–5 it is seen that when $x_2 = 12$, 10 units of output can be produced with 3 units of input Number 1; 20 units can be produced with 5 units of input Number 1; 30 units can be produced with 6 units of input Number 1; 40 units can be produced with 8 units of input Number 1; and 50 units with 11 units of input Number 1. As output is increased in 10-unit increments, the quantity

FIGURE 10–5

ISO-PRODUCT CONTOURS—DIMINISHING RETURNS

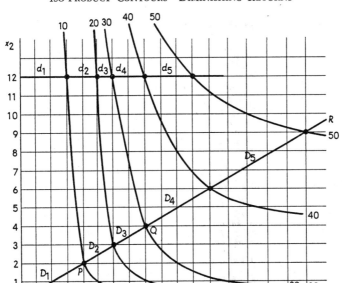

of input Number 1 required increases first at a decreasing rate, then at an increasing rate. The first 10-unit increase in output (from 0 to 10) requires the addition of three units of input Number 1 (from 0 to 3), the second 10-unit increase in output requires the addition of 2 units of input, the third 10-unit increase in output requires the addition of 1 unit of input, the fourth requires the addition of 2 units, and the last requires the addition of 3 units. In general, if the distances d_1, d_2, d_3, d_4, and so forth, form an ascending series, i.e., $d_1 < d_2 < d_3 < d_4 \ldots$, then we have the phenomena of diminishing returns to the variable factor for all outputs that can be produced with input Number 2 employed at its fixed level. If they were to form a descending series, we would have increasing returns to the variable factor for all such outputs and a violation of the law of diminishing returns. The law of diminishing returns contends that always there exists some point beyond which these distances will form an increasing series. In Figure 10–5 it is seen that $d_1 > d_2 > d_3 < d_4 < d_5 <$ etc., indicating that when x_2 is fixed at 12, there is increasing returns to the variable input Number 1 up to about 25 units of output, beyond which there is diminishing returns.

Mathematically, diminishing returns imply that there exists some values of x_1 and x_2 beyond which $\partial^2 f / \partial x_1^2 < 0$ and $\partial^2 f / \partial x_2^2 < 0$.

A phenomenon which is altogether different from diminishing returns is that of returns to scale. Diminishing returns is concerned with how output changes with changes in an input when other inputs are held constant. *Returns to scale* is concerned with how output changes when proportional simultaneous changes are made in *all* inputs, and there is no generally accepted law or principle requiring returns to scale eventually to decline. Some processes show increasing, some constant, and others decreasing, returns to scale. Still other processes may, over different ranges of output, show all three kinds of returns.

In Figure 10–5, returns to scale are represented by reference to the straight line OR through the origin. Observe that if we begin with any input combination, such as that represented by the Point $P(x_1 = 4$, $x_2 = 2)$, then any proportional increase in *both* inputs must be on the line OR. For example, if both inputs are doubled, the new input combination is represented by the Point Q. Beginning at Point P if both inputs are increased $3/2$ times (to $x_1 = 6$ and $x_2 = 3$) it is seen that output increases by a factor of 2 (from 10 to 20). Over this range there is increasing returns to scale. Beginning at Q if both inputs are increased $3/2$ times (to $x_1 = 12$ and $x_2 = 6$) output increases by a factor of $4/3$ (from 30 to 40) showing decreasing returns to scale. In general if $D_1 > D_2 > D_3 > D_4$ etc., the process shows *increasing returns to scale* at all output levels. If $D_1 = D_2 = D_3 = D_4$ etc., the process shows *constant returns to scale* at all outputs. If $D_1 < D_2 < D_3 < D_4 <$ etc., the process shows *decreasing returns to scale* for all outputs. In the example of Figure 10–5 the process shows increasing returns to scale at first, then constant returns to scale, and finally decreasing returns to scale.

The question of returns to scale is related to the mathematical concept of a homogeneous function. The production function $y = f(x_1, x_2)$ is said to be homogeneous of Degree 1 if an increase in all inputs by the same proportion, say a, increases output by the proportion a. That is, the production function is homogeneous of Degree 1, and therefore exhibits constant returns to scale for all outputs, if

$$(10.5) \quad ay = f(ax_1, ax_2), a > 1.$$

If the production function is not homogeneous of Degree 1, and shows either increasing or decreasing returns to scale, then

$$(10.6) \quad \beta y = f(ax_1, ax_2), a > 0, \beta > 0.$$

If $\beta > a$ we have increasing returns to scale, while if $\beta < a$ we have decreasing returns to scale.

10.8. The Cost Equation and Iso-Cost Contours

Just as the production function is a means of introducing essential technological data into production planning, the cost equation is a means of introducing economic data into production planning. In choosing the best technique of production, the essential economic data in the decision are the purchase prices of the productive inputs. If there are only two inputs to a process and w_1 is the price of input Number 1 and w_2 is the price of input Number 2, then the total cost equation is

$$(10.7) \quad C = w_1 x_1 + w_2 x_2.$$

The product $w_1 x_1$ is the total expenditure on x_1 units of input Number 1, while the product $w_2 x_2$ is the total outlay on input Number 2.

Equation (10.7) can be mapped in the plane of x_1 and x_2 by considering all those combinations of x_1 and x_2 that can be purchased with given total outlays. In Figure 10–6 is shown the iso-cost contours for total outlays of \$12, \$24, and \$36 when $w_1 = \$4$ per unit and $w_2 = \$6$ per unit. The contour for a total outlay of \$12, for example, is simply a graph of the linear equation $4x_1 + 6x_2 = 12$. Note that lower iso-cost lines correspond to lower total cost outlays.

Two important characteristics of iso-cost contours should be carefully noted. First, since more x_1 cannot be purchased with a fixed total

FIGURE 10–6

ISO-COST CONTOURS

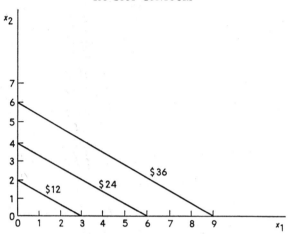

outlay without buying less x_2, these contours slope down to the right. Specifically, the numerical value of this slope is given by the ratio of the price of input Number 1 to the price of input Number 2, that is:

$$(10.8) \quad \frac{\partial x_2}{\partial x_1} = -\frac{w_1}{w_2}.$$

In constructing iso-cost contours and seeing how they change in response to input price changes, it is useful to bear in mind that the x_1 intercept of an iso-cost line is given by the ratio C/w_1, and the x_2 intercept is given by the ratio C/w_2. These characteristics are shown in Figure 10–7. An increase in the price w_1 causes the iso-cost line to pivot in a

FIGURE 10–7

ISO-COST CONTOURS—COST CHANGING

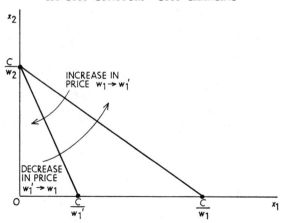

clockwise direction around the x_2 intercept point C/w_2. A decrease in w_1 causes the line to shift in a counterclockwise direction around the x_2 intercept point. Similarly, changes in w_2 cause the iso-cost line to rotate around the x_1 intercept point C/w_1.

10.9. The Least-Cost Input Combination

Our analysis has now progressed sufficiently to enable a solution to be given to one of the basic problems of production planning. How is the input combination determined which will allow a given specified

FIGURE 10–8

THE LEAST-COST INPUT COMBINATION

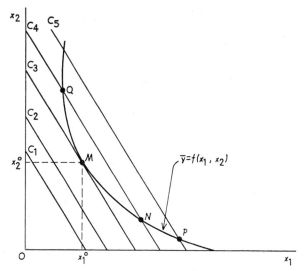

output to be produced at least total cost? Suppose, in general, that the production function is given by $y = f(x_1, x_2)$ and let the required rate of output by $y = \bar{y}$. Then the expression $\bar{y} = f(x_1, x_2)$ defines one of a family of iso-product contours such as that shown in Figure 10–8. This contour represents the locus of all input combinations (x_1, x_2) that will produce $\bar{y}$ units of product. On the same scale is shown representative members of the family of iso-cost lines given by the total cost equation $C = w_1x_1 + w_2x_2$. The problem is to choose that input combination (x_1^0, x_2^0) which will allow $\bar{y}$ units to be produced, that is, satisfies the relation $\bar{y} = f(x_1^0, x_2^0)$, and at the same time renders cost, C, a minimum. It will be seen that the combinations represented by the Points P, N, M and Q in Figure 10–8 will, among countless others, allow $\bar{y}$ units to be produced. However, the combination N is certainly better than P, since it lies on a lower cost line than does P. Similarly, the combination M is better than either N or P. If a movement in the direction of the Point Q from M is made, it is clear that cost will increase since higher iso-cost contours correspond to larger total cost outlays. The combination (x_1^0, x_2^0) at M is clearly the best as this combination lies on the lowest iso-cost contour that will permit $\bar{y}$ units to be produced. The total cost for this input combination is C_3 dollars.

This solution is often referred to as the tangency solution, since the best combination occurs where the iso-product contour is just tangent to an iso-cost line. This requires that $f_1/f_2 = w_1/w_2$, where $f_1 =$ marginal productivity of Input 1 and $f_2 =$ marginal productivity of Input 2.

10.10. The Minimum Cost-Output Relation

In the previous chapter the cost-output curve was derived for a process in which there was only one variable input and hence no problem of choosing the best input combination. In processes employing two or more substitutable inputs, the situation is more complicated since cost depends not only on output but the choice of inputs in producing any given output. Under the condition that inputs are employed in the best combinations, i.e., so as to minimize the cost of producing each level of output, it is then possible to derive a relationship between minimum total cost and the level of output.

To derive such a cost curve, consider the contour map of Figure 10–9A. Six iso-product contours for outputs of 10, 20, 30, 40, 50, and 60 are shown along with the iso-cost contours corresponding to the minimum cost means of producing each of these outputs. For example, the minimum cost input combination for producing 10 units is represented by the Point S, and the cost of purchasing that combination is $30 since the iso-cost line through the Point S corresponds to an outlay of $30. An output of 20 units is seen to be produced at a cost of $40, when the best technique is used, and so forth. Given input prices are assumed, therefore the iso-cost lines are all parallel with the same slopes.

In Figure 10–9B the costs associated with each of the indicated levels of output is shown plotted. The curve connecting these points is the relationship between total cost and output *on the assumption that each level of output is produced at minimum cost.* If cost were not minimized at each output, a higher, and entirely different curve would be obtained.

Whether the cost curve in Figure 10–9B is a short-run or long-run cost curve depends upon the inputs which are considered variable in the

FIGURE 10–9A

A SCALE LINE

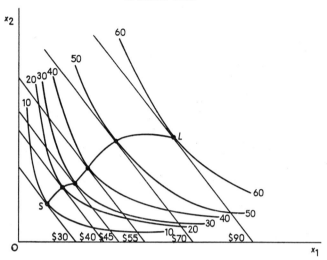

analysis. If x_1 and x_2 are the *only* inputs to the process and one (or both) of them are capital inputs, then our relationship is a long-run cost curve or planning curve. If x_1 and x_2 are both current inputs and there is one or more capital inputs to the process that are considered fixed in drawing the x_1, x_2 contour map, then the resulting cost curve would be of the short-run variety.

FIGURE 10–9B

A TOTAL COST CURVE

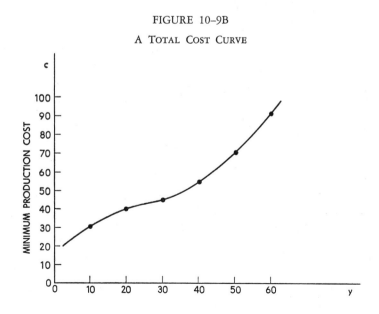

Suppose we consider a long-run interpretation of this cost curve. Then the line *SL,* connecting the points representing the minimum cost input combinations in Figure 10–9A, is often called the *scale line,* as it shows the effect of changing the scale of output on the combination of inputs which minimizes cost. Both the scale line and the cost curve are straight lines in the special case of constant returns to scale when the production function is homogeneous of Degree 1. Note, in comparing Figures 10–9A and 10–9B, that over the range of output for which the production function shows increasing returns to scale, the total cost curve is concave from below, that is, rises at a decreasing rate. This means that marginal cost falls with output in this range. Over the range of output for which the production function shows decreasing returns to scale, the total cost curve is convex from below and marginal cost rises. It is seen therefore that the U-shaped marginal cost curve can be directly related to returns to scale where two substitutable inputs are employed in production.

10.11. *Capital Inputs in the Production Function*

Thus far the analysis of production has not been explicit regarding the period of time during which inputs are consumed and outputs are produced. In the production function of Equation (10.1) x_1 and x_2 are normally thought of as current or flow inputs, involving rates of consumption in physical units per unit of time, while y is the rate of output per unit of time. The cost Equation (10.7) then gives the cost of production per unit time. However, as will be evident in the next chapter, there are many production functions that arise in applied work that reflect substitution as between current or flow inputs and capital or stock inputs. In such cases the cost Equation (10.7) cannot be written in such a simple form.

For example, suppose the production function is:

$$(10.9) \quad y = f(x_1, X_2) ,$$

where x_1 is the consumption per year of a current input such as labor, and X_2 is the stock of a capital good such as some kind of equipment used in production. Now, if w_1 is the price of input Number 1, then $w_1 x_1$ is the total annual cost of purchasing x_1 man-hours of labor per year. But if W_2 is the price of the durable machinery input, the product $W_2 X_2$ is the investment outlay for X_2 units of machinery rather than a cost per year.

If no other inputs are required by the process, then the production of y units of output per year necessitates an outlay of $w_1 x_1$ dollars per year for labor, and an investment outlay of W_2X_2 dollars for machinery. Because the time base for these two types of expenditures is different, they cannot be added to give total cost as was done in Equation (10.7). The investment sum W_2X_2 must first be converted to an equivalent cost *stream,* or cost on current account. To do this we have to know how often the equipment has to be replaced.

Suppose in the first instance that the equipment is of infinite durability, that is, never has to be replaced, and that the process is expected to produce y units of output per year indefinitely into the future. This assumption implies an infinite planning horizon. Then if i is the rate of interest, we wish to find the constant annual income stream that has a present value of W_2X_2 dollars. This is obtained by using Equation (8.8) in Chapter 8 in which $V = W_2X_2$. That is, an income stream of $i\,W_2X_2$ dollars per year, indefinitely into the future, has a present value of W_2X_2. The annual cost, including invested capital is then

$$(10.10) \quad C = w_1x_1 + i\,W_2X_2 .$$

From Equation (10.10) it is seen that $i\,W_2$ takes the place of w_2 in Equation (10.7). The unit investment cost of equipment is W_2, but the *annual* unit cost of equipment is $i\,W_2$, which sum can be multiplied by X_2 and added to the annual cost of labor to give total annual cost.

The minimum cost input combination in this case can be determined graphically as in Figure 10–8 except that w_2 is replaced by $i\,W_2$, and x_2 is replaced by X_2. This procedure would yield a solution to the firm's *long-run production planning problem* and would be relevant only for a firm which had not yet purchased any equipment, or for a firm considering an expansion in its existing equipment capacity. Once the investment in equipment is made, say $X_2 = X_2^0$ units of equipment are acquired, then the term $i\,W_2X_2 = i\,W_2X_2^0$ in Equation (10.10) is no longer variable with X_2 except as changes in the original capacity are considered. Once $X_2 = X_2^0$ is fixed, the term $i\,W_2X_2^0$ becomes a *fixed cost,* and short-run variations in output can be met only by varying the level of x_1.

Consider next the case in which the equipment has a life of L years, at the end of which time all units have to be replaced. Let it again be assumed that the process is expected to produc a constant flow of output, y per period, indefinitely into the future. Under these conditions the firm, faced with the long-run decision of determining the volume of equipment capacity to install, must incur an initial investment outlay of W_2X_2 dollars, and thereafter a *replacement* investment outlay of W_2X_2 dollars every L years. The initial investment outlay has a present value (at the beginning of the operation) of W_2X_2 dollars. The first replacement outlay has a present value of $W_2X_2(1+i)^{-L}$ dollars, if i is the rate of interest [see Equation (8.4) of Chapter 8]. The second replacement outlay has a present value of $W_2X_2(1+i)^{-2L}$ dollars, and so forth, indefinitely into the future. The present value of all future investment outlays is, therefore,

$$W_2X_2 + W_2X_2(1+i)^{-L} + W_2X_2(1+i)^{-2L} + \ldots$$

This expression is a simple geometric progression with constant ratio $(1+i)^{-L}$, which can be summed to give:

$$\frac{W_2X_2}{1-(1+i)^{-L}}.$$

This sum can in turn be converted into its equivalent constant income stream if it is multiplied by i [see Equation (8.8) of Chapter 8]. Therefore, the equivalent annual cost of all future investment outlays for X_2 units of equipment is simply,

$$\frac{i\,W_2X_2}{1-(1+i)^{-L}},$$

and the equation for total annual cost for this case can be written

$$(10.11) \quad C = w_1x_1 + \frac{i\,W_2X_2}{1-(1+i)^{-L}}.$$

From Equation (10.11) we see that for equipment requiring replacement every L years, the unit annual cost of equipment is,

$$\frac{i\,W_2}{1-(1+i)^{-L}},$$

which replaces w_2 in Equation (10.7) and $i\,W_2$ in Equation (10.10). With these modifications, the minimum cost input combination can be determined as in Figure 10–8. That is, given the rate of output, y, the life of equipment L, the interest rate i, the price of capital W_2, and the price of labor w_1, we can determine $x_1 = x_1^0$ and $X_2 = X_2^0$.

10.12. The Input-Output Equilibrium of the Firm

From the analysis of this chapter and the preceding one, it is now possible to set forth the complete conditions for the simultaneous determination of the firm's best input combination and best rate of output.

It has been shown that a necessary condition for determining the best input combination is to adjust the employment of the two inputs until the ratio of their marginal productivities is equal to the ratio of their respective prices, that is, until $f_1/f_2 = w_1/w_2$. If this condition is put in the equivalent form

$$(10.12) \quad \frac{w_1}{f_1} = \frac{w_2}{f_2},$$

it can be given a very useful interpretation. Since $f_1 = \partial f/\partial x_1$ is the rate at which output increases with increases in the use of input Number 1, while w_1 is the unit cost of increasing input Number 1, it follows that the ratio w_1/f_1 measures the rate at which cost increases as a result of increasing output by employing more of input Number 1. Stated differently, it is simply the marginal cost (with respect to output) of employing input Number 1. Similarly, the ratio w_2/f_2 measures marginal cost of employing input Number 2. Therefore the condition (10.12) states that the two inputs are employed in their best combination when their marginal costs are equal, and in equilibrium, these two ratios are interpreted as marginal (production) cost, dC/dy (or MC) in Chapter 9.

Under this interpretation we can write

$$(10.13) \quad \frac{dC}{dy} = \frac{w_1}{f_1} = \frac{w_2}{f_2}.$$

However, in Chapter 9, Equation (9.7), it was shown that a necessary condition determining the profit maximizing rate of output was for marginal revenue to equal marginal cost, that is

$$(10.14) \quad \frac{dR}{dy} = \frac{dC}{dy}.$$

Therefore, from (10.14) and (10.13) we have

$$(10.15) \quad \frac{dR}{dy} = \frac{w_1}{f_1} = \frac{w_2}{f_2}.$$

The second equality is necessary to insure operation at least cost, while the first equality is necessary for profit maximization, taking account of demand effects. In this equation, remember that marginal revenue dR/dy, depends upon output y, while the marginal productivities f_1 and f_2 depend, in general, on x_1 and x_2. Therefore (10.15) supplies us with two equations relating the three decision variables y, x_1, and x_2. A third relation is necessary to determine completely best input-output production policy. This relation is the production function

$$(10.16) \quad y = f(x_1, x_2).$$

Equations (10.15) and (10.16) together determine the firm's optimal production level and the best technique for achieving that output.

APPENDIX: THE THEORY OF COST AND PRODUCTION—MATHEMATICAL ANALYSIS

The theory of cost and production was developed by graphical methods in the main body of this chapter. Such methods have their greatest usefulness in helping us to understand the theory, but are not suitable for computational purposes when the production function involves more than three variables. This Appendix is concerned with a mathematical analysis of the theory.

10.A.1. *Mathematical Statement of the Theory of Cost and Production*

Again, let us consider the three variable production function,

$$(10.A.1) \quad y = f(x_1, x_2),$$

and the total cost equation

$$(10.A.2) \quad C = w_1 x_1 + w_2 x_2 + F .$$

For generality a fixed cost element, F, is included in the total cost equation. If there are only two inputs to the process then of course F is zero. If there are more than two inputs, only two of which are being considered as variables, then F stands for the cost of the fixed inputs. Mathematically, the problem of least-cost production, is to minimize the cost Equation (10.A.2) subject to the *constraint* $y = \bar{y}$ (a constant) in Equation (10.A.1). (In other words, we minimize the cost of producing a given output, $\bar{y}$.) This is a *constrained* minimization problem. One way of finding necessary conditions for a minimum is to perform differential variations in $y = f(x_1, x_2)$ and $C = w_1 x_1 + w_2 x_2 + F$. We have, from the production function,

$$(10.A.3) \quad dy = d\bar{y} = \frac{\partial f}{\partial x_1} dx_1 + \frac{\partial f}{\partial x_2} dx_2 = f_1 dx_1 + f_2 dx_2 = 0 .$$

Equation (10.A.3) describes differential movements in x_1 and x_2, that will produce a constant output. It states in differential form that a given output objective is to be achieved, i.e., differential alterations in x_1 and x_2 must be constrained to move along a given iso-product contour.

Also we have, from the cost equation

$$(10.A.4) \quad dC = w_1 dx_1 + w_2 dx_2 ,$$

which describes the effect on C of differential adjustments in x_1 and x_2. Now, if we are to find the point at which cost is a *minimum* it is *necessary* (but not sufficient) that $dC = 0$. That is, we want

$$(10.A.5) \quad dC = w_1 dx_1 + w_2 dx_2 = 0 ,$$

which expresses the condition that incremental adjustments in x_1 and x_2 causes no net change in total cost.

From (10.A.3) and (10.A.5) we can write:

$$(10.A.6) \quad -\frac{\partial x_2}{\partial x_1} = -\frac{dx_2}{dx_1}\bigg|_{y=\bar{y}} = \frac{f_1}{f_2} = \frac{w_1}{w_2} \quad \text{or} \quad \frac{w_1}{f_1} = \frac{w_2}{f_2} \quad \text{or} \quad \frac{f_1}{w_1} = \frac{f_2}{w_2} \,.$$

This condition is often called the marginal condition for choosing the best technique of production. It states that the marginal rate of substitution of x_1 for x_2 must equal the ratio of the price of x_1 to the price of x_2. In the form $f_1/w_1 = f_2/w_2$ the condition states that cost is at a minimum if we employ inputs Number 1 and Number 2 up to the point at which the last dollar's worth of input Number 1 yields the same addition to output as the last dollar's worth of input Number 2. Since f_1 and f_2 are in general functions of both x_1 and x_2, the condition $f_1/w_1 = f_2/w_2$ defines a relationship between x_1 and x_2. This relationship is simply the locus of the points of tangency between the iso-product and iso-cost contours, i.e., the scale line shown in Figure 10–9A.

Conditions similar to that in (10.A.6) are obtained when there are more than two inputs. If we had n inputs, there would be $n - 1$ conditions of the form:

$$(10.A.7) \quad \frac{f_1}{w_1} = \frac{f_2}{w_2} = \ldots = \frac{f_n}{w_n} \,.$$

If we solved the equation $f_1/w_1 = f_2/w_2$ together with the production function constraint $\bar{y} = f(x_1, x_2)$ we could obtain x_1^0 and x_2^0, the quantities of the two inputs which will simultaneously produce $y = \bar{y}$ and minimize cost. Graphically this solution would amount to finding the intersection of the scale line with the particular iso-product contour for $y = \bar{y}$. The solution values x_1^0 and x_2^0 so obtained will be functions of the prices w_1 and w_2, and the output level $\bar{y}$, i.e.

$$(10.A.8) \quad \begin{cases} x_1^0 = h_1(w_1, w_2, \bar{y}) \\ x_2^0 = h_2(w_1, w_2, \bar{y}) \end{cases}$$

where the h's merely stand for functions.

By substitution into (10.A.2) we get

$$(10.A.9) \quad C = w_1 h_1(w_1, w_2, \bar{y}) + w_2 h_2(w_1, w_2, \bar{y}) + F \,,$$

which shows how the minimum attainable cost of production depends upon input prices and the level of output.

There is another somewhat more elegant mathematical method for solving constrained minimization (or maximization) problems, known as the Lagrange multiplier method. By this method expression (10.A.2) is minimized subject to the constraint in (10.A.1) by forming a new expression to be minimized, call it ϕ of the form

$$(10.A.10) \quad \phi = w_1 x_1 + w_2 x_2 + F + \lambda[\bar{y} - f(x_1, x_2)] \,,$$

where λ is called a Lagrange "undetermined" multiplier. This expression for ϕ can be regarded as a function of the three variables x_1, x_2 and λ, and necessary conditions for a minimum of ϕ can be obtained by setting the partial derivatives

$$\frac{\partial \phi}{\partial x_1}, \frac{\partial \phi}{\partial x_2}, \frac{\partial \phi}{\partial \lambda}$$

equal to zero. This gives

$$\frac{\partial \phi}{\partial x_1} = w_1 - \lambda f_1 = 0 .$$

$$(10.A.11) \quad \frac{\partial \phi}{\partial x_2} = w_2 - \lambda f_2 = 0 ,$$

$$\frac{\partial \phi}{\partial \lambda} = \bar{y} - f(x_1, x_2) = 0 .$$

The first two conditions in (10.A.11) can be written in the form

$$(10.A.12) \quad \frac{w_1}{f_1} = \frac{w_2}{f_2} = \lambda ,$$

which will be recognized to contain the condition previously obtained in (10.A.6). The last condition in (10.A.11) is simply the production function constraint. Therefore, the simultaneous solution of the three equations in (10.A.11) yields immediately the best input combination $x_1{}^0$ and $x_2{}^0$, and a value for λ whose interesting interpretation is developed in the next section.

10.A.2. The Relation between Cost Minimization and Profit Maximization

In Chapter 9 on page 130 it was shown that the profit maximizing rate of output is the one which equates marginal revenue and marginal cost, i.e., $dR/dy = dC/dy$. In (10.A.6) above we have developed a condition for cost minimization in the choice of the quantities of each of two inputs to employ. These two sets of conditions can be combined to determine simultaneously the best rate of output and best quantities of inputs to employ.

To show this we need to relate marginal cost dC/dy to the condition (10.A.6) or (10.A.7). In general, by taking total derivatives, the ratio of a small variation in cost dC to a small variation in output dy can be written

$$(10.A.13) \quad \frac{dC}{dy} = \frac{w_1 dx_1 + w_2 dx_2}{f_1 dx_1 + f_2 dx_2} .$$

Now, if only variations in output which are made at least cost are to be considered, it is necessary to impose the conditions (10.A.12). If these conditions are written $f_1 = w_1/\lambda$ and $f_2 = w_2/\lambda$ and substituted in (10.A.13), we get

$$(10.A.14) \quad \frac{dC}{dy} = \frac{w_1 dx_1 + w_1 dx_2}{\frac{w_1 dx_1}{\lambda} + \frac{w_2 dx_2}{\lambda}} = \left(\frac{w_1 dx_1 + w_2 dx_2}{w_1 dx_1 + w_2 dx_2} \right) \lambda = \lambda = \frac{w_2}{f_2} = \frac{w_1}{f_1} .$$

Hence, it has been shown that if the least cost input combination is employed at each level of output, then λ, the Lagrange multiplier is equal to marginal cost, and marginal cost is equal to the ratios w_1/f_1 and w_2/f_2. The full conditions for determining the optimum rate of output and optimum employments of each of two inputs are thus

$$(10.A.15) \quad \frac{dR}{dy} = \frac{w_1}{f_1} = \frac{w_2}{f_2}.$$

The ratios of the prices of each input to their marginal productivities must be equal to each other, and to marginal revenue.

10.A.3. An Example

In order to illustrate the above theory, suppose the production function has the simple form:

$$(10.A.16) \quad y = 6(x_1 x_2)^{1/3},$$

and let the input prices be $w_1 = \$0.25$, $w_2 = \$2$, and $F = \$50$. Hence:

$$\frac{\partial y}{\partial x_1} = 2x_1^{-2/3} x_2^{1/3}, \quad \text{and} \quad \frac{\partial y}{\partial x_2} = 2x_1^{1/3} x_2^{-2/3}.$$

If we substitute these marginal productivity functions and the above prices into the conditions (10.A.6) then

$$(10.A.17) \quad x_1 = \frac{w_2}{w_1} x_2 = 8x_2.$$

Solving (10.A.16) and (10.A.17) for x_1 and x_2 gives

$$(10.A.18) \quad \begin{cases} x_1^0 = 8\left(\frac{w_1}{w_2}\right)^{1/2}\left(\frac{y}{6}\right)^{3/2} = 8\left(\frac{y}{12}\right)^{3/2} \\ x_2^0 = \left(\frac{w_1}{w_2}\right)^{1/2}\left(\frac{y}{6}\right)^{3/2} = \left(\frac{y}{12}\right)^{3/2}, \end{cases}$$

corresponding to (10.A.8.) above. For each output y, (10.A.17) gives the combination of x_1 and x_2 which will minimize cost.

The relationship between minimum total cost and the level of output can be obtained by substitution from (10.A.18) into the cost equation (10.A.2) as follows:

$$(10.A.19) \quad C = w_1 x_1^0 + w_2 x_2^0 + F = (8w_1 + w_2)\left(\frac{w_1}{w_2}\right)^{1/2}\left(\frac{y}{6}\right)^{3/2} + 50 = 4\left(\frac{y}{12}\right)^{3/2} + 50.$$

Note from (10.A.19) that marginal cost is given by

$$(10.A.20) \quad \frac{dC}{dy} = \frac{1}{2}\left(\frac{y}{12}\right)^{1/2}.$$

In (10.A.14) it was proved that marginal cost must equal the ratio of each input to its marginal productivity if the inputs are employed in their best combinations. Let us then evaluate w_1/f_1 and w_2/f_2 for this example, by substitution from (10.A.18). The result is:

$$(10.A.21) \quad \begin{cases} \dfrac{w_1}{f_1} = \dfrac{.25}{2x_1^{-2/3}x_2^{1/3}} = \tfrac{1}{2}\left(\dfrac{y}{12}\right)^{1/2} \\[2ex] \dfrac{w_2}{f_2} = \dfrac{2}{2x_1^{1/3}x_2^{-2/3}} = \tfrac{1}{2}\left(\dfrac{y}{12}\right)^{1/2} \end{cases}$$

which is equal to marginal cost as expected.

Now assume that the price of the product is $p = 2$. Then total revenue $R = 2y$. We can determine the profit-maximizing rate of output from the condition that marginal cost equals marginal revenue as follows:

$$(10.A.22) \quad \frac{dC}{dy} = \tfrac{1}{2}\left(\frac{y}{12}\right)^{1/2} = \frac{dR}{dy} = 2, \text{ or } y = 192 \,.$$

QUESTIONS AND EXERCISES

1. Show graphically that if two inputs are perfect substitutes, then depending upon the relative prices of the inputs, least-cost production requires either the one or the other input to be used. Under what conditions would a firm be indifferent as to which of the inputs it used?

2. Show that if two inputs each have to be used in fixed proportion to output, then the input combination for least cost production is not affected by the relative prices of the inputs.

3. If the production function is given by $y = Ax_1x_2 + B$, where A and B are constants, w_1 is the price of input No. 1, and w_2 is the price of input No. 2, determine expressions for the amounts of x_1 and x_2 which will minimize the cost of producing y. Determine total cost as a function of y under these conditions.

4. Repeat Question 3 assuming the production function is $y = Ax_1x_2^2$.

5. Which of the following production functions show increasing returns to scale? Decreasing returns? Constant returns?

    (1) $y = Ax_1^{\frac{1}{2}}x_2^{\frac{1}{2}}$.
    (2) $y = \tfrac{1}{2}x + 10$.
    (3) $y = Ax_1x_2$.
    (4) $y = 3x_1 + 5x_2$.
    (5) $y = Ax_1^{\frac{1}{2}}x_2^{\frac{1}{2}}$.
    (6) $y = \sqrt{-Ax_1^2 - Bx_2^2 + Cx_1x_2}$.

6. The production function for a heat transmission process is

$$yx_1 - \frac{280}{.01381 - .000595X_2} \,,$$

where x_1 is heat input rate, y is heat output rate, and X_2 is quantity of insulation. Sketch the iso-product contour for $y = 10,000$. Show that

$$\frac{\partial y}{\partial x_1} > 0 \,, \quad \frac{\partial y}{\partial X_2} > 0 \,, \quad \text{and} \quad \frac{\partial X_2}{\partial x_1} < 0 \,.$$

7. A firm has two plants. Plant 1 has a variable cost curve $C_1(y_1)$, where y_1 is output. Plant 2 has variable costs $C_2(y_2)$, where y_2 is output. For a given total output $y = y_1 + y_2$, deduce conditions for a minimum total cost allocation of production between the two plants.

Chapter
11

THE THEORY OF COST

AND PRODUCTION

CONTINUED: APPLICATIONS

It is beyond the scope of the present book to go into the construction of production functions for entire firms making products involving many complicated processes and stages. However, there is nothing to prevent us from showing how possibilities of input substitution arise in several simple, and familiar, processes of production. The actual algebraic form of the production function for a few processes will be stated, while for other more complicated processes, the technological basis for input substitution will be explained to give the reader some idea of the breadth of applications of production theory. Some examples of how such production functions can be derived from technological data and equations are presented in the Appendix to this chapter.

11.1. Agricultural Production Functions

Some of the earliest pioneering work in the empirical study of production functions was done in the field of agriculture where there is a firm biological basis for expecting output to depend in an important way on the combinations of feed or fertilizer nutrients employed in the production of meat and crop products. In the production of corn and other grain crops, the two fertilizer nutrients, nitrogen and phosphate, are important determinates of crop yields. For example, one carefully controlled experiment in corn fertilization yielded the following production function:[1]

(11.1) $y =$
$$-5.68 - 0.32x_1 - 0.42x_2 + 6.35\sqrt{x_1} + 8.52\sqrt{x_2} + 0.34\sqrt{x_1x_2} ,$$

where $x_1 =$ pounds of nitrogen applied per acre per year, $x_2 =$ pounds of phosphate applied per acre per year, and $y =$ yield of corn in bushels per acre per year. In this application both inputs are current inputs. The

---

[1] See Earl O. Heady, "An Econometric Investigation of the Technology of Agricultural Production Functions," *Econometrica*, April, 1957, p. 252.

164

student can readily verify that Equation (11.1) possesses the characteristics of a production function as set forth in Chapter 10. The iso-product curves for output rates of 40, 60, 80, 100, and 120 bushels per acre are shown in Figure 11–1.

Given this production function and the prices of nitrogen and phosphate fertilizer, the least-cost combination of the two fertilizers

FIGURE 11–1

Iso-Product Contours for Corn Production

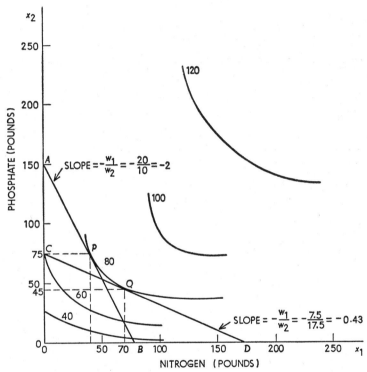

can be determined for any desired corn yield. Suppose, for example, that nitrogen costs 20 cents per pound, and phosphate costs 10 cents per pound. Then the iso-cost lines have a slope of −2. If the production target is 80 bushels per acre, then the least-cost input combination is the point of tangency between the iso-cost line AB and the iso-product contour for an output of 80, or Point P as shown in Figure 11–1. The solution is 75 pounds of phosphate per acre and 40 pounds of nitrogen. If the price of nitrogen were to fall to 7.5 cents per pound and the price of phosphate were to rise to 17.5 cents per pound, it would pay to substitute nitrogen for phosphate in the fertilizer dose. The new equilibrium would be at Q using 45 pounds of phosphate and 70 pounds of nitrogen.

The production functions for numerous other agricultural products have been determined for a variety of conditions. The production of alfalfa has been related to the potash and phosphate fertilizers used, pork production has been related to the quantities of soybean oilmeal and corn used as feed, and milk production has been related to such feed variables as forage and grain concentrate. Such production function studies have made major contributions to rational production planning in agriculture.

11.2. *Transportation Production Functions*

Two examples of production functions in the transportation area arise in connection with the transmission of natural gas by pipeline, and the transmission of electricity by power line. A complete economic analysis of these processes is far from simple, but certain aspects of the production problems associated with these processes can be studied by means of the three variable production function.

The process of electrical transmission can be simplified by assuming that there are just two major inputs, electrical energy (at the power plant source) and transmission cable. The output is electrical energy at the consumer end of the power line. The schematic diagram in Figure 11–2 illustrates various components of the productive process. In this conception of the process, note that the two inputs are of a fundamentally different character. Cable is a capital good, a "stock" input, that is not consumed as output is delivered. The electrical energy input is a flow input with respect to time, and is "consumed" continuously as output is delivered. The process involves one current and one capital

FIGURE 11–2

THE ELECTRICAL TRANSMISSION PROCESS

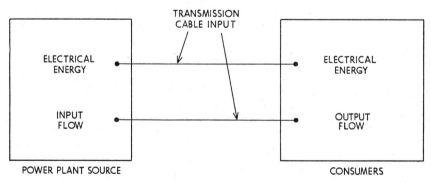

input; therefore the analysis of Section 10.10 in the preceding chapter is relevant to this application.

In analyzing this process the first step is to choose units of measurement for the output and inputs. The obvious way to measure electrical energy input and output is in kilowatt-hours. If the distance over which electrical energy is to be transported is fixed, then variation in the "quantity" of cable can only occur by virtue of the possibility of choosing among different wire sizes in the design of the power line. Hence, the variable "cable" could be measured by its cross-sectional area, or, since both cable weight and volume is proportional to its area, cable could be measured in either pounds or cubic feet. Using these input measures, what are the substitution possibilities between cable and electrical energy input and why do they arise? To answer this, suppose a given quantity of electrical energy is to be delivered to customers. This requirement can be met with an almost unlimited number of different combinations of the two inputs. It is a well-known engineering phenomena that the resistance of a transmission wire to the flow of electricity is greater the smaller is the cross-sectional area of the wire. But, the greater the resistance of the wire, the greater the energy loss from heat generated in the wire. Therefore, the smaller the area of the wire (or the smaller the volume or weight of wire used) the greater must be the input of electrical energy to meet any specified level of electrical energy output. Hence, the greater the input of wire, the less is the energy lost in transmission, and therefore the smaller is the input of electrical energy required to meet any level of output.

An iso-product contour for the process, as described, is shown in Figure 11–3. x_1 is the kilowatt-hour input of electrical energy, and X_2 is the quantity of wire used (in cubic feet for example). If this contour is for an output of 10,000 kilowatt-hours, then the larger is X_2, the nearer will the contour approach $x_1 = 10,000$, since larger wire implies lower energy loss in transmission. But no matter how large X_2 is, an output of 10,000 kilowatt-hours could never be produced with less than 10,000 kilowatt-hours input. A lower bound is thus set upon the extent to which wire can be substituted for electricity in this process.

If w_1 is the unit cost of generating energy, then w_1x_1 is the total cost of electrical power input per unit of time. If W_2 is the unit cost of cable in, say, cents per cubic foot, then W_2X_2 is the total investment in cable. Therefore, the cost of one input involves an outlay per unit time, the other is a one-shot investment outlay, and the two cannot be added without conversion to an equivalent base. It is assumed that transmission cable lasts indefinitely, does not deteriorate with use and

FIGURE 11–3

ISO-PRODUCT CONTOURS FOR ELECTRICAL TRANSMISSION

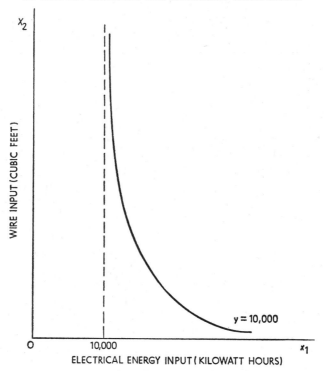

requires no upkeep, then the investment outlay for cable provides capital services indefinitely into the future. Under these assumptions, Equation (10.10) in Chapter 10 gives the total annual cost of operating the process, that is

$$(11.2) \quad C = w_1 x_1 + i\,W_2 X_2 .$$

If electrical energy is valued at $0.05 per kilowatt hour, $i = 6$ per cent and $W_2 = \$1.00$ per pound, then total cost is: $C = .05x_1 + .06X_2$ dollars per year.

The transmission of gas by pipeline has many close similarities with power-line transmission, and could be analyzed in a similar way. In order to emphasize a somewhat different aspect of transmission process problems the gas transmission process will be simplified by considering only the two inputs, compressor capacity and pipeline capacity. Compressor or pumping capacity, X_2 will be measured in horsepower, while pipe capacity X_1 could (as in the case of transmission cable) be measured by either cross-sectional area or weight, for a given length of pipeline.

The mechanism whereby compressor horsepower and pipe size

are substitutable is very similar to the character of the substitution possibilities arising in power-line transmission. The smaller the pipe used, the greater the energy loss in the form of heat due to friction in the pipe, and therefore the greater the compressor horsepower necessary to pump gas through the pipeline. The iso-product contours for a particular gas transmission process[2] are shown in Figure 11–4.

FIGURE 11–4

Iso-Product Contours for Gas Transmission

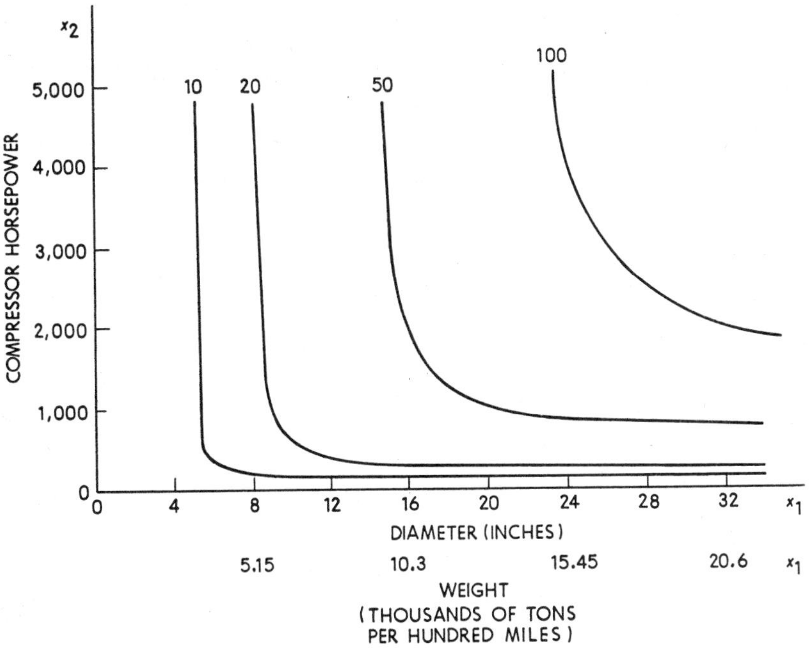

11.3. Manufacturing Process Functions

The tool engineer is continually confronted with problems of determining the most economical cutting speed for machine tools, computing the power requirements of machine tools, and estimating the consumption of cutting tools through wear and breakage. Such problems are essentially economic in character, in the sense that cost is typically used as the criterion for determining the best engineering method or design. Many of these problems involve input substitution possibilities and can be analyzed using the tools of production theory.

[2] See Hollis B. Chenery, "Engineering Production Functions," *Quarterly Journal of Economics,* November, 1949, p. 524. The authors are indebted to the Harvard University Press for permission to use Figure 11–4.

For example, it is. well known that in metal-cutting processes, such as drilling, milling, turning, and so forth, the life of cutting tools depends on cutting speed. Due to this technological phenomenon it is possible to substitute machines for cutting tools in metal fabrication processes. Any specified output of finished manufactured pieces can be produced by using fewer machines, and increasing the cutting speed of the machines. This reduces the stock of machine requirements but the consumption of cutting tools increases due to the greater cutting speed. Consequently, by appropriate variation in cutting speed, it is possible to substitute cutting tools for machines or machines for cutting tools. If x_1 represents the consumption of cutting tools per month, X_2 represents the stock of machine tools used, and y represents the output of finished pieces per month, then the form of the production function for this process can be written,

$$(11.3) \quad y = Ax_1^a X_2^{1-a} \quad A > 0 \; ; 0 < a < 1 \, ,$$

where A and a are constants depending upon the amount of material that has to be cut to produce a finished piece, the type of metal being machined, the hardness, strength, and other properties of the cutting tools, and other technical factors. The derivation of this function from engineering data is shown in the Appendix. The constant, a, in Equation (11.3) is usually quite small, varying in value from 0.05 to 0.25. From the form of Equation (11.3) it will be evident that tool consumption and the stock of machines are substitutes over a broad range. Also note that the process shows constant returns to scale, that is, if both inputs are increased in the same proportion output is increased by that same proportion.

Processes for the manufacture of chemicals and petroleum products frequently exhibit very complex input substitution possibilities. For example in many chemical reactions the percentage yield of product for given "charges," as they are called, of raw material reactants, can be increased by supplying heat to the process. Increasing the percentage yield means that less of the raw-material reactants are required to produce any specified amount of product. Hence, increasing the heat supplied to the chemical reaction saves on raw-material reactants. This implies substitution between raw materials and fuel for each level of output.

APPENDIX

The purpose of this Appendix is to show how the production functions for the transmission of electrical energy, and for metal-cutting processes, discussed in the main body of this chapter, can be derived from engineering laws, under simplified assumptions. For example, to simplify the power-line problem the analysis will assume that the electrical energy produced is in the form of direct rather than alternating current.

11.A.1. *Production of Electrical Energy*

If P_0 is the power output required of a transmission line, P_i is the power input at the generating end of the line, and P_L is the power loss in transmission due to resistance in the line, then the fundamental energy-balance equation underlying the process is

$$(11.A.1) \quad P_0 = P_i - P_L .$$

This equation simply states the fundamental physical principle of the conservation of energy. The power output of the system must equal the power input less all power losses.

From the laws governing the behavior of electricity in circuit networks, if I is the electric current flow in the line, and R is the electrical resistance of the line, then

$$(11.A.2) \quad P_L = I^2 R .$$

Or, if E_0 is the fixed voltage at which customers require power to be delivered to them, then, for direct current

$$(11.A.3) \quad P_0 = E_0 I \text{ or } I = \frac{P_0}{E_0} ,$$

from the principles of electric circuits. Substituting for I from (11.A.3) into (11.A.2) gives

$$(11.A.4) \quad P_L = \left(\frac{P_0}{E_0}\right)^2 R .$$

The resistance R of a transmission cable is related to the cross-section area of the cable, A, the round-trip length of the line, which is $2L$ for a line L feet long, and what is called the coefficient of conductivity of the wire, σ, as follows:

$$(11.A.5) \quad R = \frac{2L}{\sigma A} .$$

Observe that cable resistance is inversely proportional to its cross-sectional area. In Equation (11.A.5), L can be regarded as fixed, while σ can be regarded as fixed once the cable material is chosen. That is, σ depends upon whether copper, aluminum, or some other substance is chosen as cable material and its numerical value can be determined by consulting engineering tables. We will assume that σ is fixed, but it is worth noting that the choice of cable type is itself an economic decision.

Substituting for R from (11.A.5) into (11.A.4) gives

$$(11.A.6) \quad P_L = \left(\frac{P_0}{E_0}\right)^2 \frac{2L}{\sigma A} .$$

From (11.A.6), Equation (11.A.1) can be written

$$(11.A.7) \quad P_0 = P_i - \left(\frac{P_0}{E_0}\right)^2 \frac{2L}{\sigma A}.$$

All that remains is to transform the engineering variables of Equation (11.A.7) into economic input variables, that is, variables with which we can associate prices. For this process we have output $y = P_0$, while input Number 1, electrical energy, is simply $x_1 = P_i$. If A is the cross-sectional area of the cable in square feet, then input Number 2, cable, measured in cubic feet, is given by

$$(11.A.8) \quad X_2 = 2LA .$$

Therefore, by substitution in (11.A.7) we get the production function:

$$(11.A.9) \quad y = x_1 - \left(\frac{y}{E_0}\right)^2 \frac{4L^2}{\sigma X_2}.$$

Since E_0, L, and σ are constants, we can let $K = \dfrac{4L^2}{\sigma E_0{}^2}$ and write (11.A.9) in the form:

$$(11.A.10) \quad y = x_1 - \frac{Ky^2}{X_2}.$$

From (11.A.10) it is seen that, given y, x_1 and X_2 can be substituted over a broad range.

11.A.2. Choice of Power-Line Design

If we assume that the capital input, wire, is of infinite durability, then the cost function can be written as in Equation (11.2). The economic design problem is to minimize Equation (11.2) subject to (11.A.10). As was shown in the Appendix to Chapter 10, this is equivalent to minimizing

$$(11.A.11) \quad \phi = w_1 x_1 + i W_2 X_2 + \lambda \left[y - x_1 + \frac{Ky^2}{X_2} \right].$$

Note in this case that the production function (11.A.10) turns out to be an implicit function of y. That is, y is not expressed as an explicit function of x_1 and X_2. But this creates no difficulties in applying the Lagrange multiplier technique. The production function in implicit form is simply multiplied by the Lagrange multiplier, λ, and added to the cost function to form the ϕ function in (11.A.11). Minimizing ϕ, with respect to x_1, X_2 and λ (for given y) yields

$$(11.A.12) \quad w_1 - \lambda = 0$$

$$(11.A.13) \quad i W_2 - \lambda \frac{Ky^2}{X_2{}^2} = 0$$

$$(11.A.14) \quad y - x_1 + \frac{Ky^2}{X_2} = 0 .$$

From (11.A.12) and (11.A.13) by eliminating λ and solving for X_2, we have

$$(11.A.15) \quad X_2{}^0 = y\sqrt{\frac{w_1 K}{i\, W_2}}\,.$$

Then, by substitution into (11.A.14)

$$(11.A.16) \quad x_1{}^0 = y\left(1 + \sqrt{\frac{i\, W_2 K}{w_1}}\right).$$

These equations provide the best quantities of wire and electrical energy input as functions of output requirement, input prices, and the discount rate.

11.A.3. The Production Function for Metal-Cutting Processes

Let V be the cutting speed of a machine in feet per hour. For example, a cylindrical bar of metal may require turning on a lathe, in which case V is the lineal feet of travel of the cutting tool along the bar being machined. If T is the life of a cutting tool in machine hours, then the empirical engineering formula relating tool life and cutting speed is

$$(11.A.17) \quad VT^a = b\,,$$

where a and b are constants depending upon the depth of cut, type of metal, and so forth.[1]

If X_2 stands for the stock of metal-cutting machines to be used, and x_1 the total consumption per hour of cutting tools, then by definition:

$$(11.A.18) \quad x_1 \equiv \frac{X_2}{T}\,.$$

T has dimensions [machine hours/tools] while X_2 has the dimensions [machines]. Therefore, x_1 has the dimensions $\left[\dfrac{\text{tools}}{\text{hours}}\right]$, that is total tools consumed per hour. In Equation (11.A.18) it is assumed for simplicity that after T hours of service the life of a cutting tool ends beyond recovery, and cannot be repaired or resharpened.

If m is the total number of lineal feet of metal that must be removed in machining to produce a finished piece, then m/V is the number of machine hours required per piece. Therefore, if y is the total output per hour of finished pieces, using X_2 machines, then y is equal to X_2 divided by the ratio m/V, that is, by definition:

$$(11.A.19) \quad y \equiv \frac{X_2 V}{m}\,.$$

Substituting for T from (11.A.18) into (11.A.17) and for V from (11.A.19) into (11.A.17), and solving for y in terms of x_1 and X_2, gives

[1] See American Society of Mechanical Engineers, *Manual on Cutting of Metals,* 1952, pp. 313–20, for a discussion of Formula (11.A.17), and an approach to the economics of metal cutting dealing directly with engineering variables.

$$(11.A.20) \quad y = \frac{b}{m} x_1{}^a X_2{}^{1-a} = A x_1{}^a X_2{}^{1-a}$$

where $A = b/m$. Equation (11.A.20) provides the production function of economic theory for a simplified metal-cutting process, based on the technological relation between tool life and machine speed given in Formula (11.A.17). The latter engineering formula provides the foundation for the substitution possibilities implied by Equation (11.A.20).

11.A.4. A Production Function for a Batch Production Process

Many processes in the chemical, petroleum, metal and food product industries are characterized by the fact that production takes place in lots or batches for storage, with sales being met out of such inventory stores. Typically, in such processes, a production lot is made in a chemical reactor or some processing machine, the machine is then cleaned, adjusted, and set up for the next batch-run. In the meantime, sales are met out of the inventory accumulated in the production of the last lot. We shall illustrate this process by deriving its production function. The production rate, p, will be assumed given and the resulting production function will exhibit substitution between warehouse space X_2, and set-up labor x_1.

Suppose we assume that the inventory level accumulated by the end of each batch-run is Q, and that the rate of sales from inventory is y (y is the output rate of the warehouse-production system). During a batch production run, the machine produces for inventory at the rate p, while inventory is being depleted by sales at the rate y. The net rate of inventory accumulation is thus $p - y$. While the machine is idle and being cleaned, adjusted, etc., inventories are being depleted at the rate y. The manner in which inventories vary over the production cycle is illustrated in Figure 11–5. If the peak inventory accumulation is Q, then the operating time for the machine is $\frac{Q}{p-y}$, while the period of inventory run-down is $\frac{Q}{y}$. We assume that the inventory is depleted to zero before a new batch is started. Idle or down-time for clean-up, adjustment, servicing, set-up, etc. is assumed to be θ, which cannot be larger than $\frac{Q}{y}$. That is, the inventory run-out time must be long enough to allow for the down-time.

If we let N be the number of cycles run per year, with the time for each cycle being $\frac{Q}{p-y} + \frac{Q}{y}$, then we can write the fundamental scheduling relationship

$$(11.A.21) \quad N\left(\frac{Q}{p-y} + \frac{Q}{y}\right) = 1 .$$

That is, the number of cycles per year is the reciprocal of the time required (in fractions of a year) to complete each cycle.

If H man-hours per cycle are required to perform the set-up operation,

FIGURE 11-5

VARIATION OF INVENTORIES OVER PRODUCTION CYCLE

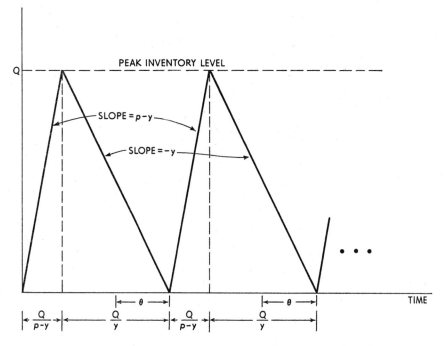

and if K square feet of warehouse space are required per unit of product, we can write

$$(11.A.22) \quad x_1 = HN,$$

$$(11.A.23) \quad X_2 = KQ,$$

where x_1 is man-hours labor input per year and X_2 is total square feet of warehouse capacity. Eliminating N and Q from (11.A.21) gives the production function

$$(11.A.24) \quad \frac{p x_1 X_2}{p - y} = KHy,$$

where p, K, and H are given technical parameters, and $p > y$ if we are not to exceed the capacity of the process.

The cost function for this process can be written in the usual form

$$(11.A.25) \quad C = w_1 x_1 + w_2 X_2,$$

where w_1 is the price of labor per man-hour and w_2 is annual cost of a unit of warehouse space. If warehouses last L_2 years, and require no upkeep, then $w_2 = \dfrac{i\,W_2}{1 - (1 + i)^{-L_2}}$ in accordance with the discussion of Section 10.11, Chapter 10.

QUESTIONS AND EXERCISES

1. In Figure 11–3 showing an iso-product contour for electrical energy transmission, there is a lower bound on x_1, equal to 10,000 kilowatt-hours. Should
there also be a lower bound on X_2 in the delivery of 10,000 kilowatt hours
of electricity? Why or why not?

2. Show that $\dfrac{\partial X_2}{\partial x_1} < 0$, and $\dfrac{\partial^2 x_2}{\partial x_1{}^2} > 0$ for the production functions shown in
Equations (11.3) and (11.A.20).

3. The results of a fertilizer experiment show that the production of a grain
crop in bushels per year, Z, varies with the number of pounds per year of
fertilizer applied, x_1, according to the relation

$$Z = (a + bx_1)^{\frac{1}{2}} \cdot$$

Derive the production function for this crop for the two inputs, fertilizer, and
land.

4. The production of ethyl acetate under certain conditions is governed by the
equation

$$\frac{y^2}{(1.5x_1 - y)(2.0x_2 - y)} = 4.0 ,$$

where x_1 = pounds of acetic acid input, x_2 = pounds of ethyl alcohol input,
and y = pounds of ethyl acetate produced. Determine the ratio of acetic acid
to ethyl alcohol which minimizes the cost per pound of ethyl acetate if
acetic acid costs $.08 per pound and ethyl alcohol costs $.06 per pound.
What happens to the ratio if acetic acid falls to $.04 per pound?

5. Consider the implicit production function:

$$y\left(\frac{100,000}{100x_1 - y}\right) - 100,000X_2 = 0 .$$

Sketch iso-product contours for $y = 1,000,000$ and $2,500,000$. Show that the
process exhibits decreasing returns.

6. A wide class of important empirical production functions is described by the
general function

$$y = K\left[ax_1^{-b_1} - (1 - a)x_2^{-b_2}\right]^{-\frac{1}{c}} ,$$

where K, a, b_1, b_2 and c are constants. Deduce the marginal productivity
functions for x_1 and x_2. Show that when

$$b_1 = b_2 = c = 0 , \quad \frac{\partial y}{\partial x_1} = \frac{aKy}{x_1} , \quad \frac{\partial y}{\partial x_2} = \frac{(1 - a)Ky}{x_2} .$$

Verify that these are the marginal productivity functions for the production
function $y = Kx_1{}^a x_2{}^{1-a}$. Hence, as $b_1 = b_2 = c$ is allowed to approach zero,
the general production function above achieves the constant returns form
$K x_1{}^a x_2{}^{1-a}$. If $b_1 = b_2 = b \neq c$, show that the above production function
gives increasing, constant, or decreasing returns according as $b \gtreqless c$.

Chapter 12

LINEAR PROGRAMMING AND THE ANALYSIS OF PRODUCTION

In recent years a new, and very powerful, technique of analyzing production decision problems has gained wide application in industry. This technique is known as *linear programming*. In this chapter the basic principles of linear programming will be set forth, using graphical methods, and the connections and similarities between this new technique and the theory of cost and production set forth in Chapter 10 will be developed.

12.1. Linear Programming and the Choice of Optimal Production Technique

It will be recalled in our discussion of the production function in Chapter 10 that we encountered the case of "limitational inputs," that is, production processes in which the inputs had to be combined in fixed proportions. In this connection the iso-product contour map was developed in Figure 10–3. To illustrate the application of linear programming to problems of choosing the best input combination, a slight generalization of this case will be considered in which a product can be produced by any of several processes, and for each process inputs must be combined in fixed proportions.

Consider a construction firm owning both bulldozers and power shovels. Either of these two kinds of equipment can be used on most dirt-moving jobs. Suppose that on a typical earth-moving job bulldozers require 1 man-minute of labor per cubic yard of earth moved, and 1.5 gallons of fuel per cubic yard of earth moved. If y is the cubic yards of dirt moved per day, x_1 is the input of labor in man-minutes per day, and x_2 is the input of fuel in gallons per day, then the following equations describe the input-output characteristics of the bulldozer process:

$$(12.1) \quad \begin{cases} x_1 = y \\ x_2 = 1.5y . \end{cases}$$

177

For the same type of earth-moving job suppose power shovels require 2 man-minutes of labor per cubic yard of earth moved, and 1 gallon of fuel per cubic yard of earth moved. Using the same notation as before, the following equations describe the input-output characteristics of the power-shovel process:

$$(12.2) \quad \begin{cases} x_1 = 2y \\ x_2 = y \ . \end{cases}$$

Now, each of these processes taken *separately* exhibits iso-product contours like those encountered in any productive process in which in-

FIGURE 12–1

ISO-PRODUCT CONTOURS FOR TWO SEPARATE PROCESSES FOR
EARTH MOVING

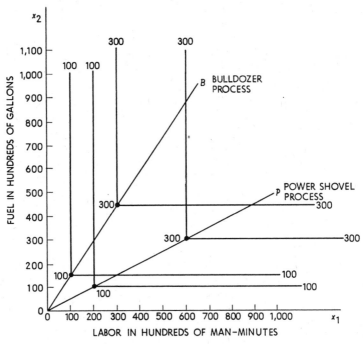

puts must be combined in fixed proportions. In Figure 12–1 is shown, superimposed on the same diagram, the iso-product contours for each of these two processes, for outputs of 100 and 300 cubic feet per day. However Figure 12–1 does not provide a complete representation of the input possibilities, since in addition to considering the bulldozer and power-shovel processes separately, there is the technical possibility of operating the two processes in parallel combination. That is, there is nothing of a technological character to prevent our construction firm from using both bulldozers and power shovels in any desired combination to perform a given earth-moving task. Such an integration of the two processes requires Figure 12–1 to be modified.

Consider Figure 12–2 in which the two rays *OB* and *OP*, whose slopes represent the ratios at which the two inputs must be combined in each process, have been reproduced from Figure 12–1. The scale laid

FIGURE 12–2

DERIVATION OF ISO-PRODUCT CONTOURS FOR COMBINATIONS
OF TWO PROCESSES FOR EARTH MOVING

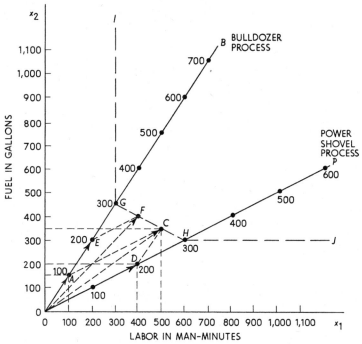

off along each ray represents the output that would result if the indicated input combinations were employed in that process. For example, 300 units of output can be produced by the bulldozer process when 300 man-minutes of labor are expended and 450 gallons of fuel consumed. Similarly, 300 units of output can be produced with the power-shovel process when 600 man-minutes of labor and 300 gallons of fuel are used. But 300 units of output can also be produced by employing the two processes in combination. For example, we could produce 100 units of output with the bulldozer process and 200 units of output with the power-shovel process.

In Figure 12–2 the length of the "vector" $\overrightarrow{OA}$ represents 100 units of output by the bulldozer process while the projections of this vector on the horizontal and vertical axes give the amounts of the two inputs required, 100 and 150 units respectively. Similarly, the vector $\overrightarrow{OD}$ represents 200 units of output by the power-shovel process, and its projection on the axes identifies the input requirements of the process at this output. Now, combining or adding the two processes together is equivalent geometrically to adding the vector $\overrightarrow{OA}$ to $\overrightarrow{OD}$, or, since $\overrightarrow{OD}$ equals $\overrightarrow{AC}$, to adding $\overrightarrow{OA}$ to $\overrightarrow{AC}$ giving $\overrightarrow{OC}$ a vector representing a total output of 300 units and whose projections on the axes give the total input requirements of the two processes together. Therefore, Point C represents a point on the iso-product contour for an output of 300 units which is obtained by operating the bulldozer process at an output level of 100 units and the power-shovel process at an output level of 200 units.

By the same arguments we could employ the bulldozer process at an output level of 200 units, and the power-shovel process at an output level of 100 units. The vector $\overrightarrow{OF}$ would represent the addition of the two processes at these levels, and F would be another point on the iso-product contour for an output of 300 units. If the two processes were completely divisible, then any point on the line GH would represent an output of 300 units that could be obtained by combining the two processes by the method described. Hence, the line segment GH is that part of the iso-product contour representing all possible ways in which the two processes can be combined to produce 300 units. Since each process is "limitational," that is, excesses of either input can contribute nothing to production, the line segment IG would represent the portion of the iso-product contour corresponding to excesses of fuel available for the bulldozer process. Similarly, HJ corresponds to excesses of labor available for the power-shovel process. The complete iso-product contour for 300 units of output is given by $IGHJ$. At every output level a similar iso-product contour can be drawn.

The above reasoning could be applied to any number of processes requiring any numbers of different inputs, provided the processes were all "linear," that is, each input requirement was proportional to the output level, and the processes could be operated in combination without altering the structure of input requirements. For example, in Figure 12–3 there are shown several iso-product contours for three different processes for producing a product.

If the price of input Number 1 is w_1 and the price of input Number 2 is w_2, then

$$(12.3) \quad C = w_1 x_1 + w_2 x_2$$

represents production cost as a function of x_1 and x_2. In Figure 12–3 the two dotted lines represent two different iso-cost contours. If it is desired to produce 300 units at lowest cost, it is necessary to find the point on the iso-product contour for 300 units of output through which the lowest iso-cost contour passes. In the diagram it is seen that an out-

FIGURE 12–3

ISO-PRODUCT CONTOURS FOR THREE PROCESSES,
AND THE CHOICE OF BEST TECHNIQUE

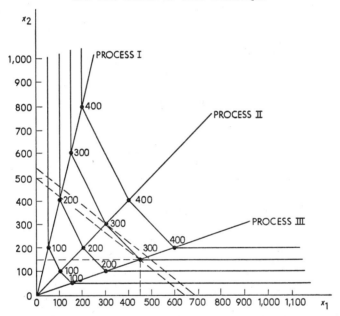

put of 300 units can be produced at least cost by using Process III at $x_1 = 450$ and $x_2 = 150$. Note that the relative prices w_1 and w_2, and therefore the slope of the iso-cost contours, can shift over a fairly considerable range without altering the least-cost equilibrium point. However, if w_1 rises sufficiently relative to w_2, then Process II would be most economical. A still further rise in w_1 relative to w_2 could make Process I the most economical. Note that in the two-input case, if production is carried out at least cost, there will never be more than one process employed.

It should be observed that the iso-product map of Figure 12–3 exhibits a form of input substitution that is a very close cousin to the input substitution characterizing the production function. However, the *mechanism* of substitution is different. In Chapter 11 we found that the mechanism of input substitution in the gas and electrical power transmission production functions was energy loss due to friction. This underlying physical principle gave rise to continuous input substitution possibilities. In input-output problems to which linear programming applies, the mechanism of substitution is the existence of distinct alternative processes, and inputs are substitutable through the device of being able to choose among these alternative processes with different input consumption characteristics. This is one of the major distinctions between linear programming and the production function analysis.

The special assumptions underlying linear programming as applied to input analysis may be summarized as follows:

1. The ratio at which inputs must be combined for any particular process is the same for all levels of output. This is why the rays drawn from the origin in Figure 12–3 are straight lines.
2. Since inputs must be combined in fixed proportions it follows that each process exhibits constant returns to scale, that is, a doubling of all inputs causes output to double. This is why the points representing the output scale along the rays in Figure 12–3 are evenly spaced.
3. If any two processes are used in conjunction, they will neither interfere with nor enhance the productivity of each so that the input requirements and outputs resulting from combined use of the two processes at any level of operation can be found by adding the inputs and outputs of the individual processes. This is the "additivity" postulate which enabled us to deduce that any point on the line *GH* in Figure 12–2 represented an input combination which would result in the production of 300 units of output. The additivity postulate is not satisfied if there is any possibility of a more efficient reorganization of production as a consequence of the combined operation of two or more processes.

12.2. Linear Programming and the Choice of Optimal Product Mix

An important class of problems to which linear programming applies is concerned with the choice of how much to produce of each of several products with given facilities. One such problem arises in production machine shops in which there are available certain numbers of each of several different types of metalworking machines. On the other hand, several different products requiring machine time on several different machines can be produced. The problem is to allocate machine time among these various products so as to maximize profit.

To illustrate this machine scheduling problem, assume there are two products and two machines. Suppose product No. 1 requires 0.2 machine hours and product No. 2 requires 0.1 machine hours on machine type No. 1. If y_1 is the output per day of product No. 1 and y_2 is the output per day of product No. 2, then the number of machine hours per day required on machine type No. 1 is $0.2y_1$ for product No. 1 and $0.1y_2$ for product No. 2. The total requirements on machine type No. 1, $0.2y_1 + 0.1y_2$, cannot exceed the available capacity of these machines. This capacity is equal to the stock of machines of type No. 1 times the

FIGURE 12–4

MACHINE SCHEDULING AND THE CHOICE
OF BEST PRODUCT MIX

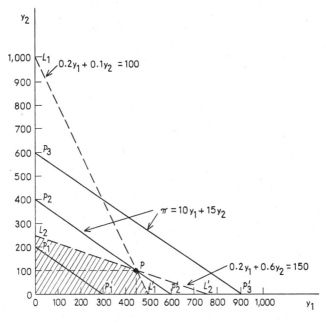

number of machine hours each can be operated per day. Suppose the total daily machine-hour capacity of machine type No. 1 is 100. Then this capacity restriction can be expressed in the form of the following inequality:

$$(12.4) \quad 0.2y_1 + 0.1y_2 \leq 100 .$$

That is, total machine-hour requirements may be less than, or equal to, but cannot exceed, available capacity. In Figure 12–4 the line L_1L_1' represents the equation $0.2y_1 + 0.1y_2 = 100$. Therefore any point *on* or *below* this line represents a combination of y_1 and y_2 which satisfies the restriction in (12.4).

If product No. 1 requires 0.2 machine hours while product No. 2

requires 0.6 machine hours on machine type No. 2, and if the available capacity of machine type No. 2 is 150 machine hours per day, then the capacity restriction on this machine is

$$(12.5) \quad 0.2y_1 + 0.6y_2 \leq 150 \, .$$

In Figure 12–4 the equation $0.2y_1 + 0.6y_2 = 150$ is represented by the line $L_2L'_2$. Any point *on* or *below* this line represents a combination of y_1 and y_2 which satisfies the restriction (12.5).

There is one other set of restrictions on our variables which are important in most problems of economic analysis as well as in linear programming. These restrictions are that the outputs y_1 and y_2 of each of the two products cannot be negative. That is, we can permit zero or positive solutions, but never negative solutions. These nonnegativity restrictions can be written

$$(12.6) \quad y_1 \geq 0 \, ; \quad y_2 \geq 0 \, .$$

Geometrically, these restrictions require that we consider only points which are above the horizontal axis and to the right of the vertical axis in Figure 12–4.

The inequality restrictions contained in (12.4), (12.5), and (12.6), taken together, define the set of points contained in region OL'_1PL_2 shown in Figure 12–4. Every point in this region represents a feasible or possible output combination. It represents all those production possibilities which are technically achievable, given machine capacities and the characteristics of the two products to be made.

As a first approximation let us assume that the net profit per unit from the production of each of these two products is constant, that is independent of the quantities produced. Suppose in fact, that the profit on product No. 1 is $10 per unit and the profit on product No. 2 is $15 per unit. Then total profit per day from the production of y_1 and y_2 is

$$(12.7) \quad \pi = 10y_1 + 15y_2 \, .$$

Equation (12.7) is called the criterion function. That is, maximization of π is the criterion used to allocate machine capacity between the two products. Equation (12.7) is graphed in Figure 12–4 for three different profit levels. The line P_1P_1' represents all those combinations of y_1 and y_2 yielding a profit of $3,000 per day. P_2P_2' represents a profit level of $6,000 per day, while P_3P_3' represents a profit level of $9,000 per day. These lines represent three different iso-profit contours. Maximization of profit implies choosing y_1 and y_2 so as to be on the highest profit contour without violating the restrictions (12.4), (12.5), and

(12.6), that is, without going outside the production possibility region OL'_1PL_2. It is evident from Figure 12–4 that the most profitable allocation of machine time occurs at P when $y_1 = 450$ and $y_2 = 100$, since the highest profit contour passing through a point in the production possibility region is P_2P_2'. The production of 450 units of product No. 1 requires $0.2 \times 450 = 90$ hours per day on the type No. 1 machine and $0.2 \times 450 = 90$ hours per day on the type No. 2 machine, while the production of 100 units of product No. 2 requires $0.1 \times 100 = 10$ hours per day on the type No. 1 machine and $0.6 \times 100 = 60$ hours per day on the type No. 2 machine. Therefore machine No. 1 time is allocated 90 hours to product No. 1 and 10 hours to product No. 2, while machine No. 2 time is allocated 90 hours to product No. 1 and 60 hours to product No. 2.

In this example there was no unused capacity. That is, the full available capacity on both machines was used. However, if profit per unit on product No. 1 had been \$2 and on product No. 2 had been \$8, then the slope of the iso-profit lines would have been greater (less negative) than the slope of L_2L_2'. As a result the most profitable allocation would have been at L_2 with $y_1 = 0$ and $y_2 = 250$, in which case machine No. 2 time would have been fully utilized, but only $0.1 \times 250 = 25$ hours or $\frac{1}{4}$ of the available machine No. 1 time could be used profitably.

The analysis of this section has been concerned with the application of linear programming to a problem in multiproduct firm analysis. A more general nonlinear analysis of the multiproduct firm can be developed by an extension of the concept of the production function.[1] Linear programming applies only when the quantity of each input required can be expressed as a linear combination of the quantities of the various outputs produced.

12.3. *Algebraic Statement of the Linear Programming Problem*

All linear programming problems have the same general mathematical form whether they be concerned with the choice of best input combination, the best output mix, or other allocation decisions. In all cases there is a criterion function which is to be optimized (maximized or minimized). This function is linear in the variables, which represent the objects of choice in the problem. These variables are sometimes

---

[1] If there are two outputs y_1 and y_2, and two inputs x_1 and x_2, then y_1, y_2, x_1, and x_2 are technologically related in production. This can be expressed functionally by writing the production function, in implicit form, as follows: $F(y_1, y_2, x_1, x_2) = 0$.

called "activity levels." Suppose, for example, that we have three variables, Y_1, Y_2, and Y_3. Then if the problem is one of maximization, there will be a criterion function of the form

$$(12.8) \quad z = C_1Y_1 + C_2Y_2 + C_3Y_3$$

to be maximized, where C_1, C_2, and C_3 are constants. Bear in mind, however, that there can be any number of variables. For example there might be fifty variables instead of three.

In linear programming there is also a set of linear constraints in the form of equalities or inequalities (more-than or less-than relations), which involve the variables of the problem. These constraints taken together constitute a description of the technological possibilities which govern the choice of specific values for the variables of the problem. One set of such restrictions limits this choice to only positive values of the variables. This is an important characteristic of allocation problems. Another set of restrictions provides an equation or inequation for each distinct requirement in the problem. For example, in the machine scheduling problem if there were 10 different machine types required to produce one or both of the products, then there would have been ten inequations of the form (12.4) and (12.5) instead of two.

Suppose there are four distinct requirements in a maximization problem. Then the technological restrictions on the choice of Y_1, Y_2, and Y_3 can be written

$$(12.9) \quad
\begin{cases}
\quad\quad\quad\quad\quad Y_1 \geq 0 \\
\quad\quad\quad\quad\quad Y_2 > 0 \;\}\text{nonnegativity conditions} \\
\quad\quad\quad\quad\quad Y_3 \geq 0 \\
a_{11}Y_1 + a_{12}Y_2 + a_{13}Y_3 \leq b_1 \\
a_{21}Y_1 + a_{22}Y_2 + a_{23}Y_3 \leq b_2 \\
a_{31}Y_1 + a_{32}Y_2 + a_{33}Y_3 \leq b_3 \;\}\text{technical conditions} \\
a_{41}Y_1 + a_{42}Y_2 + a_{43}Y_3 \leq b_4
\end{cases}$$

The a's and b's in (12.9) are constants. The a's are technical coefficients and the b's are the requirements or capacity limits on the utilization of each distinct activity.

Note that there is no requirement that the number of restrictions or inequations be equal to the number of variables. Mathematically, the existence of inequalities and the possibility that one or more variables may take on zero values, precludes any such requirement. This is where linear programming differs in a significant way from the mathematics of simultaneous equations.

Since it is not unusual, in practice, to encounter linear programming problems involving hundreds of variables, it would appear that the solution to such problems would be extremely difficult to obtain. However, such is not the case for the reason that extremely efficient computational techniques have been developed for solving linear programming problems. There is a general technique called the "simplex method" which can be used very efficiently to solve any such problem. Also there are several special techniques that are even more efficient for solving certain frequently encountered, specialized linear programming problems.[2] As a result of the availability of these very efficient computing techniques, many linear programming problems can be solved quickly with a desk calculator, even though the number of variables is large. These techniques also lend themselves readily to solution by automatic computing machines where the number of variables is very large and new solutions have to be repeatedly computed because of changes from week to week in the data and conditions of a problem.

12.4. *Industrial Applications of Linear Programming*

Linear programming represents a particular mathematical technique for formulating and solving problems concerned with the most efficient allocation of scarce resources to alternative ends. It is a technique which is gaining increasing application to allocation problems arising in manufacturing, transportation, and agriculture. The following constitutes a partial list of such applications, and indicates the breadth of service this new tool has rendered in solving business decision problems:

1. *Gasoline Blending.* There are numerous applications of linear programming to petroleum refining. One application is to the problem of blending gasolines. In such blending, several different kinds of partially refined oil, called blending stocks, each with distinct chemical and physical properties, are mixed together to produce gasoline of a given grade. The typical refinery produces several premium and regular grades of gasoline. The result of a particular combination of blending stocks is to produce a gasoline with certain major characteristics, such as volatility, octane rating, and sulphur content. These characteristics of the product are approximately expressible as linear combinations of the

---

[2] Several expositions of these computing techniques are available in the literature. The standard source is T. C. Koopman (ed.), *Activity Analysis of Production and Allocation* (New York: John Wiley & Sons, 1951). Less advanced discussions are contained in C. W. Churchman, R. L. Ackoff, and E. L. Arnoff, *Introduction to Operations Research* (New York: John Wiley & Sons, 1957), and E. H. Bowman and R. B. Fetter, *Analysis for Production Management* (rev. ed.; Homewood, Illinois: Richard D. Irwin, Inc., 1961).

characteristics of the blending stocks.[3] For example, if 100 gallons of blending stock with a sulphur content of 0.18 per cent are blended with 200 gallons of stock with a sulphur content of 0.09 per cent, the result will be 300 gallons of gasoline with a sulphur content of

$$\left(\frac{100}{300} \times 0.18\right) + \left(\frac{200}{300} \times 0.09\right) = 0.12 \text{ per cent .}$$

Knowing the unit costs of each of the blending stocks, one can also express the cost of a given gasoline grade as a linear combination of the amounts of each of the blending stocks used to produce that grade. Hence, one can use linear programming to determine the minimum-cost blend which will meet given product quality specifications. For example, one might solve for the minimum-cost blend that will have not more than 0.10 per cent sulphur, not less than an 86 octane rating, and not less than a certain volatility index.

2. *Product Transportation Scheduling.* One of the earliest applications of linear programming was to the so-called "transportation" problem faced by the multiple-plant firm serving several markets. The typical form of this problem is as follows:

a) Given amounts of product are available for shipment at each plant.
b) Given amounts of product are to be received at each market (for example, a city) served by the firm.
c) Given the transportation cost per unit of product from each plant to each market, the problem is to determine how much product to ship from each plant to each market so as to minimize the total outlay for transportation service.

Condition *a* gives rise to a set of linear inequalities—one for each plant—which state that the total shipments out of any one plant cannot exceed the quantity of product available at that plant. Condition *b* leads to a set of linear inequalities—one for each market or receiving point—which state that the total shipments received at any one market cannot be less than the sales requirements of that market. Condition *c* states the objective to be achieved subject to the restrictions provided by conditions *a* and *b*.

3. *Production Scheduling.* A typical production scheduling problem, to which linear programming may be applied, requires certain expected sales requirements to be met in each of several future sales periods. For example, one might forecast monthly sales of a product over a period of one year. These sales forecasts would then become the

---

[3] For octane rating the assumption of linearity is actually rather crude, but there are methods of modifying linear programming techniques to handle such nonlinearities.

sales requirements in each month, which in turn can be met out of inventory holdings of the product accumulated from excesses of production over sales in previous months, or out of current production. Current production might be further broken down into regular time and overtime. The problem then becomes one of scheduling regular and overtime production and inventory holdings, for each month in the planning period, so as to minimize the total of production plus inventory cost necessary to satisfy the sales requirements of each period.

4. *Feed Mixing.* A problem very similar to the gasoline-blending problem is known as the "minimum-cost, adequate-diet" problem. The task is to mix various food items such as soybean meal, grains, and additives to produce a feed product that provides the minimum daily requirements of each of various nutrients for cattle, hogs, or poultry. The problem is to blend that combination of available feed items that minimizes the cost of satisfying the protein, mineral, vitamin, and other nutrient requirements of the animal in question.

The preceding examples are only a few of the many applications of linear programming that have been developed in recent years. It is a relatively new tool that will undoubtedly find wider and wider industrial application as the problems of production planning become more complex and more difficult to solve satisfactorily without the aid of systematic methods of analysis. Our purpose here has been merely to introduce the basic elements of programming. Before the student can make any effective use of programming tools he must study the various applications in greater detail, as well as the various techniques for solving problems involving large numbers of variables.[4]

QUESTIONS AND EXERCISES

1. Figure 12–3 shows a linear programming iso-product map. Does it show diminishing returns? Increasing, constant, or decreasing returns to scale?
2. The following table gives the machine-hour requirements per unit of output for two products and two machines:

	Product 1	Product 2
Machine 1.............	0.2	0.1
Machine 2.............	0.1	0.4

[4] In very recent years there has developed a considerable literature on what is called "dynamic programming." This is a more general approach to allocation decision processes than linear programming in that it is able to handle both linear and nonlinear programming problems—the latter of course being extremely important in most economic analysis. A good general reference is Richard Bellman, *Dynamic Programming* (Princeton, New Jersey: Princeton University Press, 1957).

The available time on Machine 1 is 200 hours, and on Machine 2 is 300 hours. If the net profit on Product 1 is $5 per unit, and on Product 2 is $8 per unit, what are the most profitable amounts of the two products that should be produced?

3. In Problem 2, if the available capacity on Machine 2 rises to 400 hours, what is the effect on the solution.

4. What happens to the solution in Problem 2 if the unit profit on Product 1 rises to $6?

5. Suppose the diet for broiler chickens consists of soybean oil and grain. Suppose further that the three important nutrients in this diet are protein, vitamins, and minerals. The following table gives the protein, vitamin and mineral content of one pound of grain and one pound of soybean oil.

	Grain	Soybean Oil
Protein...............	0.3	0.1
Vitamins.............	0.2	0.4
Minerals.............	0.2	0.1

Suppose the minimum daily requirements of a chicken flock for each of these nutrients is as follows:

Protein — 60 units
Vitamins—100 units
Minerals— 50 units

If grain costs 10 cents a pound and soybean oil costs 20 cents a pound, find the minimum cost adequate diet for this chicken flock.

6. In Problem 2 what happens to the solution if we double the capacity of both machine types? Why?

7. In Problem 5 what happens to the solution if the cost of grain increases to 20 cents a pound?

8. What happens to the cost of feeding the flock in Problem 5 if the minimum daily requirements of each nutrient is doubled?

Chapter 13

THE THEORY OF THE FIRM
AND THE ECONOMIC
SYSTEM

In analyzing competitive market price in Chapters 2 through 6 it was necessary to introduce certain important behavior hypotheses concerning business enterprises. Having just completed in Chapters 8 through 12 an analysis of the individual firm in terms of optimal production decision behavior, it should now be possible to deduce these earlier hypotheses from our deeper analysis of the decision problems of the individual firm. If our models of the market process are to be consistent with our model of rational firm behavior, it is important that it be possible to show how certain assumptions contained in the earlier models can be deduced or derived from our analysis of the firm. In other words we should be able to "close the loop" by showing how the theory of markets can be tied in with the theory of the firm.

For example, in analyzing the formation of competitive market prices the concept of supply was introduced. According to this hypothesis, the higher the market price of a competitively produced commodity, the greater will be the quantity of the commodity that will be produced and offered for sale. It follows that if the theory of the firm is consistent with the theory of markets, this supply relationship concerning markets should be derivable as a result (a theorem) from the deeper theory of the firm lying behind the concept of market supply.

Similarly, in analyzing the determination of factor or input prices in competitive markets it was stated that the demand for a product gives rise to a demand for any input required in the production of that product. Therefore, out of our theory of the firm's choice of the best input combination in production it should be possible to derive the firm's demand for an input.

The purpose of this chapter is to show briefly how these connections between the theory of the firm and the theory of markets can be established.

13.1. *The Supply Curve of an Individual Firm under Pure Competition*

In Chapter 9 it was shown that the most profitable rate of output for the firm in pure competition is that output for which marginal cost, *MC*, is equal to product price, *p*. This equilibrium is illustrated graphically in Figure 13–1. At the price *p* the most profitable short-run output is *y*. Under these conditions, the firm will be earning a pure

FIGURE 13–1

THE SUPPLY CURVE OF THE INDIVIDUAL FIRM

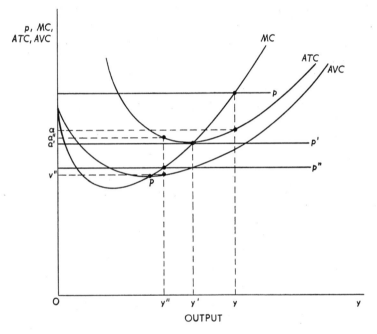

profit above all costs of production, including "normal" profits, of $p - a$ dollars per unit of output or total pure profits of $(p - a)y$. If price persisted at this level, the existence of pure profits would, in competitive industries, serve as an inducement for new firms to enter, causing industry output to expand and price to fall. If price were p' it would pay the firm to employ its fixed facilities somewhat less intensively by contracting output to y' where average total cost is $a' = p'$, and pure profits are zero. At the price p' the best that the firm can do is to make only normal profits, which are included in the definition of the average total cost curve. At the price p'' the optimum rate of output is y'', at which production level the firm will make losses of $a'' - p''$ dollars per unit of output or total losses of $(a'' - p'')y''$ dollars. Thus the optimum rate of output in the short run may be a loss minimizing output. In the long run if the price p'' persisted firms would be forced to drop out of the industry, and as the industry contracted, industry output would fall and price would rise, tending to restore normal profits.

Notice, however, that under these conditions the firm would eventually, but not immediately, drop out of production. The reason for this is that even at the price p'' and the corresponding rate of output y'', the firm is earning something above its directly variable costs. After variable expenses of $v''y''$ dollars have been made, the firm is obtaining short-run earnings of $(p'' - v'')y''$ dollars. This represents a return on the firm's investment in fixed facilities, which permits the firm to recover, through production and sale, all or at least a portion of its capital investment. However, since fixed costs, including interest on the investment and normal profits, are not covered, there is no incentive for the firm to reinvest in the enterprise once the existing facilities are no longer serviceable and require replacement for production to continue. On the other hand the firm would not drop out of production immediately if price were below average total cost, since its fixed costs are a sunk cost—a cost that has already been incurred whether production takes place or not. Therefore, if the firm were to drop out immediately, it would obtain no further return at all on its fixed investment. It is much preferable to obtain some recovery of capital than no recovery at all.

If price were below, and expected to remain below, P, the point of minimum average variable costs, then the firm cannot even cover its directly variable costs and has no choice but to shut down immediately. This would be the situation when a trucking company could not earn enough to pay the costs of drivers and fuel.

From this analysis it will be seen that the profit-maximizing (or loss-minimizing) firm will always adjust output along its marginal cost curve until $p = MC$ for prices above the point P. For prices below the point P the firm will produce zero output. It follows that the marginal cost curve, starting at the point P, represents the firm's output response behavior to changes in market price. In other words, it represents the individual firm's supply curve of a product.

13.2. The Supply Curve of an Industry

The theoretical supply curve for a purely competitive industry can be determined by simple addition if the supply curves (marginal cost curves) of all the firms, actually or potentially, producing a given product are known. In the short run the supply curve of the industry is the horizontal sum of the marginal cost curves of the individual firms in the industry. That is, the quantities that the firm will find it profitable to produce at a given market price, say p, are added together to find the quantity supplied to the market at the price p. The same procedure is followed for every price that might conceivably prevail in the market. The result is a short-run supply schedule of the industry. In the long run, additional firms may enter or existing firms may leave the industry, depending upon whether the industry is abnormally profitable or unprofitable. Consequently, in the long run, changes in price cause corresponding changes in industry output for *two* reasons: (1) the output of each firm in the industry is altered in response to price changes, and (2) new firms may enter or old firms may leave the industry.

These considerations are illustrated in Figure 13–2. In this diagram it is assumed that the lowest cost firms in the industry are represented by the cost curves in Graph I on the left side of the figure. The minimum expected long-run price necessary to induce these lowest cost producers to invest in production in this industry is P_1'. At this price, if N_1 firms, with the cost characteristics of Graph I, enter the industry, aggregate output is $Y_1' = N_1 y_1'$ and S_{L1} is a point on the long-run supply curve. Once these firms have entered the industry, the short-run supply curve $S_1 S_1$ is the horizontal sum of the N_1 marginal cost curves MC_1. In the short run these firms will produce along MC_1, if product price is above P_1. Below P_1 the industry will produce no output even in the short run, since P_1 does not cover the average variable costs of the lowest cost group of firms in the industry.

Graph II in Figure 13–2 is assumed to represent a group of firms with costs somewhat greater than the lowest cost producers in I. The fact that some firms have higher costs than others may be attributable to a variety of circumstances. Some firms may have certain natural advantages due to the use of a superior raw material as in mining where the mines vary in ore quality or in agriculture where the soil varys in fertility. Certain firms may have an advantage due to more effective management or a more favorable location. In the example, the Group II firms will not find it to their advantage to invest in the industry unless the long-run price is expected to be P_2' or greater. Once this group of firms has invested in the industry the short-run supply curve becomes $S_2 S_2$. If there are N_2 of the Group II firms, the short-run industry supply curve is the horizontal sum of the N_1 Group I marginal cost curves, MC_1, and the N_2 Group II marginal cost curves, MC_2. Aggregate out-

FIGURE 13–2

DERIVATION OF INDUSTRY SUPPLY CURVES

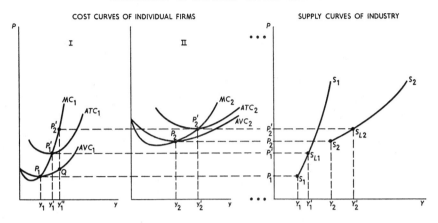

put at P_2 is then $N_1 y_1' + N_2 y_2 = Y_2'$, and a second point of the long-run industry supply curve is S_2. At the price P_2' it is seen that the Group I firms appear to earn a "pure profit" of $P_2'Q$ per unit. This is not considered a profit by the economist but rather a return or rent to "institutional advantage." Thus, in copper mining the high-yield low-cost mines command a greater market value because of this return due to differential productivity. By continuing the indicated derivation procedure for still higher cost firms we can generate a series of long-run supply points, S_{L1}, S_{L2}, S_{L3}, . . . , and a series of short-run supply curves. If we imagine a continual gradation of individual firm cost curves from the lowest cost producer through ever higher cost curves, the corresponding short-run and long-run supply curves will be smooth and continuous, as shown in Figure 4–1 (p. 38).

13.3. The Demand for an Input

Ultimately, inputs are demanded because they are productive, but in order to state how much of any input a firm will demand at any price (its demand curve for the input), a behavior objective for the firm is required, and again we assume profit maximization. In the theory of cost and production this is reflected in the assumption that a firm attempts to minimize the cost of producing any given output. For simplicity of exposition in what follows, we will derive the firm's demand for input on the assumption that output is held constant, and then indicate the modifications necessary to account for changes in the level of output induced by changes in input prices.

It has been shown that if the inputs to a firm or process are substitutes for each other, a necessary condition for the minimum cost production of any given level of output is that

$$\frac{w_1}{f_1} = \frac{w_2}{f_2},$$

for a three variable input-output productive process. This equilibrium is
illustrated in Figure 13–3A by the point P. Therefore when the price
of input Number 1 is w_1 and the price of input Number 2 is w_2, the
firm will consume x_1 units of input Number 1. The association of the

FIGURE 13–3

DERIVATION OF INDIVIDUAL FIRM DEMAND FOR AN INPUT

A   B

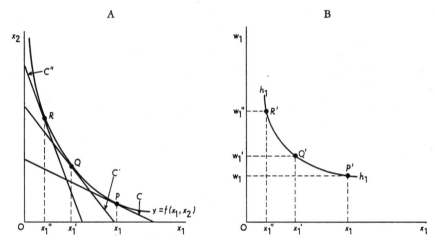

demand quantity x_1 with the price w_1, given w_2 and y, is represented by
the point P' in Figure 13–3B. If the price of input Number 1 rises to
w_1', the lowest achievable cost shifts from C to C', input Number 2 is
substituted for input Number 1, and the equilibrium quantity of input
Number 1 becomes x_1' at the point Q in Figure 13–3A. The quantity
x_1' is now associated with the price w_1' and is represented by the point
Q' in Figure 13–3B. If the price of input Number 1 were still higher,
say w_1'', cost would be minimized at R in Figure 13–3A, and the corresponding input-demand point would be R' in Figure 13–3B. The
points P', Q', R' are three points on the firm's demand curve for input
Number 1, $h_1 h_1$.

Note that the demand curve $h_1 h_1$ was derived on the assumption
that the price of input Number 2, and the level of output remained
unchanged. In general, as was shown in the Appendix to Chapter 10,

the demand for input Number 1 is a function of the prices of both inputs and the level of output, the latter, in turn being determined by the price of the product. Similarly, the demand for input Number 2 depends upon each input price and output. That is,

$$(13.1) \quad \begin{cases} x_1 = h_1(w_1, w_2, y) \\ x_2 = h_2(w_1, w_2, y) \end{cases}$$

A more comprehensive analysis of the demand for an input would go two steps further. First it would account for the changes in y induced by changes in w_1. When any input price increases, this may increase marginal cost which, in turn, would require a decrease in y in order to maintain the $p = MC$ equilibrium. Second, it would account for the fact that if the marginal cost curves of individual firms increase, this decreases industry supply and causes an upward readjustment of price. Short of an analysis of all these repercussions the demand curve derived in Figure 13–3B shows how the "law of demand" as applied to an input is based upon the concept of input substitution.

Having derived the input demand curve for an individual firm, the theoretical total demand curve for an input becomes simply the horizontal summation of all the individual firm demand curves for that input.

13.4. The Demand for Investment Goods

It will be recalled that in our analysis of production (Chapter 10) we studied the problem of best input combinations when one of two inputs to a process is a capital good. To simplify the analysis suppose the capital good is infinitely durable so that the cost function can be written

$$(13.2) \quad C = w_1 x_1 + i W_2 X_2$$

where w_1 is the price of the current input (such as labor), W_2 is the price of the durable capital input, and i is the market rate of interest on long-term money capital. We seek a relationship between the rate of interest and the amount of capital which the firm will find it most profitable to employ. "Capital" could be measured in physical units, X_2, or value units, $W_2 X_2$.

If the interest rate were i' then the cost function would be $C = w_1 x_1 + i' W_2 X_2$ and the firm would find it most profitable to invest $W_2 X_2'$ dollars in a stock of X_2' units of the capital good, as represented by the point P in Figure 13–4A. The amount of investment undertaken by the firm, $W_2 X_2'$, is associated with an interest rate i'

FIGURE 13-4

DERIVATION OF INDIVIDUAL FIRM DEMAND FOR INVESTMENT CAPITAL

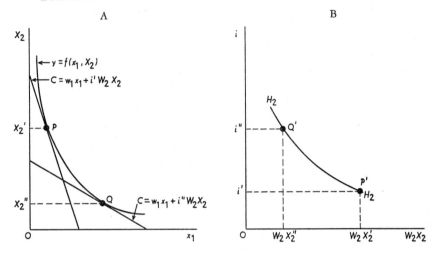

and is represented by the point P' on the firm's investment demand schedule in Figure 13–4B. If the rate of interest were $i'' > i'$, the cost of capital to the firm would be greater relative to the cost of labor and the firm would find it profitable to use more labor and less of the capital good. Thus at i'' the firm would employ X_2'' units of capital at point Q of Figure 13–4A. Consequently, an investment level of W_2X_2'' would be associated with an interest rate of i'', as represented by Q' in Figure 13–4B. A still higher rate of interest would further discourage potential investment outlays for the capital input. If P', Q' and other such points are joined by a line we have the resulting investment demand curve for one type of capital input, H_2H_2.

Observe again that certain other factors, notably y, w_1 and W_2, have been held constant in deriving the schedule H_2H_2. Therefore, in general, investment outlay W_2X_2 will be a function of all these parameters.

13.5. The Firm and the Industry: Technological Change in Agriculture

As an illustration of the connections between the theory of the firm and the theory of markets, we shall apply some of the tools developed in this and in earlier chapters to a discussion of the problems of the agricultural industry.

American agriculture has often been said to be plagued with two outstanding economic characteristics in the years since World War II.

The demand for agricultural products, particularly grain crops, is said to be relatively inelastic, and the production of these products has experienced exceedingly rapid technological advance. In developing our illustrative analysis, we shall suppose that the product is corn, and we will adhere to the following three *assumptions:*

1. The demand for corn is assumed to be inelastic.
2. The major dynamic force to which the industry must adjust is assumed to be technological improvement.
3. The significant economic effect of technological improvement is of course to lower the unit costs of production in individual firms adopting the improvements. This can occur in many ways. We shall assume the direct effect of technological improvement is to lower ATC and move the minimum point of ATC to the right. Hence, the optimum-sized firm is assumed to increase as a consequence of technological advances in machinery, fertilizer development, and hybrid seeds.

These assumptions are in accord with commonly accepted views in agriculture. Note, however, that we are greatly simplifying the problem of agriculture by isolating only a few factors for study. Obviously, population growth, with its expanding demands for food and fiber, are also important factors in the analysis of agriculture. Such qualifications should be borne in mind during the analysis to follow.

In Figure 13–5A, MC and ATC represent the marginal cost and average total cost curves for the typical normally profitable firm before the technological advance. The individual firm's demand is perfectly elastic at the price P determined by the intersection of DD and SS in Figure 13–5B. Individual firm production is y_0 per year, and industry output is Y_0. As firms begin to adopt improved machinery, fertilizer and seeds average total costs tend to shift down and to the right as indicated by ATC'. Temporary pure profits are enjoyed by the firms first introducing the new technology. But as more and more firms adopt the new techniques we know from our derivation of the industry supply curve in Figure 13–2. that this general decline in the average total cost curves of individual firms will cause a corresponding increase in industry supply (the supply curve moves down or shifts to the right giving a greater supply quantity at each price). Thus, in Figure 13–5B, we get an increase in supply from SS to $S'S'$. This causes price to fall from P to P', and even the firms who have adopted the new technology to get the advantage of the lower ATC' curve find that they are making losses. These losses may drag on for several years depending upon the mobility of labor and capital resources into other industries. Eventually, however, as some firms are driven out by losses the supply curve of corn is de-

FIGURE 13–5

TECHNOLOGICAL CHANGE IN AGRICULTURE

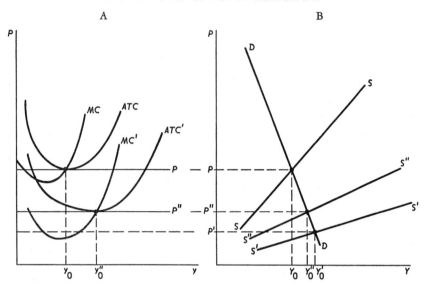

creased, and price increases until supply becomes $S''S''$. Price is now P'' and the industry is just normally profitable. But if demand DD is inelastic, as we have assumed, it means that the gross income of corn producers $P''Y_0''$ is smaller than its previous level PY_0. Hence, the net effect of the technical improvement is to (*a*) lower price, (*b*) increase average firm size, (*c*) decrease the number of firms in the industry, and (*d*) decrease industry gross income. If individual firm gross income rises, that is if $Py_0 < P''y_0''$, as indeed has been the tendency, with industry gross income falling, it means that the number of firms which must leave the industry to restore normal profitability may be quite large. It is often argued that this is precisely the situation in agriculture today. If normal profitability is to be maintained in the absence of price supports, there must be a substantial annual migration of families from the farms to other industries. This, of course, suggests that a government policy designed to encourage the movement and retraining of human resources now in agriculture into such labor scarce areas as the growing personal service industries, would be much wiser than a policy of price supports. Agricultural price supports provide an incentive for such resources to remain in agriculture, causing excessive capacity and a surplus of the supported commodities.

The conclusions of our analysis are tempered somewhat by the fact that demand, DD, also tends to rise due to population growth. An analysis taking account of shifting demand as well as supply would, however, yield the same general conclusions, provided only that the rate of technological advance more than offset the effect of rising demand.

QUESTIONS AND EXERCISES

1. Draw supply and demand schedules for the product of an industry.
   - *a*) Directly to the left of this diagram draw a graph of the perfectly elastic demand curve that is faced by a typical firm in this industry, showing how this individual firm demand curve is related to the supply and demand conditions for the industry as a whole.
   - *b*) In the diagram for the individual firm, draw in the average total cost and marginal cost curves for a typical firm under the assumption that the industry is in long-run equilibrium.
   - *c*) Suppose now that there is an increase in industry demand. Trace through the effects of this increase in demand on the industry and the typical firm by reference to the two diagrams.

2. In the digram of Figure 13–3A assume, when the price of input No. 1 rises from w_1 to w_1', that it no longer pays to produce an output y. Instead, assume that the best rate of output is $y' < y$. Draw a new diagram analogous to Figure 13–3A, which contains the iso-product contour for y', and which shows how the purchase of x_1 is effected by the combination of an increase in w_1 and the resulting reduction in output. How is Figure 13–3B modified when we relax the assumption that output is held constant?

3. Regions and industries that have suffered economic decline have been given relief by various means through congressional legislation. "Distressed areas" have been given priority for receiving defense contracts, tariffs have been employed to reduce foreign competition, and the prices of certain raw materials and agricultural products have been bolstered by government stockpiling. An alternative proposal has been a program to subsidize the moving and retraining of employees from regions or occupations in economic decline to those that are growing. Analyze and contrast the possible short- and long-run effects of the two types of programs.

4. Reconstruct the analysis of Section 13.5 for an industry whose demand is relatively elastic, and in which technological change does not affect the equilibrium size of the firm, that is, the *ATC* curves simply shift vertically downward. Compare the results of your analysis with the conclusions of Section 13.5.

Chapter 14   MONEY AND BANKING

In the first thirteen chapters of this book, our concern has been with the forces that determine the prices of particular commodities. Such detailed studies belong to the branch of economics called microeconomics. We now turn to another branch of economics. This branch of our study is called macroeconomics, and it is concerned with the broad interrelationships which exist in the economy—wide aggregates and averages, for example, total output, total consumption expenditures, the average level of prices, and the total quantity of money in circulation. The study of macroeconomics has greatly deepened our understanding of what determines the general level of economic activity—the level of employment and total income—in a private enterprise economy.

In Chapter 6 we analyzed some interrelationships which exist in the economic system by referring, for illustration, to a circular flow diagram of economic life. The assumptions made for that diagram and the description of the interrelationship of economic forces which accompanied it were very specific. It should be recalled that money as such played a neutral role; there were neither increases nor decreases in the average of all prices coming from changes in the role of money. Furthermore, no provisions were made for growth in the economy, or for instability leading to inflation or depression. It is now necessary to alter our simple assumptions by considering the effect of changing the money supply, of alterations in the extent of saving and investment which occur for the economy, of the impact of government spending and taxation, and of the role of international trade and finance.

14.1. The Functions of Money

The major economic phenomena with which we have concerned ourselves thus far have been specialization and exchange. In order that specialization may take place, there must be a means for the specialist to exchange the result of his productive effort for the products produced by others. It has already been indicated that the extent of specialization is limited by the extent of the market. Of very great importance to the economist is the development of the devices by which exchange is carried on. One of the principal economic institutions of the modern world is the institution of money as a means for facilitating exchange. Without some kind of money, exchanges could only be carried on by means of bartering. It does not require much imagination to think of the difficulties which would be encountered if each party to an exchange had to have, at the moment the exchange took place, commodities of equal value and desirability wanted by the other partner to the transaction. In fact, even in primitive societies, some device for facilitating exchange was developed. For instance, on the island of Yap, giant circular stones were used for "money," in that exchanges were reckoned in terms of the passing of possession of these immovable stones from one party to another.

Today, the primary functions of money are for facilitating exchanges. Money acts as a *medium of exchange.* Money can be received and paid for the desired amount, quality, style, size, at the time and place of receiving goods. This lessens the time and effort required in exchange and removes the necessity of there being a double coincidence of wants as is required under barter.

Secondly, money acts as a *standard of value.* It serves as a measuring standard to determine the value of goods. The values of goods which are physically very different, with uncomparable units of measurement, may be compared in terms of money.

Arising out of the two primary functions of money come two additional functions. Money acts as a store of value and as a standard for deferred payments. Even in the normal act of exchange, money holds value until the next transaction in which the holder spends his money. Over a longer period of time, money has been an imperfect store of value, in that its own worth is subject to change. As a standard of deferred payment, one may contract to pay a specific sum, valued in terms of money, at some future time.

An adequate definition for money, then, might be one which says that anything is money that is generally accepted as a medium of exchange, a standard of value, a store of value, and a standard for deferred payments. When nothing better suffices, people have used cigarettes, tobacco, buckskin, sea shells, metal, and paper as money. Whatever is acceptable to the people of an economy for performing the functions of money has been made money. It should be apparent, then, that money does not acquire its acceptability and its own value from the intrinsic worth of the commodities used for money but from something else, its relative scarcity and its universal acceptability. After an examination has been made of the monetary system of the United States, we shall return to the problem of the determination of the value of money.

14.2. Monetary System of the United States

The two major classes of money which perform the above functions in the United States and, indeed, in any modern economy, are national currency and demand deposits subject to check (checking accounts). The tabulation in Table 14–1 shows the distribution of the money supply of this country by type of money.

TABLE 14–1

UNITED STATES MONEY, IN CIRCULATION, BY KINDS

December 31, 1961

	Money in Circulation* (In Millions of Dollars)
Federal Reserve notes	28,694
Treasury currency—total	5,224
Standard silver dollars	346
Silver certificates and Treasury notes of 1890	2,090
Subsidiary silver coin	1,622
Minor coin	614
Other Treasury currency	552
Total Federal Currency	33,918
All banks, demand deposits subject to check.† (Dec. 27, 1961)	143,630

    * Outside Treasury and Federal Reserve banks. Includes any paper currency held outside the continental limits of the United States.
    † Excluding interbank deposits.
    Source: *Federal Reserve Bulletin.*

The major classes of national currency in circulation today are Federal Reserve notes and silver certificates. The monetary gold is held by the U.S. Treasury, principally at Fort Knox, Kentucky, and is represented in paper form by gold certificates which are held by the Federal Reserve banks. These gold certificates are, in turn, the legal reserves of the Federal Reserve banks against Federal Reserve notes and deposits, as will be explained in Chapter 15. The few gold certificates still in circulation may be presumed to be lost or hoarded. The standard silver dollars, subsidiary silver coin (halves, quarters, and dimes), and minor coin are self-explanatory. The other Treasury currency includes United States notes, Federal Reserve bank notes, and national bank notes, which exist as a carry-over from monetary laws of earlier days.

The Federal Reserve notes are issued by the Federal Reserve banks, under requirements which will be examined in the next chapter. It can be said here that the Federal Reserve banks are bankers' banks which act as regulators of the monetary system. The silver certificates are issued in small denominations, $1, $2, $5, and $10. This currency is issued by the U.S. Treasury and is based upon Treasury purchases of silver.

By far the most important form of money in this country, and, indeed, in all modern national economic systems, is the demand deposits which are held by private commercial banks. A majority of payments is made by means of checks, not through the payment of cash. In fact, it has been estimated that about 90 per cent of all transactions, by volume, are effected through the use of checks. Consequently, the major part of our analysis of the money supply has to do with the determinants of the amount and activity of demand deposits as a form of money.

One should recognize the difference between demand deposits and savings deposits of banks. One can spend a demand deposit without going near the bank, by merely writing checks for payments of various sorts. Savings deposits, on the other hand, can be spent only by withdrawing those deposits from banks in the form of cash or checks. A savings deposit is not money, even though it is "near-money" because of the ease with which it may be converted into money.

14.3. Commercial Banks

The beginning student of money and banking usually has the preconceived notion that banks have the primary function of lending out the savings of their depositors. This is the primary function of a very limited class of banks, the *savings banks,* or the savings departments of banks. They accept the savings of people and invest the proceeds in high-grade securities of various sorts. In this manner they are able to diversify the small savings of many persons into a variety of investments, and hence collect the savings of the community and spread the risks of investment over a variety of undertakings. The savings banks, like other financial intermediaries, put the liquid savings of people into borrowers' hands and thus increase the velocity with which money is used. In our study of the monetary system, this type of bank will not be of primary interest.

Our major interest is in *commercial banks,* which in our monetary system are able to *create money* in the form of demand deposits subject to check. Their primary function is to make loans, mostly to the business community, in the form of demand deposit credit, which is nothing more than the granting of the right to write checks. Since checking accounts are the most important component of the money supply of the country, it is important for us to understand just how the commercial banking system functions and to what extent commercial banks have the power of creating money.

When a commercial bank makes a loan, the initial effect of the loan is an addition to the money supply in the form of the demand deposit which is created. An example of the change in the statement of condition of a commercial bank as the consequence of a loan transaction appears, for illustration, below.[1] There is a loan made by a commercial bank, evidenced by the increase in the asset, Loans, by the amount of $10,000. The bank gives the borrower credit in the form of a deposit. Therefore, the liability of the bank, Demand Deposits, also increases, by $10,000. At the same time, the borrower's statement of condition will have changed by an increase in its assets, Demand Deposits, $10,000, and an increase in its liabilities, Notes Payable, $10,000. In this transaction it should be noted that all that has happened is that the borrower has exchanged his credit (a note), which is not generally acceptable as money, for the bank's credit (a demand deposit), which is more generally acceptable as money. When the borrower writes checks against that deposit he is spending without having drawn cash from the bank.

COMMERCIAL BANK

ASSETS		LIABILITIES	
Loans..................	+$10,000	Demand deposits..........	+$10,000

PUBLIC (Borrowers)

ASSETS		LIABILITIES	
Demand deposits in comm'l bank...........	+$10,000	Notes payable to comm'l bank.................	+$10,000

A borrower from a savings bank, on the other hand, is given a check on *another bank,* a commercial bank, as is shown in the figures which follow. This is because the savings bank is not authorized to hold checking accounts, or demand deposits subject to check. Borrowers of

---

[1] Assets are property and property rights which an organization owns; liabilities are claims against the organization. When there is an addition to assets there must be an increase in liabilities or a decrease in other assets in order for the statement of condition to show that all assets are owed to others in the form of liabilities. Similarly, a decrease in one asset requires either a decrease in liabilities or an increase in other assets. Also, for an increase in liabilities, there must be a decrease in other liabilities or an increase in assets. For a more detailed explanation of a balance sheet, that is, a statement of assets and liabilities, see Chapter 7, Section 7.5.

large sums are then given checks on other banks, the commercial banks, in which the savings bank keeps funds which it is willing to loan. The borrower from the savings bank, by receiving the check, becomes the holder of a deposit in the commercial bank, and the savings bank reduces its deposit with the commercial bank by the amount of the check.

COMMERCIAL BANK

ASSETS	LIABILITIES
	Demand deposit of savings bank..................−$10,000
	Demand deposit of sav. b'k debtor..............+$10,000

PUBLIC (Borrowers)

ASSETS	LIABILITIES
Demand deposits in comm'l bank...........+$10,000	Notes payable to savings bank.................+$10,000

The borrower from the savings bank does not receive a newly created deposit, since there is no net change in commercial bank demand deposits.

What happens to the deposit after it has been spent, through the writing of checks, is important for us to recognize, for it is here that the reality of the creation of deposits by commercial banks becomes clear.

14.4.   The Clearing of Checks

There are about 13,500 commercial banks in the United States today, and, although less than one half of these banks are member banks of the Federal Reserve System,[2] a majority of bank deposits are held in banks which are "member banks." Other banks may keep balances with the Federal Reserve banks; member banks are required to keep balances on deposit with the "Fed," as the system of Federal Reserve banks is called.

One of the principal tasks of the Federal Reserve banks is the handling of a national check collection system. If the check on the commercial bank referred to in Section 14.3 is sent to a party who is located in another city, he will deposit or cash that check at a bank in his own locality. That bank will, quite probably, send the check, along with other out of town checks received that day, to the Federal Reserve bank of its district. The commercial bank (hereafter called Bank B) will receive an increase in its deposit with its Federal Reserve bank by the amount of the check, either immediately or within two days, de-

[2] A description of the organization and functions of the Federal Reserve System appears in the next chapter.

pending on how remote the paying bank is from the bank which first received the check. If the check is drawn on another bank in the same Federal Reserve district, the Federal Reserve bank will forward the check to the paying bank where the deposit of the drawer of the check will be reduced by the face value of the check. The paying bank will be required to remit to the Federal Reserve bank payment for the check, which will decrease the deposit balance of the commercial bank with the Federal Reserve. Consequently, Bank B will have increased its balance with the "Fed" by the amount of the check and the paying bank, Bank A, will have had its balance at the "Fed" reduced by the amount of the check. If the check was for $10,000, the change in balance sheets for the two banks involved will be as follows:

BANK A

ASSETS		LIABILITIES	
Deposit with the Federal Reserve bank (legal reserves)	−$10,000	Deposits	−$10,000

BANK B

ASSETS		LIABILITIES	
Deposit with the Federal Reserve bank (reserves)	+$10,000	Demand deposits	+$10,000

FEDERAL RESERVE BANK

ASSETS		LIABILITIES	
		Member bank reserve account	
		Deposits of Bank A	−$10,000
		Deposits of Bank B	+$10,000

It seems that a bank may not lend money which it does not possess, for the writing of checks against deposits causes the deposits to be extinguished and cash or reserves to be withdrawn from the bank. Before this idea is accepted too matter-of-factly, we should hasten to point out that not all of the checks being written on Bank A during one day must be paid by Bank A through a reduction of its cash or reserve balance. There will also be checks being received at Bank A for deposit. These checks will be forwarded for payment, and the clearing process may have the effect of bringing about an approximate balance between the checks which are received and those which are paid. In such a case there would be little or no change in the size of the item "Deposit with the Federal Reserve banks." It would follow that if all banks are expanding their loans at approximately the same rate, there is little need for excess reserves on the part of the lending banks, for the clearing mechanism brings about an offset of checks being received or paid in with those being paid out.

Two other aspects of bank clearing should be mentioned. In the first place, the original check may have been deposited with another bank in the vicinity of the bank on which the check is drawn. In this case it is possible that the two banks involved are members of the same clearinghouse. At the clearinghouse each bank presents daily the checks which it has honored and which are drawn on other members of the clearinghouse. Here too, payments tend to equal receipts, with differences only being required to be settled through the payment of cash, at regular intervals.

In the second place, the checks which are forwarded to a Federal Reserve bank for collection may be payable in another Federal Reserve district. In this event the check is mailed to the Federal Reserve bank of the district of the bank on which the check is drawn, and collection is made as above. The Federal Reserve banks daily inform the Interdistrict Settlement Fund in Washington, D.C. of the value of checks on other Federal Reserve districts which they have mailed for collection. The Interdistrict Settlement Fund makes a bookkeeping entry of the amounts involved, and differences are settled by the bookkeeping transfer of the ownership of a sum of gold certificates which is held by that Fund for that purpose.

Finally, depositors of a bank may present their checks to be paid in cash at the counter of the bank on which the checks are drawn. Unless there is a change in the holding of cash on the part of the local community as that cash is spent, it will be returned to banks as cash deposits by the merchants who have received it. Consequently, the banks need only sufficient cash to meet the time differences between withdrawals and redeposits, under ordinary conditions. As a matter of actual practice, banks only hold about 2 per cent of deposits in the form of cash to cover withdrawals which might take place.

14.5. *Earnings vs. Liquidity and Solvency*

A bank must meet all current claims for cash. As a consequence, the managers of banks are required to keep sufficient cash on hand to meet immediate and normal claims and to be able to convert a sufficient volume of earning assets into cash, as the need may arise, to meet any future and abnormal withdrawal of cash. The assets of the banks will be divided among primary reserves and earning assets. The primary reserves consist of cash in the bank, balances with banks, including reserves deposited with the Federal Reserve banks, and cash items in process of collection. Balances with banks will be the balances held at the Federal Reserve banks, as mentioned above, plus any balances maintained in other banks as a convenience for normal banking business. Cash items in process of collection will consist of the checks which have been honored but which have not yet been paid by the banks on which they are drawn or for which credit in another bank has not yet been granted. These items in the assets of a bank are essentially liquid.

Earning assets represent loans and investments on which the bank receives interest. From the point of view of earnings, it is desirable that primary reserves be as small as possible and that earning assets be invested at as high a rate of interest as possible. From the point of view of liquidity, it is desirable that primary reserves be large and that earning assets be invested in easily salable values, even though the interest rate on highly liquid investments may be low. From the point of view of solvency it is necessary that earning assets not be sold at a loss when it is necessary to convert them into cash, for a decline in asset values such that the liabilities of the bank exceed the assets would bring insolvency and failure.

Failure of many bankers in time past to maintain the necessary liquidity has resulted in bank regulation. Today, all banks must keep a certain percentage of their deposits as required reserves. The required reserves of Federal Reserve member banks are made up of cash on hand and deposits kept with the Federal Reserve banks of their districts. The required reserves are the most nonliquid of bank assets, since they are required to be held. However, the pooling of the required reserves of many banks at the Federal Reserve banks makes it possible for the Federal Reserve banks to make loans to commercial banks and savings banks which are in need of cash to meet the claims of depositors.

In the past, runs on banks have taken place when depositors feared that their banks might be unable to meet their claims. Since not all banks can convert earning assets into cash at once, for there must be some holder of cash to whom the assets can be sold, widespread bank panic has led to the failure of otherwise sound banks. This danger to the banking system has been lessened by the creation of the Federal Reserve System, to which banks can go to borrow against certain assets, and by the creation of the Federal Deposit Insurance Corporation. The Federal Deposit Insurance Corporation insures deposits, up to $10,000 per depositor, in insured banks. The F.D.I.C. will give the depositors cash or a deposit in a sound bank in the event the insured bank fails. The very existence of this assurance has ended the periodic waves of bank panic that once swept the country.

14.6   The Generation of Bank Credit

There are two limits to the creation of deposits by banks. These are the bankers' own prudence and the legal reserve requirements imposed on the banks. The bankers' prudence establishes the size of *working reserves* that the banks hold. The reserve requirements establish the size of *required reserves* which the banks must have. Legal reserves are made up of all of the cash on hand, both till money and vault cash, plus the amount on deposit with the Federal Reserve bank of the district. The difference between this sum and the amount the bank is required to maintain is called the excess reserve or the working reserve. This includes the till money or cash that turns over regularly plus any excess in the reserves deposited with the Federal Reserve bank. However, the size of cash on hand as till money and vault cash holdings is kept as small as possible in order to minimize the danger of loss through theft, because most loans result in the writing of checks rather than the withdrawal of cash against the deposits created by the loan, and because most investments of banks represent purchases of securities acquired in the money market of the big cities rather than through local over-the-counter purchases. Therefore we are able to generalize that the funds available for the expansion of bank credit are the excess reserves in the Federal Reserve banks.

Let us assume that a bank has $1,000,000 of demand deposits against which it must keep 20 per cent required reserves (savings deposits are here ignored, although small required reserves must be held against them as well), and that available legal reserves are $300,000. Since,

$$ER = LR - RR$$

where ER = excess reserves, LR = available legal reserves, and RR = required reserves, and with r = reserve requirements, then

$$ER = \$300,000 - (.20)(\$1,000,000), \text{ or}$$
$$ER = \$300,000 - \$200,000 = \$100,000 .$$

The bank has $100,000 of excess reserves against which it can make loans or invest. This $100,000 represents the basis for an increase in loans by $100,000 above the amount that the bank has been lending, all of which may be withdrawn through the check collection system. However, the bank's required reserve position would remain unimpaired, for other reserves and other deposits would be unaffected. The procedure of a bank with $100,000 in excess reserves making loans in the amount of $100,000 is illustrated as follows:

BANK A

ASSETS		LIABILITIES	
Excess reserves.......	$100,000		
(1) Loans..............	+ 100,000	Deposits...............	+$100,000

The loans will result in the writing of checks against the deposit which has been created. These checks will be cleared through the Federal Reserve bank (2):

F.R.B.

ASSETS	LIABILITIES	
	Deposit (Bank A).......	−$100,000
(2)	Deposit (Bank B).......	+ 100,000

Consequently the condition of Bank A will change as follows:

BANK A

ASSETS		LIABILITIES	
(3) Excess reserves.......	−$100,000	Deposits...............	−$100,000
Loans..............	$100,000		

Bank B, with added deposits and legal reserves (4), given a 20 per cent reserve requirement, will be able to create loans and deposits (5) which, when the deposits are withdrawn (6), will have completed the following steps:

BANK B

ASSETS		LIABILITIES	
(4) Reserves............	+$100,000	Deposits...............	+$100,000
(5) Loans..............	+ 80,000	Deposits...............	+ 80,000
(6) Reserves............	− 80,000	Deposits...............	− 80,000

However, the step (6) above would only be accomplished after the Federal Reserve bank had reduced Bank B's reserve deposit by $80,-000 in favor of still other banks, called here Bank C. Bank C will be able to go through similar steps with the new reserves received through the deposit of checks with it:

BANK C

ASSETS		LIABILITIES	
(7) Reserves............	+$80,000	Deposits...............	+$80,000
(8) Loans..............	+ 64,000	Deposits...............	+ 64,000
(9) Reserves............	− 64,000	Deposits...............	− 64,000

The total of demand deposits created thus far in the process of expansion through the banking system on the basis of the original $100,000 of excess reserves has been $100,000 + $80,000 + $64,000 and, for Banks D and E, it would extend to + $51,200 + $40,960. The total quantity of demand deposits or checking accounts that could be created as the series continues would approach

$$100,000[1 + .8 + (.8)^2 + \ldots] = \frac{100,000}{0.20} = 500,000$$

or, in general,

$$ER_0[1 + (1 - r) + (1 - r)^2 + \ldots]; \text{ or } \frac{ER_0}{r}$$

where ER_0 = initial excess reserves in the banking system and r = reserve ratio required against demand deposits.[3] Thus, the total position of all banks combined as a result of the existence of the initial excess reserves of $100,000 would be:

ALL BANKS

ASSETS		LIABILITIES	
(10) Reserves	$100,000	Demand deposits	+$500,000
Loans	+ 400,000		

The banking *system,* by creating bank deposits on a fractional reserve basis, has been able to create additions to the money supply. That such additions to the money supply have come into existence during and since World War II can be demonstrated by reference to Table 14–2.

TABLE 14–2

ALL COMMERCIAL BANKS IN THE UNITED STATES, PRINCIPAL ASSETS AND
LIABILITIES, SELECTED DATES
(Amounts in Millions of Dollars)

	Dec. 30, 1939	Dec. 31, 1945	Dec.27, 1961†
ASSETS			
Cash Assets*	22,474	34,806	52,330
Loans	17,238	26,083	125,230
U.S. government obligations	16,316	90,606	66,480
Other securities	7,114	7,331	23,900
Total Loans and Investments	40,668	124,020	215,610
Other Assets	2,074	1,486	6,350
Total Assets	65,216	160,312	274,290
LIABILITIES AND CAPITAL ACCOUNTS			
Interbank deposits	9,874	14,065	16,570
Demand deposits	32,513	105,921	143,570
Time deposits‡	15,331	30,241	81,960
Total Deposits	57,718	150,227	242,100
Other Liabilities	613	1,135	9,770
Capital Accounts	6,885	8,950	22,420
Total Liabilities and Capital Accounts	65,216	160,312	274,290

* Cash assets include balance with banks including Federal Reserve banks.
† Preliminary.
‡ Time deposits include and are mainly savings deposits.
Source: *Federal Reserve Bulletin.*

The expansion of bank credit to the extent shown above is possible, on a given basis of excess reserves, only if there is no increase in

[3] The sum of the geometric series $S_n = 1 + (1 - r) + (1 - r)^2 + \ldots + (1 - r)^{n-1}$ can be written $S_n = \dfrac{1 - (1 - r)^n}{1 - (1 - r)}$ and $\lim_{n \to \infty} S_n = \dfrac{1}{1 - (1 - r)} = \dfrac{1}{r}$.

the holdings of cash by the general public as a consequence of the increased volume of checking accounts in existence and only if each bank is completely willing and able to lend and invest in securities to the amount of its excess reserves. For if any leakage of the excess reserves into cash held by the public took place, the extent of that leakage would reduce the amount of excess reserves available for the expansion of bank credit. Similarly, any holding of the excess reserves by banks as increased working reserves would have the effect of limiting the expansion of bank credit which could take place.

Furthermore, it is important to realize that expansion and contraction in the total money supply comes as a result of demand deposit increases when more new loans are being incurred than there are outstanding loans being paid off, and demand deposits decrease when more loans are being paid off than new ones are being incurred. The expansion in money supply since 1939 is largely attributable to the considerable increase in the size of bank held debt, including Federal Reserve credit, in the twenty-two years between the end of 1939 and the end of 1961.

14.7. Demand Deposit Money and National Currency

The money supply of the country is made up of national currency, M, and demand deposit money, M'. Total money is, therefore,

$$M_T \equiv M + M' .$$

Except in extremely unusual cases, M_T increases only when M' increases. The analysis in the section above implies that M, national currency in circulation, does not increase when a loan is made. The increase in the money supply of the country takes place in the form of the increase in demand deposits of banks as a consequence of the expansion of bank credit in the country on the basis of excess reserves.

When national currency in circulation increases, it is at the expense of demand deposits. More checks are being written for cash than there is cash being deposited in banks, as shown by the changes which take place for a bank, Bank A, and for the public, in the accompanying partial balance sheets.

BANK A

ASSETS		LIABILITIES	
(11) Cash................	−$1,000	Demand deposits...........	−$1,000

PUBLIC

ASSETS		LIABILITIES
(11) Demand deposits......	−$1,000	
(11) Cash................	+ 1,000	

If the bank feels that its holding of cash for till money and vault cash is being seriously depleted by cash withdrawals, it can withdraw cash from the Federal Reserve bank. If it withdraws Federal Reserve notes, a Federal Reserve bank liability, Federal Reserve notes outstanding increases, and another liability, the reserves of member banks, decreases. If the commercial bank withdraws other cash, such as subsidiary silver coin, the Federal Reserve bank loses an asset and reduces its liabilities.

The total changes in the position of the commercial bank, Bank A, could be shown as follows, where (11) refers to the withdrawal of cash by the public and (12) shows the replenishment of cash by the commercial bank through the withdrawal of cash from the Federal Reserve bank when the commercial bank draws on its excess reserve.

BANK A

ASSETS		LIABILITIES	
(11) Cash	−$1,000	Demand deposits	−$1,000
(12) Reserves	− 1,000		
(12) Cash	+ 1,000		

For the Federal Reserve bank, the changes in its statement of condition might reveal the following:[4]

F.R.B.

ASSETS		LIABILITIES	
(12) Treasury currency	−$100	Federal Reserve notes	+$ 900
		Deposits (Bank A)	− 1,000

Whenever there is a net drain of cash into the hands of the public, such as occurs at the Christmas shopping season, the banks rebuild their cash on hand by converting a portion of their reserve deposit assets into cash. The Federal Reserve banks supply this cash. It is the ability of the Federal Reserve authorities to supply additional cash to meet seasonal or unusual needs that gives the banking system its liquidity and provides for elasticity in the supply of cash in the country. If a bank needing cash has no excess reserves on which to draw it will have to sell some of its earning assets or borrow from the Federal Reserve bank, or other lenders. It is through its ability to control the access of banks to Federal Reserve deposits that the Federal Reserve authorities are able to control the money supply of the country.

[4] Note that the division between Federal Reserve notes and Treasury currency is a purely arbitrary one for purposes of illustration only. The division could be made in any fashion.

QUESTIONS AND EXERCISES

1. The following member banks, all in the same Federal Reserve district, receive checks on other banks to the following extent:

Received by ↓	Drawn on⟶ Bank A	Bank B	Bank C	Bank D
Bank A	—	11,000	25,000	13,000
Bank B	13,000	—	11,000	25,000
Bank C	27,000	12,000	—	10,000
Bank D	10,000	17,000	22,000	—

By how much are member bank reserve accounts in total diminished? By how much is the reserve account of each bank altered?

2. A commercial bank has the following items in its balance sheet: Cash $15,-000, capital accounts $100,000, investments $250,000, deposits $850,000, loans $560,000, surplus $50,000, balance with Federal Reserve bank $125,-000, building $50,000.

   a) Arrange the items in proper balance sheet form.

   b) Has it too small an amount of cash on hand to meet ordinary needs?

   c) If the required reserve ratio is 15 per cent, what is the size of excess reserves?

   d) By how much would asset values have to shrink for the bank to become insolvent?

   e) Which are primary reserves? Earning assets?

3. A bank with $150,000 of excess reserves has the following operations performed in one hour of the working day: (a) cash withdrawal $80,000 (b) checks drawn on other banks received for deposits $60,000; (c) loans made $50,000; (d) cash deposits $30,000.

   (1) Trace each operation by showing appropriate changes on the bank's balance sheet.

   (2) What is the size of excess reserves at the end of the hour if required reserve ratio is 15 per cent?

4. A bank has $100,000.00 of excess reserves. Trace the expansion of bank credit made possible from these excess reserves, using balance sheet charts, with the stipulation that: for Banks A and B the required reserve ratio, r, is 20 per cent; for banks from C on, the required ratio is 10 per cent; at Bank D, borrowers withdraw one half of their borrowings in cash which does not return to the banking system.

5. Get one of the published statements of the bank where you keep your checking account. Determine the size of needed cash balances based on normal requirements, the reserve ratio, the size of excess reserves (use current reserve requirement ratio) and the ratio between liabilities and capital accounts.

6. A student deposits checks from home at his local bank twice a month. He withdraws all of his account prior to each new deposit by means of writing a series of checks for ordinary expenses.

   a) What kind of investment can the bank make with this active balance?

   b) Are there any costs for the bank in administering this account?

Chapter
15

MONEY AND BANKING
(Continued)

15.1. *The Organization of the Federal Reserve System*

In the description of the factors which lead to changes in the money supply, we have made repeated reference to the Federal Reserve System, to the member banks, and to the Federal Reserve banks. The principal structural elements of the Federal Reserve System are the Board of Governors of the Federal Reserve System, the twelve Federal Reserve banks in twelve Federal Reserve districts, and the member banks. When the Federal Reserve System was created, by national law, in 1913, there was considerable expression of fear in the country of the power which a single central bank, located on Wall Street, would have over the money supply. As a compromise of opposing political points of view, twelve central banks were established; nevertheless, it was essential that there be one unified control agency for policy purposes. Therefore, the original law, and subsequent amendments to it, created the Board of Governors of the Federal Reserve System, with substantial powers to control the operation and policies of the twelve banks.

The Board of Governors consists of seven members, each appointed by the President of the United States, to serve a fourteen-year term. The appointment by the President has the effect of making the members of the Board independent of the wishes of any of the banks or other private interests of the country. At the same time, the length of the term of office helps to keep the Board members free from political control. In the hands of the Board of Governors lie powers over the management of each of the Federal Reserve banks, and, to a certain extent, over the member banks. Their principal importance to us, however, lies in the powers they possess to control the expansion of bank credit, to which we shall refer more extensively later.

The twelve Federal Reserve banks, one for each of twelve Federal

Reserve districts into which the country has been divided, hold the legal reserves of the member banks of their districts. These Federal Reserve banks are owned by the member banks, in that each member bank is required to subscribe 6 per cent of its own capital stock and surplus, one half of which is paid in, to capital stock in its Federal Reserve bank. Dividends on this stock are limited by law to an annual return of 6 per cent on the paid-in stock, at par value. Consequently, the member banks, as owners of the Federal Reserve banks, are limited in their influence over the policies of the Federal Reserve banks toward the making of greater profits. Each Federal Reserve bank has nine directors, three of whom are appointed by the Board of Governors, and six are selected by the member banks of the district. The chairman of the Board of Directors of a Federal Reserve bank is one of the three members who is appointed by the Board of Governors. He is the Federal Reserve agent for that bank. In addition, the president and vice-presidents of the Federal Reserve banks, who are their executive officers, are appointed by the Boards of Directors for each bank but subject to the approval of the Board of Governors.

The member banks, besides owning the stock of the Federal Reserve banks and holding deposits (defined as legal reserves) in the Federal Reserve banks, are subject to examination by Federal Reserve bank examiners and must obey the laws and rules set up for member banks. All national banks, banks which have received their charters from the national government, are member banks of the Federal Reserve System. State banks and trust companies may become member banks if they wish to do so and comply with the requirements for membership. About 85 per cent of bank deposits in this country are held by member banks of the Federal Reserve System.

In addition, the Federal Open Market Committee consists of the seven members of the Board of Governors plus five of the twelve Federal Reserve bank presidents. It supervises the open-market operations of the Federal Reserve banks through an open-market operations manager whose office is located at the Federal Reserve Bank of New York. There is also the Federal Reserve agent for each Federal Reserve bank who controls the issuance of Federal Reserve notes, superintending the collateral which is placed as security behind the notes. Finally the Federal Advisory Council includes men appointed from each of the twelve Federal Reserve banks. It meets periodically with the Board of Governors in a purely advisory capacity, to assist it in its function of controlling the expansion of credit in the United States.

15.2. The Operations of the Federal Reserve System

The Federal Reserve banks are bankers' banks; together they make up the *central bank* of the United States. As such, their primary interest is in the control they possess over the expansion of the money supply. They do not, except under special provisions of the law, make loans or hold deposits of the general public, but they do hold the deposits of the member banks and extend loans and rediscount eligible paper[1] for member banks. In addition, the Federal Reserve banks issue money, in the form of Federal Reserve notes, to supply the principal part of the national currency of the country. They carry on operations necessary to the smooth functioning of the American banking system and the

TABLE 15–1

STATEMENT OF CONDITION OF THE FEDERAL RESERVE BANKS
December 31, 1961
(In Billions of Dollars)

ASSETS		LIABILITIES	
Gold certificates	16.6	Federal Reserve notes	28.8
Currency	.3	Deposits:	
Federal Reserve credit:		Member bank reserve account	17.4
Discounts and Advances	.2	U.S. Treasurer—general account	.5
U.S. government securities	28.9	Other deposits	.6
Other Assets	6.5	Other liabilities and capital accounts	5.2
Total Assets	52.5	Total Liabilities	52.5

Source: *Federal Reserve Bulletin.*

convenience of the United States Treasury. These are the operations of the Federal Reserve check collection system, the wire transfer service, and activities performed as fiscal agent of the Treasury. The Federal Reserve Board supervises the operation of the member banks, establishing rules under the law for the regulation of the activity of the member banks and their officers and directors. The major function of the Federal Reserve System is making available and controlling the legal reserves of the commercial banks, by which it attempts to assure the liquidity of commercial banks and at the same time provide an elastic money supply to cover the nation's varying needs for money to promote maximum economic stability and full employment in the country.

An analysis of a statement of condition of the twelve Federal Reserve banks will help us to understand the way in which these functions are carried out. In Table 15–1, the leading asset is gold certificates.

[1] Eligible paper represents evidences of loans to business of good quality, due to the form of the paper and the time it has to run.

United States law requires that all monetary gold be held by the U.S. Treasury. Against that gold the Treasury has issued gold certificates, backed 100 per cent by gold, to the Federal Reserve banks. When gold is purchased by the Treasury, payment is made by check. These checks are forwarded to the Federal Reserve banks by the banks which have received them on deposit, where the deposit of the U.S. Treasurer is decreased by the amount of the checks, and the deposits of the commercial banks which had received the checks are increased by the amount of the checks. When the Treasury forwards to the Federal Reserve banks gold certificates issued against that gold, the Treasury's deposit balance with the Federal Reserve is replenished. In this way the receipt of gold from newly mined gold or gold imports adds to the money supply of the country,[2] in that it results in the increase in the size of member bank reserve accounts, at least part of which will be excess reserves and which can then become the base for multiple expansion of bank credit. Similarly, an outflow of gold from the country, with a contraction of gold certificate holdings by the Federal Reserve banks, would cause a decrease in legal reserves of member banks and a possible multiple contraction in bank credit.

The foregoing analysis of the mechanism by which new gold becomes money in the form of deposits in member banks and increased reserve balances in Federal Reserve banks is illustrated with the series of statements of condition which appear, as follows:

PUBLIC

(Gold Mining Companies or Importers of Gold)

ASSETS	LIABILITIES
(1) Gold holdings........ —$1,000,000	
(1) Checks on U.S. Treasury........... + 1,000,000	
(2) Checks on U.S. Treasury........... − 1,000,000	
(2) Demand deposits......+ 1,000,000	

In (1) gold is sold to the U.S. Treasury for checks on the Treasurer of the United States. In (2) the checks on the Treasurer of the United States are deposited in banks, and can later be drawn on to effect payments.

The commercial banks receive the checks on the Treasurer of the United States as a deposit by customers in (2). These checks are honored by the Federal Reserve bank, the fiscal agent of the U.S. Treasury, in (3). Part of the reserve deposit of the member banks becomes re-

---

[2] Gold purchases are a minor source of additions to money supply under ordinary conditions as compared with the creation of deposits through loans by commercial banks.

COMMERCIAL BANKS

ASSETS		LIABILITIES
(2) Cash items in process of collection..........+$1,000,000		Demand deposits.........+$1,000,000
(3) `` − 1,000,000		
(3) Reserves............+ 1,000,000		
[required reserves... (r) ($1,000,000)]		
[excess reserves.. $(1−r)$ ($1,000,000)]		

quired reserves against the increased deposit, and the remainder becomes excess reserves and as such are the potential basis for an expansion in the money supply.

The Federal Reserve banks charge the deposit account of the U.S. Treasury when they honor the checks issued for the gold (3). The reserve accounts of the member banks are increased by the amount of the checks (3). When the U.S. Treasury issues gold certificates to the Federal Reserve banks, its deposit balance with the Reserve banks is restored (4). In the meantime, the Treasury holding of gold has been increased and its Federal Reserve deposit account decreased by the purchase of the gold (1).

FEDERAL RESERVE BANK

ASSETS		LIABILITIES
(3)		U.S. Treasury deposit......−$1,000,000
(3)		Member banks reserve deposits.............+ 1,000,000
(4) Gold certificates......+$1,000,000		U.S. Treasury deposit......+ 1,000,000

U.S. TREASURY

ASSETS		LIABILITIES
(1) Deposits with F.R.B...−$1,000,000		
(1) Gold...............+ 1,000,000		
(4) Deposits with F.R.B...+ 1,000,000		Gold certificates.........+$1,000,000

Observe the following conclusions which can be derived from the above analysis:

1. U.S. Treasury gold-buying policy is not a cost to the American taxpayer. The Treasury pays for the gold out of deposits obtained from tax receipts, as in transaction (1) above, but by issuing gold certificates on the gold the Treasury rebuilds its deposit to the previous level, as in transaction (4), by "monetizing" gold.

2. Treasury purchases of gold have an inflationary effect on the economy in that *a*) the quantity of money in circulation is increased directly by an amount equal to the value of the gold purchased, and *b*) commercial bank excess reserves are increased, thus providing a base on which further additions to the money supply can be made by commercial bank loan activity.

3. Insofar as the Treasury purchases gold, the supply of money in the economy is not responsive to the needs of the community but instead is responsive to the output of U.S. gold mines and shifts in the pattern of international trade.

4. Treasury policy of standing ready to purchase all gold offered to it at a pegged price of $35 per ounce has the effect of maintaining an artificial demand for gold, thereby restricting the industrial uses of gold and diverting resources of other industries to gold mining. Gold purchase policy amounts to price supports for the gold-mining industry analogous to the support price program in agriculture, with somewhat similar consequences. Furthermore, the establishment of an unlimited market for gold, at $35 an ounce, at the U.S. Treasury has had the effect of causing the value of gold to be determined by the value of the dollar, rather than the reverse, as so many persons have supposed.

The Federal Reserve banks are required to keep at least a 25 per cent gold certificate reserve against their deposits, and Federal Reserve notes in circulation. In addition, the Federal Reserve bank must deposit with its agent as collateral against Federal Reserve notes received from him for issue, 100 per cent collateral consisting of any or all of the following: notes arising from member bank borrowing, U.S. securities bought in the open market, and gold certificates. At the time of the statement of condition shown on page 219, the ratio of gold certificate reserves to deposit and Federal Reserve note liabilities combined was 35.1 per cent. In other words, the Federal Reserve banks could, if they deemed it desirable, create considerably more deposits and Federal Reserve note liabilities.

The currency held as an asset by the Federal Reserve banks consists of Treasury currency which has been received and will be disbursed in the ordinary course of banking business, as was indicated in the previous chapter. Federal Reserve credit includes the loans, discounts, advances, and investments of the Federal Reserve banks. When the Federal Reserve banks acquire these assets they at the same time create liabilities, principally member bank reserve deposits. It is through control over the size of Federal Reserve credit that the Board of Governors and the Federal Open Market Committee control the expansion and contraction of commercial bank credit. An analysis of these controls will appear later. The principal remaining asset is "cash items in process of collection," to the extent of about $6.1 billion. It represents checks which have been received for collection but which have not yet been paid by the banks upon which they are drawn.

The liabilities of the Federal Reserve banks include the principal part of the national currency of the country, the Federal Reserve notes. Repeated reference to the issuance of Federal Reserve notes has been made. In summary, they represent liabilities of the Federal Reserve banks; they are backed by gold certificates and by debt instruments; and when they are issued, member bank reserve balances are extinguished. Expansion and contraction of the volume of Federal Reserve notes takes place in accordance with the needs of the country for cash. The only limits on their issuance, for all practical purposes, are the limits imposed upon the ability of the member banks to avail themselves of Federal Reserve credit. This, in turn, has a much more powerful limiting effect on the volume of demand deposits which member banks may hold.

We are familiar with the member bank reserve accounts. They include the required reserves and excess reserves examined in the previous chapter and subject to further examination later. The U.S. Treasury general account is maintained at a working minimum. It is replenished by the payment of taxes by means of checks and through the sale of U.S. securities paid for by checks and through the deposit of gold certificates, and it is depleted when the Treasury draws upon its Federal Reserve deposits. Other deposits include foreign central bank deposits and nonmember bank clearing accounts.

Other liabilities of the Federal Reserve banks include "deferred availability cash items," about $3.8 billion on December 31, 1961. This represents the checks which the Federal Reserve banks have received for collection from the banks of the country and for which reserve deposit credit has not yet been given. The Federal Reserve "float" is the difference between "uncollected cash items" among the assets of the Federal Reserve banks and "deferred availability cash items," in this instance about $2.3 billion, and represents additions to reserves of member banks granted prior to the final collection of the checks by the Federal Reserve banks.

15.3. *Federal Reserve Control over Bank Credit Creation*

The expansion of bank credit by commercial banks might be classified into two categories: primary credit expansion and secondary credit expansion. *Primary credit expansion* refers to the expansion of bank credit by means of the employment of excess reserves, which do not originate from Federal Reserve credit extension, for creating deposits when loans are made or investments acquired by the commercial banks. To the extent that the commercial banks possess excess reserves, then, they do not have to go to the Federal Reserve banks to acquire funds that will permit them to make additional loans. In such an event, the Federal Reserve authorities have two methods available for controlling the access of customers of the banks to credit.

Selective Credit Controls. One of these methods of intervening between the commercial banks and the borrowing public is through the employment of *selective credit controls.* By this is meant the regulation of selected uses for borrowed funds. The establishment of margin requirements for the purchase of securities is a privilege of the Board of Governors of the Federal Reserve System, under Regulations T and U. For instance, on August 5, 1958, margin requirements were raised to 70 per cent from a previous 50 per cent of the market value of securities. The margin requirements were raised again, on October 16, 1958, to 90 per cent. This meant that a purchaser of a security needed to have 90 per cent of the market value of the stocks he wished to purchase financed with his own funds and could borrow, either at his bank or through his broker, only 10 per cent. The intention was to limit the extension of bank credit for stock market speculation. Later, on July 28, 1960, margin requirements were lowered to 70 per cent. Similarly, in times past, Regulation W has been in effect to limit the extension of installment credit, by establishing minimum down payments and maximum payment time for purchases of automobiles and appliances. During the Korean War, Regulation X limited the extension of bank credit for the financing of the purchase of new residences, by establishing minimum down payment and maximum repayment periods. In all of these cases of the employment of selective credit controls, the primary purpose of the control is to regulate a specific purpose for borrowing with a specific intention in mind—to keep the stock market liquid, to avoid overexpansion of installment credit, or to reduce activity in the house-building industry. There is, however, an over-all effect on the total volume of loans that the banks can make, as well as the direction of the loans, when such controls are employed.

Moral Suasion. Another way that the Federal Reserve authorities have for intervening between the banks and their customers is more intangible than the employment of selective credit controls. This is the use of *moral suasion.* Moral suasion means that the Federal Reserve authorities make suggestions to the member banks about the ways that they should employ their reserves. There is the implication that failure to comply with the suggestions may mean that the rights and privileges of Federal Reserve System membership will be taken away from the offending banks. One example of the widespread use of moral suasion was the creation of "Voluntary Credit Restraint Committees," with the co-operation of the American Bankers Association, at the start of the Korean War period in 1950 under which banks were requested to make loans only for productive purposes and not to finance speculation.

Aside from the employment of moral suasion or of selective controls over the making of loans by commercial banks, the Federal Reserve banks have no other means of regulating primary credit expansion. However, this does not mean that commercial banks are completely free to loan any excess funds they may have. For one thing, they feel restraint in terms of the desire for liquidity and solvency as well as earnings. When market interest rates are low or when there is widespread pessimism over the future of business operations in the country, commercial banks may keep large excess reserves. But when expectations are good and the interest rate is high, the banks are likely to be loaned up to the hilt, because of the profits that might be earned from high-interest rate loans and investments and because of the sanguine attitude toward the future.

This variation in the extension of bank credit, on the part of the commercial bankers, may run counter to the wishes of the Federal Reserve control authorities, the Board of Governors of the Federal Reserve System, who feel charged with the responsibility for maintaining the proper level of bank credit in the country. Then one, or a combination, of three additional powers for controlling money supply are likely to be employed. These three control devices are designed to influence the ease with which the commercial banks may draw upon Federal Reserve credit, and they may also create the need to do so. Hence they refer to *secondary credit expansion,* credit expansion which comes from the employment of Federal Reserve credit, the effect being intended to force the commercial banks to obey the will of the regulating authority with respect to limiting the expansion of credit. And these devices convert secondary credit expansion into possible primary credit expansion when the desire is to make money "easy" or to induce bankers to expand the volume of loans which they are willing to extend.

Changes in the Required Reserve Ratio. The Federal Reserve Act, as amended, authorizes the Board of Governors of the Federal Reserve System to change within certain limits the size of required reserves which member banks must keep against deposits. These limits are shown in the accompanying table.

Reserve city banks are in large cities, and country banks are all other member banks. Reserve requirements have been changed twenty-one times since the end of World War II. When reserve requirements are lowered, required reserves are decreased and excess reserves increased. Consequently, the member banks may, if they wish, increase their loans, and, through the multiple expansion of bank credit, the total volume of deposits thereby created can reach an amount equal to the additional excess reserves divided by the new required reserve ratio against demand deposits.

Conversely, when it is desired to prevent additional primary credit expansion on the basis of existing excess reserves, the reserve requirement can be increased, up to the limit allowed by law, thus converting excess reserves into required reserves and preventing the potential ex-

	Lower Limit	Upper Limit	In Effect, Jan. 1, 1962
Time deposits:			
All member banks...........	3%	6%	5%
Demand deposits:			
Reserve city banks..........	10	22	16½
Country banks.............	7	14	12

pansion of credit. It is also, of course, possible to force a contraction in the volume of bank credit to take place by increasing reserve requirements to such an extent that all excess reserves become required reserves. The banks must, in addition, reduce the volume of deposits which they hold, because of the increase in the required reserve ratio to a point beyond one where the banks possess sufficient reserves. In this event, as each bank attempts to reduce demand deposits, it does so by allowing old loans to mature without making new loans. Hence, as deposits are extinguished through the repayment of loans, the banks become holders of a smaller quantity of demand deposits.

A bank may attempt to increase its legal reserves to the required amount but not decrease the volume of demand deposits which it holds. It could do this if it sold some of its earning assets. If it can be assumed, for the moment, that the sale of assets is not made to the Federal Reserve banks, the purchaser will pay for the assets with a check on his own bank. Through the clearing mechanism this will reduce the holding of legal reserves by some other bank, which will, in turn, have to contract its deposits or sell assets. For the banking system, the only solution for a problem where required reserves exceed legal reserves held is for the banks to contract the volume of demand deposits. The consequences for the total volume of bank credit will be similar to that illustrated on page 229 for the effects of open-market sales by the Federal Reserve banks. For the system, the formula which illustrates the necessary reduction in demand deposits or the reduction in the potential for the creation of demand deposits on the basis of what were once excess reserves would be the same formula applied for expansion, but in reverse:

$$\text{Potential change in demand deposits} = \frac{-ER_0}{r}$$

where ER_0 is the decrease in size of excess reserves and r is the reserve ratio which must be applied to demand deposits.

Open-Market Operations. The open-market operations of the Federal Reserve banks are controlled by the Federal Open Market Committee. The Federal Reserve banks are authorized to buy and sell on the open market (*i.e.,* not through regular depositors) bank acceptances and U.S. government securities. The bank acceptances are bought only for the purpose of creating a liquid bank acceptance market; they are not of interest to us. The U.S. securities are bought and sold in the open market as a device for monetary management. Let us consider the consequences of open-market sales of such securities.

The buyers of the securities do so through brokers and dealers and are not specifically aware that the seller is the Federal Reserve banks. The open-market operations manager also operates through recognized dealers in U.S. government securities. If the commercial banks are the buyers, then the following adjustments in bank statements of condition would take place, on the basis of the sale of $1,000,000 of securities by the Federal Reserve banks:

F.R.B.

ASSETS	LIABILITIES
(1) U.S. government securities..........−$1,000,000	Deposits of member banks..−$1,000,000

as the Federal Reserve banks receive checks of the member banks for payment and collect them by reducing the reserve balances of the banks by the amounts of the checks. And,

COMMERCIAL BANKS

ASSETS	LIABILITIES
(2) Reserves with F.R.B...−$1,000,000	
(2) U.S. government securities..........+ 1,000,000	

The reduction in legal reserves would be accompanied by no change in deposits in the banks and no change in required reserves. However, excess reserves, which may otherwise have become the basis for multiple expansion of bank credit, will have disappeared as the Federal Reserve banks reduced Federal Reserve credit and excess reserves of banks.

If members of the public (individuals, corporations, insurance companies) are the buyers of the securities, the effect on the Federal Reserve banks would be the same as indicated above, but the changes for the commercial banks would be quite different. The Federal Reserve banks would receive payment for the securities with checks drawn on member banks. These checks would be collected by the device of reducing member bank reserve balances by the amount of the checks. Member bank statement of condition would change as follows:

COMMERCIAL BANKS

ASSETS	LIABILITIES
(3) Reserves with F.R.B...−$1,000,000	Demand deposits..........−$1,000,000

For the public, the change in a "statement of financial condition" would be as follows:

PUBLIC

ASSETS	LIABILITIES
(1) U.S. government	
securities...........+$1,000,000	
(1) Demand deposits......− 1,000,000	

Since demand deposits decrease, the required reserves will decrease by r (ΔDD). The remainder of the decrease in member bank reserves will have to be either in excess reserves or in legal reserves which are still required reserves. If the former is the case, the net effect is the same as if the banks themselves had purchased the bonds, as far as potential credit expansion is concerned. Excess reserves decrease by $(1-r)\$1,000,000$ and money in the hands of the public decreases by $\$1,000,000$. Since potential expansion of demand deposits for any volume of excess reserves is ER_0/r and in this case the potential expansion is decreased by $[(1-r)ER_0]/r$ and the actual decrease is ER_0, with $ER_0 = \$1,000,000$, potential plus actual decrease in money supply is $\$1,000,000/r$. For example, with 20 per cent reserve ratio required, the money supply that is possible on the basis of original legal reserves is decreased by $\$5,000,000$.

If the banks on which the checks are drawn do not have any excess reserves they must rebuild their reserves by the amount of $(1-r)\$1,000,000$ which they will accomplish by selling earning assets (4):

Commercial Banks A

ASSETS	LIABILITIES
(3) Reserves with F.R.B.............. $-\$1,000,000$	(3) Demand deposits......$-\$1,000,000$
(4) Reserves with F.R.B.......$+(1-r)(\$1,000,000)$	
(4) Loans and in- vestments....$-(1-r)(\$1,000,000)$	

This will affect other banks (5)

Commercial Banks B

ASSETS	LIABILITIES
(5) Reserves with F.R.B.......$-(1-r)(\$1,000,000)$	(5) Demand deposits.....$-(1-r)(\$1,000,000)$

which will, in turn, cause them to sell assets to replenish their required reserves with effects on themselves (6) and other banks as follows (7) and (8):

Commercial Banks B

ASSETS	LIABILITIES
(5) Reserves with F.R.B.......$-(1-r)\ (\$1,000,000)$	(5) Demand deposits.....$-(1-r)(\$1,000,000)$
(6) Reserves with F.R.B.......$+(1-r)^2(\$1,000,000)$	
(6) Loans and in- vestments...$-(1-r)^2(\$1,000,000)$	

Commercial Banks C

ASSETS	LIABILITIES
(7) Reserves with F.R.B.......$-(1-r)^2(\$1,000,000)$	(7) Demand deposits.....$-(1-r)^2(\$1,000,000)$
(8) Reserves with F.R.B.......$+(1-r)^3(\$1,000,000)$	
(8) Loans and in- vestments...$-(1-r)^3(\$1,000,000)$	

and so on throughout the banking system until the contraction in the volume of demand deposits becomes $(\$1,000,000)/r$.

In other words, just as there can be a multiple expansion of bank credit under a fractional reserve banking system, similarly, there can be brought about a multiple contraction of bank credit, of like maximum proportions.

If the Federal Open Market Committee wishes to see the money market eased, it may order the purchase of U.S. government securities on the open market. In this event, exactly the reverse of the effects of open-market selling takes place. The amount of Federal Reserve credit will be increased by the amount of the security purchases, member bank reserve balances will be increased by a like amount, and actual and potential expansion of commercial bank deposits will be a multiple of the increase in reserve balances, by an amount determined by the required reserve ratio.

Changes in the Rediscount Rate. Changing the reserve requirements and buying and selling in the open market are quantitative instruments of credit control. They cannot, by their nature, select the banks and the kinds of credit which it is desired to effect. However, there is one more instrument which tends to have the effect of making the quantitative controls specific in application. This is the device of changing the rediscount rate.

Each of the twelve Federal Reserve banks announces its own rediscount rate, but the rediscount rate which it selects must be approved by the Board of Governors of the Federal Reserve System. We can say, in effect, that the Board of Governors determines rediscount rates. The rediscount rate is the basic rate of interest which a Federal Reserve bank will charge for loans to commercial banks. When banks are deficient in reserves they may turn to the Federal Reserve banks to rediscount or borrow in order to replenish their reserves, either to acquire funds with which to make loans or to build their reserves up to the required amount. If the rediscount rate is high, the commercial banks will be reluctant to acquire funds in this fashion, and they will charge high interest rates to their own customers. If the rediscount rate is low, they may feel encouraged to use the lending capacity of the Federal Reserve banks to finance themselves if the need should arise, and they will charge lower interest rates to their own customers. Consequently, the rediscount rate is a weapon for controlling the willingness of banks to make loans and for establishing the position of the range of interest rates which exist in the market.

Actually, there is very little discounting or borrowing from the Federal Reserve banks to finance normal banking operations. There are two reasons for this. In the first place, banks tend to think of the Federal Reserve banks only as lenders of last resort, and, to supplement this attitude, the Federal Reserve bank enforces an unwritten rule, the taboo on continuous borrowing. In the second place, the number of financial institutions in the country is so great that individual banks are able to find purchasers of their portfolios of loans and securities when they need to outside of the Federal Reserve banks. However, when money is tight, the volume of rediscounting and borrowing from the Federal Reserve banks increases substantially. Since the Board of Governors possesses the power to make money tight through its other controls, it is able to force the banking community to recognize the changes which take place in the rediscount rate. Consequently, the rediscount rate has acquired a significance out of proportion to the percentage of all loans which involve Federal Reserve loans and advances to banks. Today, the changes in the rediscount rate are watched as signals of the feeling of the Board of Governors toward the money market and its attitude toward easing or tightening money.

When the quantitative controls over bank credit are employed, a bank may turn to the Federal Reserve bank for funds through rediscounting eligible paper. Although the Federal Reserve authorities feel their responsibility as a lender of last resort, they may admonish a bank for pursuing an unwise credit policy and they may refuse to rediscount for banks which are not "acceptable" because of their behavior in the money market. The coupling of the admonishments, that is, moral suasion, with the threat of withdrawing the rediscounting privilege, is used as a mechanism for converting the broad quantitative controls over the money supply into qualitative controls over the purposes for which bank loans are made.

In summary, then, the commercial banks are the principal creators of money in the economy, through their creation of demand deposits. The volume of demand deposits outstanding may, at a maximum, be a multiple of the required reserves which the commercial banks must hold. The Board of Governors of the Federal Reserve System and the Federal Open Market Committee are able to enforce rather specific controls over the extent of the expansion of bank credit. It is possible for them to reduce the size of excess reserves and thus cut down on the allowed amount of primary credit expansion. By rediscounting for banks and by buying and selling government securities on the open market, the Federal Reserve banks give or withdraw access to Federal Reserve credit and therefore to secondary expansion of bank credit. Since the Federal Reserve banks are not operated primarily for profit, it is possible for them to exercise their power over the commercial banks of the country to regulate the volume of money in the interests of a stable money supply, to expand the money supply to meet the needs of an expanding economy, and to maintain a rate of interest for funds which helps to maintain stability in the size of the national income. Additional reference to the use of *monetary policy* as a policy for creating economic stability in the country will be made in Chapter 21.

15.4. *The Equation of Exchange*

The assumptions involved in the analysis of the means by which the banking system determines the volume of money in the country include the assumption that the amount of money in existence has an important influence on the level of economic activity. Just what that importance is will be better realized by a brief analysis of the determinates of the value of money. However, in analyzing general economic activity it is important to bear in mind the distinction which exists between money as a *stock* (the quantity of money) and money as a *flow* (the volume of payments made by a given quantity of money).

The question arises, "What does a given quantity of money mean in terms of the volume of exchanges which it facilitates?" Obviously, the same $10 bill can, in the course of a year, effect a great many purchases and sales. Since the level of economic activity is closely associated with the volume or rate at which exchanges are taking place, there remains a "missing link" (or several missing links) between the quantity of money and the level of activity in the economic system.

In order to capture the essence of the notion that a given quantity of money can do relatively more or less work—in terms of the number of exchanges facilitated—it is useful to introduce the concepts of the *velocity* of money and the *equation of exchange.* Suppose we let P be the average price of all commodities and services sold during a year, q be the total number of transactions in which goods and services are marketed during the year, M_T be the total quantity of money of all kinds in circulation, and v be the velocity of money (the average times per year that a unit of money changes hands in the above exchanges). Then the equation of exchange, which is really an identity states that

$$(15.1) \quad M_T v \equiv Pq .$$

Pq is the total money value of *all* transactions in the goods and services, q.

The usual usage, and that which will be employed in Chapters 16 through 21 of this book, is one which establishes a relationship between national product and the total quantity of money of all kinds in circulation. In these chapters national product will be identified as the final value of goods and services produced in the country, less allowances for the extent to which the stock of capital goods in the country has worn out and been replaced with part of total production. This value will be called *net national product.* It can be identified as PQ, where Q is the physical quantity of *net* production, which multiplied by its average price becomes net national product. PQ is smaller than the total value of all transactions by an amount which is generally regarded as being a factor of ten or twelve. If that factor is identified as α, then

$$(15.2) \quad \alpha PQ \equiv Pq, \text{ and}$$
$$(15.3) \quad M_T v \equiv \alpha PQ .$$

If the term V is used to identify the income (or net national product) velocity of money, that is, the national income divided by the amount of money in circulation, then

$$(15.4) \quad M_T V \equiv PQ, \text{ and}$$

$$(15.5) \quad V \equiv \frac{PQ}{M_T} \equiv \frac{v}{\alpha}.$$

The equation of exchange reveals that there may be several different and causal relationships between money supply and the level of economic activity. In the first place, if v and P do not change, an increase in M_T would be accompanied by an increase in q. In other words, the volume of trade would be related to the quantity of money. During a depression, it is possible that an increase in the amount of spending power, in the form of money, would allow for and act as a stimulus to an expansion in economic activity and recovery from the depression. In the second place, the constants in the identity might be v and q, in which case the level of prices would vary with the quantity of money. During peak prosperity, with full employment, it may be impossible for the volume of trade to increase beyond existing levels; then an increase in money supply might merely have the effect of increasing the price level. An increase in money would cause inflation. If neither P nor q could increase, under price control and rationing during wartime, for example, an increase in M_T could only be accompanied by a decrease in the rate of turnover of money, v. Similarly, a change in the rate of turnover of money, v, with no change in supply of money, M_T, could be accompanied by an increase in the price level, in the volume of transactions, or both. Unfortunately, an identity can never tell us what the causal connections between the parts of the tautology are. For this reason, it is important for us to know more about the factors underlying the determination of v.

15.5. Motives for Holding Money

The reciprocal of the velocity of money, $1/v$, has an interesting and useful interpretation for us in our attempt to discover the factors which influence the velocity of money. If v is the number of times, on the average, that a dollar changes hands in the course of a year, then $1/v$ can be thought of as the average period of time that a dollar "rests" or is held between successive payments, or $1/v$ is simply the "period of turnover" of money. That is,

$$(15.6) \quad M_T \equiv \theta P q,$$

where θ is $1/v$.

Armed with this interpretation of $1/v$ it is easier to understand what kinds of human *behavior* influence the magnitude of v. If $1/v$ is the average time that a unit of money is held, then clearly the velocity of a given quantity of money in circulation is vitally affected by people's willingness or desire to hold money. The "demand" for *money to hold* determines $1/v$ and hence v. It is customary to consider three classifications of motives for holding money.

1. *The Transaction Motive.* Perhaps the quantitatively most important reason that people have for holding money is to bridge the gap between their income receipts and their expenditures. If all of our purchases were made at the very instant we received our income payments, we would not hold any money for transaction purposes. Suppose an individual gets paid once a month, and pays out all of his income continuously throughout the month. Then the profile of his money holdings over time will be as is shown in Figure 15–1.

FIGURE 15–1

PROFILE OF AN INDIVIDUAL'S MONEY HOLDINGS OVER TIME

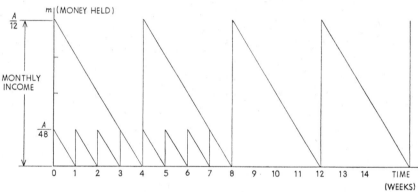

If our individual receives an annual income of A dollars per year paid in equal monthly installments of $A/12$ dollars, then his average "demand" for money to hold is $m = \frac{1}{2}(A/12)$. If he is paid four times per month, then $m = \frac{1}{2}(A/48)$.

Obviously, the transactions requirements of the community for money depends strongly upon institutional factors such as the frequency of wage payments, the availability of banking facilities, and transportation and communication facilities. However, given a certain set of institutional factors, which undoubtedly change very slowly under ordinary conditions, differences in the transactions needs for money, over time, develop in accordance with two other factors. One of these is the price level and the average size of income payments. With a price level in the country at one time which is considerably higher than the price level at another time, the transactions needs for money will be higher also. The other factor is the size of national income, which indicates the number of persons who are employed and the number of transactions for which money is being spent. When there is full employment in the country, and times are prosperous, there is a greater volume of money held for transaction purposes than when employment and production are at low levels. This is one of the reasons that the Federal Reserve authorities are concerned with maintaining a volume of money in the country which is consistent with the needs of the economy from one phase of growth in production and employment to another.

2. *The Precautionary Motive.* Some money may be held as a precautionary measure to take care of uncertain situations which may arise, such as illness, loss of job, or a slump in a firm's normal sales rate while expenditures continue at the former rate. Here money is held, not to meet planned expenditures, but to have in case it should be needed to meet unexpected expenditures. The size of holdings of money for precautionary purposes depends to a considerable extent on the changing psychology of the people. When there is fear of the future, and uncertainty exists as to what future events may hold, people tend to hold a large amount of money, as a liquidity buffer against any unforeseeable contingency.

3. *The Speculative Motive.* Some money holdings may be influenced by expected changes in the average level of prices. When the price level is expected to fall, it is to the advantage of individuals and businesses to hold their assets in the form of money or "near-money" rather than in physical goods such as real estate, automobiles, inventories, machines, and securities, the values of which are expected to fall in terms of money. Similarly, if the price level is expected to rise, it is better to hold assets in the form of physical goods, the money value of which is rising. Thus, when the price level is rising, the demand for money to hold decreases, and money turns over rapidly. During a period of hyperinflation in a country, when prices are rising very rapidly, no one wishes to hold money for any time at all. The money holdings may lose a large part of their value in half a day. As a consequence, the very speed with which money changes hands contributes to the inflation.

Both the precautionary motive for holding money and the speculative motive can be thought of as a desire for liquidity. Therefore, both of these motives are grouped together and are called the *liquidity-preference* motive for holding money. Other things being equal, the individual or firm would rather hold its possessions in liquid form. The desire to be "liquid" is overcome by the payment of interest for the use of money. A range of interest rates would exist partly in accordance with the liquidity of the investment. Those investment instruments which can be liquidated readily will carry the lowest rates of interest, other risks being neglected, and those investments which are "frozen" for some time would carry higher interest rates.

An increase in the "demand" for money to hold because of any of the above motives will *decrease V*. If at the same time the quantity of money in circulation is constant, then the equation of exchange indicates that the price level and/or output must decline. The relative impact upon P and/or Q depends upon considerations which will be taken up in subsequent chapters.

15.6. *Index Numbers*

In making calculations of PQ it is possible to conceive of the collection of figures on all physical production and to determine what all of the prices are and by this means to multiply production by prices to get the total value, PQ. Actually, no such thing is practically possible. Instead, *index numbers* of production and prices are employed. An index number is merely an expression of the change in a numerical value over what it was in a base period, shown as a percentage. The numerical value may itself be an average of a number of similar values which are grouped together because of a common relationship which they possess. Such, for example, would be an index number of wholesale prices or an index number of industrial production. In order to interpret an index number properly, it should be borne in mind what it is and how it is constructed.

The Federal Reserve Index of Industrial Production is, for example, an index number created by determining the percentage changes since the base period in the production of a number of different commodities. The base period is average annual production for 1947–1949. Each of these separate percentage figures, called a production relative, is given a weight in determining the average percentage figure which is the index number being constructed for the entire group. This weight is assigned to each production relative in accordance with its importance, as conceived by the creators of the index, among all of the production relatives which are being included. The weights for that index are listed monthly in the *Federal Reserve Bulletin*. The index number created from these average relatives is, then, a weighted average index number. Even here, the relative importance of each of the commodity groups being measured changes from period to period, so that a decision has to be made as to what weights should be employed, the weights of the base period or of the current period or a combination of both. Furthermore, the index number finally determined is not an index number of all industrial production but only of the production of the items included in the preparation of the index number. If it is carefully drawn, however, so that the items involved are representative ones, sensitive to changes in the economy in a manner deemed to be equivalent to the sensitivity of other, unincluded items, the resulting index number may be interpreted as being an index number of all industrial production rather than only an index of the measured items.

The same problems are true for an index number of prices. There is the problem of selection of items to include, the problem of weighting, the problem of changes in the commodities being measured, such as quality changes, the problems associated with the representativeness of the sample for all prices in the same category (e.g., retail prices, wholesale prices, prices which farmers pay, prices which farmers receive, etc.). The most publicized price index number in this country is the "Index of Consumer Prices," prepared by the Bureau of Labor Statistics from prices collected for a considerable range of commodities, grouped into eight major categories of products and services, and collected in forty-six cities of the country. Although this index number then only shows a weighted average of the percentage changes in the prices which are being measured, with all of the difficulties of collection, interpretation, and averaging which have been mentioned, it is accepted as the guide for policy determination in labor-management contracts for "escalator" clauses in wage agreements, by politicians and policy makers in their assessment of the changing price level, and by householders generally in measuring their welfare. Nevertheless, for any one individual or group, the retail price index is an inexact measurement of how changing prices affect that party's purchases.

QUESTIONS AND EXERCISES

1. What happens to the total quantity of money and the legal reserves held by commercial banks when citizens pay their taxes to the federal government? Show the appropriate balance sheet diagrams.

2. Show by appropriate balance sheet diagrams the consequence of the sale of gold abroad by the U.S. Treasury.

3. Can the deflationary effect of the outflow of gold from the United States be offset by the Federal Reserve authorities? Explain, using the balance sheet diagrams.

4. The following is a partial balance sheet (consolidated) for member banks:

Cash....................	$ 100,000	Demand deposits........	$5,000,000
Deposits with the Federal			
Reserve banks........	1,500,000		
Loans..................	2,000,000		
U.S. Government Securi-			
ties................	3,000,000		

Assume that bank reserve requirements are at the Federal Reserve minimum and that the average is about equal to that of the Reserve city banks.

If the kind of condition revealed by the statement above had been present for some months, show by reference to at least two of the items on the balance sheet what is probably the state of the economy, indicating your reasons.

5. *a*) Assume that the banking system is loaned up (no excess reserves) with deposits of $120 billion and a reserve requirement of 20 per cent. What could happen to the total money supply if the FRB lowered the reserve requirements to 16⅔ per cent and sold $4 billion in bonds on the open market?

   b) Assume that reserves are $25 billion and the banks are loaned up with reserve requirements of 12½ per cent. What would happen to the money supply if the FRB, in order to combat inflationary forces, raised reserve requirements to 16⅔ per cent and sold $1 billion of bonds in the open market.

   c) Assume that deposits are $124 billion, reserves are $25 billion and the reserve requirement is 12½ per cent. What would happen to the money supply if the FRB lowers reserve requirements to 10 per cent and buys $2 billion of bonds in the open market? What would happen to loans of member banks?

6. Show the effect on the size of v (velocity of turnover of money) of:

   a) A speed-up in the clearing of checks due to the use of closed circuit television for identification between banks in different cities.

   b) The continuous outflow of gold from the United States.

   c) The outbreak of war in Europe.

   d) A shift from weekly to monthly pay for most industrial laborers.

   e) Abandonment of the withholding feature of income tax collection.

7. Given the table:

Commodity	Price, Base Period	Price, Current Period	Weight
A....................	$ .10	$ .15	3
B....................	5.00	6.00....................	10
C....................	50.00	32.50....................	10
D....................	200.00	250.00....................	2
E....................	.25	.10....................	15
			40

Find the index number of prices for the current period by determining the:

a) Percentage change in the aggregate of prices.

b) Unweighted arithmetic mean of price relatives.

c) Weighted arithmetic mean of price relatives.

Chapter 16

NATIONAL INCOME AND
ITS COMPONENTS

The foundations for an analysis of the determinants of the level of total national income will be laid in this chapter and carried through in Chapters 17 and 19. We have analyzed the forces determining the composition of national income and its allocation to the factors of production producing it, but what determines the total volume of production? Before we can answer this question we need to develop some basic concepts of national income.

During the last quarter century economists have made increasing use of national income concepts both as indicators of the status or well-being of an economy and as tools of analysis. However, there are many concepts of "national income," each with its own special usefulness. In this chapter we shall distinguish three such concepts, gross national product, net national product, and disposable income. We shall then briefly discuss real income versus money income.

16.1. Gross National Product

The economic processes, which we have been studying, result in the creation of goods and services, on the one hand, and in money incomes on the other. It was seen, in Chapter 5, that the hiring of any productive resource by a business firm represents a cost to the business firm and at the same time is income earned by the owner of the productive service. Thus we say that the incomes (wages, salaries, rent, dividends, and profits) of the owners of the productive resources are derived from, and are the compensation for, the role which the factors play in the production of goods and services.

The essential relationship between the creation of goods and services and the simultaneous generation of money income was seen in the simplified circular flow economy discussed and illustrated in Chapter 6. There we saw that the operation of the economic system could be viewed as a flow of money payments from the resource owners to the business community in payment for a flow of products. At the same time, there was a flow of money payments (income) from the business community to the owners of the resources in payment for a flow of productive services received by the businesses and used in the production of goods and services. The act of production, it was seen, results in the creation of income.

It is noted, in the circular flow diagram, that the total of money payments received by business firms is equal to the total amount paid out by the business firms to cover all of the costs of production, remembering that profits are properly a cost of production and that they may be positive or negative. The money value, at current market prices, of all final goods and services produced in any given period (usually a year) is called the gross national product, GNP. Since the end-product prices are equal to the total costs of production, it is obvious that gross national income is necessarily equal to the total costs of production—it is really just two ways of looking at the same economic phenomenon. Thus, in order to measure the gross national product—which we have defined as the market value of all final goods and services produced—we may use either the product approach or the income approach. First, the gross national product may be measured by adding together the market values of all the final goods and services produced by the economic system during a given period of time; this is called the product approach. Second, we may add together all incomes earned by the factors of production in creating the final goods and services, plus certain taxes and transfer payments and capital consumption allowances; this is called the income approach. In terms of the circular flow concept, it really doesn't matter whether we choose to measure the gross national product as a product flow or an income flow.

The gross national product does not include all goods produced. Large quantities of goods sold in any given period are intermediate goods which enter as raw materials (for example coal in the production of steel), or semifinished goods (for example, motors in washing machines). While flour sold to a baker is an intermediate product, flour sold to a housewife is a final product. Thus if a product is resold by the purchaser, we call it an intermediate product, and it is not part of gross national product; but if the product is not resold, we call it a final product and it is a part of gross national product. In the same way washing machines sold to consumers are part of GNP, but we do not also include in GNP the value of the paint, sheet steel, and electric motors that go into the washing machines. However, the electric motors that are sold directly to consumers for their own use (do-it-yourself enthusiasts) are included in the GNP. All these considerations are introduced in order to avoid double counting. GNP is *not* the total volume of purchases or total transactions. Note that full-employment GNP gives an estimate of total production capabilities of an economic system. Such an estimate would be very useful to defense officials who would like to know the maximum productive capacity available in an emergency.

16.2. Net National Product

In the above concept of GNP there still remains some "double counting," for we have made no adjustment for the depreciation or wearing out of equipment. Over any period of time the total value of the stock of capital goods declines as it is used in the production of goods and services. Hence the output of capital goods in any period is not a net contribution or addition to the value of the total stock of capital goods in the economic system. Net national product, NNP, is a measure of the net money value of the national output, and is obtained from GNP by deducting a figure which is called capital consumption allowance (CCA), the money value of the depreciation and obsolescence in the stock of capital goods during the particular period. That is,

$$(16.1) \quad NNP \equiv GNP - CCA .$$

Net national product, unlike gross national product, is not the measure of the sum total of all final goods and services produced; rather it measures only the net additions to the values already on hand at the beginning of the period. An economic system always has on hand a certain stock of capital goods and equipment and certain inventories of intermediate and finished goods produced in previous periods of production. These stocks of capital goods will be used by the business firms in the production of goods and services and as they are used their value will normally decrease. This process is called capital consumption, and the capital so used up in production must be replaced before we can measure the net money value of the national output. Note that the net national product gives an estimate of the value of final goods and services available to be consumed by various purchasers, while maintaining intact the economy's productive capacity; thus this concept may be more relevant than GNP when considering the capacity of our economy under long-run "cold-war" international relations.

16.3. Disposable Income

For many purposes the most significant national income concept is that of disposable income, which we define as the income earned by the owners of the factors of production that is available for spending or saving. Disposable income does not include business saving, i.e., undistributed corporate profits, as business savings are not available to the individuals for spending or saving. In passing from the net national product to disposable income, there are many items which must be added and subtracted. Thus goverment interest payments represent income paid to individuals which is not for services performed in production. Consequently, such payments are part of disposable income but are not part of net national product. On the other hand, business and personal taxes represent income earned by employed individuals which is not paid out to individuals. Hence such sums are part of net national product but are not a part of disposable income. Similar considerations apply to social security contributions, veterans' benefit payments, indirect business taxes, and so forth.

Our purposes will be adequately served without going into the complete details of national income accounting as developed by the Department of Commerce.[1] We have summarized the official national income statistics in an appendix to this chapter. Since taxes bulk very large as the major difference between net national product and disposable income, let us simplify the system by assuming that disposable income is equal to the net national product minus taxes. If $Y = \text{NNP}$, $Y_d =$ disposable income, and $T =$ taxes, then

$$(16.2) \quad Y_d \equiv Y - T .$$

16.4. An Important Identity

The net national product can be viewed from the product side or the income side, in exactly the same way as we earlier viewed the GNP. If we approach the NNP from the income side, the income receipts can be divided into the following categories: a) the use of income for consumption expenditures by households; b) the use of income for taxes by businesses and households; c) the use of income to make savings by businesses and households. Therefore, if we let $T =$ taxes, $C =$ consumption, $S =$ net savings, and $Y =$ net national product, then

$$(16.3) \quad Y \equiv C + T + S .$$

Equation (16.3) says that the receipts from the sale of the net national product are used to pay for consumption expenditures, to pay taxes and to save.

If the net national product is approached from the product side the goods and services produced can be divided into the following three

---

[1] National Income: Supplement to Survey of Current Business, 1947, 1951, 1954.

categories: *a*) consumer's goods purchased by households; *b*) investment goods purchased by businesses; *c*) goods of all kinds purchased by the government (including in this term all levels of government, national, state, and local). If we let $C =$ consumption goods, $I =$ net investment, and $G =$ government purchases, we have:

$$(16.4) \quad Y \equiv C + G + I .$$

If we combine (16.3) and (16.4), it follows that

$$(16.5) \quad Y \equiv C + T + S \equiv C + G + I .$$

Since the amount of income used to buy consumption goods must be equal to the amount of goods purchased by households, we can subtract C from both sides of (16.5) and we have

$$(16.6) \quad T + S \equiv G + I .$$

This says that the sum of tax collections by the government and the savings by businesses and households is equal to the sum of government expenditures on goods and services and net investment expenditures. If $G = T$, that is, if government expenditures are equal to tax collections (the government is neither increasing nor decreasing the national debt), then we have

$$(16.7) \quad I \equiv S ,$$

if we subtract G from the right-hand side of (16.6) and T from the left. Equation (16.6) is called an identity, a truism. It states that that part of NNP which is not spent on private consumption must either be paid out in taxes or saved. The part of NNP which is not composed of consumption goods must be either goods purchased by government or net investment. Equation (16.7) says that if government spending is equal to taxes collected, then that part of income saved is equal to net investment. These identities give an important starting point for our subsequent analysis of aggregate income determination in the following chapter.

16.5. Investment—Gross and Net

In Section 16.2 we pointed out that the difference between gross national product and net national product is the capital consumption allowance. This is the difference between gross and net investment. The term gross investment, as we shall understand it in income accounting and analysis, refers to the purchase of newly produced capital goods. By investment we mean real investment in capital goods and *not* financial investment, as when one buys a stock or bond. Notice that real investment involves the generation of income while financial investment represents the transfer of a certificate of ownership—such as a bond or stock. Income is not generated when financial investment is made.

Included in gross investment are such things as producer's durables or machinery and equipment. Goods going to increase inventories—the stock of finished and semifinished goods which businesses have on hand —are also part of gross investment. If inventories are growing, this item will be positive, but if businesses are retrenching and cutting back on the amount of inventories carried, the item will be negative. Inventory investment may also be negative if businesses are selling goods faster than they can replace them, causing stocks to fall. Expenditures on new construction goods such as plants, residential houses, and business buildings are also included in gross investment. At this point we will also mention net foreign investment, which refers to our sales of goods to foreign countries minus their sale of goods to us, as a part of gross investment. However, in the chapters immediately following, we will not consider foreign investment but will postpone it until we analyze international trade.

The term net investment (I as we will call it) refers to gross investment less capital consumption allowances. There is a net increase in the stock of capital goods in an economic system whenever total capital goods purchased for investment purposes exceeds the depreciation or wear on the existing stock of capital goods. Under certain circumstances net investment may be negative, and consumption plus government purchases will exceed net production. We have noticed that net investment in inventories will be negative whenever inventories are falling; furthermore, net investment may be negative even in the plant and equipment category, since it is possible for depreciation to exceed investment in new plant and equipment. Capital goods may wear out faster than they are replaced. This situation occurred in the United States in 1933, during the worst of the depression years of the Thirties. Net private investment was also negative in 1943, during World War II, when we drew on our capital stock to help fight the war.[2] In our subsequent analysis we will be mostly concerned with net rather than gross investment. If I' = gross investment, then

$$(16.8) \quad I \equiv I' - \text{CCA} .$$

It should be observed that net investment is a flow, i.e., a rate of change with respect to time. If we let K be the total value of the stock of capital in existence in an economy at a given time, then

$$(16.9) \quad dK/dt = I \equiv I' - \text{CCA} ,$$

[2] See Table 16–4 in the appendix to this chapter.

and $dK/dt \gtreqless 0$ according as $I' \gtreqless$ CCA. The stock of capital in existence in an economy may grow or decline through time and the rate of change of K with time is simply what we call net investment. This is illustrated in Figure 16–1.

If net investment in an economy is zero, then that economy will be just exactly consuming its net national product or income. The capital stock will be replaced from time to time as the buildings, machines, etc., are used up but there will be no net addition to the stock of capital

FIGURE 16–1

NET INVESTMENT AND THE STOCK OF CAPITAL

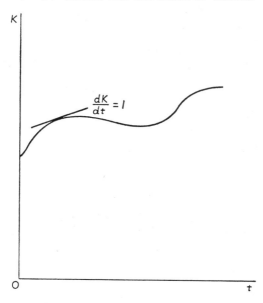

and the society will be essentially stationary. In the more usual case, net investment is positive. In this instance, there is a growing society that is more than replacing its worn-out capital stock each year, with the annual net addition being the net investment.

Today there is widespread concern with economic growth—growth not only in the absolute size of national income but in the per capita real income. As we will analyze later, growth in an economy's capital stock—net investment—plays an important role in bringing about a rising per capita real income. The last case, that of an economy with negative net investment, occurs when an economy wears out its capital stock faster than it is being replaced. An economy may consume more than it is currently producing, that is, live off its capital stock for some time, but if the process is continued the net national product (or national income) will certainly decrease.

16.6. Savings—Gross and Net

In national income analysis, savings is defined to mean not spending out of current disposable income receipts. An individual has a certain disposable income. He can use this disposable income to purchase consumption goods or not spend it—that is, save it. Savings may be held in such forms as bank deposits and currency, U.S. savings bonds, government bonds, insurance, corporate stocks and bonds, and mortgages. If S = net savings, then from (16.2) and (16.3) we have

$$(16.10) \quad S \equiv Y_d - C \equiv Y - T - C,$$

where Y_d = disposable income, Y = NNP, T = taxes, and C = total household expenditure for consumption goods. A certain amount of saving takes place in the business sector in the form of undistributed profits; thus total net saving is composed of personal saving and business saving. Also businesses regularly set sums aside out of their current receipts which represent their estimate of the depreciation of capital equipment. If we add these capital consumption allowances to net saving we have what we call gross saving:

$$(16.11) \quad S' \equiv S + \text{CCA}.$$

If we combine (16.1), (16.5), (16.8), and (16.11), we have

$$(16.12) \quad \text{GNP} \equiv \text{NNP} + \text{CCA} \equiv C + T + S' \equiv C + G + I'.$$

All of these income concepts are brought together in the appendix to this chapter where data for selected years are presented.

16.7. Money Income versus Real Income

Thus far we have discussed the various national income concepts in money terms, but the importance of the various concepts as indicators of economic well-being depends upon what the dollar will buy. If all prices and all incomes were increased a hundredfold overnight, leaving production unchanged, national income would appear to have increased a hundredfold; but now each dollar would have only the real purchasing power of the old penny. Surely one would not want to say we were better off after such an inflationary rise in the money value of national income. For example, in the United States the money value of the gross national product increased almost six and one-half times from 1933 to 1953, from $56 billion to $365.4 billion. Part of this tremendous increase was illusory, being the result of a general increase in prices during the two decades.

In earlier chapters we saw that price changes are the inevitable result of changing supply and demand conditions in markets where competition prevails. Increasing demand or diminishing supply tends to bring about higher prices, and decreasing demand or increasing supply tends to bring about lower prices. Furthermore, changing prices stimulate buyers and sellers to change their offers to buy or sell. Higher prices tend to stimulate production and discourage buying, while lower prices tend to stimulate buying and discourage production. Prices are the regulators that tend to keep production and consumption in line with each other in a private enterprise economy, and in the performance of this function it is quite common for some prices to be rising while other prices are falling.

However, when prices of all goods and services are going up, it is not because everything is worth more, but because the dollar (or

TABLE 16–1

DEFLATING MONEY GNP TO COMPUTE REAL GNP

Year	Money GNP in Current Dollars (Billions)	Price Index 1954 = 100	Real GNP in 1954 Prices (Billions)
1933.....	56	44.2	$56 × 100/44.2 = $126.7
1953.....	365.4	99	$365.4 × 100/99 = $369.1

Source: Based on *Economic Report of the President*, 1961.

other unit of currency) is worth less. Suppose an automobile costs $500 and a bicycle costs $10; this means that an automobile is worth 50 bicycles or a bicycle is worth one fiftieth of an automobile. Should prices of everything increase ten times, then automobiles would sell for $5,000 and bicycles for $100 each. An automobile would still be worth fifty bicycles; their exchange (or relative) value would remain the same. But clearly something has happened to the value of the dollar. Its real purchasing power has been cut tenfold—that is what we call inflation. The opposite situation in which prices fall and the purchasing power of the dollar rises is called deflation. During the 1930's the United States experienced a long and severe deflation, but since the end of World War II the general problem facing the nations of the world has not been deflation but rather inflation. We shall return to this problem when we consider some of the weapons the government has at its disposal in combating deflation and inflation.

If the value of the dollar keeps changing, as it has, how can we utilize national income statistics when we wish to compare the amounts of goods and services available to the economy at different points of time? Table 16–1 shows how we can allow for the fact the price level rose more than twofold between 1933 and 1953. To compute the change in *real* gross national product (expressed in dollars of constant purchasing power) as distinct from *money* gross national product (expressed in dollars of changing purchasing power), we must "deflate" the money figures by dividing them by an index of the price level. By this means we find that real 1933 gross national product was $126.7 billion if expressed in constant 1954 prices rather than $56 billion

FIGURE 16–2

COMPARISON OF MONEY AND REAL GNP, U.S., 1929–1960

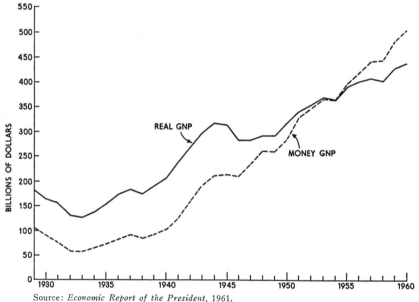

Source: *Economic Report of the President,* 1961.
* Real GNP calculated in 1954 prices.
† Money GNP calculated in current prices.

expressed in 1933 prices, and 1953 GNP, in constant 1954 dollars, was equal to $369.1 billion. Thus real gross national product had almost tripled between 1933 and 1953 rather than increasing by six and one-half times.

Figure 16–2 summarizes the different movement of real and money gross national product in the United States since 1929.

APPENDIX TO CHAPTER 16

A SUMMARY OF THE OFFICIAL NATIONAL INCOME STATISTICS

The Department of Commerce publishes gross national product and national income statistics in considerable detail. From time to time during the year the department publishes estimates of the various incomes and annually it publishes the July issue of the *Survey of Current Business* as the National Income number. In this issue the national income accounts are treated in great detail, sector by sector, and students are urged to study this issue with care. However, here we shall present only a summary account of gross national product and show how the various national income concepts are related.

As we pointed out earlier, the gross national product total published by the Department of Commerce is a measure, at current prices, of the flow of final

TABLE 16–2

THE TWO WAYS OF COMPUTING GROSS AND NET NATIONAL PRODUCT, FOR 1960
(In Billions of Dollars)

Income Approach		*Product Approach*	
Compensation of employees	$293.7	Personal consumption Expenditure	$328.9
		Durable goods	$ 44.3
Income of unincorporated enterprises (adjusted)	36.2	Nondurable goods	152.4
		Services	132.2
Income of farm proprietors	12.0		
		Gross private investment	75.4
Rental income of persons	11.7	New construction	$ 40.7
		Producers durable equipment	27.5
Net interest income	18.4	Change in business inventories	4.2
		Net foreign investment	3.0
Corporate profits, before taxes	45.0		
Corporate profits tax $22.3			
Dividends 14.1		Government purchases of goods and services	100.1
Undistributed profits 8.6			
$45.0		Federal	
Inventory valuation adjustment	0.0	National defense $ 45.5	
		Other 8.0	
Indirect business taxes	45.6	State and local 47.2	
Statistical discrepancy	−1.3		
Net national product	$461.3		
Capital consumption allowances	43.1		
Gross national product	$504.4	Gross national product	$504.4

output resulting from the economic activity of American residents during a selected accounting period, usually a calendar year. Viewing gross national product from the output point of view first, we know that total output is either purchased by consumers, investors, or the government. See Table 16–2. Consumption purchases are further roughly classified as durable goods, nondurable goods, and services. In 1960, with a gross national product of $504.5 billion, personal consumption expenditures totalled $328.9 billion, of which $44.3 billion was spent on durable goods, $152.4 billion on nondurable goods, and $132.2 billion on services. During the same period, gross private investment totalled $75.4 billion. This is further broken down into new construction $40.7 billion, of which $21.1 billion was nonfarm residential construction, and all other construction totalled $19.7 billion. Business firms purchased $27.5 billion of producers' durable equipment, and the change in business inventories added $4.2

billion to investment. Net exports of goods and services equaled $3.0 billion in 1960. The last major category making up GNP is government purchases of goods and services which totaled $100.1 billion in 1960. This total was made up of $52.9 billion by the federal government—$45.5 billion for national defense and $8.0 billion for all other items—and purchases totalling $47.1 billion by state and local governments.

At the beginning of the chapter we pointed out that gross national product can be viewed from the point of view of the product output or of the income earned in the production of that output. Utilizing the earnings approach, the gross national product is equal to the sum of the earnings of the owners of the factors of production plus certain taxes and the capital consumption allowances.

TABLE 16-3

RELATION OF GROSS NATIONAL PRODUCT AND NATIONAL INCOME STATISTICS,
FOR SELECTED YEARS
(In Billions of Dollars)

Items	1929	1933	1943	1953	1958	1960
Gross national product	104.4	56.0	192.5	365.4	444.2	504.4
Less:						
Capital consumption (primarily depreciation)	8.6	7.2	10.9	26.5	38.1	43.1
Equals:						
Net national product	95.8	48.8	181.6	338.9	406.1	461.4
Less:						
Indirect business taxes	7.0	7.1	12.7	30.2	39.4	45.6
Business transfer payments	0.6	0.7	0.5	1.4	1.8	1.8
Statistical discrepancies	0.3	0.9	−1.7	1.3	−1.7	−2.6
Plus:						
Subsidies less current surplus of government enterpr.	−0.1	(n.a.)	0.2	−0.4	1.1	0.5
Equals:						
National income	87.8	40.2	170.3	305.6	367.7	417.1
Less:						
Corporate profits and inventory valuation adjustment	10.1	−2.0	23.8	37.3	37.4	45.1
Contributions for social security	0.2	0.3	4.5	8.7	14.8	20.7
Excess of wage accruals over disbursements	—	—	0.2	—	—	—
Plus:						
Gov. transfer pay	0.9	1.5	2.5	12.9	24.5	27.3
Net interest paid by government	1.0	1.2	2.1	5.2	6.2	7.8
Dividends	5.8	2.1	4.5	9.2	12.4	14.1
Business transfer pay	0.6	0.7	0.5	1.4	1.8	1.8
Equals:						
Personal income	85.8	47.2	151.4	288.3	360.3	402.2
Less:						
Personal taxes	2.6	1.5	17.8	35.8	42.4	50.4
Federal	1.3	0.5	(n.a.)	32.4	36.7	43.2
State and local	1.4	1.0	(n.a.)	3.4	5.7	7.2
Equals:						
Disposable personal income	83.1	45.7	133.5	252.5	317.9	351.8
Less:						
Consumption expenditures	79.0	46.4	100.5	232.6	293.5	328.9
Equals:						
Personal saving	4.2	−.6	33.0	19.8	24.4	22.9

In 1960 compensation of employees came to a total of $293.7 billion, while the income of unincorporated enterprises (business and professional income) after adjustment for inventory valuation changes was $36.2 billion. During the same period farm proprietors received an income of $12.0 billion. Persons receiving rental income earned an income of $11.7 billion and net interest payments to individuals were $18.4 billion. Also part of gross national product are corporate profits before taxes, an estimated $45 billion in 1960. Corporate profits before taxes are further broken down to corporate tax liability $22.3 billion, dividend payments $14.1 billion, and undistributed profits $8.6 billion. Also included in GNP are indirect business taxes of $45.6 billion and capital consumption allowances (mainly depreciation) of $43.1 billion. The two ways of computing gross national product are estimated independently by the Department of Commerce. If all their estimates were perfect the totals for gross national product would be the same for both the product approach and the income approach. However, many of the estimates are approximations and the two estimates for GNP are frequently not the same; therefore usually an item called "statistical discrepancy" appears to reconcile the two estimates. In 1960 the item "statistical discrepancy" appears on the income side as −$1.3 billion.

We, like many economists, prefer to use national income to refer to net national product. However, our guiding rule is to obtain concepts that are used in the analytical model which is developed in Chapters 17 and 18. In this appendix, we will show how the official Department of Commerce statistics of national income are interrelated.

TABLE 16–4

USES OF NATIONAL OUTPUT
(In Billions of Dollars)

	1929	1933	1943	1953	1958	1960
C:						
Personal consumption.................	79.0	46.4	100.5	232.6	293.5	328.9
S':						
Gross savings........................	16.7	.6	5.1	47.0	57.6	73.9
CCA: Capital consumption allowances...	8.6	7.2	10.9	26.5	38.1	43.1
S_p: Personal saving....................	4.2	−.6	33.0	19.8	24.4	22.9
S_b: Business saving (Undistributed corp. profits and inventory valuation adjustment)......................	2.9	−4.6	5.4	7.8	6.5	8.6
S_g: Govt. saving....................	1.0	−1.4	−44.2	−7.1	−11.4	1.9
S_p': Gross private saving $S_p' = S' - S_g$..	15.7	2.0	49.3	54.1	69.0	72.0
S:						
Net savings $S = S' - CCA$............	8.1	−6.6	−5.8	20.5	19.5	30.8
T':						
Gross taxes..........................	11.3	9.3	49.2	94.9	115.2	139.1
T_i: Indirect taxes.....................	7.0	7.1	12.7	30.2	39.4	45.6
T_b: Direct taxes (business).............	1.4	.5	14.1	20.2	18.6	22.3
T_p: Direct taxes (personal)*............	2.8	1.8	22.3	44.5	57.2	71.1
Less T_r:						
Govt. transfers, interest and subsidies....	1.7	2.6	4.8	19.2	33.1	39.1
T:						
Net taxes $T = T' - T_r$.................	9.6	6.7	44.4	75.7	82.1	100.0
Statistical discrepancy....................	0.1	.9	−1.7	3.0	−0.4	+1.6
GNP = $C + S' + T$....................	104.4	56.0	192.5	365.4	444.2	504.4

* Direct personal taxes includes all contributions to social insurance.
Detail will not necessarily add to the totals because of rounding.

An alternative way of organizing the data concerning the national income is not concerned with the relationships between various income concepts but is developed logically around the uses of national income—that is, the gross income is either consumed, saved, or paid to the government in taxes.

The movement of the various components of gross national product for selected years is presented below.

TABLE 16–5

GROSS NATIONAL PRODUCT
(In Billions of Dollars)

	1929	1933	1943	1953	1958	1960
Durable goods	9.2	3.5	6.6	29.8	37.3	44.3
Nondurable goods	37.7	22.3	59.3	116.1	141.6	152.4
Services	32.1	20.7	34.7	81.7	114.3	132.2
C:						
Consumption purchases	79.0	46.4	100.5	230.5	293.2	328.9
New construction	8.7	1.4	2.3	25.8	35.5	40.7
Residential (nonfarm)	(3.6)	(0.5)	(0.9)	(11.9)	(18.0)	(21.1)
Other	(5.1)	(1.0)	(1.4)	(13.8)	(17.4)	(19.6)
Producers' durable equipment	5.8	1.6	4.0	24.3	23.1	27.5
Net change in business inventories	1.7	−1.6	−0.8	0.3	−2.0	4.2
Net foreign investment	0.8	0.2	−2.2	−2.0	1.2	3.07
I':						
Gross private investment	17.0	1.6	3.4	48.3	57.8	75.4
Federal expenditures on goods and services	1.3	2.0	81.2	59.5	52.6	52.9
National security	(n.a.s.)	(n.a.s)	(80.4)	(51.5)	(44.8)	(45.5)
Other	(n.a.s.)	(n.a.s.)	(1.5)	(8.4)	(8.3)	(8.0)
State and local	7.2	6.0	7.4	24.9	40.8	47.2
G:						
Government purchases of goods and services	8.5	8.0	88.6	84.4	93.5	100.0
GNP:						
Gross national product $(C + I' + G)$	104.4	56.0	192.5	363.2	444.5	504.4
Minus CCA	8.6	7.2	10.9	26.5	38.6	43.1
Equals NNP: Net national product $(Y = C + I + G)$	95.8	48.8	181.6	336.7	405.9	461.4
I:						
Net investment $(I = I' − \text{CCA})$	8.4	−5.6	−7.5	21.8	19.7	32.3

* Less than $5 million. Details may not add to total due to rounding.
n.a.s.—Not available separately.
Source: *Economic Report of the President*, 1961.

INCOME IDENTITIES

The alternative ways of computing gross national product can be summarized in a series of identities which form the basis for the subject of the following chapter—the theory of income determination. The following notations will also be used in the following chapters.

GNP—Gross national product
   Y—Net national product (national income)
   Y_d—Disposable income

CCA—Capital Consumption allowances
   W_p—Personal income receipts
   C—Personal consumption

S_p—Personal saving
T_p—Direct personal taxes
T_b—Direct business taxes
S_b—Business saving
S'—Gross saving
S_p'—Gross private saving
S—Net saving
G—Government purchases
S_g—Government saving (surplus or deficit)

T_i—Indirect taxes
T'—Gross taxes
T—Net taxes
T_r—Government transfer payments
I'—Gross investment
I—Net investment
I_d—Net domestic investment
I_f—Net foreign investment

From the product approach, we have (using 1960 figures):

$$(16.A.1) \quad \text{GNP} \equiv C + I' + G ,$$
$$504.4 \equiv 328.9 + 75.4 + 100.1 .$$

The income generation side gives us:

$$(16.A.2) \quad \text{GNP} \equiv W_p + T_b + S_b + T_i + \text{CCA} ,$$
$$504.4 \equiv 383.8 + 22.3 + 8.6 + 45.6 + 43.1 .$$

When we examine how income is used we observe that income is either spent for goods and services, saved, or used to pay taxes. Therefore, we have:

$$(16.A.3) \quad W_p \equiv C + S_p + T_p - T_r .$$

Identity (16.A.2) then becomes:

$$(16.A.4) \quad \text{GNP} \equiv C + S_p + T_p + T_b + S_b + T_i + \text{CCA} - T_r .$$

Gross investment is given as

$$(16.A.5) \quad I' \equiv I_d + I_f + \text{CCA} .$$

Substituting this in (16.A.1), gives us

$$(16.A.6) \quad \text{GNP} \equiv C + G + I_d + I_f + \text{CCA} .$$

Setting Identity (16.A.4) equal to Identity (16.A.6) (since they are both GNP), and subtracting C from both sides gives us:

$$(16.A.7) \quad S_p + S_b + \text{CCA} + T_p + T_b + T_i - T_r \equiv G + I_d + I_f + \text{CCA} ,$$
$$22.9 + 8.6 + 43.1 + 71.1 + 22.3 + 45.6 - 39.1 \equiv 100.1 + 29.3$$
$$+ 3.0 + 43.1 ,$$

that is, gross private saving plus net taxes is identical to government spending plus gross investment.

Government saving is equal to net government receipts minus expenditures, or

$$(16.A.8) \quad S_g \equiv (T_p + T_b + T_i - T_r) - G ,$$
$$1.9 \equiv 71.1 + 22.3 + 45.6 - 39.1 - 100.1 .$$

Substituting Identity (16.A.8) into Identity (16.A.7), shows that in national income accounting gross savings is defined to be equal to gross investment:

$$(16.A.9) \quad S_p + S_b + S_g + \text{CCA} \equiv I_d + I_f + \text{CCA} ,$$
$$22.9 + 8.6 + 1.9 + 43.1 \equiv 29.3 + 3.0 + 43.1 .$$

If we then subtract the capital consumption allowances from gross saving and gross investment, we observe that net saving is identical to net investment:

$$(16.A.10) \quad S_p + S_b + S_g \equiv I_d + I_f ,$$
$$22.9 + 8.6 + 1.9 \equiv 29.3 + 3.0 .$$

Furthermore, net national product (national income) is equal to gross national product minus the capital consumption allowances:

$$(16.A.11) \quad Y \equiv GNP - CCA ,$$
$$461.3 \equiv 504.4 - 43.1 .$$

Let net taxes, T, be defined as:

$$(16.A.12) \quad T \equiv T_p + T_b + T_i - T_r ,$$
$$99.9 \equiv 71.1 + 22.3 + 45.6 - 39.1 .$$

Then disposable income is given as:

$$(16.A.13) \quad Y_d \equiv Y - T ,$$
$$361.4 \equiv 461.3 - 99.9 .$$

Since we have used the figures as reported in the July, 1961 issue of the *Survey of Current Business,* the two sides of the identity are not always equal because of the presence of a statistical discrepancy and rounding errors.

QUESTIONS AND EXERCISES

1. "The gross national product does not include all goods produced." Explain.
2. How are disposable income, net national product, and gross national product related?
3. Discuss the difference between money income and real income. If the value of the dollar changes, how can we utilize national income statistics when we wish to compare the amounts of goods and services available to the economy at different points in time?
4. The price index for the following years is:

1929	70.0
1933	54.0
1943	77.3
1947	100.0
1953	119.0
1956	124.9
1958	133.4
1960	137.8

Calculate the gross national product in 1947 prices, for years given in Table 16–5. Compare the change in real GNP with money GNP from 1929–1933. 1929–1960.

5. By suitably combining the appropriate figures listed below, calculate the following:
   a) GNP
   b) NNP, Y
   c) Disposable income, Y_d

d) Gross investment, I'
e) Net investment, I
f) Gross savings, S'
g) Net savings, S
all in billions of dollars.

   1. Personal expenditures on durable goods........................ 35
   2. New construction.. 34
   3. Personal savings.. 18
   4. Net foreign investment...................................... 3
   5. Government transfers.. 18
   6. Personal expenditures on services...........................100
   7. Net change in business inventories.......................... 4
   8. Undistributed corporate profits............................. 8
   9. Indirect business taxes..................................... 35
10. Producers' purchases of durable equipment.................... 30
11. Contributions to social security............................ 14
12. Capital consumption allowances.............................. 35
13. Personal taxes.. 40
14. Personal expenditures on nondurable goods...................135
15. Corporate profits tax liability............................. 23
16. Federal government purchases of goods and services........... 50
17. State and local government purchases of goods and services....... 34

6. Bring the tables "Gross National Product" (Table 16–5) and "Uses of National Output" (Table 16–4) up to date.

Chapter	CONSUMPTION, SAVING,
17	AND THE MULTIPLIER

In the preceding chapter we developed the concept of national income and its important components: investment, saving, consumption, government purchases of goods and services, and tax receipts. Our next task will be to show how these aggregate variables are related through the behavior of households in adjusting their consumption expenditures, businesses in deciding how much to spend on investment goods, and both households and businesses in adjusting their holdings of money. A discussion of the economic influence of governmental activities will be postponed, for the moment. Our purpose now is to go beyond the anatomy of national income to see what determines the level of the national income at any point in time, and what causes it to rise or fall. This chapter deals with the relationship between consumption and income, or what is technically called the consumption function, its characteristics, and its objective and subjective determinants. The functional relationship between consumption and income is considered as one of the strategic relationships affecting the economic behavior of the economy as a whole. In this analysis the stress is placed upon the level of income as determined by the interaction of the forces influencing saving and investment.

As a first step in explaining the determinants of the equilibrium level of income we will abstract from the effects of government, that is, we will be studying an economic system in which both tax receipts and government expenditures are equal to zero (i.e., $T = G = 0$). After we have explored this first approximation to the economic system in this and in the next chapter, we will introduce and take account of the effect of taxes and government expenditure on the levels of income and employment. We will also discuss the various ways in which government, through fiscal and monetary policy, can affect the level of income and employment. You will notice that we are also leaving out of the account at present the effects of international trade, that is, we are

256

considering what is called a closed system—an economy in which the trading, production, and consumption are all undertaken within the system. The effects of international trade on the domestic level of income and employment will be considered later.

17.1. The Individual Propensity to Consume

In the simplified national income accounting in the last chapter we said that the net national product minus net taxes was equal to disposable income. In our present model, since $T = G = 0$, $\text{NNP} \equiv Y_d$, where Y_d is disposable income. We have the following identity

$$(17.1) \quad Y_d \equiv C + S \equiv C + I .$$

This says that disposable income can be divided into spending on consumer goods and saving; and, in product terms, the value of the product produced by the recipients of this disposable income can be divided into consumption goods and investment goods. For the moment we shall ignore the factors determining the volume of investment (they will be considered in the following chapter) and concentrate on consumption. We want to discover what it is that determines the amount of money which a community spends on consumption goods.

Now, the volume of consumption in a country clearly depends on the consumption decisions of individual members of the community. The sum total of the amounts which separate individuals spend on consumption is the amount spent by the community as a whole. This may sound obvious, but it is desirable not to overlook the importance of these individual decisions.

For the individual family, income appears to be the most important single determinant of consumption and saving. As disposable income increases, a family's consumption also increases, but not by as much as in the increase in disposable income. The validity of this relationship is substantiated by personal experience and by consumption and income statistics. For example, consider the 1953 family data in Table 17–1.

The relationship between disposable income and consumption, which is called the propensity to consume, or the consumption function $[c = c(y_d)]$[1] may be represented very clearly graphically. If values for disposable income (y_d) are plotted along the horizontal axis, consumption (c), and savings (s), along the vertical axis, the line which

---

[1] As pointed out in Chapter 1, $c(y_d)$ is read as c of y_d, not as c times y_d. This method of notation is used to indicate that consumption is some function of disposable income, but the exact form of the function is not given. We are using lower case letters to indicate family data.

relates consumption and income represents the consumption schedule or the propensity to consume $c = c(y_d)$. The data given in Table 17–1 are plotted in Figure 17–1.

In Figure 17–1, the $45°$ line traces out what the consumption function would look like if all of the family's disposable income were used for consumption purposes; i.e., consumption spending, measured from the origin on the vertical axis, is exactly equal to the associated disposable income, measured from the origin on the horizontal axis. The position of the consumption function with reference to the $45°$ line im-

TABLE 17–1

DISPOSABLE INCOME, CONSUMPTION, AND SAVINGS*

y_d Disposable Income (After Taxes)	$c = c(y_d)$ Consumption Expenditures	$s = y_d - c(y_d)$ Net Savings
$1,000	$1.100	−$100
2,000	2.050	− 50
3,000	3,000	0
4,000	3,900	100
5,000	4,780	220
6,000	5,650	350
7,000	6,500	500
8,000	7,300	700

* Adapted from projections of the 1950 Bureau of Labor Statistics Survey. For the projections see "The Consumer Markets, 1954–59," *Fortune*, August, 1954.

mediately shows whether or not the family has positive or negative saving. If the consumption function lies above the $45°$ line, it means that the family is spending more on consumption that its disposable income and its dissaving is equal to the difference between the consumption function and the $45°$ line. Similarly, if the family's consumption function lies below the $45°$ line it means that the family has positive savings, it is spending less on consumption that the whole of its disposable income. Again, the amount of current savings is measured by the difference between the consumption function and the $45°$ line. Where the two lines meet, the family's saving is zero.

From this relationship between the consumption function and the $45°$ reference line we can derive another function—the saving function, which is equal to disposable income minus the consumption function, $s = y_d - c(y_d)$. The savings function in Figure 17–1 thus intersects the x axis at the level of disposable income at which the family has zero savings. The vertical distance in Figure 17–1 between the s curve and

FIGURE 17–1

CONSUMPTION AND SAVINGS FUNCTIONS

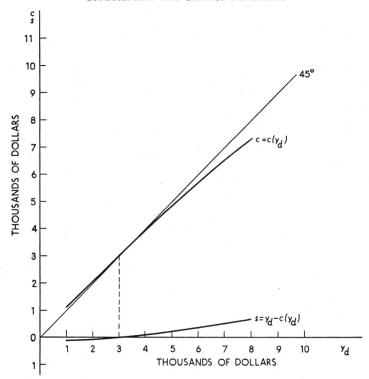

the disposable income axis (x axis) is exactly the same as the distance between the consumption function and the $45°$ reference line.

17.2. The Marginal Propensity to Consume

It is a common observation that as an individual's income rises, he usually spends a part of the increase for consumption and saves part. When we explain the determination of the level of national income we will attach much importance to the extra amount spent on consumption if an individual receives an increase in income. This idea or concept has been termed the marginal propensity to consume. The data in Table 17–1 has been used to construct Table 17–2, which includes the marginal propensity to consume. Disposable income is given in Column 1, and the accompanying consumption is shown in Column 2. As income increases from $1,000 to $2,000, consumption rises from $1,100 to $2,050. The increase in income is $1,000 and the increase in consumption is $950, therefore the additional consumption is .95 of the additional income. The marginal propensity to consume is there-

TABLE 17–2

THE MARGINAL PROPENSITIES AT VARIOUS INCOME LEVELS

	y_d	c	MPC $\Delta c/\Delta y_d$	s	MPS $\Delta s/\Delta y_d$
A	$1,000	$1,100		−$100	
			$\frac{950}{1000} = .95$		$\frac{50}{1000} = .05$
B	2,000	2,050		− 50	
			$\frac{950}{1000} = .95$		$\frac{50}{1000} = .05$
C	3,000	3,000		0	
			$\frac{900}{1000} = .9$		$\frac{100}{1000} = .1$
D	4,000	3,900		100	
			$\frac{880}{1000} = .88$		$\frac{120}{1000} = .12$
E	5,000	4,780		220	
			$\frac{870}{1000} = .87$		$\frac{130}{1000} = .13$
F	6,000	5,650		350	
			$\frac{850}{1000} = .85$		$\frac{150}{1000} = .15$
G	7,000	6,500		500	
			$\frac{800}{1020} = .8$		$\frac{200}{1000} = .2$
H	8,000	7,300		700	

fore .95 when income rises from $1,000 to $2,000. We notice that as the level of income rises the marginal propensity to consume decreases, from .95 to .8 in Table 17–2.

17.3. The Marginal Propensity to Save

An individual's income is divided between consumption and saving. In the same manner any increase in income an individual receives is either consumed or saved. Therefore we find another concept which relates changes in income and changes in saving—the marginal propensity to save. Because an increase in income is either consumed or saved, the marginal propensity to consume plus the marginal propensity to save always add up to 1. In geometrical terms the marginal propensity to consume is the slope of the consumption function in Figure 17–1, and the marginal propensity to save is the slope of the savings function in Figure 17–1. Notice that at point A, Table 17–2, where the individual has an income of $1,000, and spends more than his income on consumption, the marginal propensity to consume is less than 1. This means that while the individual spends more than his total income on consumption, if this same individual receives an increase in income he will not spend all of this increase in income on consumption.

17.4. The Aggregate Propensity to Consume

To study what determines national income, we are not so much interested in individual behavior as in the behavior of the whole community, but the same principles that apply to individuals will apply to the aggregate community. Aggregate income is not the only factor determining aggregate consumption, but it does appear to be one of the most important. We will assume that consumption behavior is such that a definite and fairly stable functional relationship exists between a community's disposable income and the amount the community spends on consumption. Thus we have, for the community as a whole,

$$(17.2) \quad C = C(Y_d) ,$$

where C represents the functional relationship between disposable income and consumption.

The data presented diagrammatically in Figure 17–2 illustrates the

FIGURE 17–2

AGGREGATE DISPOSABLE INCOME AND CONSUMPTION,
U.S., 1929–1960

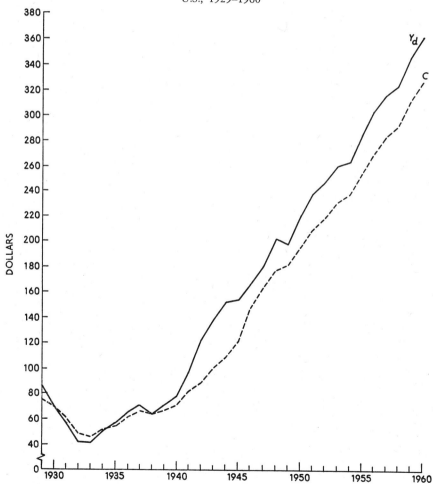

very close relationship that has existed between consumption and disposable income in the United States during the period 1929–1960.

17.5. The Schedule of the Propensity to Consume

Since consumption is a function of disposable income, it follows that one can construct a schedule (the propensity to consume) showing how much will be consumed at various levels of disposable income. We are here assuming that it is a stable schedule over some time period. In Table 17–3 the first column records various possible levels of disposable income (Y_d) and the second column refers to various amounts of consumption expenditure out of current disposable income (C). The whole schedule relating various amounts of disposable income and consumption is called the propensity to consume or simply the con-

TABLE 17–3

CONSUMPTION SCHEDULE
(In Billions of Dollars)

Disposable Income Y_d	Consumption $C = C(Y_d)$
50	60
100	100
150	140
200	180
250	220
300	260
350	300

sumption function. There are a number of assumptions we can make about the shape and the nature of the schedule of the propensity to consume of a modern community that appear to be rather realistic.

First, it is reasonable to suppose that as a community's income rises its consumption will rise too. We can suppose, further, on good ground, that if income rises by a given absolute amount, say $1,000, consumption will rise by a smaller absolute amount, that is, when income increases consumption will increase too, but not, as a rule, by so much as income has increased.

This may be put mathematically; where dY_d represents a very small increase in income, and dC represents the resulting increase in consumption, then dC/dY_d will be positive but less than 1, that is $1 > dC/dY_d > 0$. dC/dY_d is known as the community "marginal propensity to consume." It shows the change in the community's consumption with respect to a very small change in the community's disposable income. Since aggregate savings equals disposable income minus consumption, we have

$$(17.3) \quad S = Y_d - C,$$

and $dS/dY_d = 1 - dC/dY_d$ is the community marginal propensity to save, as the change in aggregate income is either consumed or saved and what is saved is the remainder.

Thus we can illustrate both the aggregate propensity to consume and the aggregate propensity to save on the same diagram. Figure 17–3

FIGURE 17–3

AGGREGATE CONSUMPTION AND SAVINGS FUNCTIONS

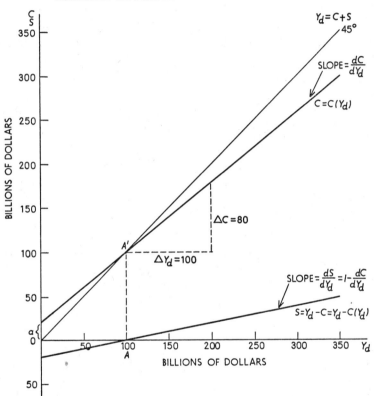

shows in diagrammatic form the consumption schedule of Table 17–3. Aggregate savings and consumption are measured vertically and disposable income is measured horizontally. The $45°$ reference line indicates what the aggregate consumption function would look like if, in the aggregate, disposable income were completely used to purchase consumption goods, leaving a zero level of savings. The distance between the consumption function, at any given level of disposable income, and the $45°$ line represents aggregate savings. Many attempts have been made statistically to find the precise form of the consumption function.

These studies indicate that many factors in addition to income affect the level of consumption. However, at present we shall consider only the relationship between income and consumption, leaving other possible variables for later inclusion in the analysis. Specifically, we shall take the consumption function to be of the form

$$(17.4) \quad C = a + bY_d .$$

On this simplifying assumption, consumption is a linear function of disposable income. This explains the constant slope of the consumption curve in Figure 17–3. The consumption curve slopes upward to the right, indicating that consumption increases as disposable income increases. At the point A', where the consumption curve intersects the 45° line, savings equal zero, and the community consumes exactly its entire disposable income.

In Table 17–3, this break-even point occurs where disposable income is equal to $100 billion. At levels of income lower than $100 billion the community has negative savings, but it has positive savings at levels of disposable income greater than $100 billion. The savings curve, in the lower part of Figure 17–3 is simply the complement of the consumption curve, inasmuch as savings equals disposable income minus consumption.

The form of the consumption function we have employed in Figure 17–3 (a sraight line: $C = a + bY_d$) embodies the assumption that every addition to income involves a constant addition to consumption. The marginal propensity to consume, dC/dY_d, is a constant and equal to b in our example. If we had chosen a nonlinear consumption function the marginal propensity to consume would not have been constant. We will return to the marginal propensity to consume again when we investigate the change in the level of income which occurs in response to a change in investment.

For other problems we might be interested in another attribute of the consumption function, the average propensity to consume. The average propensity to consume is defined as the ratio of consumption expenditure to disposable income, C/Y_d, for any level of disposable income. In Table 17–3, if Y_d is equal to $100 billion, consumption is also equal to $100 billion; C/Y_d equals 1. If Y_d equals $200 billion, C is $180 billion, and C/Y_d is .9, etc. We notice that the proportion of income spent on consumption decreases as community disposable income rises, while the proportion of disposable income saved increases as the level of income increases.

17.6. Determinants of the Propensity to Consume

We have ignored other factors, apart from the size of aggregate disposable income, which may affect the community propensity to consume. We have taken the propensity to consume as a schedule of the various amounts that consumers as a whole will spend on consumption goods for a corresponding schedule of disposable incomes, at a given time and over a given period, say one year. We have abstracted from other factors which may affect the amount a community will spend on consumption, such as price changes, actual and expected.

If community expectations are that prices will rise, this expectation will tend to raise the proportion of income spent for consumption, since the quantity of goods that a dollar will buy will be less in the future than in the present. Thus the propensity to consume line will shift upwards. For our simplified consumption function, this means that a will increase and perhaps b will also increase. The reverse will occur if community expectations are that prices will fall.

17.7. Tastes and Habits

Normally we assume that the ultimate goal of consumption is to provide satisfaction to the consumer. On this basis one might well imagine that we should include some measure of satisfaction in our formulation of the consumption function. However, as yet, we do not have a simple measure of taste. Furthermore, we generally assume that consumers' tastes do not change radically from year to year and therefor appear as a constant factor in the consumption function. If community attitudes toward thrift do change, the consumption function will shift upward or downward depending on whether the community is becoming less or more thrifty.

17.8. The Distribution of Income

As we pointed out, the community consumption schedule is in some sense an aggregation of the individual schedules. If all consumers had exactly the same marginal propensity to consume, the distribution of income would be unimportant; but as long as we think people at different levels of income do have different marginal propensities to consume, the distribution of income will affect the community consumption function. The position of the consumption function presupposes a given distribution of income. A change in the distribution of income toward greater equality will tend to raise the propensity to consume of the community as a whole. If a rich man's marginal propensity to consume is lower than that of a poor man, then a redistribution of income that shifts income from the rich man to the poor may be expected to raise the total level of consumption expenditure in the community.

For example, let us assume there is a community of 100 persons, 50 of whom have incomes of $8,000 each and the other 50 have incomes of $2,000 each. Further, let us assume that Tables 17–1 and 17–2 describe the relationship between disposable income and consumption for each of the individuals. Under these conditions total income is $500,000, with $467,500 used for consumption purposes and $32,500 saved. Now let us assume the aggregate income is redistributed so that each individual will have the same income, $5,000. Table 17–1 tells us that each person will now save $220, so aggregate saving will fall to $22,000 and aggregate consumption will rise to $478,000, in our hypothetical community. Thus the redistribution of income in our example raised the aggregate propensity to consume.

However, there appears to be less variation in the marginal propensity to consume than in the average propensity to consume between people in the upper and lower income brackets. One estimate indicated that if all consumers in the United States had the average income, consumption would be increased by about 4 per cent.

17.9. Determination of the Equilibrium Level of Income

We are now prepared to pull together the various elements that help determine the equilibrium level of national income. By an equilibrium level of income we mean a level of income such that there is no tendency to move from this level, once it is attained, unless conditions change. Practically all modern economists agree that one of the most important factors in causing income and employment to fluctuate is investment. This is based on the belief that consumption expenditures tend to be a much more stable component of income than investment expenditures. Indeed, it is argued, the key to understanding fluctuations in income and employment is to be found in the great variability of investment expenditures.

At this point, however, our aim is much more modest. In this first model we shall investigate the determination of the equilibrium income in a purely private enterprise economy, an economy in which the government neither taxes nor spends, where the distribution of income does not change, tastes are given and unchanged, and the price level remains constant. This is a model of a very simple economy, but one in which the essential forces determining the level of income can be isolated. Provisionally, we shall also assume that the amount of private investment is given and unchanged, that is, investment is constant irrespective of the level of income. Later on we shall deal specifically with the determinants of investment, but for the moment we shall hold investment constant in our economic system.

In order to find the equilibrium level of income under the above conditions, let us restate Equation (17.1), which is an identity:

$$(17.1) \quad Y_d \equiv C + I .$$

We now substitute on the right-hand side of Equation (17.1) the value of C given in Equation (17.4), which is the consumption function, a behavior relation, and write $\bar{I}$ for I, since we have assumed the amount of private investment to be given and constant. We then have:

$$(17.5) \quad Y_d = (a + bY_d) + \bar{I} .$$

Equation (17.5) is not an identity but is based on the behavior implied in the consumption function. Then if we subtract bY_d from both sides of Equation (17.5), we obtain:

$$(17.6) \quad Y_d - bY_d = a + \bar{I} .$$

Next we divide both sides of Equation (17.6) by $(1 - b)$ and we have:

$$(17.7) \quad Y_d = \frac{1}{(1 - b)} (a + \bar{I}) .$$

This solution of the equations tells us what the equilibrium level of income would be if we knew the given level of investment and the numerical value of the constant a and of the community's marginal propensity to consume, b. Using the consumption schedule in Table 17–3 and assuming the given $\bar{I}$ to be $30 billion we can construct an arithmetical example of the determination of the level of aggregate income.

In Table 17–4, we observe the equilibrium level of income is $250 billion, that is $Y_d = 250 = C + \bar{I} = 250$. This is the only level of income that will maintain itself unchanged, where the sum of consumption expenditure plus investment add up to the total of disposable income. A study of Table 17–4 gives us an understanding of the process by which the economy reaches the equilibrium level of income. Suppose the consumers, in the aggregate, expected to receive an income of $150 billion. With this level of income, the consumption function in Table 17–4 tells us that the individuals together would spend $140 billion for consumption. Added to this $140 billion consumption expenditure is the $30 billion for investment, making a total expenditure of $170 billion on goods and services during the period, with a corresponding rise in the level of income. With income running at the $170 billion level the expenditure on consumption would rise since the previous rate of spending was based on a lower level of income. Consumers would prefer to consume more out of the new, higher level of income. The increased consumption would in turn push the level of income still higher, with this process of expansion continuing until income reached a level of $250 billion.

However, if the individuals in the community expected a level of income higher than the equilibrium level, we would observe the op-

TABLE 17–4

HYPOTHETICAL INCOME DETERMINATION
(In Billions of Dollars)

Y	$C(Y_d)$	$\bar{I}$	$C + \bar{I}$
50	60	30	90
100	100	30	130
150	140	30	170
200	180	30	210
250	220	30	250
300	260	30	290
350	300	30	330

posite adjustment, *viz.* contraction. Suppose the members of the economy, in the aggregate, expected total income to be $350 billion. With this rate of income the desired rate of consumption would be $300 billion per period. This rate of consumption plus the given rate of investment of $30 billion would give a total rate of spending on goods and services of $330 billion—thus the level of income would fall. As the level of income fell, the desired rate of expenditure on consumption would also decline and income would fall again. This process of contraction would continue until the equilibrium level of income was reached, where $Y_d = C(Y_d) + \bar{I}$.

This process is shown graphically in Figure 17–4. In the upper part of Figure 17–4 we have added the given amount of investment from Table 17–4 to the consumption function of Figure 17–3. The equilibrium level of income is found where income equals consumption plus investment. In Figure 17–4 this occurs at the point where the 45° line (along which income equals output) intersects the $C + \bar{I}$ line. Alternatively, we can find the equilibrium income using the savings function of Figure 17–3. In the lower part of Figure 17–4 the constant

FIGURE 17–4

EQUILIBRIUM INCOME

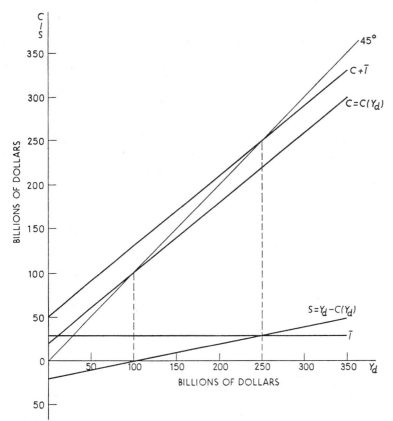

amount of investment is constructed as a straight line and the savings function is based on the data in Table 17–4. The equilibrium level of income is given by the intersection of the savings function and the investment line. At this rate of income, the desired level of savings is equal to the rate of investment. The equilibrium condition, therefore, is

$$(17.8) \quad Y_d - C(Y_d) = \bar{I} .$$

17.10. The Equality of Savings and Investment

The desire to save in relation to income and the desire to invest determine the equilibrium level of income for the economy as a whole, just as the desire to sell and the desire to buy, as functions of price, determine the equilibrium price of a good or service in a market. Let us examine the relationship between savings and investment and the adjustment function involved.

We recall from the previous chapter that actual savings and actual investment are always identically equal, Equation (16.7). This accounting equality of savings and investment follows from the definition of savings as equal to income minus consumption expenditures and of investment as equal to net national product minus consumption goods. Since income earned is equal to the value of the goods produced and the amount spent on consumption is equal to the value of the goods sold for consumption purposes, we have the accounting equality of savings and investment. This accounting identity holds good regardless of whether the economic system is in or out of equilibrium. If there were nothing more than this accounting identity of savings and investment in national income analysis, the relationship between savings and investment would have a very limited role to play.

Equation (17.8) is more than an accounting identity that is always true; it states the condition that must be satisfied in order to reach the equilibrium level of income, that is, a condition characterized by the equality of *planned* savings and investment (as opposed to actual savings, which may deviate from the desired level). The functional equality of savings and investment makes use of the functional concept of savings (the savings function) and emphasizes the importance of the behavior of the individuals in the economic system. Thus the functional equality of savings and investment [as expressed in Equation (17.8)] means that individuals react to income variations in such a way that their desires to save and to invest (which we will discuss in the following chapter) are reconciled in the working out of their reactions and adjustments to income changes. In our present simplified model, the functional equality of savings and investment is the final result of a process of adjustment among savings, investment, and income. Let us examine the adjustment process, using the data in Table 17–5.

The first two columns of Table 17–5 beginning on the left, make up the savings function; the third column gives the value of investment, which we have assumed to be constant, and the last column shows the divergence between planned savings and planned investment, at various levels of income. We may interpret Table 17–5 as follows. If the planned amount of investment exceeds the planned amount of savings, at a given level of income, income will expand. If we look at the reaction in terms of the circular flow of income, more will be added to the income stream by the behavior of the investors than will be deducted from the income stream by the behavior of the savers. Income will continue to change until the divergence has been eliminated. In

Table 17–5 the divergence between planned investment and planned savings is equal to zero when income is equal to $250 billion. In the following chapter, when we analyze the general equilibrium of income, consumption, investment, savings, and the rate of interest, we will use the savings function rather than the consumption function for purposes of convenience only. The determination of the equilibrium level of income may be explained in terms of either function.

TABLE 17–5

INCOME DETERMINATION USING A SAVINGS FUNCTION
(In Billions of Dollars)

Y_d	$S = Y_d - C(Y_d)$	$\bar{I}$	$\bar{I} - S$
50	−10	30	40
100	0	30	30
150	10	30	20
200	20	30	10
250	30	30	0
300	40	30	−10
350	50	30	−20

17.11. *The Investment Multiplier*

The importance of investment is emphasized when we realize than an increase in private investment, given the consumption function, will cause income to expand, and a decrease in investment will cause it to contract. This should not appear surprising, since, as we pointed out earlier, investment is one part of total output. But our theory of income determination gives us a more startling result. Income analysis shows that increases in investment can give rise to more than proportional increases in income. The amplified effect of investment on income is called the "multiplier."

To satisfy yourself that a given increase in investment causes a larger increase in income, suppose in the graphical illustration in Figure 17–4 that the given, and constant, investment increases from $30 billion to $60 billion, and then compute the resulting increase in income.

The multiplier shows the ratio between an increase in equilibrium income and the increase in investment which has given rise to it. If we employ the conventional notation using dI to represent a given increase in investment and dY_d the resultant increase in income, and k to designate the multiplier, then the multiplier is defined as

$$(17.9) \quad k = \frac{dY_d}{dI}; \text{ thus, } dY_d = kdI .$$

It is easy to show that the value of the multiplier is determined by the community's marginal propensity to consume. Consider the relationship $Y_d = C + I$, where C is a function of income. Then, $I = Y_d - C$,

$$\frac{dI}{dY_d} = 1 - \frac{dC}{dY_d}.$$

Therefore,

$$(17.10) \quad k = \frac{dY_d}{dI} = \frac{1}{1 - \dfrac{dC}{dY_d}} = \frac{1}{1 - MPC} = \frac{1}{MPS}.$$

In terms of the consumption function we used in Equation (17.7) to determine equilibrium income, we have

$$(17.11) \quad Y_d = \frac{1}{(1 - b)} (a + \bar{I}).$$

Again we shall use dI to represent a change in investment and dY_d the corresponding change in income. As we increase investment from $\bar{I}$ to $(\bar{I} + dI)$, income will increase from Y_d to $(Y_d + dY_d)$. Let us make this substitution in equation (17.11).

$$(17.12) \quad Y_d + dY_d = \frac{1}{1 - b} (a + \bar{I} + dI).$$

If we subtract equation (17.11) from equation (17.12) we have

$$(17.13) \quad dY_d = \frac{1}{1 - b} dI.$$

From this we see that dY_d/dI (the multiplier k) depends upon the value of the marginal propensity to consume, b, for

$$(17.14) \quad dY_d/dI = \frac{1}{1 - b}.$$

Thus, the larger is the value of the marginal propensity to consume, the larger is the value of the multiplier.

We should remember, however, that we are concerned with an economic process and not simply an algebraic manipulation. The relationship between k (the multiplier) and the marginal propensity to consume can be derived less formally, and with more economic meaning as follows:

a) Suppose businesses decide to increase their investment expenditures by some increment, say ΔI billion dollars. This money will be paid out for construction goods, inventories, equipment, etc. The recipients of this expenditure will have their incomes increased by $\Delta_1 Y_d = \Delta I$ billion dollars. That is if $\Delta I = 1$, there will be a $1 billion increase in incomes when this money is paid out to individuals.

b) If the aggregate marginal propensity to consume (b) or $\Delta C / \Delta Y_d$ equals 80 per cent, then on the average we would expect the recipients of the $1 billion increase in income to spend $0.8 billion on consumer goods, and to increase their savings by $0.2 billion. Thus at the second round the recipients of this $0.8 billion increase in spending will experience an increase of $0.8 billion in their incomes. At the second round $\Delta_2 Y_d = $0.8 billion, or in general $\Delta_2 Y_d = b\Delta I$.

c) These people will then spend, on the average, 80 per cent of $0.8 billion, that is 80 per cent of the increase in their incomes, or $0.64 billion (since the marginal propensity to consume or b was taken to be equal to 80 per cent). Thus at the third round $\Delta_3 Y_d = $0.64 billion, or in general $\Delta_3 Y_d = b^2 \Delta I$.

d) This process continues, tending to lead to a cumulative increase in income given by

$$\begin{aligned} \Delta Y_d &= \Delta_1 Y_d + \Delta_2 Y_d + \Delta_3 Y_d + \ldots \\ &= \Delta I + b\Delta I + b^2 \Delta I + \ldots \\ &= \Delta I (1 + b + b^2 + b^3 + \ldots) \end{aligned}$$

The multiplier is then

$$k = \frac{\Delta Y_d}{\Delta I} = \frac{1}{1 - b}$$

since

$$\frac{1}{1 - b} = 1 + b + b^2 + b^3 + \ldots$$

Even with the simple model we have studied, considerable insight is given for the economic implications of such things as changes in a community's desire to save or fluctuations in the rate of private investment. In this chapter we took investment as a constant and fixed amount; it is now time to consider investment demanded, the subject of the following chapter.

17.12. Government Taxation and Expenditures

Thus far in our discussion of the determination of the equilibrium level of income we have assumed that the economy we are studying is a very simple one, an economy in which the government neither taxes nor spends, where the distribution of income is constant, tastes are given and unchanged, the price level is constant, and business saving and foreign trade is negligible. Provisionally, we have also assumed that private investment is a given and unchanged amount. At this point we wish to relax these assumptions slightly and consider the impact of government expenditures and taxation on the determination of the equilibrium level of income.

Under these conditions income will be earned in the production of goods and services purchased by consumers, investors, and the government.

$$(17.15) \quad Y \equiv C + I + G .$$

With the addition of government taxation, aggregate income will be used to buy consumption goods and services, part of income will be used to pay taxes, and the remainder is saved.

$$(17.16) \quad Y \equiv C + S + T .$$

In order to isolate the effects of government expenditures and taxation on the equilibrium level of income in the simple economy we are studying, let us first assume that government expenditures increase from zero to some positive amount, but that tax receipts remain at zero. Then we will assume that tax receipts increase from zero to some positive amount, and observe what happens to the equilibrium level of income in each case.

In order to find the equilibrium level of income, in our simple economy, let us begin with Equation (17.15):

$$(17.15) \quad Y = C + I + G .$$

We now substitute on the right-hand side of the equation the value of C given earlier in Equation (17.4) and write $\bar{I}$ for I, since we are still assuming that the amount of private investment is a given constant. We also assume that G is given, presumably by political action in the various levels of government. We now have:

$$(17.17) \quad Y = (a + bY_d) + \bar{I} + G .$$

In Chapter 16 we pointed out that disposable income is equal to national income minus net taxes,

$$(16.2) \quad Y_d \equiv Y - T ;$$

therefore, let us substitute the quantity $(Y - T)$ for Y_d in Equation (17.17). Then if we subtract the quantity bY from both sides of Equation (17.17), we have:

$$(17.18) \quad Y - bY = a - bT + \bar{I} + G .$$

Next we divide both sides of Equation (17.18) by $(1 - b)$ to obtain:

$$(17.19) \quad Y = \frac{1}{(1 - b)}(a - bT + \bar{I} + G).$$

This solution tells us what the equilibrium level of income would be if we knew the given level of investment, the numerical value of the constant a, the value of the community's marginal propensity to consume, and the given levels of government expenditure and taxation. In the present case we have assumed net taxes to be equal to zero, so the term concerned with taxes, bT, drops out, giving us:

$$(17.20) \quad Y = \frac{1}{(1 - b)}(a + \bar{I} + G).$$

Using the consumption schedule and assumed level of investment given in Table 17–4 as a starting point, let us assume that government expenditures are given as $50 billion per year, and then examine what happens to the hypothetical level of income.

TABLE 17–6

HYPOTHETICAL INCOME DETERMINATION (G added)
(In Billions of Dollars)

Y	$C(Y_d)$	$\bar{I}$	G	$C + \bar{I} + G$
50	60	30	50	140
100	100	30	50	180
150	140	30	50	220
200	180	30	50	260
250	220	30	50	300
300	260	30	50	340
350	300	30	50	380
400	340	30	50	420
450	380	30	50	460
500	420	30	50	500
550	460	30	50	540
600	500	30	50	580
650	540	30	50	620
700	580	30	50	660

We observe that the equilibrium level of income is now $500 billion. This is the only level of income that will maintain itself unchanged, period after period. Previously, we pointed out in Equation (17.8) that the equilibrium condition required that the desired rate of savings be equal to the rate of investment—taken as given. With the addition of government expenditures to our simple model, notice that the equilibrium condition has also been altered. In equilibrium we observe that $Y = C(Y_d) + \bar{I} + G$. In our simple model, aggregate income is equal to disposable income, as we have assumed taxes are equal to zero; therefore, if we subtract consumption from both sides of the equation we have:

$$(17.21) \quad Y - C(Y_d) = \bar{I} + G .$$

Now the desired rate of savings is equal to investment plus government expenditures, not investment only. It is implicitly assumed in this case

FIGURE 17–5

EQUILIBRIUM INCOME (*G* added)

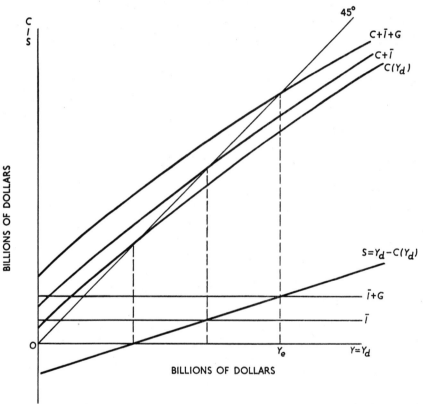

that the government finances its purchases by the sale of bonds to the individuals. Thus savings acts as an offset to both investment and government expenditures. This process is shown graphically in Figure 17–5.

Instead of having the government finance its purchases by the sale of bonds to the general public, let us assume that taxes are levied in an amount to equal government expenditures, that is, assume that $T = \$50$

billion in our simple example. The result of adding taxes to the system is presented in Table 17–7.

The equilibrium level of income has now shifted to $300 billion per year. We observe that when we added government expenditure to our simple model, aggregate income increased, but when we added government tax receipts to the model, aggregate income was reduced. With the addition of taxes, the equilibrium condition is again altered. In-

TABLE 17–7

HYPOTHETICAL INCOME DETERMINATION (With positive G and T)
(In Billions of Dollars)

Y	T	$C(Y_d)$	$\bar{I}$	G	$C + \bar{I} + G$
50	50	20	30	50	100
100	50	60	30	50	140
150	50	100	30	50	180
200	50	140	30	50	220
250	50	180	30	50	260
300	50	220	30	50	300
350	50	260	30	50	340
400	50	300	30	50	380
450	50	340	30	50	420
500	50	380	30	50	460

stead of requiring that desired savings be equal to investment plus government spending, we now observe that desired saving plus taxes must be equal to investment plus government expenditures, that is:

$$(17.22) \quad Y - C(Y_d) + T = \bar{I} + G .$$

In our example we assumed that both taxes and government expenditures were equal to $50 billion; therefore, desired savings and investment were equal. If, however, the government had either a deficit or a surplus, savings and investment would not be equal to each other.

The impact of the government will be explored more fully after we have developed the general equilibrium of investment, consumption, income, interest, and money, but even with this simple model one gains considerable insight to the effect of government spending and taxing on the rest of the economy.

QUESTIONS AND EXERCISES

1. Aggregate disposable income appears to be a very important determinant of the level of aggregate consumption. What other factors might also influence the aggregate consumption function?

2. If the aggregate consumption function is $C = 40 + \frac{4}{5} Y$ and the level of investment is given at $40 billion, what is the equilibrium level of income?

a) If investment increases to $45 billion, what is the equilibrium level of income?

b) If investment then falls to $35 billion, does the aggregate level of income fall? How much?

c) Using the above figures, what is the value of the multiplier?

3. Using the consumption function $C = 40 + \frac{4}{5} Y$, derive a savings function. Construct a savings schedule from the function. Taking investment as given and equal to $40 billion, use the savings function to determine the equilibrium level of income.

Assume that as a result of people desiring to save *more* out of each dollar the consumption function becomes $C = 40 + \frac{3}{4} Y$. What happens to the equilibrium level of income ($I = $40 billion)? Did the shift in the consumption function change the value of the multiplier from what it was in Problem 17.2?

4. Suppose the consumption function shifts to $C = 35 + \frac{4}{5} Y$. If investment remains at $40 billion, what is the equilibrium level of income? Is the new level higher or lower than in Problem 17.2? Than in the last part of Problem 17.3? Did the shift of the consumption function alter the value of the multiplier? Compare with Problem 17.3, and explain the results you observe.

5. The multiplier is concerned with an economic process and is not simply the result of an algebraic manipulation. Explain the statement.

6. Suppose that every person in an economy suddenly decided to increase their savings. Would aggregate savings increase? Explain your answer.

7. In Chapter 16 it was shown that actual savings and actual investment are always equal, and yet in Chapter 17 it is said that the relationship between savings and investment determines the aggregate level of income. How can this be?

THE GENERAL EQUILIBRIUM OF INVESTMENT, CONSUMPTION, INCOME, INTEREST, AND MONEY

Chapter
18

In the preceding chapter we examined the consumption and savings functions and the determination of the equilibrium level of income on the basis of a given level of investment. In this chapter we shall consider another component of aggregate demand—private investment, that is, the demand for goods to be used to further production and not as final goods for consumption purposes. In the previous chapter we showed how income was determined, given the propensity to consume and the level of investment. Now we ask, "What determines the level of investment?" The rate of investment spending, I, is an extremely volatile variable in income analysis, and it is, therefore, very difficult to make a simple postulate concerning the determinates of investment which will yield a stable functional relationship between investment, I, and other readily measurable variables. First we shall consider investment activity as a simple independent variable, and then as a function of the rate of interest and the expected rate of profit. Then we shall ask, "What determines the rate of interest?" Finally we shall bring the various economic behavior functions we have examined together into a basic model of the economic system and study the general equilibrium of investment, consumption, income, interest, and money.

18.1. *Autonomous Investment*

Part of the total demand for investment goods does not seem to be dependent upon either the level of income or the rate of interest but rather upon such factors as changes in technology and government policy. Some public utility investment, investment which occurs in direct response to inventions, and a certain amount of "long-range" investment (such as research and development) fits in this category, which we term "autonomous investment." As such, autonomous investment may be written

$$(18.1) \quad I = \bar{I}$$

279

where $\bar{I}$ is a constant given by technology and public policy. For this part of the investment function the rate of investment does not vary with the level of income or with the rate of interest. Total autonomous investment remains the same irrespective of what happens to income or the rate of interest. Figure 18–1 represents such autonomous investment.

In Figure 18–1, disposable income, Y_d is measured on the horizontal axis, and investment (equal to autonomous investment) is meas-

FIGURE 18–1

AUTONOMOUS INVESTMENT

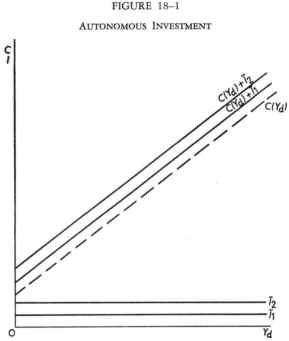

ured on the vertical axis. Since autonomous investment does not vary with the level of income, it is represented by a horizontal line paralleling the income axis. Two levels of autonomous investment are represented in Figure 18–1, $\bar{I}_1$ and $\bar{I}_2$. A movement from $\bar{I}_1$ to $\bar{I}_2$ is an upward shift of the autonomous investment function representing a higher rate of autonomous investment.

If we again assume that government spending is zero, aggregate demand for goods and services will consist of the sum of consumer buying and investment buying. Thus we can add the autonomous investment function $(\bar{I})$ to the consumption function $C(Y_d)$, which gives us the aggregate demand at various levels of income. In Figure 18–1 this is the $C(Y_d) + \bar{I}_1$ line. In the same way we can add the larger invest-ment represented by $\bar{I}_2$ to $C(Y_d)$ to give us the higher level of aggre-gate demand $C(Y_d) + \bar{I}_2$. For purposes of income determination all we would need to introduce into Figure 18–1 would be the $45°$ line and the equilibrium level of income would be given by the intersection of the $45°$ line and the appropriate consumption plus investment line (as in Figure 17–4 of the preceding chapter), depending upon the level of autonomous investment in our present model. While this simplified eco-nomic model, with only autonomous investment, gives very little insight into the normal peacetime economic system, it is very applicable in a war economy, or centrally planned economy, in which the level of in-vestment is conditioned by military objectives or by government plan-ning.

18.2. The Investment Demand Function

The variability of private investment is linked with variation in business expectations regarding the profitability of new investment projects. If we assume that the state of business expectations is constant, then we can postulate an investment demand schedule relating private investment with the rate of interest. This part of the total investment demand schedule has been called the *marginal-efficiency-of-capital* schedule. With the rate of interest taken to be an independent variable, we may analyze the functional relation between various amounts of in-vestment and various rates of interest.

The marginal efficiency of capital is equivalent to what business-men call the expected rate of profit and refers to the expected rate of profit of a new capital asset. As we have pointed out before, investment refers to the purchase of a new capital asset and not to the purchase of a stock or bond. As it is used here, the word "efficiency" refers to the effectiveness or profitability of investment, that is, the rate of return over cost. The word marginal is used to mean incremental or additional. Thus the marginal efficiency of a particular kind of capital asset means the highest rate of return over cost expected from an additional unit of that particular kind of capital asset. In the same manner the marginal efficiency of capital in general is the highest rate of return over cost ex-pected from producing a marginal or additional unit of the most profit-able of all types of capital assets.

Looking at the problem of the determination of investment in the simplest manner, it is readily apparent that a businessman might be expected to make any investment he thinks will be profitable. But how does the businessman determine this profitability? At this point we shall examine general principles only. The problem of the profitability of investment for the individual firm has been discussed earlier.[1] Let us consider the case of a firm trying to decide whether or not to purchase a certain machine. The firm can expect to receive certain revenues from the use of the machine each year that it owns the machine. Also, the firm will incur certain expenses in connection with using the machine as long as the firm owns the machine. If we subtract the stream of costs from the stream of revenues, we have a stream of net returns received by the firm for the use of the machine.

However, the stream of net returns received by the firm will not be all profit. It is obvious that the firm will need to set the original cost of the machine against the stream of net returns. But, is this all? What of the financing cost? Further consideration of the problem indicates that the stream of net returns must also cover the cost of financing the original purchase of the machine. This is very clear if the firm borrows the money to make the purchase. In this case the firm must pay interest until the loan is repaid, and clearly this is a charge against the revenue created by the use of the machine.

If, however, the firm does not borrow the money but uses its own money to finance the purchase of the machine, it does not incur interest charges, but it does incur an alternative cost in that the firm must forego alternative uses of the money. Instead of using the money to buy a machine, the firm could make a loan to some other firm and receive interest on that loan. This lost interest, then, is properly a charge against the stream of net returns when the firm finances its own investment.

Assume for the moment that the firm borrows the money to buy the equipment. We can then ask the question, "At what rate of interest could the firm borrow the money to buy the equipment and still break even?" As we have seen, this question really asks, "What rate of interest makes the present value of the stream of returns equal to the purchase price?" Obviously the firm will not buy the equipment unless the rate of yield is greater than the interest rate it has to pay on the money it borrows. At any one time a number of different investment opportunities are open to a firm with differing rates of yield. If these varying investment opportunities are ranked according to the rate of yield, there will be a certain amount at a relatively high yield, a greater amount at a lower yield, and a still larger amount at a still lower rate of yield. If we plotted these investment opportunities with the rate of yield on the vertical axis and the amount of investment on the horizon-

---

[1] See Chapter 9.

tal axis, we would have a schedule of the marginal efficiency of capital for the individual firm concerned.

The volume of investment varies inversely with the rate of return for two reasons. First, an increased amount of investment in a certain kind of capital, for example motels, tends to reduce the rate of return, because the new motels will have to compete with the existing motels for customers. We know from our earlier supply and demand analysis that if the supply of any good is increased, given the demand conditions, the price of the good will tend to fall. This is true for the services of capital goods as well as for consumer goods. Thus, increased investment tends to increase the supply of the particular capital good (motels) with a consequent tendency for the price of the output produced by the capital good to fall. As price falls, with unchanged cost conditions, the net return per unit of capital falls—that is, the marginal efficiency of capital falls. Second, the marginal efficiency of capital may fall with increased investment in any particular capital good, since the increased output of the capital good, say motels, may increase the cost of production of motels, which would reduce the stream of net returns. Cost may be pushed up as a result of a rise in prices of factors of production as increased investment increases the demand for the needed factors. With unchanged supply conditions for the factors, the increased demand would tend to push up factor prices.

If we imagine similar computations on the part of all the businessmen and firms in the economy and if we added together the investment opportunities open to the businessmen, we would have a marginal-efficiency-of-capital schedule for the economy as a whole. A graph representing such a schedule is shown in Figure 18–2.

From the above discussion we may infer that the amount of new investment in capital goods is a decreasing function of the rate of interest. Clearly, a businessman will not borrow money to buy a machine if the rate of yield or the marginal efficiency of capital is less than the rate of interest. Given the marginal-efficiency-of-capital schedule, we could determine the amount of investment demanded if we knew the rate of interest, since investment will be pushed to the point where the marginal efficiency of capital is equal to the rate of interest. We may write this as

$$(18.2) \quad I = g(i) \,,$$

to indicate that investment is a function of the rate of interest. Since investment is a decreasing function of the rate of interest, $dI/di < 0$, for a very small increase in i.

FIGURE 18–2

A HYPOTHETICAL MARGINAL-EFFICIENCY-OF-CAPITAL SCHEDULE

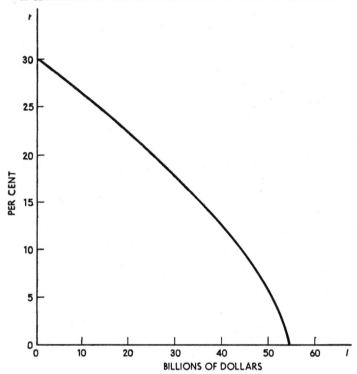

If we add the autonomous investment schedule to the marginal-efficiency-of-capital schedule, we will have the aggregate investment demand schedule for the economy, thus:

$$(18.3) \quad I = \bar{I} + g(i) .$$

This aggregate function will still be some function of the rate of interest, so we can substitute a new function for the aggregate investment function, as:

$$(18.4) \quad I = I(i) ,$$

which indicates that the aggregate investment will vary with the rate of interest, given the autonomous investment.

Let us assume that the graph shown in Figure 18–3 represents the investment demand function for the economy. Given this investment demand schedule, if the rate of interest, i, were 25 per cent, the businessmen in the community would want to invest $25 billion in capital goods. If the rate of interest was reduced to 20 per cent, aggregate investment would be $37 billion, while if the rate of interest fell

FIGURE 18–3

HYPOTHETICAL INVESTMENT DEMAND FUNCTION

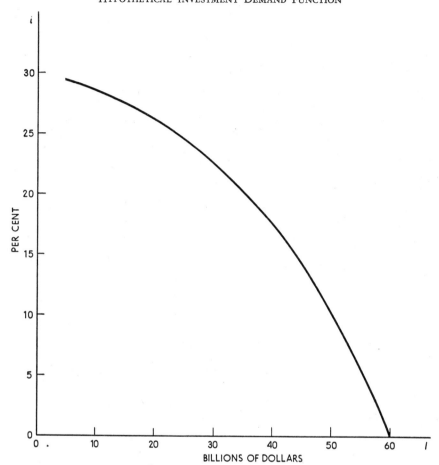

to 4 per cent, investment would be at the rate of $57 billion. Thus, given the investment demand schedule, the amount of investment is determined, given the rate of interest. Our next object, then, is to analyze the determination of the rate of interest.

While the above analysis is perfectly correct as far as it goes, a great deal is concealed under the assumption of given expectations on the part of businessmen. We said that investment was determined by the rate of interest and the marginal efficiency of capital. The marginal efficiency of capital in turn depends upon the present cost of capital goods and expected net returns, which, in turn, depend upon expected costs and expected revenues. Thus, as businessmen revise their cost and revenue expectations, the marginal efficiency of capital schedule may shift around, resulting in a changed level of investment at every possible level of the rate of interest.

In a more complex model of the economic system, the relationship between changes in aggregate demand and investment would also be considered. Part of total investment may be induced by changes in the rate of aggregate spending on final goods and thus this part of investment is some function of changes in aggregate income. As aggregate income, Y (consumption plus investment plus government demand for final goods), increases, additional investment is induced. However, we shall not consider this aspect of the investment function in our basic model of the economic system in order to keep the model as simple as possible without losing any of the essential properties of the system and thus to isolate the important elements in the system which help determine the economic variables.

In developing a model of the economic system, we need, first of all, simplicity. The economic system in reality is so complicated that if all the variables in the system are included in our model, even the latest computing machines would be unable to handle it. Thus we have to simplify by making certain broad assumptions which recognize the characteristic features of many situations. Once we have made the assumptions, that is, selected the relevant functions and determined their properties, then we develop the logical interrelationships of the model. The applicability of the model to any particular situation depends upon agreement between the assumptions of the model and the conditions in the actual situation. The use of economic analysis for policy matters in any particular situation depends upon the relevance of the model.

18.3.   *The Interest Rate and the Demand for Money to Hold*

Our analysis concerning the determination of the level of investment spending led us to infer that it depended upon the investment demand schedule and the rate of interest, i.e., investment is some function of the rate of interest. But what determines the rate of interest? Interest is the price paid by the borrower to the lender of money. Earlier we said that the price of anything is determined by the forces of supply and demand, and this applies to interest as the price of money. Our first step, then, is to examine the behavior underlying the demand for money.

In Chapter 15 we distinguished three motives for holding money —(1) the transactions motive, (2) the precautionary motive, and (3) the speculative motive. The first motive gives rise to a transactions demand for money, while the second and third motives give rise to what may be called a liquidity demand for money. Part of the money held by businesses and individuals is for transactions purposes—to meet payments associated with daily transactions—and part is held as a liquidity buffer in case of a sudden and unforeseen adverse turn of events or to take advantage of changes in the price level.

The transactions demand for money, call it M_1, is probably highly correlated with the level of national income, Y. The greater is the level of national income, Y, the greater is the volume of exchange transactions, and thus the greater is the need for money to facilitate transactions. Therefore, we are led to postulate a functional relationship between the transactions demand for money and national income:

$$(18.5) \quad M_1 = D_T(Y),$$

with $dD_T/dY > 0$, where dY is a very small increase in the level of national income and $D_T(Y)$ represents the transactions-demand-for-money schedule. dD_T is the resulting increase in the transaction holdings of money. Graphically the transactions demand for money can be represented as in Figure 18–4, with national income, Y, measured on the horizontal axis and money on the vertical axis. As total income rises, from Y' to Y'' in Figure 18–4, the transactions demand for money also rises, from M_1' to M_1''. As income rises, employment and output or the

FIGURE 18–4

THE TRANSACTIONS DEMAND FOR MONEY

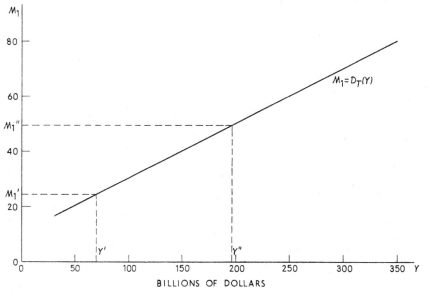

general price level or both rise; the total volume of money needed for the handling of transactions will, of necessity, also rise, given the behavior of the individuals. Individuals will be receiving greater money incomes and therefore holding greater average cash balances; business firms will also require greater balances to handle the larger volume of transactions at the same or probably higher prices.

The liquidity-preference demand for money, on the other hand, is influenced by the interest rate. Previously, we have looked at the rate of interest as the price of money—the price a borrower has to pay a lender in order to borrow money; but we can also think of the interest rate as a payment for not holding money—a payment for sacrificing liquidity. If the rate of interest, i, were zero, the only type of intangible asset that people would want to hold would appear to be money (or money equivalents). Why immobilize money in the form of government or corporation securities if the interest rate on such holdings were zero? One would be better off to hold demand deposits or cash, since one would then have all the advantages of holding the most liquid of assets. In order to induce people to own assets that have less liquidity than cash or demand deposits, some compensation has to be paid them —the interest payment. Much of the interest rate structure, i.e., the variation in the interest earnings on different kinds of financial assets can be explained by differences in the liquidity of those assets. The less-liquid assets generally have a higher interest rate to induce people to own them.

In general, the greater the average level of the interest rate the more people will be induced to own the less-liquid assets, or the more reluctant they will be to hold the nonearning asset—money. We thus have a relationship between the liquidity-preference demand for money, M_2, and the rate of interest:

$$(18.6) \quad M_2 = D_L(i) ,$$

with $dD_L/di < 0$, where di is a very small increase in the rate of interest and dD_L is the resulting decrease in liquidity holdings of money. Such a function is seen in Figure 18–5 with the rate of interest, i, measured on the vertical axis and the amount of money demanded to satisfy the liquidity-preference motive, M_2, measured on the horizontal axis.

Suppose that the rate of interest is initially equal to i', in the economic system represented in Figure 18–5. The individuals will balance the gains to be had from holding the most liquid of assets, money, against the cost of holding this money, the foregone interest returns. At the assumed rate of interest, i', an amount of money equal to OM_2' will

FIGURE 18–5

THE LIQUIDITY-PREFERENCE DEMAND FOR MONEY

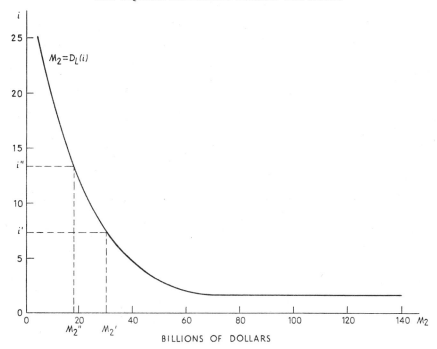

BILLIONS OF DOLLARS

be demanded by individuals to satisfy the liquidity-preference demand for money. Now suppose that the rate of interest rises to i''. The cost of holding money will now have increased. Individuals in the economy will reconsider their money holdings, in light of the increased cost, reducing the quantity of money they desire to hold to M_2'', in Figure 18–5. The increased cost of money thus restricted the amount of money people desire to hold to satisfy liquidity-preference motives.

The total demand for money in the economy is the sum of the demand for money for transactions purposes and the demand for money to satisfy liquidity-preference motives. Thus we have:

$$(18.7) \quad M_d = M_1 + M_2 = D_T(Y) + D_L(i) \,.$$

The total-demand-for-money function can be shown as a family of curves relating M_d and i for various values of Y, as in Figure 18–6. On the vertical axis we measure the rate of interest (i), with the total quantity of money demanded measured on the horizontal axis. As we saw earlier, for a given level of national income, a certain quantity of money is demanded to satisfy the transactions motive. To this is added the money demanded to satisfy liquidity-preference motives. Thus there is a separate money demand schedule for each level of income, with each schedule showing the functional relationship between the rate of interest and the total stock of money demanded, given the level of income. At higher levels of income, the transactions requirement for money rises, and the appropriate total money demand liquidity-preference curve will lie to the right. In Figure 18–6, if the rate of interest is $\bar{\imath}$, the

FIGURE 18–6

THE TOTAL DEMAND FOR MONEY

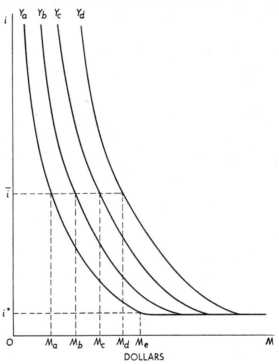

total quantity of money demanded by the economy will be M_a if total income is Y_a, M_b if income is Y_b, M_c for income Y_c, and M_d for income Y_d. However, if the level of income were taken to be Y_a and the rate of interest decreased from $\bar{\imath}$ to i^*, the total demand for money in the economy would increase from OM_a to OM_e, income remaining at Y_a, i.e., we would move along the total money demand curve Y_a, in Figure 18–6. In the first case, with income rising and the rate of interest unchanged, the increase in the demand for money would be due to a greater demand for money to satisfy the transactions motive; in the second case, with income constant and the rate of interest falling, the increase in the quantity of money demanded would be to satisfy the liquidity-preference motives. This completes our introduction of the demand side of the forces determining the rate of interest. We shall now turn to the supply side.

18.4. The Interest Rate and the Supply of Money

Since the supply of money is largely determined by the credit-creating (loaning) activity of the commercial banks, the willingness of commercial banks to expand their loans outstanding must be considered. We have already indicated, in our study of the banking system, that the willingness of bankers to extend loans is related to their excess reserve position. It would seem logical, given the profit motive, to expect that the willingness of bankers to operate near zero excess reserves, through loan expansion, is greater, the greater is the interest rate on such loans. If the loan rate of interest is very high, bankers might be inclined to expand loans until their excess reserves were so small that there would be considerable risk of having to borrow from the Federal Reserve banks to keep reserves up to the required level.

In the light of these considerations, let us introduce the hypothesis that the supply function of money is given by:

$$(18.8) \quad M_s = s(i)$$

with $ds/di > 0$, where di is a very small increase in the rate of interest and ds is the resulting increase in the quantity of money supplied. This hypothesis says that the supply of money is a function of the rate of interest and that the banking system will create more money as the rate of interest increases, other things equal. If ER_0/r is the upper limit to the amount of potential new credit that the banking system can legally create on the basis of a given volume of excess reserves, ER_0, and a reserve ratio, r, and if M_0 is equal to the actual money in circulation at a given time, then the money supply function, $s(i)$, can be expected to have the form illustrated in Figure 18–7. If M is equal to the potential upper limit to the total quantity of money that can circulate, then we can write

$$(18.9) \quad \bar{M} = M_0 + ER_0/r .$$

18.5. Impact of Monetary Policy on Money Supply

The impact of the various monetary policies pursued by the Federal Reserve System to control the monetary system, which we discussed in Chapter 15, can be illustrated through its effects on the money supply schedule, $s(i)$. Open-market operations, the buying and selling of government securities in the open market by a committee of the Federal

FIGURE 18–7

THE SUPPLY OF MONEY

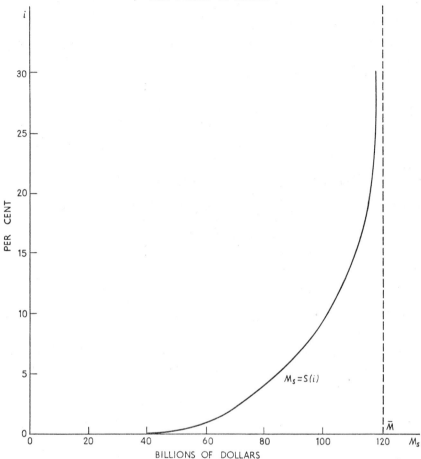

Reserve System, directly changes the quantity of money in circulation (through monetization of government debt) and indirectly by altering the total and excess reserves in the banking system. This is shown in Figure 18–8 by a shift of $\overline{M}$, the upper limit to the amount of credit that the banking system can legally create. The shift of the money supply function in Figure 18–8 from SS to $S'S'$ represents a purchase of government bonds by the Federal Reserve System, thus adding to the total quantity of reserves and moving the upper limit to credit creation from $\overline{M}$ to $\overline{M}'$. The reverse operation is shown by the shift of the money supply function from SS to $S''S''$, which represents the sale of government bonds by the system, which reduces the amount of total reserves available to the commercial banking system. In the situation pictured in Figure 18–8, if the willingness of the banking system to make loans did not change when total reserves increased from $\bar{M}$ to $\bar{M}'$, the money supply function could remain unchanged at SS, but if total reserves were reduced from $\bar{M}$ to $\bar{M}''$, the banking system would be forced to reduce credit and the supply function would be forced to shift to the left.

FIGURE 18–8

SHIFTS IN THE MONEY SUPPLY FUNCTION

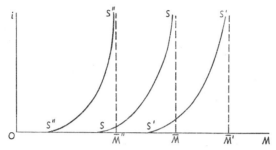

Changes in the rediscount rate by the Federal Reserve banks affect the willingness of the commercial banks to make loans on the basis of any given volume of reserves. An increase in the rediscount rate would shift the money supply function to the left, reducing the amount of money the banking system would be willing to supply at any given rate of interest. The situation would be just reversed when the rediscount

FIGURE 18–9

EFFECTS OF CHANGES IN THE REDISCOUNT RATE

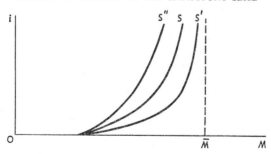

rate was lowered, with the money supply function shifting to the right indicating that the banking system was willing to create more money at any particular rate of interest. In Figure 18–9 a shift of the money supply function from SS to $S'S'$ represents the results of a decrease in the rediscount rate by the Federal Reserve banks and the shift from SS to $S''S''$ shows the results of an increase in the rediscount rate.

Changes in the required reserve ratio, r, by the Federal Reserve System shifts the upper limit to the amount of credit the banking system can create on the basis of a given amount of reserves. The shift of the upper limit to credit creation from $\bar{M}$ to $\bar{M}'$ is the result of a decrease in the reserve ratio. We have shown the money supply function also shifting to the right in Figure 18–10 as the upper limit to credit creation is

FIGURE 18–10

EFFECTS OF CHANGING THE RESERVE RATIO

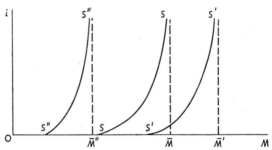

increased. The reverse situation is shown when an increase in the reserve ratio, r, shifts the upper limit to credit creation to the left, from $\bar{M}$ in Figure 18–10 to $\bar{M}''$. Such a reduction in the upper limit to credit creation is shown as bringing with it a leftward shift of the money supply function, indicating that at any given rate of interest the banking system will now be willing to supply a smaller quantity of money.

18.6. The Equilibrium Rate of Interest

This completes our discussion of the supply function of money, and we shall return to the problem of the determination of the rate of interest. Presumably, since we now have a demand function for money and a supply function for money, we could determine the price of money (the rate of interest) given this information. On the demand side we have:

$$(18.7) \quad M_d = D_T(Y) + D_L(i) ,$$

and on the supply side we have:

$$(18.8) \quad M_s = s(i) .$$

We recall from our analysis of price determination that for an equilibrium price we require that the quantity supplied at that price be equal to the quantity demanded at that price. In the present case this means we require that $M_d = M_s$ at the equilibrium rate of interest; or that:

$$(18.10) \quad M_s = M_1 + M_2 \quad \text{or,}$$
$$(18.11) \quad D_T(Y) + D_L(i) = s(i)$$

for the same value of i on both the demand and supply side. Given a particular level of national income, the demand for money can be represented by a single total money demand curve, M_dM_d, in Figure 18–11, and given the monetary policy of the Federal Reserve System, we have the supply function represented by M_sM_s. In Figure 18–11 the equilibrium rate of interest is i_0 given by the intersection of the demand for

FIGURE 18–11

THE EQUILIBRIUM RATE OF INTEREST

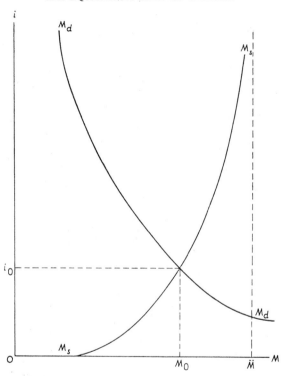

money curve, M_dM_d, and the supply of money curve, M_sM_s. At this rate of interest the quantity of money demanded and the quantity of money supplied are both equal to OM_0, the actual amount of money in circulation in the economy. This equilibrium position signifies that the economy's choice between nonearning liquid cash and earning assets (bonds, etc.) has no tendency to change. The members of the community are satisfied with the distribution of their assets between earning and nonearning varieties. If the members of the community were dissatisfied, they would either buy or sell earning assets, and the market rate of interest would be changed.

The above determination of the rate of interest is based upon a given level of income, but the level of income may change as a result of the interest rate moving toward the equilibrium value from a nonequilibrium value. The change in the rate of interest may influence the level of income via its effect on the level of investment, which in turn affects the level of income via the multiplier process. At this point we need to bring together the various functional relations we have developed and consider a general equilibrium of investment, consumption, income, interest, and money in a simplified general model of the economic system.

18.7. The Basic Model of the Economic System

Our basic model of the economic system uses the following variables, which we have discussed in Chapters 16, 17, and 18: Y, C, I, S, G, T, M_1, M_2, M_s, and i. However, we are not quite ready to analyze the economic impact of government expenditures and taxation; therefore, to eliminate the repercussions of governmental actions in our present model we assume government spending and tax receipts to be equal to zero (i.e., $G = T = 0$). This simplifying assumption will be removed in the following chapter. Since taxes are taken to be zero, disposable income is equal to total income. Y is the aggregate flow of income during a specific period, usually a year. C is the aggregate flow of spending by the community on consumer goods and services during the same specific period. I is the net flow of spending by the private sector on investment goods during the same period of time, and S is that part of Y not spent on consumption goods. M_1 represents that amount of total money held by the community to satisfy the transactions motive, while M_2 is the amount of money held to satisfy the liquidity-preference motives. M_s is the total amount of money supplied to the economy and i, the rate of interest, symbolizes the cost of financial capital, abstracting from problems of availability.

Connecting, and determining the values of the ten variables in our basic model of the economic system are the following aggregate-behavior relationships developed in Chapters 17 and 18:

(17.2) $\quad C = C(Y_d)$,
(18.4) $\quad I = I(i)$,
(18.5) $\quad M_1 = D_T(Y)$,
(18.6) $\quad M_2 = D_L(i)$,
(18.8) $\quad M_s = s(i)$,

the following identities and definitions:

(16.2) $\quad Y_d \equiv Y - T$,
(16.4) $\quad Y \equiv C + I + G$,
(16.6) $\quad S + T \equiv I + G$,

and the following special restrictions abstracting from the effects of government

$$(18.12) \quad G = 0,$$
$$(18.13) \quad T = 0.$$

If we combine (17.2), (16.4), and (16.6) we have the savings function:

$$(17.3) \quad S = Y - T - C(Y_d).$$

Combining (16.6), (17.3), (18.13), (18.4), and (18.12) we have the following equilibrium condition for the goods and service markets:

$$(18.14) \quad Y - C(Y_d) = I(i).$$

And then in the money market we have the equilibrium condition:

$$(18.10) \quad M_s = M_1 + M_2.$$

Combining (18.8), (18.5), and (18.6), we may write the equilibrium condition (18.10) as:

$$(18.11) \quad s(i) = D_T(Y) + D_L(i).$$

Equation (16.2) expresses the behavior of consumers in adjusting consumption expenditures in accordance with the level of disposable income. The investment demand function (18.4), expresses business investment behavior, based upon given expectations regarding the profitability of (or rate of return on) new investment projects. The transactions demand for money (18.5), expresses the money requirements of the community for transactions purposes. M_1 dollars are needed as a medium of exchange to facilitate the volume of transactions associated with a national income of Y dollars per year. Equation (18.6) expresses the attitude or preferences of individuals and businesses toward the holding of money to satisfy the liquidity-preference motives versus the holding of interest-bearing securities or deposits. The willingness of the banking system to create money through loan expansion is expressed in Equation (18.8).

Aggregate output is divided between consumption, investment and government purchases (16.4). In national income accounting, aggregate saving plus taxes collected by the government is identically equal to investment spending plus government purchases of goods and services (16.6). Equations (18.12) and (18.13) express our assumption that taxes and government spending are equal to zero in the present model of the economic system. The savings function (17.3), is derived by subtracting the consumption function from disposable income. In our basic model we prefer to work with the savings function rather than the consumption function, but both functions are based on the same consumer behavior. When we substitute behavior relations into the identity (16.6), it is no longer an identity but becomes an equilibrium condition (18.14) that is satisfied only when aggregate demand is equal to aggregate supply. Equation (18.11) expresses the condition that the money market is only in equilibrium when the quantity of money the banking system desires to supply is equal to the quantity of money that individuals and businesses in the economic system desire to hold.

Given the level of income, the interest rate will be driven to a level which equalizes the supply of and the demand for money. However, if at the resulting rate of interest and the given level of income, the equalization condition in Equation (18.14) is not met, the level of income will change, and then the rate of interest will be driven to a new level in order to bring the demand for and supply of money into equality again. The movement of the level of income and the rate of interest will continue until both of the conditions expressed in (18.14) and (18.11) are satisfied. Let us investigate the interrelationship more closely.

18.8. The Investment-Income-Consumption Equilibrium

In Chapter 17 we discussed the determination of the equilibrium level of income, ignoring any monetary complications. In the simple economic system we studied we saw that there is a specific level of income corresponding to each level of investment, given the aggregate consumption function, and that changes in income are related by the multiplier process to changes in investment. In this chapter we discussed the investment demand function which relates investment to the rate of interest. Now we shall summarize these relations into a single relationship, which expresses the functional relation of the rate of interest and the level of income.

Since government tax receipts are assumed to be zero, disposable income is equal to total income, and we can write (18.14) as $Y - C(Y) = I(i)$. On the left-hand side of Equation (18.14), we have the savings function and on the right we have the investment function. Now we shall find the relation between the rate of interest and the level of income using the saving function, the investment demand function, and the equilibrium condition.

Let us begin by choosing a rate of interest at random. From the investment demand schedule we find the level of investment corresponding to that rate of interest. The equilibrium condition requires that desired savings equal intended investment. Then from the savings function we find the level of income required to produce this level of savings. This gives us one point in the functional relation between the rate of interest and the level of income. This process can be repeated for any number of rates of interest, deriving a particular level of income for each rate of interest. If we plot these combinations we have what is called an *IS* curve, which expresses the functional relation of the rate of interest to the level of income. Every point on this line represents a situation in which investment equals savings and aggregate demand equals aggregate supply in the goods and services markets. Since the amount of savings varies with income levels and investment varies with interest rates, the locus of points of equality between savings and investment indicates a functional relation between income and the rate of interest, such that a lower rate of interest is associated with a higher level of income.

The *IS* relationship between i and Y can be summarized symbolically as

$$i \rightarrow I = S \rightarrow Y.$$

The rate of interest determines the level of investment *via* the investment function, and the equilibrium condition requires that intended investment equal savings, which is related to the level of income through the consumption function. Therefore i and Y are functionally related.

TABLE 18–1

DERIVATION OF A HYPOTHETICAL *IS* FUNCTION

SAVINGS FUNCTION		INVESTMENT DEMAND FUNCTION	
(1) Y (Billions)	(2) S (Billions)	(3) i	(4) I (Billions)
$ 50.0	$ 0.0	8%	$ 0.0
91.6	12.5	7	12.5
133.3	25.0	6	25.0
175.0	37.5	5	37.5
216.6	50.0	4	50.0
258.3	62.5	3	62.5
300.0	75.0	2	75.0
341.6	87.5	1	87.5

The process of deriving the functional relationship between income and the rate of interest can perhaps be better understood by working through a numerical example. Columns 1 and 2 of Table 18–1 are a savings function and Columns 3 and 4 are an investment function derived from the following equations which we will use as the savings and investment functions in our model of the economic system:

$$S = -15 \cdot 10^9 + .3Y$$
$$I = \frac{5(.08 - i) \cdot 10^9}{4 \cdot 10^{-3}}.$$

(We have chosen linear equations throughout the model in order to simplify the calculations. The functions they represent in the real economy probably are curvilinear, but the underlying principles may be developed equally well with the relatively simpler linear relations.)

Let us begin by picking a rate of interest of 7 per cent. The investment demand function tells us that with a rate of interest of 7 per cent the community would desire to invest $12.5 billion. Turning to the savings function in Table 18–1, we see that the required aggregate savings of $12.5 billion would be forthcoming from a national income of $91.6 billion. This gives us one point on the *IS* curve. With a rate of interest of 5 per cent, the desired level of investment would be $37.5 billion, which would be matched by the desired savings from a national income of $175 billion. This gives us another point on the *IS* curve—a functional relation between the rate of interest and the level of income. The same process can be repeated in the example to obtain other combinations, and thus derive the *IS* schedule relating interest and income. The *IS* schedule based on the data in Table 18–1 is given below in Table 18–2.

TABLE 18–2

IS SCHEDULE

i	Y (*Billions*)
8%	$ 50.0
7	91.6
6	133.3
5	175.0
4	216.6
3	258.3
2	300.0

The functional relationship between the rate of interest and the level of income can also be derived graphically. Figure 18–12 is the graphic representation of Table 18–1 plus the equilibrium condition that desired savings equal investment.

Again let us pick some rate of interest, say 6 per cent. At a rate of interest of 6 per cent, the investment function in Quadrant A of Figure 18–12 tells us that the economy will invest $25 billion. The equilibrium condition says that savings should equal investment; this is reflected in Quadrant B of Figure 18–12, in which a 45° line originates at the origin. We move horizontally upward from the investment function (Quadrant A) to Quadrant B and stop when we intersect the 45° line

FIGURE 18–12

DERIVATION OF THE *IS* FUNCTION

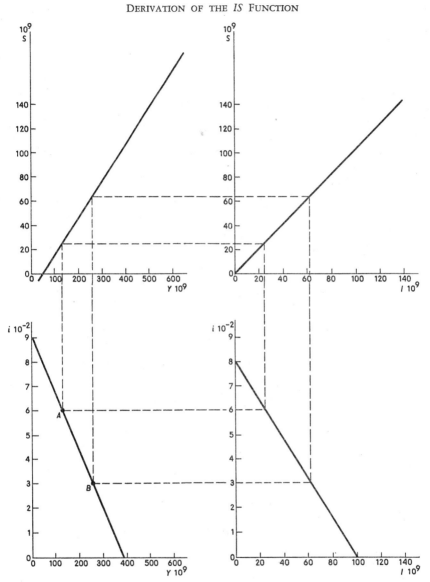

indicating savings equal investment. In Quadrant C we have the savings function, where we read off the level of income ($133.3 billion) that corresponds to the saving level of $25 billion. Then we drop down to Quadrant D and plot this income value of $133.3 billion against the interest rate of 6 per cent, with which we started—Point A in Figure 18–12.

Point B, in Figure 18–12, is found by repeating the process with an interest rate of 3 per cent. If the process is repeated for many rates of interest and the corresponding points plotted in Quadrant D of Figure 18–12 and then connected, they will produce the *IS* curve that traces out the functional relation between the rate of interest and the level of income on the condition that aggregate demand equal aggregate supply in the goods and service markets. The equation for the *IS* function is found by equating desired savings to desired investment, as required by the equilibrium condition, and solving for i in terms of Y, which gives us

$$S = -15 \cdot 10^9 + .3Y$$
$$I = \frac{5(.08 - i) \cdot 10^9}{4 \cdot 10^{-3}}$$
$$-15 \cdot 10^9 + .3Y = \frac{5(.08 - i) \cdot 10^9}{4 \cdot 10^{-3}} .$$

Therefore $i = .092 - .24Y \cdot 10^{-12}$ is the equation for the *IS* function.

Before we proceed, however, observe two things about the *IS* curve in Quadrant D of Figure 18–12: The lower the level of investment associated with any particular rate of interest in the investment demand function, the lower will be the income that corresponds to that particular rate of interest. The lower the propensity to consume (or the greater the propensity to save) the lower will be the level of income associated with any given rate of interest.

18.9. Equilibrium in the Money Market

The essential condition for equilibrium in the money market is that the quantity of money demanded by individuals and businesses in the economy be equal to the quantity of money supplied by the monetary system. This condition was written:

$$(18.11) \quad D_T(Y) + D_L(i) = s(i) ,$$

which states that the level of income, Y, determines the transactions demand for cash, $D_T(Y)$. The rate of interest is then driven to a level which brings the sum of the liquidity and transactions demand for money into equality with the supply of money as determined by bank credit creation. We see that from the transactions demand for cash, from the eagerness of the community to hold liquid cash balances, and from the eagerness of the banking system to create money by making loans, the interest rate is determined.

With this information we can trace another functional relationship between the rate of interest and the level of income, taking into account the condition that the quantity of money desired by the individuals and businesses in the economy be equal to the quantity of money supplied. The process is analogous to the derivation of the IS function.

First we choose a rate of interest at random. From the money supply function [Equation (18.8)] we know how much money will be supplied at that particular rate of interest; from the liquidity-preference demand function for money [Equation (18.6)] we know how much money the individuals in the economy will want to hold to satisfy liquidity-preference motives at the particular rate of interest. If we subtract the quantity of money held for liquidity-preference purposes from the quantity of money supplied, we have the amount of money available, at the particular rate of interest, to satisfy the transactions demand for money. When we have found the amount of these M_1 balances, the transactions-demand-for-money function gives the level of income which will be supported by the money available. This level of income can be plotted against the original rate of interest we chose, giving us one point of the functional relation between the rate of interest and the level of income. By repeating the process we can derive a series of points. When we connect these points we trace out the functional relation between the rate of interest and the level of income, with the desired demand for and desired supply of money equal, that is, the curve of all combinations of the level of income and rate of interest that are consistent with our equilibrium condition for the money market, $M_1 + M_2 = M_s$. We call this curve an LM curve.

We can summarize briefly the LM relationship between i and Y symbolically as:

$$M_s - M_2 = M_1 \leftarrow Y .$$

Given the level of income, the transaction demand for cash is determined. Both the supply of money and the liquidity-preference demand for money are functions of the rate of interest and, in turn, help determine the rate of interest. The equilibrium condition requires that the quantity of money demanded be equal to the quantity of money supplied, at the ruling rate of interest. After subtracting the quantity of money desired for liquidity-preference purposes from the total supply, we have the quantity of money available for transactions purposes. Therefore, i and Y are functionally related.

The derivation of the functional relationship between the rate of interest and the level of income using the money supply function, the transactions-demand-for-money function, the liquidity-preference-demand-for-money function, and our equilibrium condition for the money market can perhaps be better understood with a numerical example. Table 18–3 presents data for some hypothetical economy from which an *LM* curve can be derived. Columns 1 and 2 of the table give the money supply function which is given by the equation $M_s = 114.4 \cdot 10^9 + 300i \cdot 10^9$. Columns 3 and 4 give the liquidity-preference-demand-for-money schedule which is derived from the following equation,

$$M_2 = \frac{5(.091 - i) \cdot 10^9}{5 \cdot 10^{-3}}.$$

Column 5 of Table 18–3 gives the quantity of money available to satisfy the transaction demand for money at the various rates of interest. The M_1 balances are found by subtracting the quantity of money held in M_2 balances, at any given rate of interest, from the quantity of money supplied to the economy, at the same given rate of interest. Columns 6 and 7 are the transactions demand for money and is derived from the equation $M_1 = .26Y$.

TABLE 18–3

DERIVATION OF AN *LM* FUNCTION

MONEY SUPPLY $M_s = s(i)$		LIQUIDITY-PREFERENCE $M_2 = D_L(i)$		EQUILIBRIUM CONDITION $M_1 + M_2 = M_s$ or $M_1 = M_s - M_2$	TRANSACTIONS DEMAND FOR MONEY $M_1 = D_T(Y)$	
(1) i	(2) M_s	(3) i	(4) M_2	(5) M_1	(6) M_1	(7) Y
0	114.4	0	91	23.4	23.4	90
1	117.4	1	81	36.4	36.4	140
2	120.4	2	71	49.4	49.4	190
3	123.4	3	61	62.4	62.4	240
4	126.4	4	51	75.4	75.4	290
5	129.4	5	41	88.4	88.4	340
6	132.4	6	31	101.4	101.4	390
7	135.4	7	21	114.4	114.4	440
8	138.4	8	11	127.4	127.4	490
9	141.4	9	1	140.4	140.4	540
10	144.4	10	0	144.4	144.4	555.4

Let us choose a rate of interest at random, say 3 per cent, which we will assume remains constant. Given a rate of interest of 3 per cent, we find from the money supply function that $123.4 billion will be supplied. From the liquidity-preference schedule, we find that with a rate of interest of 3 per cent, the community will desire to hold $61 billion in the form of idle balances. Subtracting the $61 billion of M_2 balances from the total quantity of money supplied, $123.4 billion, we find a total of $62.4 billion available for transactions balances. Turning to the transactions-demand-for-money schedule we find that transactions balances of \$62.4 billion are associated with an aggregate income equal to \$240 billion. This gives us one point on the *LM* curve—the curve tracing out the functional relation between the rate of interest and the level of income keeping the quantity of money demanded and supplied equal.

If we choose another rate of interest, say 5 per cent, we find the supply of money equal to \$129.4 billion, M_2 balances of \$41 billion, leaving \$88.4 billion for M_1 balances, which will support a level of aggregate income of \$340 billion. If we start with a rate of interest of 8 per cent, we find a total money supply of \$138.4 billion, M_2 balances of \$11 billion, and, from Column 5, M_1 balances of \$127.4 billion. From Columns 6 and 7 we find the level of income equal to \$490 billion. Thus, we have three points on the *LM* curve, listed below in Table 18–4. The student should fill in the remaining values, utilizing the data in Table 18–3.

TABLE 18–4

LM SCHEDULE

i	Y (*Billions*)
3%	\$240
5	340
8	490

We can also derive *LM* curve graphically, in a manner similar to that used to derive the *IS* curve. Figure 18–13 uses the data found in Table 18–4 to derive the *LM* curve which, of course, are based on the equations previously given. In Quadrant A in the lower right-hand corner of Figure 18–13 we have the liquidity-preference demand for money. (Figure 18–5.) The equilibrium condition, that $M_1 + M_2 = M_s$, is found in the upper right-hand quadrant. This curve is constructed as follows: associated with any particular rate of interest is a particular quantity of M_2 balances (given by the liquidity-preference function) and a particular quantity of money supplied (given by the money supply function), if the M_2 balances are subtracted from the M_s total, the M_1 balances are found. Then we plot the resulting pair on the $M_1 - M_2$ plane of Quadrant B. If we do this for a number of rates of interest and then connect the points, we have the curve tracing out the equality of demand for and supply of money.[1] For Quadrant C, in the upper left

[1] Since the supply of money is a function of the rate of interest, there is a different total quantity of money to be allocated among M_1 and M_2 balances at each rate of interest. Graphically this could be shown as a family of lines in Quadrant B showing the total quantity of money available at various rates of interest, as in the accompanying graph. Since $M_1 + M_2 = M_s$, the line for each rate of interest has a slope of -1. In constructing

of Figure 18–13 we have the transactions demand for money (Figure 18–4), and in the lower left of Figure 18–13 we trace out the functional relation between the rate of interest and the level of income, the *LM* curve.

Again let us begin by choosing a rate of interest, say 3 per cent. Beginning in Quadrant A, we see that with a rate of interest of 3 per cent the community will desire M_2 balances equal to $61 billion. Then moving up to Quadrant B we observe that M_1 balances available are equal to $62.4 billion. Next we move to the left to Quadrant C, where the transactions-demand-for-money curve gives us the associated level

the curve representing the money equilibrium condition, only *one* point on each interest-rate line is selected. That point shows the amount of money demanded for M_2 balances and is taken from the liquidity-preference function in Quadrant A. As the rate of interest changes, M_s changes, and we move to the appropriate point on the line for each interest rate which shows M_s, given that $M_1 + M_2 = M_s$. Finally, we connect all these points, and we have the equilibrium condition shown in Quadrant B of Figure 18–13.

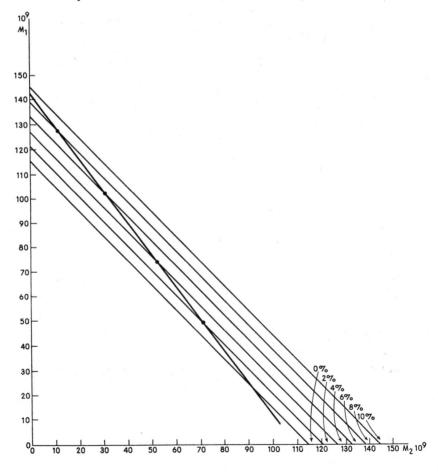

FIGURE 18–13

<small>DERIVATION OF *LM* FUNCTION</small>

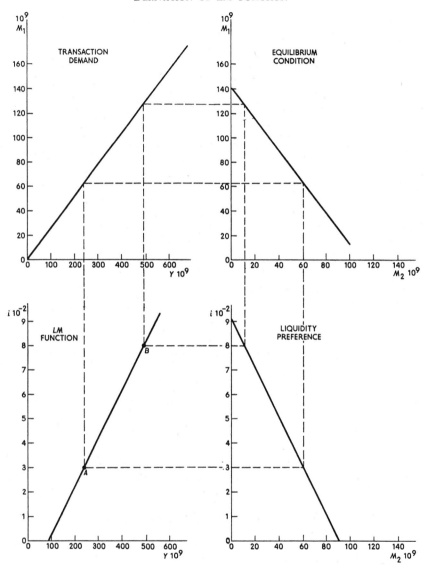

of aggregate income. This is plotted in Quadrant D as Point A, one point on the *LM* curve. Proceeding in a similar manner for a rate of interest of 8 per cent, we locate Point B, and plot it in Quadrant D of Figure 18–13. If we did the same for other rates of interest and then connected the points plotted in Quadrant D, we would have derived graphically the *LM* curve. Observe that for any given level of income, the greater the preference for liquidity on the part of the community, the higher will be the interest rate which balances the supply and demand for money. Also, for any level of income, given the money demand functions, the greater the quantity of money supplied at any rate of interest (i.e., the farther to the right the money supply function), the lower will be the interest rate on money.

The equation for the *LM* function can be derived explicitly for our model of the economy, utilizing the money supply and demand for money equations plus the equilibrium condition for the money market. We have:

$$M_s = 114.4 \cdot 10^9 + 300i \cdot 10^9$$
$$M_1 = .26Y$$
$$M_2 = \frac{5(.091 - i) \cdot 10^9}{5 \cdot 10^{-3}}$$
$$M_s = M_d .$$

After substituting the first three equations into the last one and solving for *i* in terms of *Y*, we obtain:

$$i = .2Y \cdot 10^{-12} - .018 .$$

This equation is the *LM* function in our model of the economy, showing the relationship between the rate of interest and the level of money income, based on equality between the demand for and the supply of money.

18.10. *Equilibrium of the Whole System*

We first derived the functional relationship between the rate of interest and the level of income based on equality between the desired level of savings and investment, or, equality between aggregate supply and demand in the goods and service markets—the *IS* curve. Then we derived the functional relationship between the rate of interest and the level of income based on equality between the demand for and supply of money—the *LM* curve. Neither relation by itself can give us the equilibrium values of the variables for the economic system. The model of the entire economy can be in equilibrium only if both these relationships are satisfied simultaneously—that is, only if the final values of the variables satisfies both conditions, i.e., desired savings are equal to desired investment and the demand for money is equal to the supply of money.

In order to find such an equilibrium combination of the rate of interest and the level of income we combine Quadrant D of Figure 18–12 and Quadrant D of Figure 18–13, that is, we plot both the *IS* and *LM*

FIGURE 18–14

EQUILIBRIUM OF THE BASIC MODEL

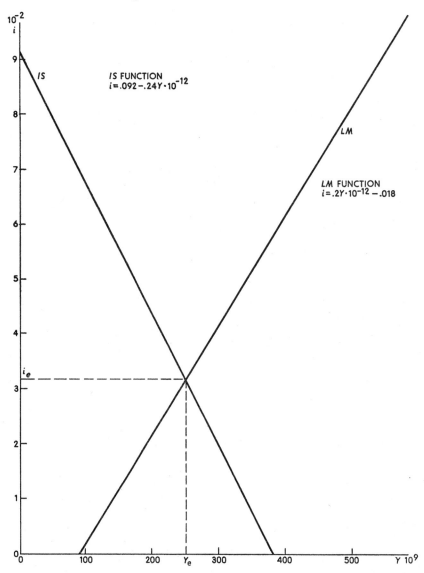

curves on the same graph, as in Figure 18–14. Only the rate of interest i_e and the level of income Y_e satisfy both of our equilibrium conditions; therefore they must be the equilibrium values. Using the data on which Figures 18–12 and 18–13 are based, it is clear that the goods and service and money markets are all in balance only at an interest rate of 3.2 per cent and a national income of $250 billion.

The same solution can be found numerically, if we combine the *IS* schedule of Table 18–2 and the *LM* schedule of Table 18–4. This is worked out in Table 18–5.

As an aid to the student in understanding the movement of our model of the economic system toward equilibrium, let us bring together

TABLE 18–5

DERIVATION OF *IS* AND *LM* SCHEDULES

IS SCHEDULE

(1) i	(2) Y (Billions)	(3) S (Billions)	(4) I (Billions)
8 %	$ 50.0	$ 0.0	$ 0.0
7	91.6	12.5	12.5
6	133.3	25.0	25.0
5	175.0	37.5	37.5
4	216.6	50.0	50.0
3.2	250.0	60.0	60.0
3	258.3	62.5	62.5
2	300.0	75.0	75.0
1	341.6	87.5	87.5
0	383.3	100.0	100.0

LM SCHEDULE

(5) i	(6) M_s (Billions)	(7) M_2 (Billions)	(8) M_1 (Billions)	(9) Y (Billions)
0 %	$114.4	$91	$ 23.4	$ 90
1	117.4	81	36.4	140
2	120.4	71	49.4	190
3	123.4	61	62.4	240
3.2	124.0	59	65.0	250
4	126.4	51	75.4	290
5	129.4	41	88.4	340
6	132.4	31	101.4	390
7	135.4	21	114.4	440
8	138.4	11	127.4	490

the data behind the *IS* and the *LM* schedules. Table 18–5 is based on Tables 18–1 and 18–3, which are derived from the equations for our model of the economy.

In Table 18–5 we see that Columns 1 and 2 are the *IS* schedule; 2 and 3 the savings schedule; 1 and 4 the investment demand schedule; 5 and 6 the money supply schedule; 5 and 7 the liquidity-preference-demand-for-money schedule; 8 and 9 the transactions-demand-for-money schedule; and 5 and 9 the *LM* schedule.

Supposing our model economy is not in an equilibrium position, what sort of path would it follow to move to equilibrium? For example, suppose we start with a level of income of $175 billion and a rate of interest of 5 per cent. A look at Table 18–5 quickly reveals that this is consistent with equilibrium in the goods and service markets, but not with equilibrium in the money market. We see that savings and investment are equal at the rate of $37.5 billion. However, at a rate of interest of 5 per cent, the money supply is $129.4 billion and the quantity of money absorbed into M_2 balances is $41 billion, leaving $88.4 billion for transactions purposes. With a rate of interest of 5 per cent, the money market would only be in equilibrium at a level of income of $340 billion. But we started with a level of income of $175 billion, which needs only $45.5 billion in money balances for transactions purposes. Thus there is an excess supply of money, at the given Y and i, equal to $42.9 billion, which will bring about competitive reduction of the rate of interest.

With a total demand for money equal to $86.5 billion ($M_1 + M_2$), at the given Y and i ($175 billion and 5 per cent), the money market would be in equilibrium only at a negative rate of interest. However, as the rate of interest falls from 5 per cent, there is a decline in the willingness of bankers to lend at the lower rate of interest, causing the money supply to shrink. Also as the interest rate falls, the quantity of money people desire to hold as idle balances increases. Given the data of our model, with a level of income of $175 billion, the demand for and the supply of money would be equal at a rate of interest of 1.7 per cent. While the money market would be in equilibrium under these conditions ($Y = \$175$ billion, $i = 1.7$ per cent), the goods and services markets would be thrown out of adjustment.

A rate of interest of 1.7 per cent would induce investors to invest $78.75 billion and bring about an expansion of aggregate income to a level of $312.5 billion. But this in turn would throw the money market out of adjustment. The increased level of income would increase the transactions demand for money, with the total demand for money increasing to $155.25 billion, an excess demand of $35.65 billion. Clearly something must change and an excess demand for money tends to push the rate of interest up. With an aggregate income of $312.5 billion, the money market would be in equilibrium with a rate of interest of 4.45 per cent. But with $Y = \$312.5$ and $i = 4.45$ per cent, the goods and services markets would be thrown out of adjustment.

With a rate of interest of 4.45 per cent, desired investment falls to a rate of $44.375 billion. Out of an income of $312.5 billion, the individuals desire to save $78.75 billion and to consume $233.75 billion.

Aggregate demand by consumers and investors thus equals $278.125 billion. The disequilibrium between the desired level of investment and savings generates pressures which reduces the level of income to $197.9 billion before the goods and services markets are again in equilibrium. However, if $Y = \$197.9$ billion and $i = 4.45$ per cent, the money market is no longer in equilibrium.

The transactions demand for money, $51.454 billion, plus the liquidity-preference demand for money, $46.5 billion, gives a total demand for money equal to $97.954 ($Y = \$197.9$, $i = 4.45$ per cent). But with i equal to 4.45 per cent the banking system would like to supply $127.75 billion. Therefore, there is an excess supply of money equal to $29.796 billion. Such an excess supply of money acts to push down the rate of interest. Given the functions we have been using in our model, the money market will be in equilibrium at a rate of interest of 2.158 per cent, if Y is equal to $197.9 billion. This change in the rate of interest, however, will again throw the goods and services markets out of equilibrium. By following through the process again we discover that the goods and service markets are brought to equilibrium at a level of income equal to $293.4 billion.

We have not yet reached the final equilibrium position, but we are very close to it. This process of adjustment may seem very rigid and mechanical, but we have followed it through to give the student an insight into the adjustments which continually take place simultaneously in all markets in the real economy. Our step-by-step approach enabled us to look at one variable at a time, but in the real economy all variables are changing at the same time. In order to completely understand the analysis, it is suggested that the student work through changes in all of the basic functions. In the next section we shall examine what happens when the investment function changes.

18.11. *A Shift of the Investment Function*

Economists have focused attention upon changes in investment as one of the more important determinants of changing income levels. Let us investigate what happens in our basic model of the economic system when the investment demand function shifts upward, assuming wages and prices remain unchanged. Specifically, let us assume that the investment demand function, given in Table 18–1 shifts in such a manner that at every rate of interest investors will desire to invest $10 billion more than previously. The new investment function is $I = 1.25(.088 - i) \cdot 10^{12}$. The investment function after the investment shift is given in Table 18–6.

The new investment function is drawn in Quadrant A of Figure 18–15 which is a copy of Figure 18–12, with the new investment function added. How will this shift in investment demand affect the *IS* function? The process of graphically deriving the *IS* function was explained in Section 18.8. If we proceed in the same manner, using the new investment function, we observe that a new *IS* curve is traced out, *IS'* in Quadrant D of Figure 18–15. The increase in investment demand has shifted the *IS* curve to the right. Picking any rate of interest at random, we observe that desired investment and desired savings are now equal at a higher level of income, that is, the level of income, associated

TABLE 18–6

HYPOTHETICAL INVESTMENT DEMAND
FUNCTION AFTER AN INCREASE
IN INVESTMENT

i	I (Billions)
8.8%	$ 0.0
8	10.0
7	22.5
6	35.0
5	47.5
4	60.0
3	72.5
2	85.0
1	97.5
0	110.0

with each rate of interest in the *IS* function, has increased. Since a greater quantity of investment is desired at each rate of interest, a higher level of aggregate income is required to bring forth the necessary higher level of savings to match the investment. The equation for the new *IS* function is $i = .1 - .24Y \cdot 10^{-12}$.

18.12. The Movement to a New Equilibrium

After the shift of the investment function, our basic model of the economic system will no longer be in equilibrium. Given the assumed data for the functions in the system, the system was previously in equilibrium with a rate of interest of 3.2 per cent, a rate of investment of $60 billion and a level of income of $250 billion. But after the increase in investment, the investors would desire to invest $70 billion at the rate of interest of 3.2 per cent; but at the level of income of $250 billion, the individuals in the community would desire to save only $60 billion. Clearly the goods and service markets are not in equilibrium.

The increased investment stimulates an increase in the level of

FIGURE 18–15

THE EFFECT OF A SHIFT IN THE INVESTMENT FUNCTION
ON THE *IS* FUNCTION

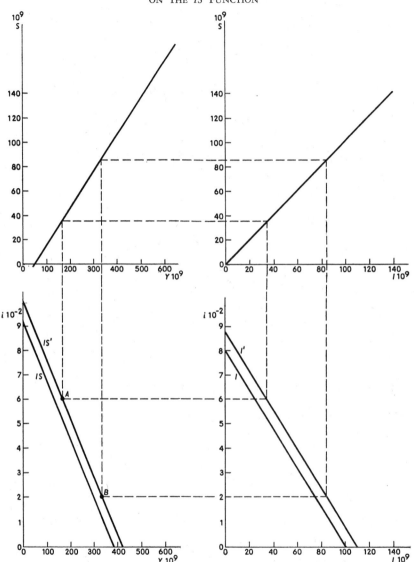

income, via the multiplier process, which in turn brings about increased
consumption expenditures. As the level of income rises, more money
is needed to satisfy transactions requirements, thus increasing the demand for money. An increase in the demand for money, with no change
in the money supply function, pushes up the rate of interest. A higher
interest rate, in turn, increases the quantity of money supplied and re-

duces the quantity of money desired to satisfy liquidity-preference motives. The process involving a rising level of income, consumption expenditures, and interest rates continues until the money market and the goods and service markets are again in balance. That is, the process of expansion will continue until the resulting rate of interest and level of income is such that desired investment is equal to desired savings and the demand for and supply of money are equal again. The shift in the equilibrium position of our hypothetical economy is illustrated in Figure 18–16, where the new *IS* function has been added. Equilibrium is given by the intersection of the *LM* curve with the new *IS'* curve: the new equilibrium *i* equals approximately 3.56 per cent and the new equilibrium level of income is $268.18 billion.

18.13. The Multiplier Again

When we discussed the investment multiplier in Section 17.11, we said the multiplier, *k*, was equal to

$$(17.10) \quad k = \frac{1}{1 - MPC} = \frac{1}{MPS}.$$

The marginal propensity to save, in our model of the economy, is equal to .3, which gives us a multiplier of $3\frac{1}{3}$. On this basis, we would expect aggregate income to increase by $33.3 billion when investment increased $10 billion. But the equilibrium income shown in Figure 18–16 is not the expected $283.3 billion, but only $268.18 billion. The increase in income was not the expected $33.3 billion, but only $18.18 billion. Therefore, the actual multiplier was 1.8 and not $3\frac{1}{3}$. The question arises, of course, why?

The increased investment demand brought with it an increase in the level of income and, consequently, an increase in the demand for money, resulting in a higher interest rate. As the rate of interest rose, investment was restrained and did not increase as much as it would have in the absence of an interest increase. The pressure of the rising interest rate thus held investment in check, which, in turn, held down the level of income from what it might have been. We note, in Figure 18–16, that if the *LM* curve was horizontal, i.e., if the monetary system was perfectly elastic, the full multiplier effect would have been observed. Our analysis in this chapter has shown that, unless the economy is operating with a perfectly elastic money supply, the actual investment multiplier will be smaller than the value based on the aggregate marginal propensity to save, and the increase in income will be less than that given by the multiplier.

FIGURE 18–16

A New Equilibrium of the Basic Model

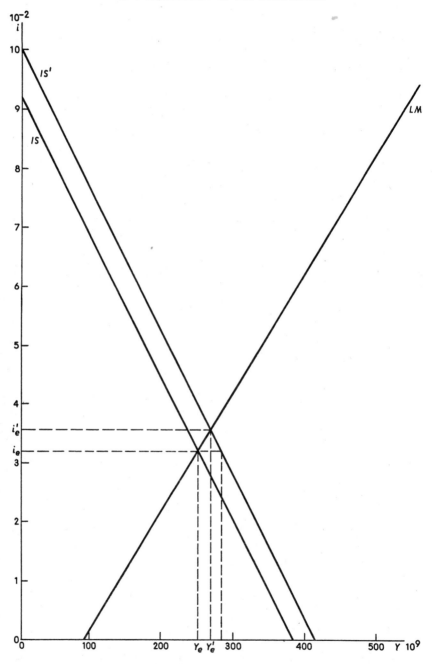

So far we have discussed and analyzed the determination of Y, the money value of the national income, rather than physical output, and employment in the economy. The analysis has been conducted with the implicit assumption that wages and prices remain unchanged. In the following chapter, we will remove this assumption and analyze the interrelationship between income, output, employment, wages, and prices.

QUESTIONS AND EXERCISES

1. Assume that the consumption function implied in Table 18–1 changes to $C = 20 + 0.7Y_d$.

   a) Construct new consumption and savings schedules, using the new function. Does the new consumption function represent an increase or decrease in thriftiness?

   b) Assuming that the other functions of our basic model remain unchanged, find the new equilibrium level of income and rate of interest. Has the level of income increased or decreased? Are investment expenditures affected?

   c) If the community's attitude toward thriftiness changes in such a manner that the aggregate consumption function becomes $C = 30 + 0.85Y_d$, what would you expect to happen to (1) the level of income, (2) the rate of interest, (3) investment, and (4) savings?

2. Assume that the transactions demand for money in Table 18–5 becomes $M_1 = 0.3Y$ and all other functions of the basic model remain as they are in sections 18.8–18.10. Then trace through the repercussions of the change in the demand for money.

3. Suppose there has been a widespread movement of vertical integrations among the firms in an economy, i.e., firms merge so that the buying and selling at intermediate levels of production are eliminated. This implies a decrease in the community's transaction demand for money. Analyze the repercussions of this change in the organization of production on the money market, i.e., the effect upon M_s, i, M_1 and M_2, and the impact in the product market, i.e., the effect upon Y, C, S and I.

4. Consider a situation in which the economy is initially in equilibrium. Now suppose there is a widespread changeover in industry from meeting wage and salary liabilities once each week to meeting them once each month. This implies a decrease in the community's transactions demand for money $M_1 = D_T(Y)$. Analyze the repercussions of this development in the money market, i.e., the effect upon M_s, i, and M_1 and M_2 and in the product market, i.e., the effect upon Y, C, S and I.

5. Suppose that people try to shift out of money and into other forms of assets such as government bonds, common stocks, etc. Analyze the impact of this behavior on both the money and product markets. Start your analysis from an initial state of equilibrium.

6. Suppose that there is a substantial increase in the investment demand for goods for inventory purposes. Trace out the impact of such a change on the money and products markets.

7. Let us assume that there has been a very strong response to an advertising campaign to increase savings. What would be the effects of such behavior on the money and products markets?

8. The following behavior equations are given:

$$(1)\ C = C(Y_d) = 20 + 0.75Y_d \qquad (4)\ M_2 = D_L(i) = \frac{0.6}{i}$$

$$(2)\ I = I(i) = 200 - 2500i \qquad (5)\ M = \$150$$

$$(3)\ M_1 = D_T(Y) = 0.25Y \qquad \text{Assume } G = T = 0$$

a) Verify, by sketching these functions, that they have the general characteristics of the behavior equations discussed in Chapter 18.

b) From these equations derive the equations of IS and LM curves discussed in Chapter 18.

c) Determine the equilibrium quantities Y_d^0, Y^0, i^0, I^0, S^0, C^0, M_1^0, M_2^0, and M^0. Solve for Y^0 and i^0 graphically by plotting the IS and LM curves.

d) Determine the effect on the IS curve of a decrease in the investment demand schedule from $I = 200 - 2500i$ to $I = 150 - 2500i$. What is resulting effect on Y^0?

e) Suppose the Federal Reserve banks, by purchasing government securities in the open market, are able to influence the willingness of bankers to make loans with the result that the supply function of money shifts from $M = 110$ to $M = 150$. Determine the effect on the LM curve and Y^0.

Chapter 19

MONEY INCOME, OUTPUT, AND EMPLOYMENT [1]

Thus far our analysis of the determination of national income and employment has been conducted within a framework that assumed constant wages and prices. As long as prices remain constant, any increase in the money value of national income also means an increase in physical output, since $Y \equiv PQ$. In the short run, with a given stock of capital, an increase in physical output will also mean an increase in employment. However, as we pointed out in our earlier discussion of national income accounting, prices do change and the more closely the economy is driven to capacity, or full employment output, the more will increases in the consumption or investment demand for goods lead to increases in the price level rather than increases in physical output and employment. Therefore, we need to develop a theoretical framework within which we can analyze money income, output, and employment together. We shall do this by expanding the basic model we have developed thus far.

19.1. Real or Money Values?

As long as prices remain constant it does not matter whether we formulate the determination of income in real or money terms but as soon as prices vary, it does make a difference whether consumption, for example, is a function of money income or real income. An increase in money income will have different effects, both on real consumption and on the money value of consumption, depending on whether prices change or not, if consumption is a function of real income. In this expansion of our basic model of the economy, we will express the various functions in such a manner that the essential relationships between

[1] Portions of this chapter including the basic model summarized in Section 19.6 draws on a paper by George Horwich and V. L. Smith, "A Reconsideration of Aggregate General-Equilibrium Theory," processed, Purdue University, School of Industrial Management, 1959.

variables are in real terms. For example, real consumption is taken to be a function of real disposable income:

$$(19.1) \quad \frac{C}{P} = a + \frac{bY_d}{P},$$

where Y_d and C are money disposable income and the money value of consumption and P is the price level. If we multiply both sides by P, we have:

$$(19.2) \quad C = aP + bY_d.$$

The money value of consumption is thus a function of the price level and the level of money disposable income. What we are assuming, in this section, is that people are not subject to money illusions. They do recognize what is happening to the real variables when prices change.

19.2. Introducing the Price Level

First we add the price level as an explicit variable in our *IS-LM* model of the economy. This is accomplished by rewriting the basic equations. Then an aggregate demand for labor is developed, based on the assumption of profit maximization, and an aggregate production function is postulated, showing the relationship between physical output and employment. An implicit supply of labor is contained in an equilibrium condition that money national income be equal to the money wage rate times employment plus the equilibrium return to the owners of capital which, in equilibrium, is equal to the rate of interest, times the value of capital. This model of an economy helps explain the determination of the level of money income, money wages, the price level, the rate of interest, output, and employment in a general equilibrium system.

Money savings is now a function of the price level and money income:

$$(19.3) \quad S = Y - C(P, Y),$$

and the money value of investment is a function of the price level and the rate of interest:

$$(19.4) \quad I = I(P, i).$$

When the desired level of savings is equated to the desired level of investment (the equilibrium condition for the *IS* function), we obtain a functional relationship between the level of money income and the rate of interest with the price level as a parameter, that is, the position of the *IS* curve, as we previously drew it, now depends on the price level and the whole curve will shift as the price level changes. The *IS* function is expressed as

$$(19.5) \quad Y - C(Y, P) = I(i, P).$$

If the price level rises, the IS curve will rotate upward, that is a given rate of interest will be associated with a higher level of money income.

In a similar fashion, the demand for speculative balances is assumed to depend upon the command over real resources, that is, with a given rate of interest, if the price level rises the demand for M_2 balances

FIGURE 19–1

A Shift of the IS Curve with Price Changes

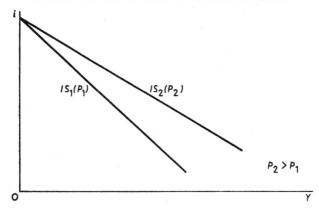

will rise proportionately in order to maintain the relationship between the rate of interest and "real" balances.

$$(19.6) \quad M_2 = D_L(i, P).$$

The demand for transactions balances remains a function of the level of money income, which reflects the change in the price level since $Y = PQ$.

$$(19.7) \quad M_1 = D_T(Y).$$

The money supply, in this expansion of our model of the economy, is equal to the given stock of money in the system, $\bar{M}$, plus the additional money the banking system is willing to create. This part of the money supply, we assume, depends upon real factors in the system, that is, the banking system is willing to create more money at a higher price level, at any particular rate of interest. This means that the banks are not subject to a money illusion, that the essential relationship is between the rate of interest and the bankers' willingness to supply monetary command over real resources. As the price level rises, however, the given stock of nominal money, $\bar{M}$, will purchase less and less goods and services. As a result, as prices rise, everything else equal, the LM curve will shift upward. In this model the money supply is given by:

$$(19.8) \quad M_s = \bar{M} + s(i, P) .$$

When the demand for money is equated to the supply of money (the equilibrium condition for the *LM* function), we now have a functional relationship between the level of money income and the rate of interest, with the price level and the given stock of nominal money as parameters. This new *LM* function is given by:

$$(19.9) \quad \bar{M} + s(i, P) = D_T(Y) + D_L(i, P) .$$

Graphically, the shift in the *LM* function, with a rise in prices, is shown in Figure 19–2.

FIGURE 19–2

A SHIFT OF THE *LM* CURVE WITH PRICE CHANGES

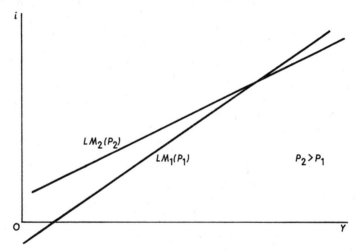

Although we now have two functional relationships between the rate of interest and the level of money income, this is not sufficient to determine them unless we assume that the price level is given. However, the price level is one of the economic variables to be determined by the operation of the economic system. We observe that the general price level does change, from time to time, and this change in the level of prices in our economy is one of the things we want to be able to explain and understand. In order to do this, we must expand our model of an economy and introduce explicitly such things as the level of employment, total output, prices, and the wage rate. At the same time, we do not want the model to get too complicated for us to handle; our goal is that of simplicity, while still enabling us to isolate and understand the fundamental relationships in our economic system.

19.3. The Demand for Labor

Accordingly, we will expand our view of the economy, building it up on the assumption that we are dealing with a competitive system in which the firms seek to maximize profits and produce a single product that may be used either for investment or consumption. This is really equivalent to using an index of production, such as the Federal Reserve Index of Industrial Production, on the assumption that the composition of output remains unchanged or makes no significant difference.

We know, from our discussion of the economics of the individual firm, that a profit-maximizing firm will hire labor up to the point where the money wage rate is equal to the value of the marginal product, under conditions of competition.

$$(19.10) \quad W = PQ',$$

where W is the money wage rate, P the price of the commodity, and Q' is the marginal physical product of labor. If we multiply both sides of Equation (19.10) by N, aggregate employment, we have the total money wages bill on the left-hand side. Since total output divided by the average product of labor is equal to total employment by definition, we may substitute $Q/\bar{Q}$ for N on the right-hand side of Equation (19.10) to give us:

$$(19.11) \quad WN = PQ' \cdot Q/\bar{Q},$$

which may be rewritten as

$$WN = PQ \cdot \frac{Q'}{\bar{Q}},$$

where Q is total output and $\bar{Q}$ is the average product of labor. If we now divide both sides of Equation (19.11) by W, the money wage rate, we have:

$$(19.12) \quad N = \frac{PQ}{W} \cdot \frac{Q'}{\bar{Q}}.$$

Equation (19.12) says that the aggregate demand for labor is equal to national income divided by the money wage rate multiplied by the share of national income going to labor. In a competitive, profit-maximizing model of the economy, the share of national income going to labor is equal to the ratio of the marginal product to the average product of labor. From Equation (19.10), it is easy to see that firms hire labor up to the point where the real wage rate is equal to the marginal product of labor. If we multiply the marginal product of labor by total employment, we have the aggregate real returns to labor. If we multiply the average product of labor by total employment, we have total output. Then if we divided the aggregate returns to labor by total output, it is clear that the share going to labor as a whole is equal to $Q'/\bar{Q}$.

19.4. The Aggregate Production Function

Next let us introduce an aggregate production function relating the output of our single commodity, Q, to the input of labor, N, and capital, K:

$$(19.13) \quad Q = Q(N, K) .$$

We assume that the production function in Equation (19.13) is of the normal form of Figure 19–3.

FIGURE 19–3

A HYPOTHETICAL PRODUCTION FUNCTION

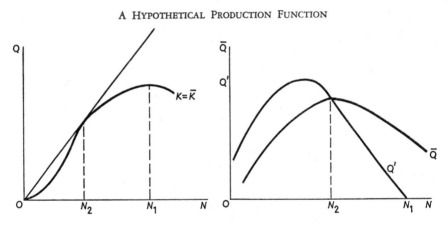

Equation (19.13) says that the output of the single good, Q, is some function of the amount of labor and capital used in the productive process. In our short-run analysis we assume the amount of capital is given and unchanged during the period, but over time the amount of capital in the economy will change. At this point in our analysis, however, we are not concerned with the factors determining growth; this will be discussed in a later chapter.

19.5. National Income Equalities

We know, from our study of national income accounting that the aggregate value of the goods purchased for consumption and net investment is equal to national income, therefore, we have:

$$(19.14) \quad Y \equiv PQ ,$$

where Y is money national income, P is the price of our single commodity (which may be thought of as the general price level), and Q is output.

Looking at the other side of the productive process, we recall that the sum of the factor payments is also equal to national income. In this simple model of the economy, with only two factors of production, the sum of the total wage payments plus the return to the owners of capital is equal to national income:

$$(19.15) \quad Y = WN + rPK .$$

In Equation (19.15) WN is the sum of the wage payments to labor while rPK is the aggregate return to the owners of capital, where K is the stock of real capital, P the price per unit, and r is the rate of return per unit of capital.

At any rate of interest, businessmen will push investment to that rate for which the net return, $r,$ is equal to the rate of interest, $i.$ This is the behavior expressed in the equilibrium condition[2]

$$(19.16) \quad i = r .$$

If the rate of interest is greater than the net return on capital, investment will fall, but if the rate of return on capital is greater than the rate of interest, investment will expand. In equilibrium the two are brought into equality.

The next equation states that in the short run the stock of capital is a given, fixed quantity,

$$(19.17) \quad K = \bar{K} .$$

Two definitions complete our simple model of a competitive economy based on profit maximization:

$$(19.18) \quad Q' = \partial Q/\partial N$$
$$(19.19) \quad \bar{Q} = Q/N .$$

Equation (19.18) defines Q', the marginal product of labor, as being the first derivative of the aggregate production function, that is the rate of change of output with respect to a very small change of labor. The average product of labor, $\bar{Q},$ is defined in Equation (19.19) as being equal to aggregate output divided by total employment.

19.6. The Basic Model

We now have a simple model of an economy consisting of ten equations, ten variables, whose values are to be determined in the work-

[2] See, for example, the treatment by A. P. Lerner in *The Economics of Control* (New York: The Macmillan Co., 1946), Chaps. 21 and 25.

ing out of the general equilibrium, and two given values. The ten equations are:

$$(19.5) \quad Y - C(Y, P) = I(i, P)$$
$$(19.9) \quad \bar{M} + s(i, P) = D_T(Y) + D_L(i, P)$$
$$(19.12) \quad N = \frac{PQ}{W} \cdot \frac{Q'}{\bar{Q}}$$
$$(19.13) \quad Q = Q(N, K)$$
$$(19.14) \quad Y = PQ$$
$$(19.15) \quad Y = WN + rPK$$
$$(19.16) \quad i = r$$
$$(19.17) \quad K = \bar{K}$$
$$(19.18) \quad Q' = \partial Q / \partial N$$
$$(19.19) \quad \bar{Q} = Q/N .$$

The ten variables to be determined as a result of the general equilibrium of our model of the economic system are Y, i, P, N, Q, W, Q', $\bar{Q}$, K, and r, that is, money income, the rate of interest, the price level, employment, aggregate output, money wages, the marginal product of labor, the average product of labor, the stock of capital, and the rate of return on capital. Given are $\bar{K}$ and $\bar{M}$, the stock of capital and that part of the stock of money that is determined outside of the system, normally by the central bank. Since K is taken as equal to $\bar{K}$ in the short run, we really only have nine variables to be determined within the system.

We recognize that Equations (19.5) and (19.9) are our familiar IS and LM functions, respectively, with the stock of money, $\bar{M}$, and the price level, P, as parameters. As we have seen, there is a different IS and LM curve for every different price level. The price level, however, is determined as a part of the equilibrium of the whole system.

The IS-LM relationship between the rate of interest and level of money income is shown graphically in the upper right-hand quadrant of Figure 19–4. Equations (19.12), (19.14), (19.18), and (19.19), may be combined to devise the aggregate demand for labor as a function of the level of aggregate money income, given the money wage rate:

$$(19.12') \quad N = \frac{Y}{W} \cdot \frac{Q'}{\bar{Q}} .$$

The relationship between the aggregate demand for labor and the level of money income is shown in the lower right-hand quadrant of Figure 19–4. The shape of the demand-for-labor function is determined by the ratio of the marginal product of labor to the average product of labor. Since we have assumed a "normal" shape for the aggregate production function, this ratio gets smaller and smaller as employment expands

FIGURE 19–4

MONEY INCOME, PRICES, OUTPUT, AND EMPLOYMENT

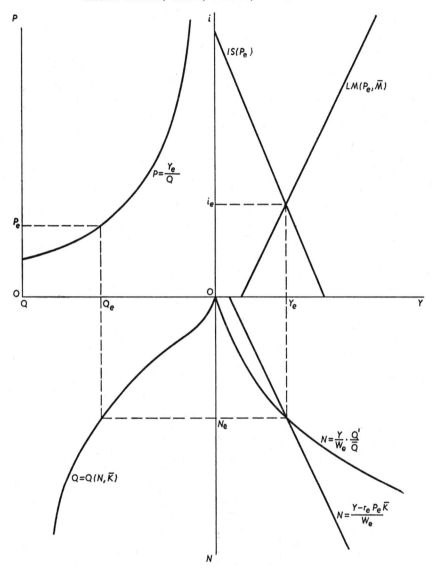

until employment reaches a level at which the marginal product of labor equals zero. Up to this point, with every increase in the level of aggregate money income more labor will be demanded, given the wage rate. But when the marginal product of labor falls to zero, the demand for labor ceases to expand with rising national money income.

19.7. The Supply of Labor

Equations (19.16) and (19.17) may be substituted into Equation (19.15) and the result rewritten as:

$$(19.15') \quad N = \frac{Y - rP\bar{K}}{W},$$

which may be considered as a labor supply function. As an aggregate labor supply function, Equation (19.15′) indicates that the quantity of labor which is offered is consistent with the wage rate, the rate of return on capital, and the behavior implied in the consumption and investment functions. This follows from the requirement that national income be equal to the sum of factor payments. We are simply requiring that the labor supply behavior be consistent with the other behavior equations in the economic system. The labor supply function is shown graphically in the lower right-hand quadrant of Figure 19–4 as a relation between the level of money income and the level of employment, given the rate of interest, the price level, and the wage rate.

When the assumption of a given stock of capital, Equation (19.17), is combined with the aggregate production function, Equation (19.13), we have a short-run relationship between the level of employment and the rate of output.

$$(19.13') \quad Q = Q(\bar{N}, \bar{K}).$$

This short-run aggregate employment-output relationship is shown in the lower left-hand quadrant of Figure 19–4.

Finally, we have the relationship between the level of money income, output, and the price level, which is obtained by rewriting Equation (19.14).

$$(19.14') \quad P = Y/Q.$$

This relationship is shown in the upper left-hand quadrant of Figure 19–4.

Figure 19–4, taken as a whole, illustrates an equilibrium position of the whole system with all of the values consistent, showing the relationship between the rate of interest, the level of aggregate money income, employment, output, and the price level.

19.8. An Alternative View of the Model

An alternative way of viewing the general equilibrium system emphasizes the relationship between aggregate employment and the wage rate, with all the other functions as a part of the total system but hidden behind the scenes. We may solve Equations (19.5) and (19.9) for i and Y, with the stock of money and the price level of parameters, which are written as

$$(19.5') \quad i = H(\bar{M}, P)$$
$$(19.9') \quad Y = N(\bar{M}, P).$$

In Equation (19.14) we see that the price level is equal to money income divided by aggregate output, therefore we can substitute Y/Q for P in the above functions. However, money income is also a function of the stock of money and the price level; therefore, we may rewrite Equation (19.14) as

$$(19.14') \quad P = J(Q, \bar{M})$$

and then substitute this function into (19.5') and (19.9'):

$$(19.5'') \quad i = H[\bar{M}, J(Q, \bar{M})]$$
$$(19.9'') \quad Y = R[\bar{M}, J(Q, \bar{M})].$$

However, according to our aggregate production function, Equation (19.13), output is a function of employment of labor and the given stock of capital, so we have:

$$(19.5''') \quad i = H(\bar{M}, J[(N, K), \bar{M}])$$
$$(19.9''') \quad Y = R(\bar{M}, J[(N, \bar{K}), \bar{M}]).$$

Next we may rewrite Equations (19.12) and (19.15) as follows:

$$(19.12') \quad W = \frac{Y}{N} \cdot \frac{Q'}{Q} \text{ and }$$

$$(19.15') \quad W = \frac{Y - iP\bar{K}}{N}.$$

Now let us substitute Equation (19.9''') for Y in Equation (19.12') which will give us:

$$(19.20) \quad W = \frac{R(M, J[(N, K), M])}{N} \cdot \frac{Q'}{Q}.$$

Our next step is to substitute Equation (19.9''') for Y, (19.5''') for i, and (19.14') and (19.13') for P in Equation (19.15'). As a result of these substitutions, we have:

$$(19.21) \quad W = \frac{R(\bar{M}, J[(N, \bar{K}), \bar{M}]) - H(\bar{M}, J[(N, \bar{K}), \bar{M}]) \cdot J[(N, \bar{K}), \bar{M}] \cdot \bar{K}}{N}.$$

Equation (19.20) represents the aggregate demand for labor as a relationship between wages and the amount of employment, with the stock of money and the stock of capital as parameters. It is based on the assumption of a profit-maximizing competitive system. The labor supply relationship in Equation (19.21) is based on the requirement that national income be equal to the sum of factor payments and that the labor supply behavior be consistent with the other behavior relations in the complete system. We thus have the complete system reduced to a wage-employment equilibrium, with the wage rate such as to bring the quantity of labor demanded into equality with the quantity of labor supplied. The relationship is expressed in money terms with the stock of money present in both the demand and supply side. Thus as the stock

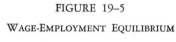

FIGURE 19–5

WAGE-EMPLOYMENT EQUILIBRIUM

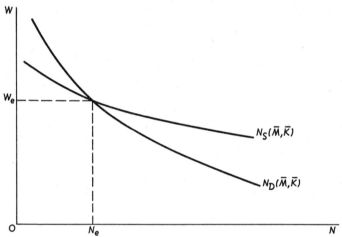

of money changes the functions will shift up or down together, changing the money wage rate but not the level of employment. Graphically, the system is shown in Figure 19–5.

This version of our model of the general equilibrium system may be likened to a clock—on the face one observes only the two hands; behind, the complete clockworks. On the surface of the wage-employment equilibrium form of our model of the economy, one observes only the supply and demand functions of labor, but beneath these two functions are all the other interrelationships of the whole economy. Once the wage rate and the level of employment are found, we can work back to find all the other variables. Since, if we know the level of employment, by (19.13) we know aggregate output. Also, if we know the level of employment and the wage rate, by (19.12′) we know the level of money income. If we know the level of money income and aggregate output, by (19.14) we know the price level, and by (19.15) we also know the rate of interest. Thus we can find all the variables in the system if we solve the wage-employment relationship.

19.9. A Numerical Model of the Complete System

Many of the interrelationships between the level of income, employment, output, and the price level may be seen more clearly if they are examined with the aid of a specific numerical example. Therefore, we will construct such an example of our basic model of the economy and then use it to explore such things as the effect on the system of an increase in the quantity of money, the effect of an upward shift of the investment function, the effect of a change in the liquidity-preference function, and the effect of a change in the savings function. (The effect of an arbitrary increase in money wages, and the effect of an arbitrary increase in the rate of return to the owners of capital.)

The savings function is assumed to be:

$$(19.22) \quad S = -3 \cdot 10^9 P + .3PQ ,$$

and the investment function is given by:

$$(19.23) \quad I = \frac{P(.08 - i) \cdot 10^9}{4 \cdot 10^{-3}} .$$

The *IS* relationship between the rate of interest and the level of income is derived from the savings and investment function, remembering that the level of money income is equal to price times aggregate output. In this example the *IS* relation is found to be

$$(19.24) \quad iP = .092P - 1.2PQ \cdot 10^{-12} \text{ or } i = 0.92 - \frac{1.2PQ \cdot 10^{-12}}{P} .$$

The *LM* function, we recall, is the relationship between the rate of interest and the level of income based upon the equilibrium condition that the quantity of money demanded be equal to the quantity of money supplied in the money market section of the economy. The supply of money is taken to be:

$$(19.25) \quad M_s = 114.4 \cdot 10^9 + 60iP \cdot 10^9 .$$

The demand for money for transactions purposes is given by:

$$(19.26) \quad M_1 = .26PQ ,$$

and the liquidity-preference demand for money is:

$$(19.27) \quad M_2 = \frac{P(.091 - i) \cdot 10^9}{5 \cdot 10^{-3}} .$$

With the above demand and supply relations in the money market, the *LM* function is equal to:

$$(19.28) \quad iP = PQ \cdot 10^{-12} + .07P - .44$$

or

$$i = \frac{PQ \cdot 10^{-12}}{P} + .07 - \frac{.44}{P} \cdot$$

The aggregate production function for our numerical model is assumed to be:

$$(19.29) \quad Q = 2HNK - AN^2 - BK^2 ,$$

with A, B, and H as given constants determined by the given state of technology in the economy. Their respective values are 10^{-5}, 10^{-13}, and $3 \cdot 10^{-9}$. In our basic short-run model, the stock of capital is given, Equation (19.17), and $\overline{K}$ is assumed to be equal to $3 \cdot 10^{11}$.

Since the marginal productivity of labor is the rate of change of output with respect to labor, i.e., the first derivative of the production function with respect to N, we have:

$$(19.30) \quad Q' = 2HK - 2AN ,$$

and the average product of labor is equal to:

$$(19.31) \quad \bar{Q} = 2HK - AN - \frac{BK^2}{N} \cdot$$

The complete system for the numerical model of the economic system consists of the following ten equations:

$$(19.24) \quad iP = .092P - 1.2PQ \cdot 10^{-12}$$
$$(19.28) \quad iP = PQ \cdot 10^{-12} + .07P - .44$$
$$(19.21) \quad N = \frac{PQ}{W} \cdot \frac{Q'}{\bar{Q}}$$
$$(19.29) \quad Q = 2HNK - AN^2 - BK^2$$
$$(19.14) \quad Y = PQ$$
$$(19.15) \quad Y = WN + rPK$$
$$(19.16) \quad i = r$$
$$(19.17) \quad K = \overline{K}$$
$$(19.30) \quad Q' = 2HK - 2AN$$
$$(19.31) \quad \bar{Q} = 2HK - AN - \frac{BK^2}{N} \cdot$$

The system includes the following ten variables $i, P, Q, N, Y, W, Q', \bar{Q},$ K, and r, plus the following constants, $\overline{K} = 3 \cdot 10^{11}$, $A = 10^{-5}$, $B = 10^{-13}$, and $H = 3 \cdot 10^{-9}$. Our basic model of the economy is thus a system of simultaneous equations with ten equations and ten unknowns. Equation (19.24) is the *IS* function, while Equation (19.28) is our familiar *LM* relationship. The next equation, (19.12), is the aggregate demand for labor based on the assumptions of profit maximization and a competitive economy. The aggregate production function is given in Equation (19.29). Equation (19.14) is the identity that national income is equal to price times quantity, while the next equation (19.15), is based on the requirement that national income is also equal to the sum total of factor payments. The condition that in equilibrium the rate of interest must be equal to the rate of return on capital is contained in Equation (19.16). Our short-run assumption is given in the following equation, and the last two equations in the system, (19.30) and (19.31), are the definitions of the marginal and average product of labor.

19.10. The General Equilibrium of the Model

In solving the system for the equilibrium values for the variables we will take advantage of the possibility of reducing the complete system to two equations representing the wage-employment equilibrium. The *IS* and *LM* functions may be solved for the equilibrium values of PQ and i, with P as a parameter to give us

$$(19.32) \quad PQ = P \cdot 10^{10} + 2 \cdot 10^{11}$$

$$(19.33) \quad i = .08 - \frac{.24}{P} \, .$$

We can then substitute these values for PQ and i as follows:

$$(19.12') \quad N = \frac{P \cdot 10^{10} + 2 \cdot 10^{11}}{W} \cdot \frac{Q'}{Q}$$

$$(19.14') \quad Y = P \cdot 10^{10} + 2 \cdot 10^{11} = PQ$$

$$(19.15') \quad P \cdot 10^{10} + 2 \cdot 10^{11} = WN + (.08P - .24) \cdot 3 \cdot 10^{11} \, .$$

The aggregate production function, after substituting the given numerical values for the constants, is equal to:

$$(19.29') \quad Q = 1800N - N^2 \cdot 10^{-5} - 9 \cdot 10^9 \, .$$

Equation (19.12') may be rewritten as

$$(19.12'') \quad W = \frac{P \cdot 10^{10} + 2 \cdot 10^{11}}{N} \cdot \frac{Q'}{\bar{Q}} \, .$$

The supply function of labor, Equation (19.15'), may be solved for W, to give us

$$(19.15'') \quad W = \frac{272 \cdot 10^9 - 14P \cdot 10^9}{N} \, .$$

We may next substitute the value for Q, given by Equation (19.29′), into Equation (19.14′) which then equals

(19.14″) $P(1800N - N^2 \cdot 10^{-5} - 9 \cdot 10^9) = P \cdot 10^{10} + 2 \cdot 10^{11}$,

and we can then solve for P:

$$(19.14''') \quad P = \frac{2 \cdot 10^{11}}{(1800N - N^2 \cdot 10^{-5} - 9 \cdot 10^9) - 10^{10}}.$$

The above value for P can then be substituted into Equation (19.12″) and (19.15″) to give us two equations in two unknowns, W and N,

FIGURE 19–6

WAGE-EMPLOYMENT EQUILIBRIUM OF BASIC MODEL

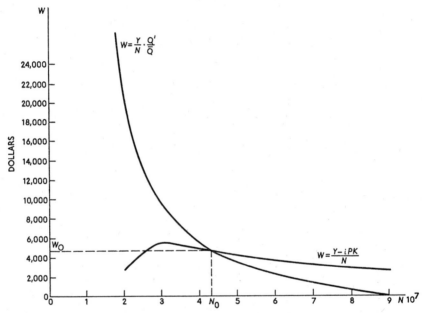

since, by Equations (19.30) and (19.31), Q' and $\overline{Q}$ are both functions of N, given $\overline{K}$. The wage-employment equilibrium is represented by

(19.12‴) $W =$

$$\frac{\left[\dfrac{2 \cdot 10^{11}}{(1800N - N^2 \cdot 10^{-5} - 9 \cdot 10^9) - 10^{10}}\right] \cdot 10^{10} + 2 \cdot 10^{11}}{N} \cdot \frac{Q'}{\overline{Q}}$$

(19.15‴) $W =$

$$\frac{272 \cdot 10^9 - 14\left[\dfrac{2 \cdot 10^{11}}{(1800N - N^2 \cdot 10^{-5} - 9 \cdot 10^9) - 10^{10}}\right] \cdot 10^9}{N}.$$

The first Equation (19.12‴) represents the demand side of the equilibrium and (19.15‴) the supply side. The supply-demand relationship provided us with the equilibrium values for the money wage rate and the amount of employment: $W_o = \$4{,}685.66$, and $N_o = 4.3118 \cdot 10^7$. Graphically the equilibrium solution of the wage-employment relation is presented in Figure 19–6.

Having found the equilibrium values for the money wage rate and the level of employment, we can proceed to find the equilibrium values of the other values. Given N, we can find Q from Equation (19.29′) and then P from Equation (19.14‴). Knowing P, we can solve for PQ, Equation (19.32), and i, Equation (19.33).

Then by Equation (19.14) we have Y. As soon as we know i, we also have equilibrium value for r, Equation (19.16). The equilibrium values for all the variables in our numerical model are as follows:

$$
\begin{aligned}
W &= \$4{,}685.66 & i &= .032 \\
N &= 43.118 \text{ million} & r &= .032 \\
P &= \$5.00 & K &= \bar{K} = 3 \cdot 10^{11} \\
Q &= 50 \text{ billion} & Q' &= 937.64 \\
Y &= PQ = \$250 \text{ billion} & \bar{Q} &= 1160.09.
\end{aligned}
$$

We can also go behind the IS and LM functions to find the equilibrium values for savings and investment, and quantity of money demanded and supplied.

$$
\begin{aligned}
S &= \$60 \text{ billion} \\
I &= \$60 \text{ billion} \\
M_s &= \$124 \text{ billion} \\
M_1 &= \$65 \text{ billion} \\
M_2 &= \$59 \text{ billion.}
\end{aligned}
$$

The aggregate return to labor, WN, is equal to $\$202$ billion, while the return to the owners of capital, rPK, is $\$48$ billion. (The amounts are rounded off to the nearest billion.)

The equilibrium position of our numerical model is illustrated in Figure 19–7. In the upper right-hand quadrant we observe the equilibrium rate of interest and level of money income, i_o, Y_o, at which both desired savings equals investment and the quantity of money demanded equals the quantity of money supplied, given the equilibrium price level, P_o. The relationship between the level of money income and the level of employment is presented in the lower right-hand quadrant. At the level of income Y_o, business firms, in the pursuit of profits, will demand the quantity of labor N_o, given the wage rate W_o; and the same quantity of labor will be supplied, given the wage rate W_o, the interest rate i_o, and the price level P_o. It is only at the level of employment N_o that the total national income is paid out to the owners of the factors of production, capital, and labor. Our aggregate production function is

FIGURE 19–7

EQUILIBRIUM OF MONEY INCOME, OUTPUT, AND EMPLOYMENT OF
NUMERICAL MODEL

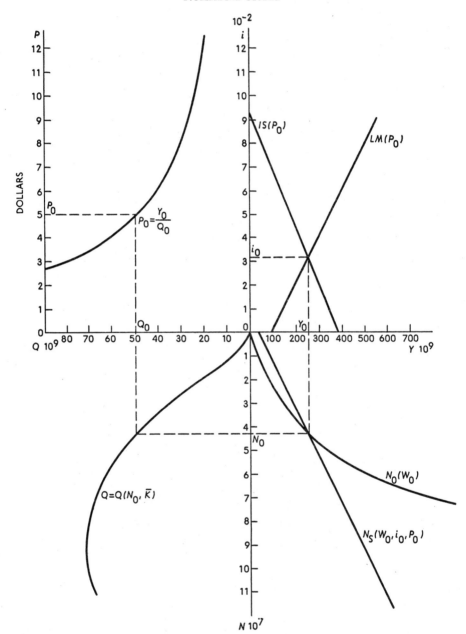

shown in the lower left-hand quadrant, and we observe that with the quantity of labor N_o output is equal to Q_o, which will be sold at the price P_o given a national income equal to Y_o.

19.11. The Effect of an Increase in the Quantity of Money

From the very beginnings of economics, economists have been interested in what happens when the quantity of money in an economic system is increased. We propose to use our model of an economic system to gain some insight into the problem. We want to remember, however, that we are dealing with a very simplified model of a competitive economic system with flexible prices, and the results of our study are strictly applicable only to such an economy. Nevertheless, the results bring out principles which have applicability to economic systems that do not deviate too widely from competitive conditions.

Specifically let us assume that the supply function of money in our model shifts to

$$(19.34) \quad M_s = 143 \cdot 10^9 + 60iP \cdot 10^9 ,$$

that is, the stock of money in the economy is increased by 25 per cent, increased in such a manner that everyone who holds money for any reason whatsoever has 25 per cent more money. As a result of the change in the money supply function, the LM equation will also shift, since with a different stock of money there will be a different level of income associated with each rate of interest to bring about equilibrium in the money market. The new LM function is given by

$$(19.35) \quad iP = PQ \cdot 10^{-12} + .07P - .55 \text{ or } i = \frac{PQ \cdot 10^{-12}}{P} + .07 - \frac{.55}{P} .$$

In this new situation, people will find they have more money than they desire to hold for transactions purposes, at the income level Y_o, and more money than they want to hold for liquidity motives, given the rate of interest i_o. The result, of course, is that the people will spend the excess money and as a result drive up the level of money income and the rate of interest will fall in the face of the excess supply of money. The level of money income will continue to rise and the rate of interest will continue to fall until the excess money is absorbed either into transactions balances or into liquidity balances.

The shift of the LM function in our numerical model, in conjunction with the unchanged IS function will give us a new equilibrium solution:

FIGURE 19–8

THE EFFECT OF AN INCREASE IN THE QUANTITY OF MONEY

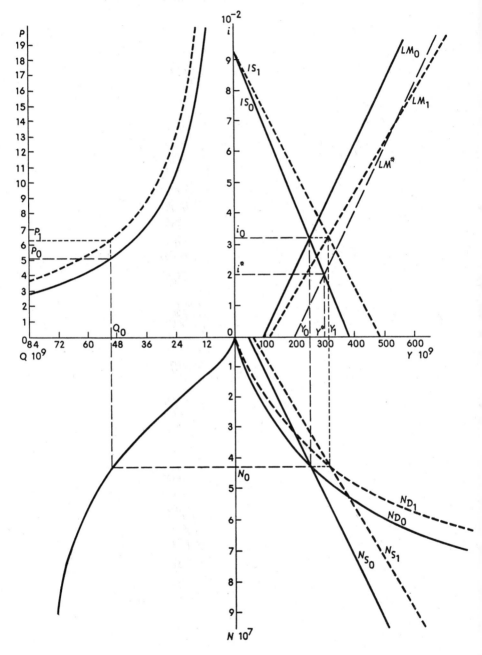

$$(19.36) \quad PQ = P \cdot 10^{11} + 2.5 \cdot 10^{11}$$

$$(19.37) \quad i = .08 - \frac{.3}{P} \, .$$

If the price level were to remain unchanged at \$5.00, it is quickly discovered that the economic system will reach equilibrium with a money income of \$300 billion and a rate of interest of 2 per cent. (This is shown in Figure 19–8 as i^*, Y^*.) However, will the price level remain constant under the altered conditions?

Obviously, under the pressure of increased money holdings and increased money income both the wage rate and the price level will rise. However, as the price level rises, the *IS* and *LM* functions will shift and continue to shift until the price level reaches a new equilibrium position.

We may again reduce the complete system to a wage-employment relationship and solve for the equilibrium wage rate and level of employment. By the same process of substitution that we used previously, the aggregate demand for labor, after the increase in the supply of money, is given by

$$(19.38) \quad W = \frac{\left[\dfrac{250 \cdot 10^9}{(1800N - N^2 \cdot 10^{-5} - 9 \cdot 10^9) - 10 \cdot 10^9} \right] \cdot 10^{10} + 250 \cdot 10^9}{N} \cdot \frac{Q'}{Q} \, ,$$

and the implicit aggregate supply of labor is equal to

$$(19.39) \quad W = \frac{340 \cdot 10^9 - 14 \left[\dfrac{250 \cdot 10^9}{(1800N - N^2 \cdot 10^{-5} - 9 \cdot 10^9) - 10 \cdot 10^9} \right] \cdot 10^9}{N} \, .$$

Remember, that although only the two variables, W and N, are expressed explicitly in these two functions, our complete economic system is embedded in the two. The wage-employment equilibrium is shown in Figure 19–9, with an equilibrium wage rate of \$5,857.08 and an equilibrium level of employment of 43.118 million. After we have found the new equilibrium values for the wage rate and employment, we can proceed to find the new equilibrium values for all the other variables in our numerical model. They are:

$$W = \$5,857.08$$
$$N = 43.118 \text{ million}$$
$$P = \$6.25$$
$$Q = 50 \text{ billion}$$
$$Y = PQ = \$312.5 \text{ billion}$$
$$i = .032$$
$$r = .032.$$

The stock of capital is, of course, unchanged, and the marginal and average products of labor also remain unchanged since output and employment remained constant.

$$S = \$75 \text{ billion}$$
$$I = \$75 \text{ billion}$$
$$M_s = \$155 \text{ billion}$$
$$M_1 = \$81.25 \text{ billion}$$
$$M_2 = \$73.75 \text{ billion.}$$

FIGURE 19–9

EFFECT OF AN INCREASE OF MONEY ON THE WAGE-EMPLOYMENT EQUILIBRIUM

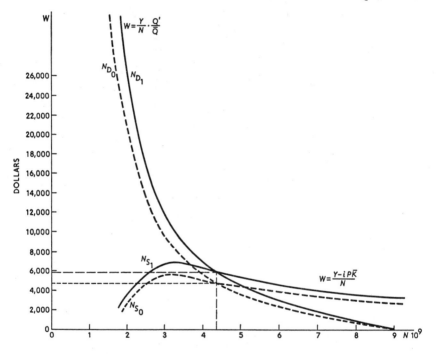

The aggregate money return to labor, WN, has increased to $252.5 billion, and the money returns to the owners of capital advanced to $60 billion.

We observe that the result of increasing the quantity of money in an economic system such as we have in our model, characterized by profit maximization, competition, and flexible prices, is an increase in all money values by the same percentage as the increase in the quantity of money but no change in output or employment. In our numerical model wages, prices, aggregate income, money saving, the money value of investment, and the monetary returns to capital and labor all in-

creased by 25 per cent. The process of spending the excess funds therefore continued until prices had risen sufficiently to eliminate the excess.
In Figure 19–8 we see that both the *IS* and *LM* functions shifted with
the rise in prices, as did the labor demand and supply functions. This is
contrasted with the expected result in the absence of price and wage
increases, where the increase in the quantity of money led to a fall in
the rate of interest and an increase in the level of money income in
which the larger income was a result of greater employment at the
existing wage rate and greater output at the existing price level. Thus
we see that an increase in the quantity of money in an economy will
only increase employment and output if the situation is such that prices
and wages remain stable. However, if prices and wages are flexible, the
increase in the quantity of money leads to inflation—an upward push
on prices and wages with no increase in employment and output.

19.12.   *Effect of an Upward Shift of the Investment Function*

Next let us use our numerical model to investigate the effect of an
upward shift of the investment function, that is, given the price level,
a higher rate of investment will be associated with each rate of interest.
Specifically, let us assume that the new investment function is given by

$$(19.40) \quad I = \frac{P(.102 - i) \cdot 10^9}{4 \cdot 10^{-3}}.$$

This new investment function, in conjunction with the unchanged savings function, gives us a new *IS* function:

$$(19.41) \quad iP = .114P - 1.2PQ \cdot 10^{-12} \text{ or } i = .114 - \frac{1.2PQ \cdot 10^{-12}}{P}.$$

In order to isolate the effect of the change in the investment function,
we are assuming that all the other functions in the model remain unchanged, thus the *LM* function continues as

$$(19.28) \quad i = \frac{PQ \cdot 10^{-12}}{P} + .07 - \frac{.44}{P}.$$

Now we can solve the *IS* and *LM* equations for the new equilibrium
values for the rate of interest and the money national income, with the
price level as a parameter in each case.

$$(19.42) \quad PQ = 20P \cdot 10^9 + 200 \cdot 10^9$$
$$(19.43) \quad i = .09 - \frac{.24}{P}.$$

These new equilibrium values for the aggregate level of money income
and the rate of interest may be substituted into the other equations of

our basic model and the complete model again reduced to two equations in two unknowns, W and N—the wage-employment relation. The shift in the investment function shifts the aggregate demand for labor to

$$(19.44) \quad W = \frac{\left[\dfrac{200 \cdot 10^9}{(1800N - N^2 \cdot 10^{-5} - 9 \cdot 10^9) - 20 \cdot 10^9} \right] \cdot 10^9 + 200 \cdot 10^9}{N} \cdot \frac{Q'}{Q},$$

and the new labor supply function becomes

$$(19.45) \quad W = \frac{272 \cdot 10^9 - 7 \left[\dfrac{200 \cdot 10^9}{(1800N - N^2 \cdot 10^{-5} - 9 \cdot 10^9) - 20 \cdot 10^9} \right] \cdot 10^9}{N} .$$

This new wage-employment relation may now be solved for the new equilibrium wage rate and aggregate employment— $W = \$4,780.82$ and $N = 48.467$ million. Figure 19–10 shows the new equilibrium position. Now that we know the new values for the wage rate and ag-

FIGURE 19–10

EFFECT OF AN UPWARD SHIFT IN INVESTMENT ON WAGE-EMPLOYMENT EQUILIBRIUM

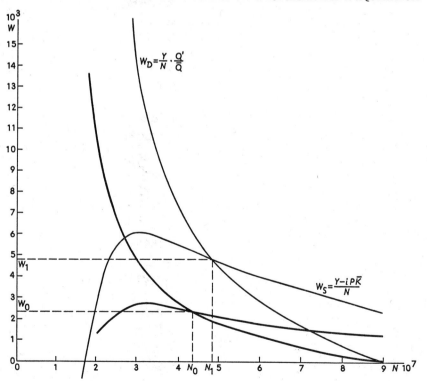

gregate employment, we can proceed to find the new equilibrium values for the other main variables in our model of the economy. They are:

$$W = \$4,780.82$$
$$N = 48.467 \text{ million}$$
$$P = \$5.755$$
$$Q = 54.75 \text{ billion}$$
$$Y = PQ = \$315.1 \text{ billion}$$
$$i = .0483$$
$$r = .0483.$$

The new equilibrium values for saving, investment, the quantity of money supplied and demanded may be found by going behind the *IS* and *LM* functions to the basic equations.

$$S = \$77.26 \text{ billion}$$
$$I = \$77.26 \text{ billion}$$
$$M_s = \$131.08 \text{ billion}$$
$$M_1 = \$81.93 \text{ billion}$$
$$M_2 = \$49.15 \text{ billion.}$$

In comparison with our basic numerical model, the values of all the variables have increased, including output and employment, but because of the rise in the price level, real income, real savings, and real investment have increased by a smaller percentage than the money values of these variables. The money value of savings and investment, for example, went up 28 per cent, but real savings and investment increased only 11.6 per cent. The monetary return to labor rises to $231.7 billion, an increase of 14.7 per cent, while the money income earned by the owners of capital jumps to $83.4 billion, up 73.7 per cent. The rise in real income to both groups is, of course, lower because of the price increase.

The new equilibrium position of our model is shown in Figure 19–11 where it is compared with the beginning equilibrium position of our numerical model. The increase in the demand for investment results in an upward shift of the *IS* function. In the absence of any price movements, the new position would have been given by the intersection of *IS** and *LM₀*, with $i = .042$ and $Y = \$300$ billion. With an unchanged price level and wage rate, the entrepreneurs in the economic system would have demanded approximately 48 million workers and would have put 54.3 billion plus units of output on the market. However, this quantity of output would have sold for a price equal to $5.52 given a national income of $300 billion. Furthermore, at the given wage rate an aggregate employment of slightly more than 50 million would be required to satisfy the requirement that the sum total of factor payments

FIGURE 19–11

THE EFFECT OF AN INCREASE IN INVESTMENT

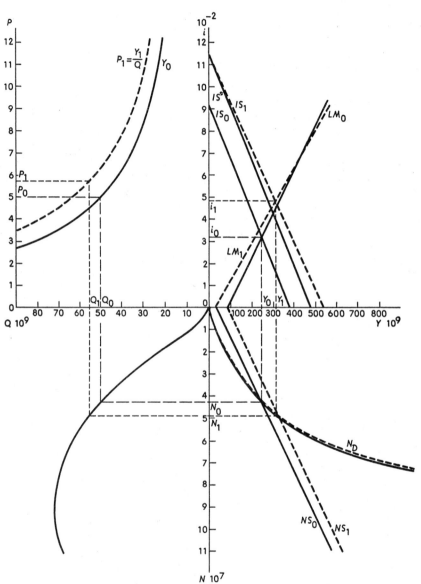

equal national income. Therefore, the price level and the wage rate have to change in order for the system to achieve a new equilibrium position.

Previously we have pointed out that the simple multiplier theory applies only if the rate of interest remains constant, and now it is clear that the price also needs to remain constant. In the example we have just analyzed—an increased demand for investment—if the rate of interest had remained constant at $i = 3.2$ and the price level had continued at $5.00, investment would have increased by $27.5 billion to $87.5 billion. With a marginal propensity to save of .3, the simple multiplier theory would give us a new equilibrium level of aggregate income equal to $341.66 billion. However, since the monetary system is not perfectly elastic, the increased demand for money would have driven the rate of interest up to 4.2 per cent, assuming the price level remained constant at $5.00. As a result of this upward movement of the rate of interest, the shift in the investment function would bring about a rise of only $15 billion, and aggregate income would rise to only $300 billion. But since prices did rise, monetary investment rose to $77.26 billion and aggregate money income to $315.1 billion, a multiplier of 3.77, if we look at the change in money investment and money income. In comparison with the $27.5 billion new investment at the old equilibrium rate of interest, we have a multiplier of only 2.36. With an unchanged rate of interest and price level the shift of the investment function would have increased real investment (money investment deflated by the price level) by 5.5 units, but, because of the change in the rate of interest and the price level, at the new equilibrium position real income had increased only 4.67 units, a multiplier of only .85.

19.13. Effect of an Upward Shift of the Savings Function

Let us now use our numerical model to investigate the other side of the savings-investment function. What would be the effect on the economic system of a change in the savings habits of the community? Specifically, let us assume that the aggregate savings function in our model of an economy becomes:

$$(19.46) \quad S = -.25 \cdot 10^9 P + .3PQ .$$

We assume that all the other equations in our basic numerical model remain unchanged. The new savings function combined with the unchanged investment function [Equation (19.23)] results in a new *IS* function:

$$(19.47) \quad iP = .081P - 1.2PQ \cdot 10^{-12}$$

or

$$i = .081 - \frac{1.2PQ \cdot 10^{-12}}{P} .$$

Thus we are substituting the new *IS* function [Equation (19.47)] for the *IS* function in our basic model [Equation (19.24)] and keeping the other nine equations in the model unaltered. What effect does an increase in thriftiness have on the values of the variables in our economic system? Will employment, output, prices, wages, etc., increase, decrease, or remain unchanged?

We can solve the *IS* and *LM* functions for the new equilibrium rate of interest and level of money income (value of final output) with the price level as a parameter:

$$(19.48) \quad PQ = 5P \cdot 10^9 + 200 \cdot 10^9$$

$$(19.49) \quad i = .075 - \frac{.24}{P}.$$

Again we may proceed by a process of substitution such as we followed with our basic model—to reduce our full system to a wage-employment relationship with one equation representing the demand side and the other equation the supply side, with two variables, wages and employment. The aggregate demand for labor becomes:

$$(19.50) \quad W = \frac{5 \left[\frac{200 \cdot 10^9}{(1800N - N^2 \cdot 10^{-5} - 9 \cdot 10^9)} \cdot 10^9 + 200 \cdot 10^9 \right]}{N} \cdot \frac{Q'}{Q},$$

and the aggregate supply of labor shifts to:

$$(19.51) \quad W = \frac{272 \cdot 10^9 - 17.5 \left[\frac{200 \cdot 10^9}{(1800N - N^2 \cdot 10^{-5} - 9 \cdot 10^9)} \cdot 10^9 \right]}{N}.$$

The new wage-employment functions are shown in Figure 19–12 and yield a new equilibrium wage rate of $4,694.40 and an aggregate employment of 40.326 million. As soon as we know the new equilibrium values for these two variables we can proceed to find the equilibrium values for all the other variables in our numerical model. These new equilibrium values are:

$$W = \$4,694.33$$
$$N = 40.327 \text{ million}$$
$$P = \$4.725$$
$$Q = 47.326 \text{ billion}$$
$$Y = PQ = \$223.6 \text{ billion}$$
$$i = .0243$$
$$r = .0243.$$

Going behind the *IS* and *LM* functions, the new values for saving, investment, quantity of money demanded and supplied are:

$$S = \$65.9 \text{ billion}$$
$$I = \$65.9 \text{ billion}$$
$$M_s = \$121.29 \text{ billion}$$
$$M_1 = \$58.15 \text{ billion}$$
$$M_2 = \$63.14 \text{ billion}.$$

As a result of the increased thriftiness of the community the upward shift of the savings function, savings and investment, in both

FIGURE 19–12

EFFECT OF AN INCREASE IN SAVING ON THE WAGE-EMPLOYMENT EQUILIBRIUM

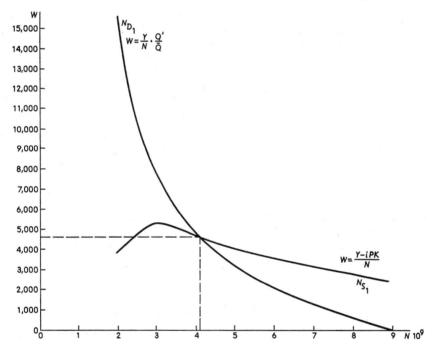

money and real terms, have increased. The rise in investment, however, is not sufficient to offset the deflationary effect of the increased savings, and, therefore, income, employment, and output have decreased. The rise in savings in the community reduced the demand for consumption goods, reducing output, employment, and aggregate income. As aggregate income fell a smaller quantity of money was needed to satisfy the transactions demand for money. Thus money was released to satisfy the liquidity demand for money. However, this excess quantity of money could only be absorbed into liquidity balances at a lower rate of interest. The rate of interest continued to fall until the individuals in the community were willing to hold the additional money in M_2 balances. As the rate of interest fell additional investment was undertaken, but not in sufficient amount to completely offset the rise in savings.

In our short-run model, an increase in the community's desire to save reduces income, output, and employment, but notice that real investment increases, which has important implications for future growth in the system.

19.14. Effect of a Shift in the Demand for Liquidity Balances

If the community's desire to hold money balances for liquidity purposes alters, how will this react upon income, output, and employment? Specifically, let us assume that the demand for liquidity balances decreases, at all rates of interest. We will then compare the new equilibrium situation with the original equilibrium position of our numerical model. Intuitively, one might expect that the system will react to such a shift in the liquidity function in the same manner as it adjusted to an increase in the quantity of money for that is really what happens. However, let us use our model to see what happens when we change the liquidity-preference function. Let us assume that the community's demand for liquidity balances shifts to:

$$(19.52) \quad M_2 = \frac{P(.0624 - i) \cdot 10^9}{5 \cdot 10^{-8}} .$$

In order to isolate the effects of the shift in the liquidity function we assume that all the other functions in our model of an economic system remain unchanged from our basic model. When we combine the new liquidity-preference function with the demand for money for transactions purposes and the supply function for money, we have the new LM function which traces out the relation between the rate of interest and the level of income, with the price level as a parameter. At every point on the LM curve the demand for money is equal to the supply of money. Our new LM curve is given by:

$$(19.53) \quad iP = PQ \cdot 10^{-12} + .048P - .44$$

or

$$i = \frac{PQ \cdot 10^{-12}}{P} + .048 - \frac{.44}{P} .$$

When this new LM function is combined with our original IS function we may solve for the new equilibrium values of the rate of interest and the aggregate money income, with the price level as a parameter:

$$(19.54) \quad PQ = 20P \cdot 10^9 + 200 \cdot 10^9$$

$$(19.55) \quad i = .068 - \frac{.24}{P} .$$

We may now substitute these new values for PQ and i in the balance of the equations of our model and, by a process of substitution, again reduce the system to two equations in two unknowns, W and N— the wage-employment relation. The aggregate demand for labor has shifted to

$$(19.56) \quad W = 20\left[\frac{\dfrac{200 \cdot 10^9}{(1800N - N^2 \cdot 10^{-5} - 9 \cdot 10^9) - 20 \cdot 10^9}}{N}\right] \cdot 10^9 + 200 \cdot 10^9 \cdot \frac{Q'}{Q},$$

and the implicit supply function of labor becomes:

$$(19.57) \quad W = \frac{272 \cdot 10^9 - .4\left[\dfrac{200 \cdot 10^9}{(1800N - N^2 \cdot 10^{-5} - 9 \cdot 10^9) - 20 \cdot 10^9}\right] \cdot 10^9}{N} .$$

The new wage-employment equilibrium, shown in Figure 19–13, confirms our intuition—money wages have increased but employment is unchanged. Since employment is unchanged, output is also unchanged. As we solve for the new values for the other variables in our model of the economic system we discover that all the money values in the system have increased by the same proportion, but employment, output, real savings, real investment, and the rate of interest are unchanged. Thus a change in the community's desire to hold money for liquidity purposes alters only the monetary values in the system but leaves the underlying real variables unchanged. The new equilibrium values for the variables are:

$$W = \$6,246.47$$
$$N = 43.118 \text{ million}$$
$$Q = 50 \text{ billion}$$
$$P = \$6.666$$
$$Y = PQ = \$333.3 \text{ billion}$$
$$i = .032$$
$$r = .032 ,$$

and back of the *IS* and *LM* functions we have:

$$S = \$80 \text{ billion}$$
$$I = \$80 \text{ billion}$$
$$M_s = \$127.19 \text{ billion}$$
$$M_1 = \$86.66 \text{ billion}$$
$$M_2 = \$40.53 \text{ billion} .$$

FIGURE 19–13

EFFECT OF A FALL IN LIQUIDITY PREFERENCE ON THE
WAGE-EMPLOYMENT EQUILIBRIUM

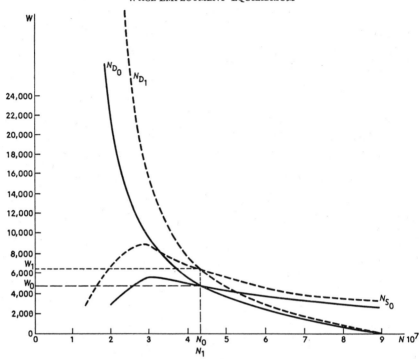

19.15. Cost-Push Inflation

There is a widespread belief that the American economy has experienced a new kind of inflation since the early 1950's. This new type
of inflation is said to be one in which prices are apparently pushed up
by the sellers in contrast to the more "classical" type in which prices are
pulled up by an excess of monetary demand. We have already observed
how prices rise when additional money is pumped into an economy, but
how can the so-called cost-push inflation occur? It has been argued that
the cost-push can arise either in the wages sector as a result of negotiated
wages or in the profits sector as a result of target-return pricing. We propose to use our basic model of an economy to gain some insight into
cost-push inflation.

19.16. Cost-Push Inflation from the Profits Side

In this variation of our model we assume that the entrepreneurs
select a particular rate of return on capital and then price their output
and adjust their demand for labor accordingly. In order to simplify the

analysis we assume that the selceted rate of return is the same for the whole economy. Obviously, our previous assumption that the aggregate demand for labor is based on the profit-maximizing efforts of the firms operating under competitive conditions has to be dropped. In our basic model, Equation (19.12) is therefore eliminated and replaced with the assumption that labor is demanded and goods produced and sold in such quantities that

$$(19.58) \quad r = \bar{r} .$$

The rest of the basic model remains unchanged. No longer is the rate of return determined as a part of the general equilibrium under competitive conditions. Instead the system adjusts to an arbitrarily determined rate of return under noncompetitive conditions. Let us further assume that $\bar{r} = 4\%$, and then proceed to find the new equilibrium values for the variables in the system. Our model of the economic system now consists of the following equations:

$$(19.24) \quad iP = .092P - 1.2PQ \cdot 10^{-12}$$
$$(19.28) \quad iP = PQ \cdot 10^{-12} + .07P - .44$$
$$(19.58) \quad r \ = \bar{r}$$
$$(19.29) \quad Q \ = 2HNK - AN^2 - BK^2$$
$$(19.14) \quad Y \ = PQ$$
$$(19.15) \quad Y \ = WN + rPK$$
$$(19.16) \quad i \ = r$$
$$(19.17) \quad K = \bar{K} .$$

The full system now includes the following eight variables i, P, Q, N, Y, W, K, and r, plus the following constants, $K = 3 \cdot 10^{11}$, $A = 10^{-5}$, $B = 10^{-13}$, $H = 3 \cdot 10^{-9}$, and the assumption that $\bar{r} = .04$. The IS and LM functions, Equations (19.24) and (19.28), may be solved for the new equilibrium values of the rate of interest and the value of aggregate output (which is equal to aggregate income) with the price level as a parameter:

$$(19.32) \quad PQ = P \cdot 10^{10} + 200 \cdot 10^{9}$$
$$(19.33) \quad i = .08 - \frac{.24}{P} .$$

However, one of our equilibrium conditions [Equation (19.16)] requires that the rate of interest be equal to the rate of return on capital. We may now combine our assumption that the target rate of return is equal to 4 per cent with the equilibrium condition and then substitute the 4 per cent into Equation (19.33) and solve for P. As soon as we have the new equilibrium value for P we may then substitute into Equation (19.32) and solve for PQ, which is equal to Y by Equation (19.14).

352 · ECONOMICS: AN ANALYTICAL APPROACH

Next we may divide PQ by P to find Q. Then knowing Q we can find N, by way of the production function [Equation (19.27)], and the given stock of capital [Equation (19.17)]. Finally, the wage rate is found by a process of substitution into Equation (19.15). The values for the variables in the system are:

$$P = \$6.00$$
$$Y = PQ = \$260 \text{ billion}$$
$$Q = 43.33 \text{ billion}$$
$$N = 36.46 \text{ million}$$
$$W = \$5,156.33$$
$$i = r = .04 \ .$$

These are the new equilibrium values for the variables in the system in the sense that they will remain unchanged until one of the behavior equations or one of the parameters is changed.

In comparison with our basic model of the economy, based on profit maximization in a competitive system with flexible prices, we observe that the change in our assumption concerning the lack of competition has resulted in a higher price level, a higher wage rate, a higher rate of interest, a higher level of money income, but a decrease in output and employment. Although money wages have risen, the price level has increased by a higher percentage, and thus real wages per employed worker have fallen. We note that the aggregate real income paid to labor as a whole has also decreased but that the aggregate real return paid to the owners of capital has increased. The change in our assumptions has thus resulted in a rise in prices and money income accompanied by a fall in output and employment—symptoms of what has been called cost-push inflation.

In the past it has frequently been suggested that an easy money policy should be employed to eliminate unemployment. The question now arises what would be the result of an easy money policy, i.e., pumping more money into the economy, in our present model? In order to explore this question let us assume that the money supply equation is shifted to:

$$(19.59) \quad M_s = 143 \cdot 10^9 + 60iP \cdot 10^9 \ ,$$

i.e., an increase of 25 per cent in the given stock of money in the economy. The new LM function then becomes:

$$(19.60) \quad iP = PQ \cdot 10^{-12} + .07P - .55$$

or

$$i = \frac{PQ \cdot 10^{-12}}{P} + .07 - \frac{.55}{P} \ .$$

Assuming all the other relations in our profits-push inflation model remain the same, we can proceed to utilize the *IS* and *LM* relations to find the new equilibrium values for the price level and the level of money income:

$$(19.61) \quad Y = PQ = P \cdot 10^{10} + 250 \cdot 10^{9}$$

$$(19.62) \quad i = .08 - \frac{.3}{P} \,.$$

Since in equilibrium $i = r$ and $r = .04$ by our assumption of target-return pricing, we can solve for P and PQ and then by a process of substitution find the new equilibrium values for the other variables. They are:

$$P = \$7.50$$
$$Y = PQ = \$325 \text{ billion}$$
$$Q = 43.33 \text{ billion}$$
$$N = 36.46 \text{ million}$$
$$W = \$6,445.41$$
$$r = i = .04 \,.$$

The effect of increasing the quantity of money in the system is to increase the price level, the level of aggregate money income, and the wage rate by the same percentage as the increase in the stock of money. However, output and employment are unchanged. Thus, in a situation of a profits-push inflation, an easy money policy only increases prices and wages without reducing unemployment.

19.17. Wage-Push Inflation

Many observers of the American economy during the last decade have argued that the cost-push type of inflation has been the most significant variety and, in the long run, the most difficult to control. It has been argued that costs are the propelling or motivating force and wage costs are dominant. Others have denied that wages are responsible and have assigned the greatest responsibility to administered prices and the profit margins they protect. We have already analyzed profit-push inflation. Now let us explore the possibility of wage-push inflation with the help of our basic numerical model of the economy.

We shall now assume that the money wage rate is determined as a result of bargaining between the employers and the workers. The employers then hire the amount of labor they desire, at the bargained wage, in order to maximize profits. Thus we are assuming an administered wage in the labor market but competition in the product market. This is just the reverse of the assumptions we made in the model illustrating profit-push inflation—in that situation we assumed competition in the labor market but an administered price in the product market. Specifically, we assume that as a result of bargaining the wage rate is set equal to $5,000.

$$(19.63) \quad W = \$5,000$$

The question now arises as to how we introduce this assumption into our basic model. We may regard Equation (19.63) as a labor supply equation, that is, the workers are willing to supply any quantity of labor demanded at the agreed upon wage. But then, we may no longer regard Equation (19.15) as the labor supply relation. With the introduction of wages determined by bargaining, we have one extra equation in our model, that is, an overdetermined system. In order to avoid this overdeterminacy we will give up Equation (19.28) as an independent relation and assume that the demand for money for transactions purposes is a residual and adjusts to whatever value is necessary in order that an equilibrium price be achieved. This means that in this model the money market adjusts to the values determined in the rest of the system. This assumption with respect to the demand for money is expressed as:

$$(19.64) \quad M_1 = aPQ .$$

Given the liquidity-preference demand for money and the supply of money as it is in our basic model, the LM function becomes,

$$(19.65) \quad iP = 5aPQ \cdot 10^{-12} + .07P - .44 ,$$

with the value of the variable a depending upon the values of P and Q as they are determined in the rest of the system.

The relevant equations for the wage-push model are now:

$$(19.24) \quad iP = .092P - 1.2PQ \cdot 10^{-12}$$

$$(19.12) \quad N = \frac{Y}{W} \cdot \frac{Q'}{Q}$$

$$(19.29) \quad Q = 2HNK - AN^2 - BK^2$$

$$(19.14) \quad Y \equiv PQ$$

$$(19.15) \quad Y = WN + rPK$$

$$(19.16) \quad i = r$$

$$(19.17) \quad K = \bar{K}$$

$$(19.63) \quad W = \bar{W} = \$5,000$$

$$(19.30) \quad Q' = 2HK - 2AN$$

$$(19.31) \quad \bar{Q} = 2HK - AN - \frac{BK^2}{N} .$$

The system includes the following ten variables i, P, Q, r, N, Y, W, Q', $\bar{Q}$, and K, plus the following constants, $\bar{K} = 3 \cdot 10^{11}$, $A = 10^{-5}$, $B =$

10^{-13}, $H = 3 \cdot 10^{-9}$, and the assumption concerning wages, $\bar{W} = \$5,000$. Then we also have Equation (19.65), with the value for the variable a determined as a residual.

In order to find the new equilibrium values in our numerical model, we need to reduce the number of equations in the system through a process of substitution. First we may substitute (19.16) into (19.24), then (19.17) into (19.15), (19.63) into (19.15) and (19.12). Next we substitute (19.14) into (19.15) and (19.12) and then (19.12) may be rewritten as

$$(19.67) \quad P = \frac{\bar{W}N}{Q \cdot \frac{Q'}{Q}},$$

which may be viewed as the aggregate supply function. In this model, Equation (19.15) is no longer considered as a labor supply function, which is given by Equation (19.63). Our next step is to substitute (19.24) into (19.15), which may then be rewritten as

$$(19.68) \quad P = \frac{\bar{W}N}{Q + 1.2Q \cdot 10^{-12} \, \bar{K} - .092_{\Lambda}},$$

and viewed as the aggregate demand for goods. The system has now been reduced to essentially a demand for and supply of goods, given the wage bargain, with the monetary sector adjusting to the results. The demand-supply equilibrium is shown in Figure 19–14.

After we solve the simplified system for the new equilibrium price level and output, we may proceed to find the new values for the remaining variables. They are:

$$P = \$5.336$$
$$N = 43.118 \text{ million}$$
$$Q = 50 \text{ billion}$$
$$Y = PQ = \$266.8 \text{ billion}$$
$$\bar{W}N = \$215.59 \text{ billion}$$
$$i = r = 3.2\%$$
$$rP\bar{K} = \$51.22 \text{ billion.}$$

In this wage-push model of the economy, with wages determined by the bargaining between employer and employee, we note that all the monetary values in the system increase in the same proportion as the increase in wages. As wages are pushed, prices and money returns also rise. Employment and output, however, are determined by the saving and investment decisions in the economy, given the state of technology, and then prices adjust to the wage level with the monetary sector allowing the necessary increase in the velocity of money. This means that in a system of this nature, labor can bargain over the money wage, but the real wage depends on real saving and real investment.

In this chapter we have expanded our basic model of the economic system to remove the implicit assumption that wages and prices are unchanged as the level of money income changes. We then used the

FIGURE 19–14

PRICE-OUTPUT EQUILIBRIUM IN THE WAGE-PUSH MODEL

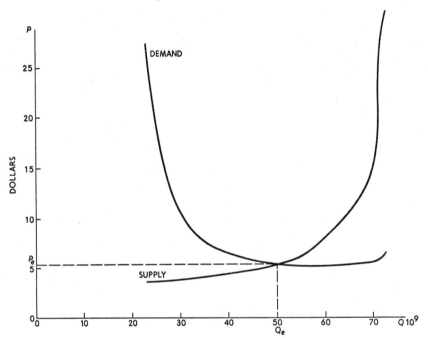

resulting wage-price model to explore the implications of changing variables in the system. We also noted that in order to have cost-push inflation it was necessary to remove our assumption of competition. The existence of cost-push inflation seems to depend upon noncompetitive conditions. We also noted that monetary policy did not seem to be an appropriate weapon to use to eliminate this kind of inflation. Other weapons are needed.

QUESTIONS AND EXERCISES

1. If the community's marginal propensity to save falls, what would you expect to happen to prices, wages, output, employment, and the rate of interest? Suppose that the saving function in Section 19.9 shifts to $S = -3 \cdot 10^9 P +$

.25*PQ*, with the other functions unchanged, find the new equilibrium values for *P*, *W*, *Q*, *N*, *r*, *I*, and *S*. What happens to real wages?

2. If the institutional arrangements of the model economy change in such a manner that less money is needed to satisfy the transactions demands for money, what would you expect to happen to wages, prices, output, and employment? Suppose the transactions demand for money shifts to $M_1 = .13Y$, while all the other equations remain as they are in Section 19.9. What happens to the equilibrium values for the variables? What happens to real wages? To the real return to the owners of capital?

3. If the stock of capital in the system increased, what would you expect to happen to wages, prices, output, and employment? Suppose the stock of capital in our model presented in Section 19.9 increases to 600 billion units, that is, it doubles. Find the new equilibrium values for the variables in the system.

4. Suppose that the stock of capital remains unchanged but that technology alters so that the constant *A* in the production function for our numerical model of the economy becomes $A = 10^{-6}$. What happens to the equilibrium values for the variables in the system?

5. Discuss the problems involved in attempting to control cost-push inflation by acting on the demand for and supply of money in the economic system. What policy would you suggest in order to control cost-push inflation?

Chapter 20 | GOVERNMENT AND THE NATIONAL INCOME

In this chapter we shall analyze the influence of the government, in our model economic system, upon the level of aggregate income, consumption, demand, and employment. In the world today by far the greatest single economic entity in each country is the government, including all its subsidiary forms. Up to now, in our model of the economic system, we have assumed government expenditures and tax receipts to be zero. We shall now remove this assumption and analyze what happens in the economic system when positive government expenditures and tax receipts are included.

20.1. Legal and Institutional Framework

The private, nongovernmental, sector of our economy feels the influence of the government through two main channels. First, through its judicial and legislative aspects, the government sets the legal framework within which private organisms carry on their economic activities. Second, through its expenditures and tax receipts, the government influences the volume of income and employment.

There are certain basic institutions that are necessary for a private enterprise economy to exist and function. The carrying on of business is hardly cenceivable without some active intervention on the part of government. Buying and selling is at the very core of an enterprise system, and this business activity could not exist without the institutions of property and contract and a judicial system in which the contracts could be enforced. Such a judicial system is maintained by the intervention of the government. A monetary system is the lifeblood of a modern economic system, and it also is maintained by the government. Thus the government intervenes in determining the working rules of the institutions of property and contract, defining rights and duties of persons in acquiring and using property. Secondly, the government establishes and maintains the monetary standard used by the individuals in the economic system. Thirdly, the government influences the general environment within which the economic system operates.

Increasingly the government has intervened more and more directly in regulating the economic processes. Acts such as Food and Drugs Act of 1906 and the Food, Drug, and Cosmetic Act of 1938, that aim to protect the consumer from misbranded and adulterated food and cosmetics in interestate trade; the Sherman Antitrust Act of 1890, the Clayton Act and Federal Trade Commission Act of 1914, and the Celler Antimerger Act of 1950, that aim to prevent monopolization of business and industry in interstate trade; the Securities Exchange Act of 1934, that aims to protect investors; the Public Utility Holding Company Act of 1935, that regulates public utility holding companies—are a few of the many pieces of legislation that contain prohibitions and restrictions on certain economic activities. With federal and state regulation of public utility companies, the government has intervened directly in the economic process with its regulation of rates. In state and federal minimum wage and maximum hour legislation and acts like the Wagner Act of 1935 (the National Labor Relations Act) and the Taft-Hartley Act of 1947 (the Labor-Management Relations Act which was an amendment of the Wagner Act), the government has played an increasingly prominent role in employer-employee relations.

There are many more pieces of legislation and court interpretations that vitally influence the operation of the economic system, and if we were engaged in a study of American economic institutions, we would investigate and analyze many of them. However, ours is not an institutional but an analytical study; therefore we shall now turn to an economic analysis of government taxing and spending.

20.2. Government Transactions with the Private Sector

All the activities above are negative in that the government determines the course of economic activity only indirectly by setting up and enforcing restrictions and prohibitions of one kind or another. Another, and more positive aspect of governmental relationship to the private economic sector exists in the governmental exchanges and transfers.

By government exchanges we mean all the buying and selling of goods and services by the various branches of the government—including the armed forces and all the civilian activity at the federal, state, and local level. In the operation of the government many different goods and services are purchased, ranging from paper clips and secretarial skills to rockets and engineering know-how. Since 1929, government purchases of goods and services have increased manyfold, from $8.5 billion to over $100 billion in 1960. As a percentage of net national product, government purchases have grown from almost 9 per cent in 1929 to over 21 per cent in 1960. (See the appendix to Chapter 16.) Government sales of goods and services, such as the sale of books and pamphlets by the government printing office and the sale of services by the post office are not very great in the United States, but such sales are large in some foreign countries where the government or government agencies own much of the country's capital goods.

Government transfer payments involve simply the transfer of assets of some kind—usually cash—from the government sector to the private sector without a corresponding flow of goods or services occurring during the same accounting period from the private sector to the government sector of the economy. For example, in the United States we have such transfer payment as social security payments, unemployment compensation and veterans' compensation payments. Transfer payments from the government to the private sector add to the disposable income available to individuals. We recall that in our national income accounting we treated government transfer payments as negative taxes—see the appendix to Chapter 16. The item taxes, T, in our model, is equal to total taxes minus transfer payments, that is, $T = Tx - Tr$, where T is net taxes, TX total taxes and Tr transfer payments.

In Section 16.4 we showed that $Y \equiv C + T + S \equiv C + G + I$, [Equation (16.5)], where Y is the net national product, C is the income expenditure by households for consumption, T is the use of income to pay taxes, and S is that part of the income not spent for consumption or used to pay taxes. On the right-hand side of the identity, C is the value of the goods and services sold for final consumption, G is the value of the goods and services purchased by the government, and I is the value of the goods purchased for net investment. We then pointed out, since the amount of income used to buy consumption goods must be equal to the amount of goods purchased for final consumption, we can subtract C from both sides of the identity in Equation (16.5) and then we have $T + S \equiv G + I$ [Equation (16.6)].

The identity in Equation (16.6) says that the sum of tax collections by the government and the savings by households and businesses is identically equal to the sum of government expenditures on goods and services and private expenditures on net investment. Notice that it is not necessary that government expenditures be equal to tax collections; they are equal only in the special case of a balanced government budget. If the government spends more than it collects, and thus increases government debt, our identity tells us that savings must be greater than net investment, greater by an amount equal to the government deficit. Thus the government deficit is financed by selling bonds to the banks or the general public.

20.3. The Basic Model with the Government Included

In previous chapters we have examined various functional relationships based on the behavior of individuals, that help determine the level of consumption and investment expenditure. The determination of the level of government expenditure and tax receipts can best be viewed as autonomous—given to the economic system. They are determined by political decisions, and then the economic impact is transmitted into the economic system via government purchases of goods and services and the alteration of disposable income. In its immediate effects on the level of economic activity, government expenditure is similar to net investment; it adds to aggregate demand for goods and services. On the other hand, taxes are similar to savings in their immediate effects on spending in that both are a part of current income not spent for consumption goods.

We propose to examine the effects of adding the government sector to our basic *IS-LM* model of the economic system by removing the assumption that $G = T = 0$. Instead we shall assume that both government expenditures and taxes are positive and may or may not be equal to each other. In all other ways our basic model will be exactly the same as it was presented, developed and analyzed in Sections 18.7 through 18.10. We shall see that the introduction of positive values for government expenditures and tax collections influences both the shape and position of the *IS* curve, and thus influences the final equilibrium position of the economic model. The *LM* function will not be changed.

20.4. Effect of G on the IS Function

In Chapter 18 we developed the functional relationship between the rate of interest and the level of income based on a functional equality of aggregate supply and aggregate demand in the goods and services markets. We shall now examine the effects of the introduction of government expenditures on our basic model. After we have traced this through, we shall introduce a positive amount of tax collections.

In Table 20–1 we have added a constant amount of government expenditures to the savings function and investment demand function of Table 18–1. Columns 1 and 2 of Table 20–1 is the savings function presented in Table 18–1; Columns 3 and 4 together make up the investment demand function presented in Table 18–1, and Column 5 is our added assumption that government expenditures are given as $20 billion and remain unchanged at that figure. Presumably this amount has been determined as the result of political decisions.

TABLE 20–1

DERIVATION OF *IGS* SCHEDULE

SAVINGS FUNCTION		INVESTMENT DEMAND FUNCTION		GOVERNMENT EXPENDITURES
(1) Y (Billions)	(2) S (Billions)	(3) i	(4) I (Billions)	(5) G (Billions)
$ 50.0	$ 0.0	8%	$ 0.0	$20
91.6	12.5	7	12.5	20
133.3	25.0	6	25.0	20
175.0	37.5	5	37.5	20
216.6	50.0	4	50.0	20
258.3	62.5	3	62.5	20
300.0	75.0	2	75.0	20
341.6	87.5	1	87.5	20

In this variation of our model of the economic system the equilibrium condition for the goods and service markets is

$$(20.1) \quad Y - C(Y_d) = G + I(i) ,$$

which is found by substituting the savings and investment functions into the identity of Equation (16.6). We now proceed, in exactly the same manner as we did in Section 18.8, to derive a new *IS* function. Let us begin by picking a rate of interest, say 7 per cent. At this rate of interest, investors desire to spend on investment goods at the rate of $12.5 billion. Adding to the investment demanded the government demand of $20 billion, we see that the required aggregate savings is equal to $32.5 billion. The savings function shows that the required aggregate savings will be forthcoming at a level of income of $158.3 billion. This gives us one point on the new *IS* curve—which we shall designate as the *IGS* function to show that government spending has been included in the model.

With a rate of interest of 3 per cent, the desired level of investment is $62.5 billion, which when added to government expenditure, gives a figure of $82.5 billion to be matched by savings. A desired level of savings of $82.5 billion would result if the level of income were $325 billion. This gives us a second point on the *IGS* curve. If this process is repeated a number of times, the *IGS* schedule given in Table 20–2 can be derived. If we compare the *IGS* schedule above in Table 20–2 with the *IS* schedule in Table 18–2, we notice that the level of income associated with each rate of interest is higher in the *IGS* schedule, by more than the amount of government expenditures.

The impact of the introduction of government expenditures is easily seen in the graphic presentation of our basic model of the economy. Figure 20–1 is essentially the same as Figure 18–12 but with the addition of government expenditures to the investment demand function in Quadrant A and the addition of government expenditures to the equilibrium condition, which now requires that desired savings be equal to desired investment plus government spending. While we examine

TABLE 20–2

IGS SCHEDULE

i	Y (Billions)
8%	$116.6
7	158.3
6	200.0
5	241.6
4	283.3
3	325.0
2	366.6
1	408.3

the impact of government expenditures separately, taxes are assumed to be zero; therefore, the savings function is unchanged.

We can now proceed to derive the *IGS* curve graphically. Let us start in Quadrant A with some rate of interest, say 7 per cent. At this rate of interest, investment demand is $12.5 billion, and government spending is $20 billion, for a total demand of $32.5 billion. In Figure 20–1 we then move up to Quadrant B where the 45° line, reflecting the equilibrium condition, tells us that the economy needs a desired level of savings equal to $32.5 billion in order to achieve equilibrium in the goods and services markets. From the savings function in Quadrant C we observe that $32.5 billion would be saved out of an income of $158.3 billion. This gives us one point in Quadrant D, $i = 7$ per cent, $Y = \$158.3$ billion, on the *IGS* curve—Point A in Figure 20–1. If we would go through the same process with a rate of interest of 3 per cent, Point B in Figure 20–1 would be found. And if we were to pick many rates of interest and work through the process of finding the level of income associated with each rate of interest we would locate many points on the *i-Y* plane of Quadrant D. In Quadrant D all these points have been connected to give us the *IGS* curve found there.

FIGURE 20-1

THE IMPACT OF GOVERNMENT EXPENDITURES

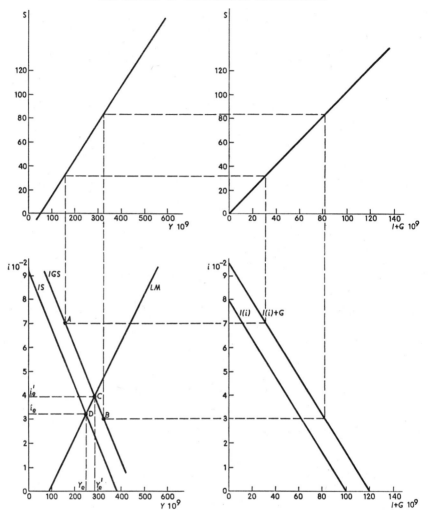

Since the money supply, liquidity-preference and transactions demand functions remain as they were in the basic model developed in Chapter 18, the *LM* curve, tracing out the functional relationship between the rate of interest and the level of income based on equilibrium in the money market, is also as it was in Section 18.9. This *LM* curve has been included in Quadrant D of Figure 20–1. We learned in Section 18.10 that the model of the whole economy can be in equilibrium only if the final values for the rate of interest and the level of income are such that desired savings are equal to desired investment and the quantity of money demanded is equal to the quantity of money supplied. Since we have added government expenditures to the model, the first condition must be altered so that desired savings are equal to desired investment plus government expenditures.

Both conditions are satisfied in Figure 20–1 at Point C where the *LM* curve (representing equilibrium in the money market) intersects the *IGS* curve (representing equilibrium in the goods and service markets). In Section 18.10 our model of the economy reached equilibrium, given our functions, with a rate of interest of 3.2 per cent and a level of income of $250 billion. Into this model we injected government expenditures equal to $20 billion. Assuming all the functions remain unchanged, what is the effect of this government expenditure?

The new equilibrium is reached with a rate of interest of 3.93 per cent and a level of income of $286.36 billion. We observe that the introduction of government spending, other things equal, increases the level of income. Notice, however, that net investment has fallen as the rate of interest rose. With the introduction of government spending, the level of income rose, increasing the quantity of money desired for transactions purposes, which helped push up the rate of interest.

The effect of the addition of government expenditures to our *IS-LM* model can also be shown explicitly, utilizing the various equations we presented in Chapter 18. The equilibrium condition for the goods and service markets now becomes

$$(20.2) \quad -15 \cdot 10^9 + .3Y = \frac{5(.08 - i) \cdot 10^9}{4 \cdot 10^{-3}} + 20 \cdot 10^9 .$$

When this equilibrium condition is solved for i in terms of Y, we have the equation for the *IGS* function:

$$(20.3) \quad i = .108 - .24Y \cdot 10^{-12} .$$

Since the *LM* function in our model is unchanged, we have the two equilibrium conditions which must be satisfied. The whole may be expressed as

$$(20.4) \quad .108 - .24Y \cdot 10^{-12} = .2Y \cdot 10^{-12} - .018 .$$

The general equilibrium solution for the model, with the addition of government expenditures, is $Y = \$286.363$ and $i = 3.93\%$.

20.5. The Addition of Taxes

Finally we need to investigate what happens to the level of income and rate of interest when we introduce tax collections into our basic model of the economy. In Chapter 17 we assumed that consumption shows a definite and fairly stable relationship between a community's disposable income and what the community spends on consumption. Thus we had:

$$(17.2) \quad C = C(Y_d) \, .$$

Disposable income, it was pointed out in Chapter 16, is equal to net national product minus taxes, where taxes are net of transfer payments:

$$(16.2) \quad Y_d \equiv Y - T \, .$$

Since consumption is some function of disposable income, we shall take the consumption function to be of the linear form assumed in Chapter 17:

$$(17.4) \quad C = a + bY_d \, .$$

If we combine Equations (16.2) and (17.4), we have

$$(20.5) \quad C = a + b(Y - T) \quad \text{or} \quad C = a + bY - bT \, .$$

Thus if $0 < b < 1$, the introduction of taxes into our basic model will change both consumption and saving. (Remember that b is the marginal propensity to consume.) Equation (20.5) tells us that when taxes are introduced into the system, consumption will fall by an amount equal to the marginal propensity to consume times the tax collections. As we shall see presently this ignores any monetary effect induced by the introduction of taxes.

In order to isolate the effects of the introduction of tax collections, we shall assume that government expenditures remain constant at $20 billion and that all the functions in our basic model remain unchanged except for the savings function, which is affected by the inclusion of the tax item. In Equation (17.3) we defined savings as

$$(17.3) \quad S = Y_d - C \, .$$

Now let us combine Equations (16.2), (17.3), and (20.2). We then have:

$$(20.6) \quad S = Y - (a + bY - bT) - T \, .$$

In our basic model we have arbitrarily chosen $a = \$15$ billion and $b = .7$ for purposes of exposition. Equation (20.6) is used to derive the savings function given below in Table 20–3. The investment demand function and the column listing government expenditures are the same as in Table 20–1, and they are repeated for convenience. We have assumed that tax receipts and government expenditures are a constant, presumably determined as a result of political actions.

By this time the student should quickly recognize that Columns 1 and 4 taken together give us the functional relationship between the rate of interest and the level of income, based on equilibrium in the goods and service markets. With tax collections added to the model, the equilibrium condition for the goods and service markets becomes the requirement that desired investment plus government expenditures must be equal to desired savings plus tax collections. When we compare Columns 1 and 4 of Table 20–3, which we shall call the *IGST* schedule, with the *IGS* schedule in Table 20–2, we notice that the level of income associated with any particular rate of interest is lower after the addition of taxes, i.e., the function has been shifted.

TABLE 20–3

DERIVATION OF *IGST* SCHEDULE

SAVINGS FUNCTION		TAX RECEIPTS	INVESTMENT FUNCTION		GOVERNMENT EXPENDITURE
(1) Y (Billions)	(2) S (Billions)	(3) T (Billions)	(4) i	(5) I (Billions)	(6) G (Billions)
$ 70.0	$ 0.0	$20	8%	$ 0.0	$20
111.6	12.5	20	7	12.5	20
136.6	25.0	20	6	25.0	20
195.0	37.5	20	5	37.5	20
236.6	50.0	20	4	50.0	20
278.3	62.5	20	3	62.5	20
320.0	75.0	20	2	75.0	20
361.6	87.5	20	1	87.5	20

The effect of the tax-induced shift of the *IS* function (now the *IGST* function) on the equilibrium level of income is seen in Figure 20–2. Quadrant A is identical to Quadrant A of Figure 20–1 and shows the addition of the investment demand function and government expenditures. In Quadrant B we again have the equilibrium condition represented and now taxes are included. The dotted line in Quadrant C represents the savings function as it has been shifted to the right by the addition of tax collections. The constant amount of taxes is then added to the savings function to derive the solid line in Quadrant C, which shows the sum of taxes and savings and the level of aggregate income associated with such a total.

By this time the graphic derivation of the *IS* curve should be clear to the student so perhaps we need not work through the details of deriving the *IGST* curve in Quadrant D. It shows the functional relationship between the rate of interest and the level of income based on equilibrium in the goods and services markets. The *LM* curve, the func-

FIGURE 20–2

THE EFFECT OF ADDING TAX COLLECTIONS TO THE MODEL

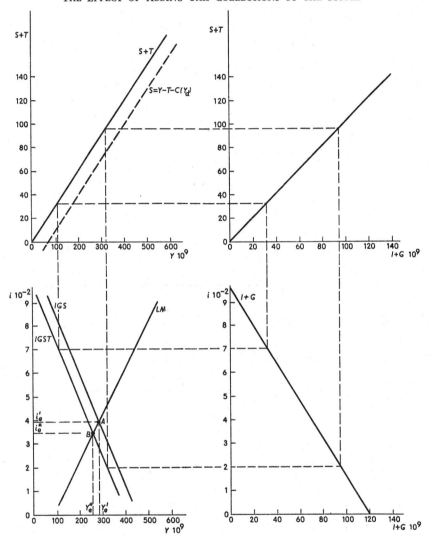

tional relationship between the rate of interest and the level of income, based on equilibrium in the money market, is also shown in Quadrant D. The equilibrium of the whole system is given by the intersection of the *LM* curve and the *IGST* curve. Only at this point do we find a rate of interest and level of income that satisfies both of our equilibrium conditions. The new equilibrium rate of interest is found to be 3.42 per cent and associated with it is a level of income of $260.9 billion.

In comparison with the equilibrium values for Y and i before taxes were introduced but including government spending, we notice that the introduction of taxes has reduced both the level of income and the rate of interest. Point A, in Figure 20–2 is the equilibrium position with only government spending added to the basic model and Point B is the equilibrium position with both government spending and taxing added to our basic model of the economy. We may conclude, then, other things equal, the addition of government spending will tend to increase the level of aggregate income, and the addition of tax collections will tend to reduce the level of aggregate income. We will use these conclusions when we consider fiscal policy in the following chapter in relation to economic fluctuations.

With the addition of tax collections to our *IS-LM* model, the equilibrium condition in the goods and service markets becomes

$$(20.7) \quad -21 \cdot 10^9 + .3Y + 20 \cdot 10^9 = \frac{5(.08 - i) \cdot 10^9}{4 \cdot 10^{-3}} + 20 \cdot 10^9 \cdot$$

When we solve this equilibrium condition for i in terms of Y, we have the new equation for what we now term the *IGST* function:

$$(20.8) \quad i = .0968 - .24Y \cdot 10^{-12} .$$

Since nothing has been altered in the monetary sector of our model of the economy, the *LM* function remains unchanged. We may now combine the *LM* and *IGST* functions to find the new equilibrium value for Y, and then utilizing the new value for Y find the new equilibrium value for i. Setting the *LM* function equal to the *IGST* function, we have,

$$(20.9) \quad .2Y \cdot 10^{-12} - .018 = .0968 - .24Y \cdot 10^{-12} .$$

The new value for Y is found to be $260.9 billion and i is 3.42 per cent.

In this section we assumed that tax collections were a constant amount, irrespective of the level of income. However, taxes might be taken as proportional to income, or progressive, that is increase faster than income. Each of these alternatives would shift the savings function and thus the *IS* function, and so, other things equal, change the equilibrium level of income.

20.6. The Impact of G and T on Wages and Prices

Up to this point we have considered the effect of government expenditures and tax collections upon the rest of the economy with the implicit assumption that the level of prices and wages was given and unchanged. In Chapter 19, however, we have observed that wages and prices do change in real life and there is advantage in being able to work with a model economy that also incorporates wage and price changes. Therefore, let us utilize the explicit model we introduced in Chapter 19 as a framework within which we will study the impact of government spending and tax collecting.

First let us examine what happens when we introduce $20 billion of government expenditures while keeping the rest of the wage-price model as it was in Section 19.9. With the addition of government spending the equilibrium condition for the goods and services markets (the *IGS* function) becomes:

$$(20.10) \quad iP = .092P - 1.2PQ \cdot 10^{-12} + .08 .$$

This new *IGS* function is then combined with the unchanged *LM* function (the equilibrium condition for the money market) and then solved for national income:

$$(20.11) \quad PQ = 10P \cdot 10^9 + 236.363 \cdot 10^9 .$$

After we have found the value for national income we substitute back into the *IGS* or *LM* function and solve for the new equilibrium value for the rate of interest:

$$(20.12) \quad i = .08 - \frac{.20364}{P} .$$

The complete system may again be reduced to two equations in two unknowns—the demand for and the supply of labor. The demand for labor is now expressed as

$$(20.13) \quad W = \frac{10\left[\dfrac{236.363 \cdot 10^9}{Q - 10 \cdot 10^9}\right] + 236.363 \cdot 10^9}{N} \cdot \frac{Q'}{Q} .$$

The new labor supply equation becomes

$$(20.14) \quad W = \frac{297.455 \cdot 10^9 - 14\left[\dfrac{236.363 \cdot 10^9}{Q - 10 \cdot 10^9}\right]10^9}{N} .$$

This reduced form of the model can now be solved for the numerical value of the wage rate and the level of employment, and then of the level of output, price, level of national income, and the rate of interest. Given the functions in our model of the economic system the new equilibrium values for the variables are found to be:

$$W = \$4{,}730.47$$
$$N = 46.71 \text{ million}$$
$$P = \$5.464$$
$$Q = 53.2598 \text{ billion}$$
$$Y = PQ = \$290.99 \text{ billion}$$
$$i = r = 4.273\% .$$

In comparison with our basic numerical model of Section 19.9, national income, wages, prices, output, and the rate of interest have all increased. Although the new level of national income is also higher than it was in Section 20.3, part of this increased income was brought about by the rise in the price level. Implicit in the analysis in the earlier sections of this chapter was a price level equal to $5.00. Notice also that as prices and wages rise under the impact of increased government spending, the rate of interest is pushed up, which will reduce the amount of real investment, although monetary investment will appear greater due to the price rise. We may conclude that part of the expansionary effect on output and employment of government spending is absorbed in pushing up prices.

Next let us add government tax receipts to our model and observe the impact on the system. Specifically, we are adding the assumptions that government spending and tax receipts equal $20 billion, the same assumption that we made earlier in this chapter when we were dealing with the *IS-LM* model of the economy. Presumably political action has determined the size of the governmental operations. The addition of tax receipts shifts the equilibrium condition for the goods and service markets to:

$$(20.15) \quad iP = .092P + .024 - 1.2PQ \cdot 10^{-12} .$$

The *IGST* function may be combined with the unchanged *LM* function and then solved for the level of national income and the rate of interest:

$$(20.16) \quad PQ = 10P \cdot 10^9 + 210.909 \cdot 10^9$$

$$(20.17) \quad i = .08 - \frac{.22909}{P} .$$

Using these new equations for national income and the rate of interest, we may proceed, by a process of substitution, to reduce the model to the demand for and the supply of labor:

$$(20.18) \quad W = \frac{10\left[\dfrac{210.909 \cdot 10^9}{Q - 10 \cdot 10^9}\right]10^9 + 210.909 \cdot 10^9}{N} \cdot \frac{Q'}{Q}$$

$$(20.19) \quad W = \frac{279.636 \cdot 10^9 - 14\left[\dfrac{210.909 \cdot 10^9}{Q - 10 \cdot 10^9}\right]10^9}{N} .$$

After solving these two equations for the new equilibrium wage rate and level of employment, we may proceed to find the new values for all the other variables in the system. They are:

$$W = \$4,692.62$$
$$N = 44.28 \text{ million}$$
$$P = \$5.132$$
$$Q = 51.097 \text{ billion}$$
$$Y = PQ = \$262.228 \text{ billion}$$
$$i = r = 3.536\%.$$

The addition of tax collections has had the result of reducing the values of all the variables, when compared to the values that resulted when government spending was added to the basic model. In comparison with the results when government spending and tax receipts were added to the *IS-LM* model (assuming wages and prices unchanged) the new equilibrium values for national income and the rate of interest are higher, but output and employment are lower because part of the rise in income is absorbed in a price rise. When prices and wages are allowed to vary, only a part of the expansionary effect of government spending is felt in enhanced output and employment, and a part of the expanded national income reflects only the upward push on prices. In a parallel fashion, the downward pressure of government taxation is reflected in lower prices and wages.

In this chapter we have explicitly introduced government spending and tax collecting into our models. As a result, new parameters were introduced and the equilibrium values of the variables in the economic system were changed. We shall find this analysis of the influence of the government on the economic system useful in the following chapter when we consider attempts to mitigate economic fluctuations of the economy.

QUESTIONS AND EXERCISES

1. "Buying and selling is at the very core of an enterprise system, and this business activity could not exist without some form of government intervention." Discuss.

2. "Government expenditure is similar to net investment; taxes are similar to savings." In what sense is this statement valid? In what sense is it false?

3. "Other things equal, the addition of government spending will tend to increase the level of aggregate income, and the addition of tax collections will tend to reduce the level of aggregate income." Explain.

4. Substitute a proportional income tax for the constant tax receipts assumed in Chapter 20, that is, $T = tY$. Assume t, the rate of tax, equals 15 per cent.

a) Write the new consumption and savings function for the model, assuming all other functions remain the same as in Section 20.5.

b) Find the new equilibrium level of income.

c) Does the government have a balanced budget in the new situation?

d) What has happened to savings and investment?

e) Assume the rate of tax is increased to 20 per cent. What happens to the equilibrium values of the variables in the money and product markets? Did they change by the same percentage as the rate?

5. Suppose the government collects $30 billion a year in taxes, spends $20 billion on goods and services, and transfers the other $10 billion a year to individuals in the community via interest on bonds, old age pensions, unemployment compensation, and other transfer payments. If all the other functions are the same as in Section 20.5, what is the equilibrium income? How does this compare with the equilibrium income found in Section 20.5? Suppose now transfer payments drop to zero, tax collections remain at $30 billion, and government expenditures on goods and services increase to $30 billion a year. What happens to the equilibrium level of income?

6. If the federal government increased its purchasing of goods and services but at the same time state and local governments reduced their buying by a greater amount, what would be the effect on the economic variables in the money and products markets?

7. After adding the government to our model of the economic system, actual savings need not always be equal to actual investment. Explain.

Chapter 21

BUSINESS CYCLES AND
COUNTERCYCLICAL POLICY

Our study of the determinates of the national income
and, therefore, the determinates of the level of employment, has developed a set of analytical tools that helps us to understand the causes
of fluctuations in economic activity, and to formulate policies aimed at
counteracting these cyclical fluctuations. History shows that our economic system has been subject to fluctuations in national income, employment, production, prices, and profits from the very beginning of our
country. There have been periods of full employment when the price
level was comparatively stable (e.g., 1922–1929) and periods of full
employment coupled with rather large inflations (e.g., most of the post–
World War II period). There have also been periods such as the 1930's
when there was widespread unemployment, and the level of production
and income was far below the potential of American technology. Millions of man-hours and machine-hours were wasted in involuntary idleness.

Numerous theories, in the history of economics, have been advanced to explain the causes of business cycles. In this chapter we shall
not consider all the various hypotheses that have been proposed. You
may do this some day if you study an advanced economics course dealing solely with business cycles. We propose here to apply the analytical
framework developed in Chapters 16 through 20 to the study of business fluctuations in terms of what might be called loosely a "typical" or
"representative" cycle in business activity. Then we shall turn to the
area of policy and investigate alternative policies available to the government in an attempt to mitigate the effects of economic fluctuations.

21.1. Development of a Boom: Demand Effects

In Chapter 18 we observe that changes in investment, other things
equal, bring about multiplied changes in the level of aggregate income,
and thus influence the level of employment of labor and machines.

Many economists believe that virtually every boom has its roots in a rising tide of new investment expenditures. The seeds of these expenditures are frequently sown in the previous depression when growth factors such as increases in population and technological improvements provided a widening need for additions to the stock of capital. Thus a boom in business activity may be triggered and stimulated by a backlog of investment demand built up during a previous depression. In the particular boom after World War II, wartime controls over private investment had also created huge pressures for investment goods when controls were lifted.

As the need for additions to the stock of capital are reflected in the purchase of capital goods, a few realized profits are made, and as other firms begin to purchase needed parts and equipment, expectations of further profits are generated. Investment is further stimulated. Employment and production pick up and a boom is underway, which may or may not surpass the previous boom period. The dominant characteristic of a boom is rising business expectations of future profits with a resulting shift to the right of the investment demand schedule. At any given level of the rate of interest, there is a heightened demand for investment goods as businesses attempt to take advantage of the expected rise in profits and prices by building up their stock of equipment, construction goods, and inventories. Such a shift in the investment demand function is shown in Figure 21–1. For example, at the rate of interest i^* the desired rate of investment spending increases from I_0 to I_1.

Since investment is a major component of national income, this increased investment spending causes a direct increase in the national income. But at higher levels of income, people spend more on consumers' goods; thus the increased investment spending causes a multiplied rise in income, via the multiplier process. These increases in national income and business sales tend to provide justification and vindication for the rising state of business expectations.

Furthermore the increases in aggregate income may induce additional investment, as we mentioned in Chapter 18, which in turn will further increase the level of income. In business-cycle literature the reaction of changes in aggregate demand upon investment is called the *acceleration principle.* A numerical example reveals the essential properties of the concept. Suppose that a machine produces ten units of some commodity per week and that current demand is for 1,000 units per week. Thus a total of 100 machines is required to supply the quantity demanded. Suppose that the machines last 20 years, then five machines a year are needed as replacements. Now suppose that next year demand increases to 1,200 per week, an increase of 20 per cent. At this point the demand for machines will increase to 25—20 machines to meet the increased demand and five for replacement. Demand in the machine industry has jumped 400 per cent as a result of a 20 per cent increase in final demand for the good. Thus the increase in demand has resulted in an accelerated demand for the machine. A little altering of our assumptions would show that it is the durability of investment goods

FIGURE 21-1

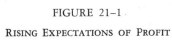

RISING EXPECTATIONS OF PROFIT

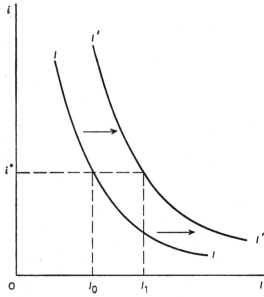

which is responsible for the acceleration effects of changes in demand, because durability is inversely related to replacement requirements. The significance of the acceleration principle is a much-debated issue in business-cycle theory and empirical proof or disproof of the principle is rather lacking. However the principle does give a revealing insight into why amplitudes of various industries can vary greatly. In our framework, the acceleration principle helps explain shifts in the investment function as income increases.

Increases in consumption spending during a boom are usually thought of as passive rather than active in nature. That is, the increase in consumption is presumed to be caused by the increase in disposable income as national income rises, and represents a passive adjustment in consumption along a given propensity-to-consume function. However, there may be some upward shift in the propensity-to-consume schedule itself. During World War II, many goods were unobtainable for civilians or in very short supply. During the war, high incomes and a scarcity of goods combined to provide a high level of savings in the community.

A backlog of demand as well as purchasing power in the form of savings and liquid U.S. government bond assets, set the stage for a

FIGURE 21–2

AN UPWARD SHIFT OF THE CONSUMPTION FUNCTION

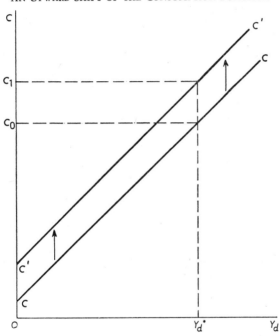

marked increase in the propensity to consume itself, i.e., an increase in the proportion of income spent on consumption over that prevailing during the war. It was this experience that led economists to revise their widely held view that the propensity-to-consume schedule was fairly stable over the course of the business cycle in addition to income varying. Such a cyclical shift of the consumption function would reinforce the shifts of the investment demand function. We see in Figure 21–2 that an upward shift of the consumption function would increase the amount spent on consumption goods from any given level of disposable income. Such a shift would create a disequilibrium in the goods and service markets, and we know from Chapter 18 that equilibrium would only be attained when income had increased sufficiently to provide the necessary level of savings to match the desired level of investment spending.

A combination of buoyant business expectations causing an upward shift in the investment demand function and an upward shift of the consumption function brings about a shift to the right of the *IS* function. Such a shift, seen in Figure 21–3, means that whatever might be the level of the interest rate on borrowed money, the level of income, supported by the volume of investment spending which is profitable

FIGURE 21–3

A SHIFT OF THE *IS* FUNCTION

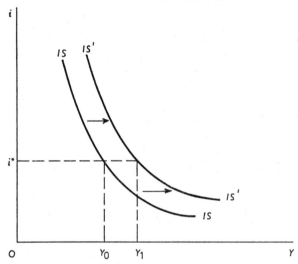

at that interest, is increased. For example, at the interest rate i^*, in Figure 21–3, the associated level of income increases from Y_0 to Y_1. The *IS* relationship, it will be remembered, is a derived rather than a fundamental relationship and takes into account the multiplier effect on income of increases in investment or shifts of the consumption function.

21.2. *Monetary Effects during a Boom*

The above demand effects or "real" effects are not the only forces making for a rise in the national income during a boom. As prosperity develops and prices rise from their previous depression lows, people may be less inclined to hold idle cash balances. If prices rise and are expected to continue rising, there will be less incentive to hold idle cash assets, the real value of which is falling and is expected to fall further. Thus, there will tend to be a shift from cash holdings and rela-

tively liquid assets such as government bonds and high-grade corporation bonds to common stock (ownership shares) and direct investment
in capital equipment and real estate. In terms of our analytical equipment, this behavior—sometimes called dishoarding of cash—lowers or
shifts to the left the liquidity demand schedule. As we see in Figure
21–4 such a reduction of the liquidity-preference demand for money
means that at any given rate of interest a smaller quantity of money
will be demanded to be held as idle balances. This release of hoarded
cash will help finance the boom by increasing the velocity of money.

As money is released from M_2 balances, it can be utilized to satisfy
transactions needs at a higher level of income. The rise in the national

FIGURE 21–4

A REDUCTION OF IDLE MONEY

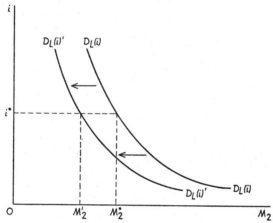

income brought on by the boom will increase the transactions requirements of the community for money, since the transactions demand for
money relates the quantity of money required for transactions purposes
to the level of income. As income rises, the average cash balances which
people desire to hold to bridge the gap between receipts and payments
will go up. Thus, some of the money released from idle balances because of the decline in the liquidity demand for money will be absorbed
by the community to meet the rising transactions requirements for
money. A reduction of the liquidity-preference demand for money,
which may be expected during the development of a boom, acts to shift
the *LM* function to the right, which will tend to increase the level of income.

During much of a boom, and in particular during the early stages,
the supply side of the money market may offer little if any significant

resistance to the development of the boom. There are likely to be large excess reserves in the banking system due to the low volume of commercial activity characteristic of the previous depression. Banks appear to raise their loan standards during periods of depression, which, of course, restricts their loan activities and thus tends to restrict the supply of money. Furthermore, the monetary authorities, desiring to contribute as much monetary stimulus as possible to the expansion, are likely to

FIGURE 21–5

AN INCREASE IN THE SUPPLY OF MONEY

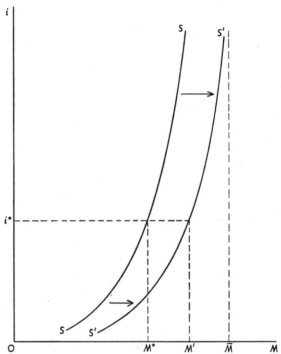

pursue "easy-money" policies. The result will be that the supply of money in the banking system will be relatively elastic, i.e., the interest rate will not rise appreciably even though there is a substantial increase in the volume of loans, and the supply schedule of money may shift to the right as the attitudes of the bankers change in the face of rising incomes and profit expectations. Such an increase in the supply of money means, as we can see in Figure 21–5, that at any particular rate of interest, a greater quantity of money will be supplied after the shift of the function. For example, the quantity of money supplied increases from M^* to M' at the rate of interest of i^* in Figure 21–5.

The net effect of a falling liquidity-preference demand for money, and an elastic, if not an increasing, supply function of bank-loan created demand deposit money, will cause an increase of the *LM* function, that is, the *LM* function will shift to the right. This function, it will be recalled, is a derived function relating the level of income to the interest rate, on the basis of equilibrium in the money market. This means

FIGURE 21–6

EFFECT OF AN INCREASED *LM* FUNCTION

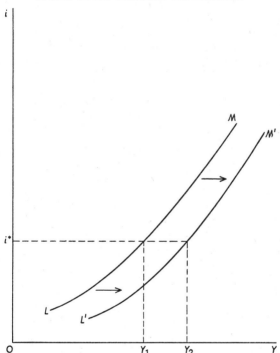

simply, that for any given rate of interest, the money released from hoarded balances and newly created by loan activities of the banking system can satisfy the transactions requirements for money at a higher level of income. For example, if the *LM* curve in Figure 21–6 is shifted from *LM* to *L'M'*, the level of income associated with the rate of interest of i^* will increase from Y_1 to Y_2.

21.3. Demand and Monetary Effects Combined

From the above discussion, it is seen that both the demand and monetary developments in the early stages of a boom are conducive to the growth of the boom. Both the *IS* and *LM* functions tend to shift to the right as a result of the various behavior responses of businesses, consumers, financial investors, and banks in the economy. Consequently, income will tend to rise, and rise sharply in some cases, with little if any deterring increase in interest rates. In some booms, interest rates may even fall during the early stages of the boom because of the increase in the quantity of money available; such a situation is shown in Figure 21–7. The new equilibrium, will, of course, depend upon the

FIGURE 21–7

A NEW EQUILIBRIUM

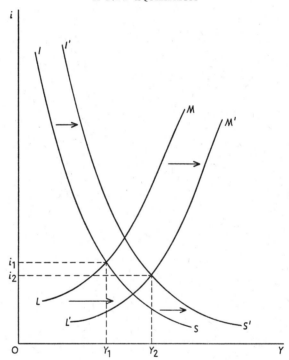

extent of the shifts of the various functions. These various behavior functions probably will continue to shift during the boom period, causing the level of income, and other variables of the economic system, to continue to change.

21.4. The Upper Turning Point—Demand Effects

As the boom continues and investment expenditures continue at a rapid pace, the stock of capital rises, since net investment, I, is simply the rate of change of the stock of capital, dK/dt. But, as we learned in Chapter 18, as the stock of capital rises, the advantages (profitablility)

of further additions to the stock of capital tend to decline. This may
not be evident to the business community at first, and the optimism
of the boom psychology may carry investment plans beyond the levels
indicated by "cooler calculations."

Eventually, however powerful the forces of expansion, uncertainty
is almost sure to develop concerning the further rise of sales and profits.
The output of newly created capacity begins to appear on the market,
adding to the supply of goods. The profits realized from the new investment may not be as large as earlier rosy expectations predicted. Further-

FIGURE 21–8

A FALL OF THE *IS* FUNCTION

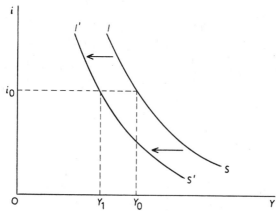

more, even if sales and profits are expected to continue at high levels,
the growth in the stock of capital caused by several years of high investment, may be sufficient to allow the expected sales, even though they
are still growing, to be produced with the existing stock of capital.

The result will be a lowering of profit expectations on the part of
businessmen which causes a shift to the left of the investment demand
schedules. But when investment expenditures decline, income payments
decline, other things equal, consumption expenditures decline, and via
the multiplier effect there is a more-than-proportional decline in the
level of national income. A reduction in the level of national income
implies falling sales, and the business community may adopt a wait-and-
see attitude and may further decrease its investment spending as uncertainty develops concerning the course of future sales and profits. There
is an increasing disinclination to undertake new commitments, which is
reflected at first in a leveling off of new orders and then a decline. The
cumulative momentum leads to depression.

The situation is further aggravated if consumers, as a result of growing uncertainty and declining income, attempt to save an increased proportion of their current incomes as protection against possible loss of their jobs. Such behavior is seen as a fall in the propensity to consume which in turn causes a further multiplied decline in income.

The combined effect of the behavior of businesses and households is to shift the *IS* schedule to the left, that is, to decrease the investment that will be carried out at any given rate of interest, to increase the rate of savings from any given level of income, and therefore to reduce the level of income that will prevail at any given rate of interest. For example, in Figure 21–8 when the *IS* curve shifts to *I'S'*, the level of income associated with the rate of interest of i_0 falls from Y_0 to Y_1.

21.5. Monetary Developments at the Upper Turning Point

Concurrent developments in the money market are likely to contribute to the upper turning point of the cycle and help bring about the subsequent downturn in economic activity. As the boom proceeds and the transactions demand for money grows with the rise in the level of income, the aggregate demand for money may grow faster than the supply of money. Consequently the tightened money supply is rationed, on the one hand by a rise in the rate of interest, and on the other by a rise in the bankers' standards of credit-worthiness. Bankers make loans on progressively less and less favorable terms. The rising commercial loan rates and more stringent collateral requirements have a direct feedback effect upon the demand for investment goods, since both higher interest rates and more stringent credit standards discourage some investment projects.

Accompanying the prosperity phase there will be, in all probability, a stock market boom. As income ascends to higher levels and prices rise, there will be an ever increasing shift on the part of individuals from holding cash to the purchase of income-yielding securities (a decrease in the liquidity-preference function as the real value of money continues to fall). This will increase stock market prices. Rising stock market prices tend to set up expectations of a further rise, and people increase their bids for stock in speculative anticipation of making gains from the increase in security prices. A speculative bubble may develop, as in the late 1920's, when security prices were carried far above the levels justified by their earnings.

Eventually, uncertainty develops as to the future trend of security prices, particularly in the face of disappointing earning records, and some security holders may unload securities to obtain the liquid asset, cash, and to avoid a capital loss, which they would sustain if overvalued securities fell in price. A general selling wave may sweep the market, in which there is an attempt on the part of large numbers of security holders to avoid capital losses by selling and shifting into cash. In terms of our analytical framework, this is represented by an abrupt upward shift in the liquidity-preference schedule. The result will be an increase in the rate of interest as the wave of selling forces down security prices, since a decrease in the price of an interest-bearing security is equivalent to an increase in the rate of interest on the security.

For example, if a bond pays an interest income of $10 per year and sells for $200, the rate of interest on the $200 purchase is 5 per cent. If

FIGURE 21-9

A LEFTWARD SHIFT OF THE *LM* CURVE

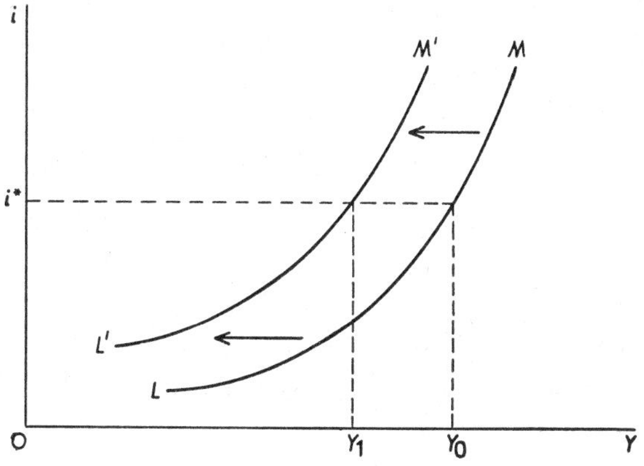

a selling wave lowers the price of the bond to $100, then the $10-per-year income yielded by the bond represents a 10 per cent rate of interest. In the new situation, corporations wishing to obtain long-term funds by selling new bond issues in the capital market will be unable to find buyers unless they offer the going rate of 10 per cent prevailing on outstanding bonds. Thus, an abrupt increase in the liquidity demand for cash caused by individuals desiring to protect themselves from plummeting security (and commodity) prices, will make it virtually impossible, or extremely costly, for borrowers to raise funds in the securities market. This, of course, is further detrimental to investment plans, the income level, and employment.

The net effect of the increase in preference for liquidity on the part of individuals and businesses in the community and the decrease in the supply of money by the banking system is to shift the *LM* schedule to the left. The level of income associated with each rate of interest is

lower. The *LM* schedule, remember, is the functional relationship between the rate of interest and the level of income, based on equality between the quantity of money demanded and the quantity supplied in the
money market. For example, in Figure 21–9, such a leftward shift of
the *LM* curve, reduces the level of income associated with an interest
rate of i^* from Y_0 to Y_1.

21.6.   Combined Demand and Monetary Effects at the Downturn

The behavior of businesses and households, resulting in falling investment demand and consumption functions, causes the *IS* curve to
shift to the left. At the same time, in the monetary area, the behavior of

FIGURE 21–10

COLLAPSE OF THE BOOM

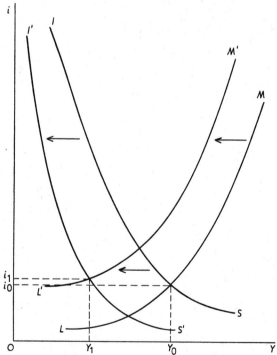

businesses and individuals is such that the liquidity demand for money
is pushed up. This increased demand, in conjunction with the behavior
of the banking system in restricting the supply of money, causes the *LM*
function also to shift to the left. The combined effect of the leftward
shifts of the *IS* and *LM* curves is such as to completely reverse the boom

and cause a cumulative fall in income and employment. Graphically, the collapse of the boom income can be shown as in Figure 21–10. As a result of the leftward shifts of the IS and LM curves to $I'S'$ and $L'M'$, income falls from Y_0 to Y_1.

The late stages of a boom are characterized by peak levels of output as the economy is driven closer to capacity output. Typically, there is some price inflation at this stage of the cycle, since increases in demand at or near full employment tend to react more strongly upon prices than on output. At the upper turning point, however, there is a tendency for output to decline more rapidly than prices. Many prices, particularly contractual obligations such as labor-management wage contracts, are very sticky in a downward direction and may cause a temporarily rigid cost structure, so that the painful process of adjusting to a decline in demand may initially take the form of output and employment reductions rather than price reductions.

21.7. The Lower Turning Point

The collapse of the boom described will not cause income and employment to fall without bound. There will be some lower limit to the amount by which investment expenditures can fall, since even in the depths of severe depression there will be a need to replace wornout equipment. Also there will be some new investment made necessary by new products and new processes. Also, the shape of the propensity to consume schedule is such as to slow down or stop the fall of income and employment. Consumption expenditures tend to fall less rapidly than income $(dC/dY_d < 1)$, and since consumption is the largest single component of income this has a retarding influence on the decline in income.

Once the decline in income is arrested, the economy may operate for several years at a low level of income and widespread unemployment of men and machines. But as depression continues, the seeds of revival are automatically sown. If net investment becomes negative so that capital goods wear out faster than they are replaced, then the stock of capital goods will fall. But even if net investment remains positive, the addition to the stock of capital will be small during the depression, while the continued growth in population, technological improvements, and new products give rise eventually to a need for larger additions to the stock of capital, even at depression levels of aggregate demand. Thus, the investment demand function moves upward again. Once investment expenditures on inventories, equipment, and construction goods start to increase, the multiplier goes to work and incomes tend to rise cumulatively. The result is a basis for revival and a movement of the economy toward a new boom and another cycle.

21.8. *Inventory Cycles*

The discussion thus far has been concerned with a typical major cycle in business activity. Superimposed upon the broad cyclical fluctuations in income and employment are minor business recessions such as occurred in 1949 and 1954 (see Table 21–1). For example, in 1949 the level of employment fell about 700,000 under its 1948 level, and net national product in the same period fell $1.9 billion. In seeking an explanation of these minor recessions, almost invariably we find the cause to be a decline in the inventory component of business investment. Thus in 1954 the slight dip in employment and net national product was accompanied by fairly steady business investment expenditures on plant and equipment (construction goods and producers' durables), but a $2.2 billion decline in inventory investment. In 1957 inventory investment declined by more than $4.5 billion, but investment in producer's durables and construction again held steady. However, in 1958, a substantial fall in the purchase of producers' durables, $7 billion, was accompanied by a much smaller fall in inventory investment, $2 billion. The 1960 recession again seemed to be primarily of an inventory nature with the other components of business investment continuing to rise. Note that the fall in investment in 1958 was offset by a substantial rise in government loan-financed expenditure on goods and services.

A study of the minor recessions, or inventory recessions as they are sometimes called, reveals that a long prosperity wave is nearly always accompanied by an overoptimistic buildup of inventories by businesses. Then, when businesses discover that they have expanded their inventories beyond the requirements dictated by their expanding sales, they cut back orders so as to reduce their inventories of goods on hand and bring inventories into line with sales. The result is a dip in total investment expenditures, which causes a dip in income and employment, but which does not develop into a general depression if the longer-run expectations of businesses are optimistic enough to maintain the level of plant and equipment expenditures. After inventories are corrected, orders are again given more freely and investment, income, and employment once again increase.

In summary, then, we can attribute major fluctuations in business activity primarily to fluctuations in investment in plant and equipment. Minor fluctuations, on the other hand, are most often attributed to fluctuations in business inventory expenditures. See Table 21–1 for changes in investment, income, and employment in selected years since 1929.

TABLE 21-1

STATISTICS OF INCOME, CONSUMPTION, INVESTMENT, GOVERNMENT TRANSACTIONS, AND EMPLOYMENT FOR SELECTED YEARS*†

Item	1929	1930	1933	1938	1941	1942	1944	1946	1947	1948	1949	1950	1953	1954	1955	1956	1957	1958	1960
1. Gross national product, GNP	104.4	91.1	55.9	85.2	125.8	159.1	211.4	209.2	232.2	257.3	257.3	285.1	363.2	361.2	391.7	414.7	433.9	444.2	501.2
2. Minus: Capital consumption allowances, CCA	8.6	8.5	7.2	7.8	9.1	10.2	12.0	11.7	14.1	16.5	18.4	20.5	26.5	28.9	31.6	34.3	37.1	38.1	43.1
3. Net national product, Y	95.8	82.6	48.8	77.4	116.8	149.0	199.4	197.6	218.1	240.8	238.9	264.6	336.7	332.2	360.1	380.4	396.8	406.1	461.4
4. Consumption, C	78.9	70.9	46.4	64.6	81.9	89.7	109.8	146.6	164.9	177.6	180.6	194.0	230.5	236.6	254.4	267.2	280.4	293.5	328.9
a) Durable goods	9.2	7.2	3.5	5.7	9.7	6.9	6.7	15.9	20.6	22.2	23.6	28.6	29.8	29.4	35.6	33.9	35.1	37.3	44.3
b) Nondurable goods	37.7	34.0	22.3	34.0	43.2	51.3	65.4	84.5	93.1	98.7	96.9	100.4	119.1	120.6	126.0	133.3	140.0	141.6	152.4
c) Services	32.1	29.8	20.7	25.0	29.0	31.5	37.7	46.2	51.3	56.7	60.1	65.0	81.7	86.6	92.8	99.9	105.4	114.3	132.2
5. Gross private investment, I'	17.0	11.0	1.6	7.8	19.2	9.7	5.0	31.7	38.6	43.1	33.1	49.0	48.3	48.0	60.2	67.3	66.9	57.8	75.4
a) Construction	8.7	6.2	1.4	4.0	6.6	3.7	2.7	10.3	14.0	17.9	17.5	22.7	25.8	27.8	32.7	33.3	33.2	35.5	40.7
b) Producers' durables	5.9	4.5	1.6	3.6	6.9	4.3	5.4	10.7	16.7	19.1	17.8	21.1	24.3	22.5	23.7	28.1	30.4	23.1	27.5
c) Inventory investment	1.7	-0.4	-1.6	-0.9	4.5	1.8	-1.0	6.1	-1.0	4.2	-2.7	7.4	0.3	-1.9	4.2	4.6	(‡)	-2.0	4.2
d) Net foreign investment	0.8	0.7	0.15	1.1	1.1	-0.2	-2.1	4.6	8.9	1.9	0.5	-2.2	-2.0	-0.4	-0.4	1.4	3.3	1.2	3.0
6. Net private investment, I	8.4	2.5	-5.6	0.0	10.1	-0.5	-7.0	20.0	24.5	26.6	14.7	28.5	21.8	19.1	28.6	33.0	29.8	19.7	32.3
7. Government loan-financed expenditure on goods and services	-1.3	0.2	1.2	0.9	3.0	30.2	49.8	-6.2	15.4	-10.1	1.1	-11.0	2.9	1.9	-7.9	-5.9	-1.6	11.4	0.0
a) Government expenditure on goods and services, G	8.5	9.2	8.0	12.8	24.8	59.7	96.5	30.9	28.6	36.6	43.6	42.0	84.4	76.6	77.0	80.2	86.6	93.5	100.0
b) Net government receipts, T	9.8	9.0	6.8	11.9	21.8	29.5	46.7	37.1	44.0	46.7	42.5	53.0	81.5	74.7	84.9	86.1	88.2	82.1	100.0
8. Labor force	49.4	50.1	51.8	55.0	57.5	60.4	66.0	61.0	61.8	62.9	63.7	64.7	67.4	67.8	68.9	70.4	70.8	71.3	72.8
a) Employment	47.6	45.5	38.8	44.2	50.4	53.8	54.0	55.3	58.0	59.4	58.7	60.0	62.2	61.2	63.2	65.0	65.3	63.9	66.4
b) Unemployment	1.6	4.3	12.8	10.4	5.6	2.7	0.7	2.3	2.1	2.1	3.4	3.1	1.6	3.2	2.7	2.6	2.7	4.7	3.9
c) Armed forces	0.3	0.3	0.3	0.3	1.6	4.0	11.4	3.5	1.6	1.5	1.6	1.6	3.5	3.4	3.0	2.9	2.8	2.6	2.5

* Items 1 through 7 expressed in billions of dollars. Item 8 expressed in millions of man-years.
† Details may not add to totals due to rounding.
‡ Less than $50 million.
SOURCE: Items 1 through 7, 1929–1955, *Survey of Current Business*, July, 1957, 1956–1960, July, 1961, National Income Number. Item 8, *Economic Report of the President*, January, 1961.

21.9. Countercyclical Policy

From the very beginning, our economic system has experienced alternate periods of prosperity and depression. The waste involved in excessive booms and busts has presented a challenge to democratic governments and brought increasing demands that the government take more responsibility for achieving a high level of employment and a stable price level. In the United States, both major political parties affirmed the responsibility of the government to fight both mass unemployment and inflation in the Employment Act of 1946. Thus far, in this chapter, we have traced through what happens during a business cycle; now we ask what weapons are available to the government to be used in its efforts to offset booms and busts.

Two major areas of policy are available. The Federal Reserve System may use monetary policy to influence the money market in an effort to smooth out economic fluctuations. Such a policy has been regarded by many as an important tool, but it does have serious limitations, particularly in a depression. The second major weapon is governmental fiscal policy, which includes such government operations as increasing or decreasing federal taxes, changing the volume of federal expenditures, and corollary expansions or contractions in the federal debt (primarily that portion not in the possession of the commercial banks).

21.10. Monetary Policy

As we pointed out in Chapter 15, the Federal Reserve System has four main methods of controlling the creation of credit in the economic system: a) changing the reserve rates, b) open-market operations, c) varying the rediscount rate, and d) moral suasion. Through these instruments of control, the Federal Reserve can influence the willingness and the ability of the banking system to create new credit money to finance business expenditures. If the level of economic activity expands too rapidly, pushing the economy into inflation, monetary demand exceeds capacity supply, at current prices. This results in a rising price level, which could be checked by the Federal Reserve System following a "tight money" policy, i.e., restricting the amount of money available to the economy, or slowing down the rate of increase of new money by reducing the ability or the willingness of the banking system to go on creating money at the current rate.

Raising the reserve ratio would reduce the upper limit to the creation of money, as shown in Figure 18–10, page 294. In our framework, this would have the effect of shifting the LM curve to the left and of raising the rate of interest associated with any given level of income. The increase in the rate of interest and the restriction of the amount of money available would have the effect of holding down or slowing down the rate of investment and thus holding monetary demand in check, or actually reducing it if the supply of money is tightened sufficiently.

A more flexible weapon is found in open-market operations. Reserves of the banking system can be destroyed and pressure brought to bear on the banking system by a suitable policy of selling bonds on the open market. In order to maintain the required reserves, the banking system can either borrow from the Federal Reserve System or not renew loans. The effect is to restrict the supply of money, which can be viewed as a leftward shift of the supply of money (shown in Figure 18–8, page 293), bringing about a leftward shift of the *LM* curve which raises the rate of interest, given the *IS* curve. Again, the consequence of the Fed's anti-inflation policy is an increase in the rate of interest, and a slowing down or reduction of the rate of investment, thus slowing down the rate of increase of aggregate demand or even reducing total money demand for goods and services.

Raising the rediscount rate—the rate at which commercial banks can add to their reserves by borrowing from the Federal Reserve System —makes it more expensive for the commercial banks to borrow from the system and signals the banking community that the banking authorities believe that the expansion needs to be slowed down. This would cause the banking system to restrict its loan activity, and the interest rate on commercial loans would tend to rise. With rising costs or with less funds available, the businesses would be forced to slow down or contract their expenditures. This can be viewed as a leftward shift of the supply function of money, but with an unchanged upper limit, as shown in Figure 18–9, page 293.

The weapon of moral suasion consists of the various influences and pressures which the banking authorities can bring to bear on the banking system in an attempt to influence the willingness of the bankers to make loans, that is, to shift the money supply function without using the first three policy measures. In periods of inflation, the banking authorities can publicly and privately try to convince the bankers that fewer loans ought to be made or that the rate of increase of loans ought to be slowed down in order that inflationary forces may be checked. The bankers may be told that unless this is done, the authorities may be forced to used stronger weapons. Appeals may be made to the bankers to act in the public interest, to exercise restraint in the granting of loans.

A policy of moral suasion may be viewed as an attempt by the banking authorities to shift the supply function of money.

The art of central banking is the use of monetary policy to induce the postponement of some investment expenditures during periods of excessive booms and to induce extra or additional investment expenditures during depressions. Thus one could say the object is to "spread out" the booms. A "tight-money" policy can be very effective in checking an inflationary boom if the monetary authorities are willing to act resolutely, but if it is not done carefully, investment may be cut back too far, resulting in undesirable excessive unemployment. The monetary authorities desire to restrict monetary demand just enough to prevent an inflationary boom but not so much as to precipitate a depression. A serious weakness exists in the ability of an "easy-money" policy to stimulate expansion, once the forces of contraction are underway. An easy-money policy is the reversal of the above policies, i.e., using open-market operations to expand reserves, lowering the required reserve ratio, and lowering the rediscount rate. The investment demand schedule may have shifted so far to the left that no feasible rate of interest is low enough to stimulate new investment. Furthermore, the banks, through their lending policy, can nullify the easy-money policy by not expanding loans and thus not expanding the supply of money. The Federal Reserve System can make reserves plentiful but cannot force the banks to make loans; therefore, an easy-money monetary policy may not be successful in the effort to prevent a slide into a depression or to extract the economy from a depression.

21.11. *Fiscal Policy, for Inflation*

We learned in the preceding chapter that the government has a very direct economic influence on the economy via its expenditures for goods and services and its receipts through tax collections. The recurrence of unemployment and inflation has led to extensive discussion of government intervention to offset the business cycle and achieve economic stability by varying its expenditure, tax, and debt policies. This deliberate manipulation of government spending, taxing, and debt is called fiscal policy. In part, fiscal policy acts directly upon government spending, and in part upon consumption and investment spending in the private sector of the economy. During the various phases of the business cycle, the government can utilize fiscal policy to restrain or stimulate aggregate demand. Normally, of course, monetary and fiscal policies are used in conjunction with each other. We have already examined monetary policy, and now we shall turn to fiscal policy.

When aggregate demand (composed of consumption, investment, and government expenditures) is tending to expand too rapidly and cause inflation, fiscal policy may be called upon in the form of increased tax collections or decreased government spending. There are additional problems involved in that Congress must decide which taxes are to be increased or which government expenditures are to be cut. Increased

FIGURE 21–11

AN INCREASE IN TAXES

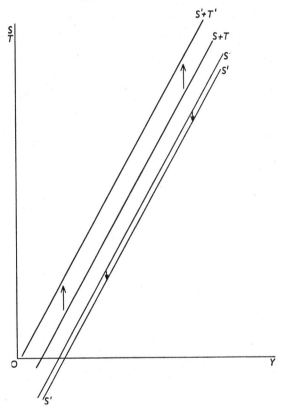

tax collections by the government, with no change in expenditures, reduces disposable income and thus consumption and saving at each level of national income. The reduction of the rate of consumption acts to reduce aggregate demand and thus to reduce the pressure toward inflation in the economic system. Because part of the increased tax collections are paid out of reduced savings, the initial reduction in consumption is less than the increase in tax collections. Diagrammatically, the increase in taxes is seen in Figure 21–11 as an upward shift of the

$S + T$ curve and a downward shift of the savings function. With a given level of government spending and a given investment demand function, the upward shift of the $S + T$ curve shifts the IS curve to the left, and, other things equal, reduces the equilibrium level of money income. For example, in Figure 21–12, the equilibrium level of money income falls from Y_0 to Y_1.

FIGURE 21–12

INCREASED TAXES REDUCE INCOME

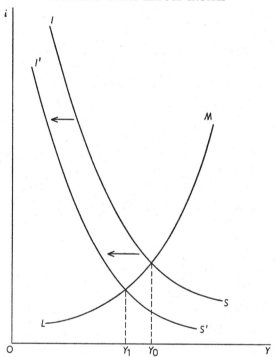

The government may also reduce, or hold in check, aggregate money demand by a reduction of government expenditures, leaving tax collections unchanged. Since the total demand for goods consists of consumer, investor, and government purchases of goods and services, the total demand can be held in check by reducing one component of total demand sufficiently to offset the growth in the other two. Such a policy of reduced government spending makes more goods and services available to satisfy consumption and investment demands. In our basic model containing the government, the condition for equilibrium in the goods and service markets is the requirement that desired investment plus government spending be equal to desired savings plus tax collections (see Section 20.5). Since we have assumed that government tax collections and the investment demand function are unchanged, when government spending is cut, the desired level of savings must also fall, if the system is to reach equilibrium. This, of course, will be achieved if the level of income falls. Graphically, this is seen as a fall of the $I + G$ curve, which, with a given savings function and tax collections, shifts the *IGST* curve to the left. Given an unchanged *LM* curve, the equilibrium level of money income will fall, reducing the monetary pressure on the limited supply of goods and therefore holding the price level in check, or slowing down its rate of increase, depending upon the size of the initial cut in government spending.

21.12. Fiscal Policy in Depression Periods

When the economy is operating at depression levels of income and employment, it is widely agreed that some governmental action is necessary to restore full employment. Monetary policy may be utilized to try to stimulate the expansionary forces in the economy, but monetary policy by itself may be insufficient; the weapons of fiscal policy may also be needed. Essentially, fiscal policies appropriate for the depression phase of a business cycle are the reverse of those used to keep a boom in check. Taxes may be reduced, government spending stepped up, or some combination may be used in order to increase the demand for goods and services and bring idle resources back into active use.

If the government reduces taxes and leaves its spending unchanged, the result will either be a budget deficit or a reduced budget surplus, probably a deficit. Such an action will increase the level of disposable income for any given level of national income (since $Y_d = Y - T$), and, given the aggregate savings function, increase the amount spent for consumption goods out of any given level of national income. An increase in consumption spending increases aggregate demand, given the investment demand function and unchanged government spending, which will give a positive push to the level of income and employment. Diagrammatically, in our basic model of the economy, this is seen as a shift to the right of the $S + T$ curve, and, consequently, the *IS* curve, which raises the equilibrium level of income with any given *LM* curve, i.e., with any given set of monetary conditions.

However, the manner of financing the governmental deficit may also affect the monetary conditions of the economy. If the government finances the deficit by printing bonds and selling them, the economic effects differ depending upon who purchases the bonds. If the bonds are sold in the open market and bought by the Federal Reserve System, additional reserves are created, which will raise the potential ceiling to credit creation. But, unless the willingness of bankers to make loans is increased, the extra reserves may remain unutilized, with no change in monetary conditions. Should the banking system be willing to create more money by making loans, the supply function of money will be increased, which may, perhaps, reduce the rate of interest and may stimulate additional investment. However, if the liquidity-preference demand for money is perfectly elastic in the range of the ruling rate of interest, all of the increased money will be absorbed into M_2 balances and the rate of interest will not fall.

If the bonds, printed by the government to finance the deficit, are sold to the commercial banks, demand deposits will rise by the amount of the deficit. Legal reserves of the banking system will remain unchanged; however, excess reserves will fall with the rise in demand deposits. The increased quantity of money may tend to reduce the rate of interest, or flow into M_2 balances with an unchanged rate of interest, or be used to repay bank-held debt and thus be destroyed. The exact result depends upon the behavior of the individuals and businesses in the economic system. The government might also finance the deficit by selling bonds to individuals, bonds which may not be purchased by banks. In this case there is no change in the total quantity of money or excess reserves. There may be an effect upon the rate of interest, since the introduction of the government bonds into the asset structure of the economy may bring about a shifting of asset holdings.

An increase in the aggregate demand for goods and services can also be brought about with an increase in government expenditures on currently produced goods and services, while leaving tax collections unchanged. It has often been suggested that the government should have a ready inventory of public works to be constructed when an increased rate of government spending is desired. In addition to increasing aggregate demand, public-works projects maintain the skills of the unemployed and, to some extent, they avoid the morale problems of direct relief. In our framework, the increase of government spending raises the $I + G$ curve, which, with a given savings function and tax collections, shifts the *IGST* curve to the right and raises the level of income, given the *LM* curve. Again, the method of financing the deficit may also influence the level of income via the monetary route.

The level of income can also be increased without a government deficit with an increase in both the rate of government spending and the rate of tax collections. Under certain conditions the equilibrium level of income will rise by the full amount of the increase in government spending.

Since $Y = C(Y - T) + I + G$, one can subtract taxes from both sides of the equation to find disposable incomes, as $Y_d = Y - T$: $Y - T = C(Y - T) + I + G - T$. Writing Y_d for $Y - T$, disposable income, and D for $G - T$, the government deficit, we have: $Y_d = C(Y_d) + I + D$. Obviously if G and T are increased by the same amount, leaving D unchanged, Y_d would be unchanged, with a given I, but aggregate income would increase dollar for dollar with the balanced increase of government spending and tax collections, since $Y = C(Y - T) + I + G$. We have here the so-called balanced-budget multiplier of unity.

However, a balanced-budget multiplier equal to unity is found only under the following special conditions: (1) the monetary system is perfectly elastic, that is, an increase in the level of income will not increase the equilibrium value of the rate of interest, and (2) the increase in government expenditures is used to purchase currently produced domestic goods and services.

21.13. The Multipliers

In Section 17.11 we learned that increases in investment can give rise to more than proportional increases in income. Many students will have already recognized that changes in governmental spending, tax receipts, and transfers can also give rise to more-than-proportional changes in aggregate income, with the change in income in the same direction as the initiating change. At this point we shall derive a more precise statement of the various multipliers involved and relate them to the various fiscal policies.

In order to find the various multipliers, let us begin with the accounting identity in Equation (16.4), $Y = C + I + G$. By combining Equation (16.4) with the linear consumption function in Equation (20.2), $C = a + bY - bT$, we obtain:

$$(21.1) \quad Y = a + bY - bT + I + G .$$

We recall from Chapter 20 that the variable, T, taxes, in our system is really government tax collections minus government transfer payments, that is, $T = Tx - Tr$. Therefore we can write Equation (21.1) as

$$(21.2) \quad Y = a + bY - bTx + bTr + I + G .$$

If we collect the Y terms, we then have:

$$(21.3) \quad Y = \frac{1}{1 - b} (a - bTx + bTr + I + G) .$$

If the government holds expenditures constant, and reduces taxes during a depression by an amount ΔTx in an effort to stimulate an expansion in income, the effect on income will be:

$$(21.4) \quad Y + \Delta Y = \frac{1}{1-b} [a - b(Tx - \Delta Tx) + bTr + I + G]$$

$$Y + \Delta Y = \frac{1}{1-b} (a - bTx + b\Delta Tx + bTr + I + G).$$

If we now subtract Equation (21.3) from Equation (21.4), we have:

$$(21.5) \quad \Delta Y = \frac{1}{1-b} (b\Delta Tx) \quad \text{or} \quad \Delta Y = \frac{b}{1-b} \Delta Tx.$$

and the taxation multiplier is:

$$(21.6) \quad K_{Tx} = \frac{b}{1-b}.$$

If the government increases its spending, while holding tax collections constant, we can derive the government expenditure multiplier as follows: Government spending is increased from G to $G + \Delta G$; income then becomes $Y + \Delta Y$:

$$(21.7) \quad Y + \Delta Y = \frac{1}{1-b} (a - bTx + bTr + I + G + \Delta G).$$

Now we subtract Equation (21.3) from Equation (21.7), and the result is:

$$(21.8) \quad \Delta Y = \frac{1}{1-b} \Delta G.$$

Therefore the government expenditure multiplier is

$$(21.9) \quad K_G = \frac{1}{1-b}.$$

Or, if the government chooses to expand the level of income by increasing government transfer payments to the private sector, the transfer multiplier is derived in the following manner: Where transfers are increased from Tr to $Tr + \Delta Tr$, income increases from Y to $Y + \Delta Y$.

$$(21.10) \quad Y + \Delta Y = \frac{1}{1-b} [a - bTx + b(Tr + \Delta Tr) + I + G].$$

$$= \frac{1}{1-b} (a - bTx + bTr + b\Delta Tr + I + G).$$

If we subtract (21.3) from Equation (21.10), we have:

$$(21.11) \quad \Delta Y = \frac{1}{1-b} (b\Delta Tr),$$

and the government transfer multiplier is given by:

$$(21.12) \quad K_{Tr} = \frac{b}{1-b} .$$

Or, the government may wish to increase the level of income without increasing the national debt, by increasing both the level of government expenditures and the level of tax collections the same amount, that is $\Delta G = \Delta Tx$. When G increases from G to $G + \Delta G$ and Tx from Tx to $Tx + \Delta Tx$, income becomes:

$$(21.13) \quad Y + \Delta Y = \frac{1}{1-b}[a - b(Tx + \Delta Tx) + bTr + I + G + \Delta G]$$

$$= \frac{1}{1-b}(a - bTx - b\Delta Tx + bTr + I + G + \Delta G) .$$

Subtracting (21.3) from Equation (21.13), we obtain:

$$(21.14) \quad \Delta Y = \frac{1}{1-b}(-b\Delta Tx) + \frac{1}{1-b}\Delta G .$$

Since $\Delta Tx = \Delta G$, we can substitute ΔG for ΔTx:

$$(21.15) \quad \Delta Y = \Delta G\left(\frac{1}{1-b}\right) - \Delta G\left(\frac{b}{1-b}\right) .$$

Simplifying (21.15), we obtain:

$$(21.16) \quad \Delta Y = \Delta G\left(\frac{1}{1-b} - \frac{b}{1-b}\right)$$

$$= \Delta G\left(\frac{1-b}{1-b}\right)$$

$$= \Delta G .$$

Therefore, the balanced budget multiplier is equal to 1.

Perhaps an example would give us a better insight as to the impact of the various fiscal measures. Let us assume that our model economy is in the depression phase of a business cycle and it is estimated that national income is $30 billion below full-employment income. Further, let us assume that the aggregate marginal propensity to consume, b, is .8. Under these conditions the tax multiplier has a numerical value of 4 $\left(21.6, K_{Tx} = \frac{b}{1-b}\right)$; therefore tax receipts would have to be cut by $7.5 billion to stimulate the economy to full employment output.

If the government chose the path of increasing its expenditures to stimulate recovery, it would have to increase its spending by $6 billion, since the government expenditure multiplier is equal to 5 (21.9,

$K_G = \dfrac{1}{1-b}$). Should the government decide to leave tax collections and spending on goods and services unchanged, but to increase transfer payments in an effort to get out of the depression, an increase of transfer payments of $7.5 billion would be necessary. The value of the government transfer multiplier in our example is 4, the same as the tax multiplier, (21.12, $K_{Tr} = \dfrac{b}{1-b}$). If the government did not want to increase the national debt, it could increase both government spending and tax collections by $30 billion to achieve a full employment level of income, with a balanced-budget multiplier of unity (21.16).

It should be noted that the most conservative of the proposals, the balanced-budget proposal, results in the largest increase in the government's share of the economy. Also, other things equal, it will require a larger deficit for the tax reduction or transfer increase policy to generate the same increase in the aggregate national income as the government spending policy. The values of the multipliers are based on the implicit assumption that the rate of interest does not rise as the level of income increases. If the rate of interest does increase, the rate of investment will be reduced and a lower level of income will be generated for given values of tax reduction, transfer payments, or government spending. The realized multipliers will be less than the above values.

21.14. Built-In Flexibility

In our economy today there are certain transfer payments and taxes that vary with the level of income, such as unemployment compensation payments, social security tax payments, and income and payroll taxes. Normally, when the level of income falls, income tax payments decrease and unemployment compensation payments increase. Therefore the induced changes in income are smaller. Built-in flexibility of this nature helps to keep recessions from developing into full-blown depressions and, during the other phase of the cycle, slows down inflationary expansion. However, the built-in flexibility reduces the values of the multipliers and thus lowers the equilibrium value of income associated with any given level of investment and increases the amount of government tax reduction, transfer payments, or government expenditures needed to generate a given increase in aggregate income.

21.15. Direct Controls

Another weapon which the government has used as an emergency measure to supplement monetary and fiscal policy, mainly during war-generated inflation, is the direct control of certain prices and, usually, wages. Usually the government attempts to hold the price level at some particular level—in World War II it was the level prevailing at the beginning of the war. A policy of this kind forces persons to save more than they really desire to save by preventing their bidding up prices for the goods and services in scarce supply. Normally, in our economy prices allocate goods and services to the various uses; but when prices are set by regulation, they no longer can act to ration the scarce goods and balance supply and demand. In such a situation scarce investment goods are usually allocated by direct controls and allocations. If the direct controls are strongly enforced and supported by the individuals in the economy, they can be successful in holding down inflation, for the moment.

The monetary authorities have also been authorized to use selective credit controls. It was pointed out in Chapter 15, that under Regulations T and U the Board of Governors of the Federal Reserve System can establish margin requirements for the purchase of securities. By varying marginal requirements, the Board can control the creation of credit for stock market speculation, which may influence business expectations and investment plans. In times past, Regulation W has been used to control the extension of installment credit for the purchase of automobiles and appliances, which has the effect of reducing aggregate demand for goods and services when minimum down payments are increased and the maximum period of repayment is reduced. Regulation X operated in a similar manner during the Korean War when it was used to limit the extension of bank credit for the financing of the purchase of new residences by establishing minimum down payments and maximum repayment periods. Selective credit controls act to restrict demand in certain particular areas, where the resources may be particularly scarce.

Continued application of direct controls to keep prices below the levels at which demand is equal to supply means that either the goods and services are allocated by forcing people to stand in line and wait for an opportunity to buy the scarce good, or by the development of black markets, or by the institution of official or unofficial systems of rationing. The controls play havoc with the basic guiding mechanism of the economy, the price system which we studied in earlier chapters. If direct controls are continued indefinitely, the result is very likely to be a serious distortion of resource allocation, loss of incentives on the part of the owners of scarce resources, including labor, and perhaps the disappearance of a free enterprise economy.

In this chapter we observed that our economy has been subject to alternating periods of prosperity and depression. We then followed through a "typical" cycle, within the framework of our analysis. In an attempt to eliminate or reduce the undesirable effects of booms and busts, the government has used monetary and fiscal policies and direct controls. While the proper use of monetary and fiscal policies may iron out the worst swings of economic fluctuations, the problem of continued growth of our economy remains, which we will examine briefly in another chapter.

QUESTIONS AND EXERCISES

1. Compare and contrast the monetary and fiscal policies appropriate for a period of substantial unemployment with the monetary and fiscal policies appropriate for a period of monetary inflation.

2. Draw up a program to counteract a cost-push inflation. Defend your program.

3. Economic observers have argued that a substantial amount of "built-in flexibility" exists in most modern economies today. Explain.

4. Since World War II, it has often been alleged that a policy of full employment is not compatible with a policy of ensuring stable prices. Under what conditions is the allegation valid?

5. Can monetary and fiscal policy completely offset business fluctuation?

6. Under what conditions might it be appropriate to use direct government controls to influence aggregate income and employment?

7. "We can attribute major fluctuations in business activity primarily to fluctuations in investment in plant and equipment. Minor fluctuations are most often attributed to fluctuations in business inventory expenditures." Use the data in Table 21–1 to see if the above statement applies to the United States since 1929.

8. It has often been argued that each expansion contains the seeds of its own destruction. Discuss.

9. Analyze the impact on the United States' economy of a substantial fall in defense expenditures by the federal government. Outline an appropriate policy.

10. Discuss the so-called balanced-budget multiplier.

Chapter 22

INTERNATIONAL TRADE
AND EXCHANGE

The analytic procedures which have been developed thus far have been concerned with price determination and with income levels and associated problems for a closed economy. That is, there has been no supposition that there is any interchange between the economy under investigation and a greater world outside of it. In this chapter we shall consider the consequences upon our analytic framework of international trade and exchange among countries, including an investigation of the bases for international trade and a brief appraisal of some of the special problems that accompany such trade and exchange.

22.1. The Fundamental Diversity among Economies of Different Nations

The differences between exchange among countries and exchange within a country come from the existence of different political and social systems. This creates three major distinguishing features. In the first place, along with differences in population and its composition and in natural and capital resources there are differences in tastes, in abilities, and in social institutions among countries. These variations affect both supply and demand within the countries for commodities and productive services and bring about different prices for these commodities and services between countries. Since the demand function has been expressed as a resultant of the interaction of the variety of prices of different goods and of the tastes and incomes of the parties entering the market, and since supply has also been expressed as a resultant of the interaction of the prices of goods and of the different inputs available, the prices of products established by the interaction of market forces will be different in different countries. Passenger cars have a different price, are purchased in a different social milieu, and are produced under different technical conditions in Europe and in the United States. Bananas have different availability and serve a different role in diet in Guatemala and in the United Kingdom.

The operation of the principle of equal advantage would lead to the price for each good and each resource becoming everywhere the same, if it were not for immobility. The second distinguishing feature is the far greater immobility of goods and resources in international trade than in domestic trade. This is particularly true for resources. Labor particularly, and capital to an important extent, do not move easily in international trade. This relative immobility of resources stems from custom, from ignorance, from fear, from artificial restrictions imposed on movement, and from transportation costs for movement among nations. There is the problem of sovereignty of nations and the different legal systems under which contracts are enforced. There is nationalism and patriotism. There is the fear of discrimination, of expropriation, and of losses arising from war. As a consequence it can be said that the trade in commodities is to an important extent a substitute for the international movement of resources.

The third distinguishing feature of international trade lies in the fact that each nation employs its own monetary system. Buyers wish to pay in the currencies of their own countries, but sellers desire payment in the currency of their countries, so that a problem of transfer of purchasing power is created. The economic consequences of these differences will be illustrated in the analysis which follows.

22.2. The Basis for Trade

An illustration of the basis for international trade and the gain in productivity which accompanies international exchange will be developed through the employment of a two-commodity–two-nation model. Many complications ensue when the analysis involves more than two commodities, more than two countries, or when more than only commodity trade is considered as a basis for international exchange. However, these complications do not destroy the validity of the underlying rationale, which is illustrated in the model developed below. These additions to the model do, however, add some interesting problems which are not the subject of this introductory economic analysis.

Let it be assumed that production employing one unit of resources could result, for the United States, in the completion of forty automobiles or of twenty loads of textiles. In the other nation, Eurasia, one unit of resources could result in the production of four automobiles or ten loads of textiles. This is illustrated by the following two-way table, or "matrix," as it is sometimes called.

		Alternative Production from One Unit of Resources	
		Autos	Textiles
(22.1)	United States	40 or	20
	Eurasia	4 or	10

The United States can produce both goods more effectively than can Eurasia, but the United States has what we call a *comparative advantage* in the production of automobiles. We mean that although the United States can produce both automobiles and textiles with fewer resources than Eurasia must employ, the greatest advantage, or comparative advantage, lies with automobile production for the United States, and the least disadvantage or comparative advantage for Eurasia is in the production of textiles. In order to demonstrate how productivity is increased when each party to a possible exchange specializes in the production of the commodity in which it possesses a comparative advantage, let us assume that the United States uses two input units of resources and Eurasia uses four input units of resources. The results would be:

		Without Trade	
		Autos	Textiles
(22.2)	United States (2 units resource)	40 and	20
	Eurasia (4 units resource)	8 and	20
	World Total	48	40

		With Trade and Specialization	
		Autos	Textiles
(22.3)	United States (2 units resource)	80	..
	Eurasia (4 units resource)		40
	World Total	80	40

Apparently, if each nation specializes in the production of that in which it possesses a comparative advantage, total world production would be increased and that gain could be divided among the countries so that all gained compared to what they would have had without trade. This specialization would take place, regardless of the superiority in the production of everything by the United States (in our model) and in spite of the existence of different monetary systems, as illustrated by the additional matrices:

Let one unit of resources be worth $100,000 in the United States and krowns (Kr.) 100,000 in Eurasia.

		Cost of Production	
		Autos	Textiles
(22.4)	United States	$ 2,500	$ 5,000
	Eurasia	Kr. 25,000	Kr. 10,000

If the *rate of exchange* was $1 = Kr.1, no trade could take place. People in Eurasia would want to purchase everything from the United States, but people in the United States would not want anything from Eurasia. However, the demand by people in Eurasia for dollars would drive the price of dollars up, in terms of krowns. If the rate of exchange exceeded Kr.2 = $1, the United States would find it less expensive to purchase its textiles in Eurasia than at home. If the rate of exchange did not reach Kr.10 = $1, Eurasia would want to purchase its automobiles in the United States. The resources released from textile production in the United States, because of foreign purchase of textiles, would be transferred to automobile production to satisfy foreign demand. Similarly, resources in Eurasia would be concentrated in textile production. The United States would pay for its textiles with automobiles. (Actually the United States would pay for its textiles with dollars which Eurasia, in turn, would use in purchasing automobiles or with krowns which the United States received from selling automobiles.) Production would be as demonstrated in Matrix (22.3) instead of the production, in the absence of international trade, of Matrix (22.2).

Suppose, for example, that the rate of exchange was $1 = Kr.5. Then, in terms of dollars, costs would be:

Cost of Production

		Autos	Textiles
(22.5)	United States	$2,500	$5,000
	Eurasia	$5,000	$2,000

and in terms of krowns, costs would

		Autos	Textiles
(22.6)	United States	Kr.12,500	Kr.25,000
	Eurasia	Kr.25,000	Kr.10,000

If the United States were to purchase twenty units of textiles from Eurasia, cost of imports to the United States would be $40,000 or Kr.200,000. If Eurasia were to purchase sixteen automobiles from the United States, cost of exports of the United States would be $40,000 or Kr.200,000. Exports of U.S. automobiles would pay for imports of Eurasian textiles.

The general determinants of comparative advantage can be expresed in the following relationship. It is assumed that price reflects production cost in each case. Let P_{1a} be the price of Commodity A in Country 1; P_{1b}, P_{2a}, and P_{2b} are, respectively, prices of Commodity B in Country 1, Commodity A in Country 2, and Commodity B in Country 2, all in terms of local currencies. Then if

$$(22.7) \quad \frac{P_{1a}}{P_{1b}} < \frac{P_{2a}}{P_{2b}},$$

Country 1 would specialize in the production and exchange of Commodity A, and Country 2 would specialize in the production and exchange of Commodity B. The student may verify Matrix (22.7) with the numerical values of Matrix (22.4).

If there are transportation costs, taxes, or other impediments to trade, such costs would raise the price of B from Country 2 entering Country 1 shown as T_b, per unit, and of A from Country 1 entering Country 2 shown as T_a, per unit. It follows that if relative production costs of (22.7) holds, and exchange possibilities become

$$(22.8) \quad \frac{P_{1a} + T_a}{P_{1b}} \geq \frac{P_{2a}}{P_{2b} + T_b},$$

then no trade would take place. The added costs of carrying on trade would wipe out the differential arising from the alternative production possibilities of the two countries which had previously favored there being trade between the two commodities.

Furthermore, balance in international trade would exist when

$$(22.9) \quad (P_{2b} + T_b)Q_b = P_{1a}Q_a$$

and

$$(22.10) \quad (P_{1a} + T_a)Q_a = P_{2b}Q_b$$

where Q_a and Q_b are the quantities of Commodities A and B exchanged, respectively.

That is to say, the price in Country 1's money of Commodity B, including transportation costs to Country 1, times the quantity of Commodity B imported by Country 1 (the total value of imports by Country 1) would be equal to the price in Country 1 of Commodity A times the quantity which it exported (the total value of exports by 1). Similarly, Country 2 pays for its imports of Commodity A, including transportation costs, with its exports of Commodity B. In the long run, if there are no other items entering into international trade, and the money of each country can be spent only in that country, international trade consists of a two-way exchange where imports are paid for by exports.

Certain truisms seem to be evident from the working of the above model:

1. International trade is a two-way proposition. A nation pays for its imports with its exports.

2. A high-productivity nation and a low-productivity nation can trade with each other under conditions in which both parties gain from the exchange.

3. There is some rate of exchange and internal price levels relationship at which international trade is possible and is in balance. If a

nation's internal prices are too high, or, in other words, its currency is overvalued by that nation in comparison with other nations' currencies, deflation at home or devaluation of the currency abroad should have the effect of stimulating the country's exports. A freely fluctuating exchange rate would always represent balance, just as freely determined market prices do not allow for the continuous existence of shortages or surpluses. However, freely fluctuating exchange rates, since they affect so many international prices, inasmuch as exchange rates are the prices of foreign monies, may be intolerable and may be subject to various forms of control. Some of these forms of control and their implications will be discussed later.

22.3. The Terms of Trade and the Gains from Trade

The *terms of trade* is the ratio representing the quantity of imports a nation gets for it exports. In the two-commodity–two-country model cited, the terms of trade must fall between two to one and two to five, the limits representing the ratios between U.S. productivity from resource inputs in automobile or textile production and Eurasian productivity ratios from production of the same commodities, respectively. If the terms of trade approach two to five, the United States is the principal gainer from the exchange. It would get close to one hundred textiles for forty automobiles. If the terms of trade were close to two to one, Eurasia would be the principal gainer from trade, in that it would receive close to forty automobiles for twenty textiles. The terms of trade are a reflection, for a country, of the ratio of prices of imports to prices of exports. This, in turn, depends on what the prices of the commodities which enter into international trade are, in each country, and on the rate of foreign exchange which exists between countries. However, in the two-commodity–two-country model used as an example, the barter terms of trade depend on the relative strength of each nation's demand for the other nation's commodity expressed in terms of the amount of the commodity which each produces itself that it is willing to give up in exchange for the other commodity. Figure 22–1 illustrates this relationship. With automobiles plotted on one axis and textiles plotted on the other axis, the line called "U.S. internal price ratio" indicates the relative prices to U.S. consumers in the absence of trade. Productive resources can produce either automobiles or textiles on a two-to-one basis. If consumers desire more of textiles, they may have them at the expense of less autos, one load of textiles having the same price as two automobiles. The *opportunity cost* of a load of textiles is two automobiles. That is, if resources are diverted from automobile production to textile production, in the United States consumers lose the opportunity to have two automobiles in order to have one load of textiles. Similarly, for Eurasia, the opportunity cost of an automobile is two and one-half loads of textiles.

In trade, each nation can do better because it can specialize in the production of the commodity in which it has the comparative advantage

FIGURE 22–1

THE TERMS OF TRADE

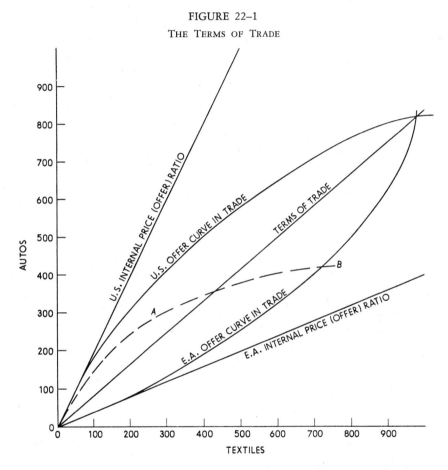

and exchange for the commodity in which it is at the greater disadvantage in production. However, as each nation acquires more of the other's specialty, it must, in turn, give up more and more of its own special product. In accordance with what we know of demand, we could say that the limited remaining supply of its own production would be cherished more, as less was left. The country would insist on receiving a larger quantity of the imported article in exchange for each additional unit of its own export. In Figure 22–1, this relationship is illustrated with the "offer curves" of each country. For example, the Eurasian offer curve indicates in its shape, convex to the horizontal axis, that Eurasia will surrender textiles, which it manufactures, in international trade with increasing reluctance for automobiles as more automobiles are acquired. Similarly, the U.S. offer curve changes in slope to illustrate the changing reluctance of the United States to acquire more and more of textiles in exchange for automobiles. For any actual volume of trade, a straight line from the offer curve drawn to the origin would show the "average rate of substitution" of one commodity for the other. Where the two offer curves intersect, the average rates of substitution are the same; the basis for trade is established; and the terms of trade are set. If the United States became less eager to trade, a new offer curve would be established, represented by the dotted line *AB* on Figure 22–1, and a new terms of trade, more favorable to the United States, would result.

The gain from trade is illustrated in Matrix (22.3) as compared with Matrix (22.2). The terms of trade depend on the strength of each nation's demand for the other's product, as illustrated in Figure 22–1. A nation could attempt to improve its terms of trade by discouraging its inhabitants from importing, thus driving down the price received abroad for imports because of lessened demand. In doing so, however, it reduces the total potential gain which could be achieved through international specialization.

22.4. The Determinants of Relative Productivity Differences

The case for international trade rests upon the existence of relative differences in productivity for different commodities among nations. If each nation had the same internal production possibilities among all commodities, there would be no basis for international trade to exist, even though one nation were more productive in everything than some other nation, for there would be nothing that the first nation would be willing to receive in exchange from the other country. The differences in productivity arise from the unequal endowments of productive resources among countries. In the first instance, there are the natural resources: climate; pastoral and tillable land; mineral, water, and forest resources. The areas of the world are differently endowed with these resources. Although there is absolute immobility of natural resources among regions, to a certain extent the disadvantages which some nations possess with respect to the possession of natural advantage can be overcome by means of technological developments. Air conditioning can create the needed humidity for textile manufacture. Irrigation can water the desert. Synthetic rubber can replace natural rubber. Nevertheless, the differences in natural resources as a basis for interregional trade will continue to persist.

With respect to labor and capital, similar differences in quantity and quality prevail. If one region of the world is possessor of a large number of unskilled laborers, that would tend to give that region an advantage in the production of commodities in which much unskilled labor is involved, for such labor would be relatively inexpensive. Another region may possess, because of earlier shifts in productivity and because of the existence of a certain set of social institutions, a rather large number of technicians. Germany, before World War I, had a great many chemists and was pre-eminent among nations in the chemicals industry. With respect to the productive resource, labor, it is a combination of numbers and "know-how" which determines relative wage structure and consequently determines in which commodities each country will possess cost advantages.

Capital, in the form of machines, buildings, power plants, automotive equipment, and any other produced goods intended for further production, is very unequally distributed throughout the world. A nation's possession of capital depends on the past savings of its people, on its current ratio of consumption to production, and on any investments which have entered the country from abroad. In a very poor country it is difficult to supply the subsistence needs of the people, to say nothing of using a part of current production for capital purposes. At the same time, there is a limit on the amount of foreign investment which such a country can absorb, inasmuch as it requires the diversion of local resources to capital purposes as well as foreign capital in order to add to the productive equipment of the country. As a consequence, some nations blessed with institutions and resources which made past capital acquisition desirable and relatively easy will possess plentiful and inexpensive capital goods of high technological capacity and other nations will not. The capital-rich nations would tend to specialize in the production of commodities in which much capital is employed and, because of the relative abundance and low cost of capital, would be able to undersell the world in the products of capital-intensive industries.

Thus we have western Europe, the United Kingdom, and the United States of America specializing in the products of capital-intensive industries. We have Argentina, Australia, and the eastern European countries specializing in the products of land, and we have India, Japan, and other heavily populated countries specializing in products where much direct labor is employed, and each of these areas of the world exchanges its surplus with the other areas of the world.

The mobility of natural resources is nil, except for the export of raw materials to the processing plants located elsewhere in the world. Labor mobility is very low because of all the usual impediments to geographic mobility: ignorance, love of home, financial cost, etc., and because of immigration barriers erected by countries. The mobility of capital is rather low as well. The added risks of foreign investment are such that differences in capital strength of nations will persist. Since the resources which result in production are unevenly distributed and will remain so, the movement of commodities in international trade helps to overcome the deficiencies which each nation possesses with respect to resources. When a foreign demand for products of labor-intensive industries is added to domestic demand, that makes the derived demand for labor greater, and that in turn helps to raise wages and improve productivity for the heavily populated areas. The same follows for the incomes which would be received by the owners of natural resources and capital. It is the exportation of their products which helps to maintain the demand for these resources and hence holds up the income from their employment.

22.5. International Payments

The problems associated with the system of international payments are related to the diversity of payments which must be rendered and to the institutions developed for converting one nation's money into another's for the purpose of rendering payment in international trade. Table 22–1 gives some idea of the complexity of the international payments market. Merchandise trade is by far the most important item in the balance of payments of the United States, but it is by no means the only one. An examination of the U.S. balance of payments for 1960 indicates that there was a "favorable" balance of trade in that year. By "favorable" is meant an excess of exports over imports, of credits over debits. It is deemed favorable in the sense that the country is owed the difference in payment rather than being obligated for the difference. The United States regularly has a favorable balance of trade.

The favorable balance of trade was partially offset by the balance on other services, the military expenditures, and partially supported by the service items which include income from foreign investments, transportation, travel, and miscellaneous services. However, the *current account* showed a positive balance of almost four billion dollars. This was not enough to finance the remainder of the items which appear in the balance of payments of the United States for 1960. The unilateral transfers or gifts made up nearly two and a half billion dollars and the outflow of U.S. capital reached a net figure of nearly five billion dollars. In addition the item "unrecorded transactions" represents the outflow of funds from the United States in the search for higher rates of return abroad or of speculative gains in foreign exchange and other markets. In consequence, the total deficit of the United States for the year 1960

TABLE 22–1

BALANCE OF PAYMENTS OF THE UNITED STATES, 1960

(In Millions of Dollars)

Exports of goods and services, total[1]	27,300
Merchandise	19,409
Services[2]	7,891
Imports of goods and services, total	23,327
Merchandise	14,722
Services	5,557
Military expenditures	3,048
Balance on goods and services[1]	3,973
Unilateral transfers (net)[3]	—2,489
Private remittances and pensions	— 848
Government nonmilitary grants	—1,641
U.S. long- and short-term capital (net)[3]	—4,965
Private, total	—3,856
Direct investment	—1,694
Long-term portfolio	—850
Short-term	—1,312
Government	—1,109
Foreign capital and gold (net)	4,129
Increase in foreign short-term assets and Government securities	2,419
Increase in other foreign assets	8
Gold sales by United States	1,702
Unrecorded transactions	—648

[1] Excluding military transfers under grants.
[2] Including military transactions.
[3] Minus sign indicates net outflow.
Source: *Federal Reserve Bulletin*, October 1961, p. 1265 and *Survey of Current Business*, September 1961, p. 8.

was approximately four billion dollars. This deficit was met by the export of 1.7 billion dollars worth of gold and by an increase in the short-term balances of foreigners in the United States of over 2.4 billion dollars. Although the United States had a favorable balance of trade it had an unfavorable balance of payments that year.

22.6. Financing International Trade

When one breaks down the subdivisions of a balance of international payments into the thousands and thousands of separate transactions which take place, and when these in turn are assigned to the various nations of the world with which the exchanges occur, it is seen that the foreign exchange market, like any over-all market, is very complicated. An oversimplified description of how one foreign exchange transaction might be handled will set the framework for the explanation of the totality. Large banks will have a foreign exchange department where bills of foreign exchange are bought and sold. Hence an importer located in New York and wishing to pay for a shipment of cutlery from England may buy a pound sterling draft at his New York bank. The draft will be an order on an account in a London bank which the importer mails to the seller in England. The British exporter merely presents this check or draft at his own bank for collection through the British clearing system. Or perhaps the importer pays with a draft on a New York bank. In this case the British exporter sells this draft to his London bank which purchases it in the hopes of being able to sell funds on New York to other of its customers in London, or to customers located anywhere else in the world. In essence, then, an import, or any other debit item, creates a demand for foreign exchange or a supply of dollars. Exports and other credits result in the creation of a supply of foreign exchange or a demand for dollars. The demand and supply of foreign exchange is derived from the demand and supply conditions that exist for the underlying transactions. In a foreign exchange market in which there is no official intervention, the rate of foreign exchange (the price of foreign bank deposits) fluctuates in accordance with the shifts in the many factors which determine demand and supply. Furthermore, in a free exchange market, a third country might pay a second country with a draft on a first country. Any deviations in cross rates of foreign exchange would be quickly extinguished by the operations of *arbitrageurs,* who would buy money where it is cheap and sell it where it is dear and, by the impact which they create on demand and supply, cause the price differentials to be quickly ironed out.

Speculators may hold as short-term capital bank balances and highly liquid short-term investments in foreign centers for the purpose of profiting by changes which they believe will take place in foreign exchange rates. Central banks and other official governmental agencies may hold short-term balances as a reserve to be available for ironing out fluctuations in exchange rates that would ordinarily occur from day to day, season to season, and year to year. The official holdings of short-term balances and of gold are called the *international monetary reserves* of a country.

22.7. The Gold Standard

Until about twenty-five years ago, the most important nations of the world were on the gold standard. Under the gold standard a nation's treasury quotes a uniform price for gold in terms of national currency and stands willing to buy or sell gold in any quantity at that price. As a consequence, any party could purchase gold and ship it to another country for sale to the Treasury, and thus acquire the money of that country. All he would lose on the transaction would be the cost of shipping the gold. As a consequence, when nations were on the gold standard, the rate of foreign exchange could not deviate from the gold par of exchange (the ratio between the gold contents of two monies) by more than the cost of shipping gold, a very small percentage change ordinarily. This created relative stability for foreign exchange rates and helped to promote the orderly growth of world trade and investment.

On the other hand, when there was a persistent outflow of gold from a country, that country would undertake measures designed to prevent the gold outflow from taking place, in order to protect its holdings of the monetary metal. These devices generally involved efforts to restrain credit expansion in order to lower prices and make exports of goods rather than gold attractive and imports unattractive. The steps involved also included upward movement in the interest rate designed to attract investment capital on short-term account and hence create an inflow of funds to offset the outflow.

The great changes in international economic relationships which were one of the consequences of World War I eventually brought an end to the gold standard as a national monetary base. The efforts to stem the outflow of gold were so restrictive that deflation and depression ensued, as was the case for England between 1925 and 1931, or were not enough to stop the persistent drain of funds, as was the case for England in 1931 and for France in 1936. Some nations deliberately left the gold standard in order to establish a different foreign exchange rate base for their trade with other countries, as did the United States in 1933.

Whatever the reasons, the international gold standard has a different position today from what it once had. Gold is still treated as an international money, but governments no longer feel constrained to buy and sell gold in unlimited quantities at set prices. The United States is the only large nation which will buy and sell gold in unlimited quantity at a set price, under certain restrictions as to purpose, however, and today most nations reckon their international monetary reserves principally in their holdings of gold and U.S. dollar balances.

22.8. *International Trade and the National Income*

A change in the balance of international payments for a country may have a marked effect upon the level of national income for that country. Also, a change in the trade balance induced by change in the internal level of income may have consequences which bring about the international transmission of the business cycle. In Chapters 16 through 21, analysis of the components of national income was made for a closed economy. That is, it was tacitly assumed that the economy under study was self-contained. Consequently, in Chapter 16, the basic identity in national income statistics was given:[2]

$$(16.5) \quad Y \equiv C + T + S \equiv I + G + C,$$

where Y is national income, C is consumption, T is taxes, S is savings, I is investment, and G is government expenditure.

Analysis was then developed in Chapters 16 through 19 based on the assumption that government could be ignored and that, as a consequence, $T = 0$, and $G = 0$. In Chapter 20, the existence of the impact of government taxing and expenditure was recognized and the model was altered to account for this more complicated system and for the closer approach to reality. As a result of the introduction of government into the model, new parameters were introduced and the equilibrium values of the variables in the system were altered.

When the role of international payments in the national income analysis is added, a somewhat similar addition to the model must be introduced. Consumption is assumed to be consumption of domestically produced goods and services. Part of income is diverted to the consumption of imports. Part of the prices received by firms for the sale of products comes from the sale of exports. If imports are equal to exports, no violence to the original model has been created by adding these additional factors. As a matter of fact, in the long run it can be assumed that the current account of the balance of payments, including unilateral transfers, must be in balance; in the long run, balance between imports and exports must exist. However, in the short run, lack of equality in the credits and debits on current account may exist because of long-term capital movements and because of changes in the size of international monetary reserves held by a country. Therefore, we must rewrite Identity 16.5 to become:

$$(22.11) \quad Y \equiv C + T + S + M \equiv C + G + I + X,$$

[2] See p. 243, in Chapter 16, Identity 16.5.

where M is imports and X represents exports. In effect, the truism of p. 243, Chapter 16, is expanded by the addition of imports and exports. Furthermore, exports may be thought of as an independent variable, responding to outside forces rather than to changes in the size of national income, at least for a first approximation. Imports, however, respond to the size of income, such that $M = f(Y)$, with $1 > dM/dY > 0$. The marginal propensity to import, dM/dY, or MPM, is a fraction of total income, rather than being a fraction of disposable income, since a certain part of government expenditures will be for imported products. As a consequence, the fraction of any increase in income which is spent on imports is temporarily lost to the economy so that MPC is smaller by the extent to which MPM is subtracted from an original concept of marginal propensity to consume. It follows that an increase in imports, other things remaining the same, will lower the level of national income. Conversely, an increase in exports, other things remaining the same, will raise the level of national income.

Investment has been divided into autonomous investment and nonautonomous investment for determining an investment demand function. Similarly, exports could be so divided, for some change in exports is induced by the change in a nation's imports. A rise in imports for Country A, for example, gives additional purchasing power to the rest of the world. To an extent, this increase in purchasing power will result in an increase in imports for the rest of the world (to be identified as Country B in this example). Country B will not increase imports by an amount equal to the increase in its exports since its MPM is less than 1. The extent to which it does increase imports, however, represents an increase in exports for Country A, in what is called a "foreign repercussion effect." Consequently, if the change in income for Country A is known, and if A's MPM is known, then B's increase in exports is known. From that, with knowledge of the increase in B's income which is represented by the increase in exports plus any increase created from the investment demand function as a result of the increase in imports, knowledge is only needed of Country B's MPM to know what the foreign repercussion effect in the form of increased exports for A will be. This in turn would generate more income in A, more imports, and so on until an equilibrium is reestablished.

The relationship between imports and exports is such that a change in economic activity in one important segment of the world tends to be transmitted to other sectors of the world, and, through the foreign repercussion effect, it tends to generate further economic change in the same direction in the originating country. The great depression of the 1930's was suffered in common by all of the countries of the world. The economic boom which has continued since World War II is common to all of the countries of the Free World. The downturn in activity in the United States in 1949 and 1954 was felt in Europe in repercussion as was the recovery of 1950–1951 and of 1955–1956. However, the recessions of 1958 and 1960–61 were not felt in Europe.

Although intended imports may equal intended exports, this is not required for income equilibrium to exist. If the two quantities are not equal, however, income equilibrium can exist only if intended investment and government spending do not equal intended saving plus taxation, and in such a fashion that the identity of Equation 22.11 is satisfied. If we again neglect the role of government in national income determination and consider only private investment and private saving, along with imports and exports, we could say that, if $X > M$, then domestic investment, I_d, must be less than domestic saving. Since $X - M$ represents the current account balance referred to above, we may call it foreign investment, I_f. Then, for equilibrium in national income the following condition must be satisfied:

$$(22.12) \quad S = I_d + I_f .$$

In all other ways, our original analysis of the equilibrium conditions for national income which have been incorporated into Chapter 18 will be the same as it was there.

FIGURE 22–2

EQUILIBRIUM INCOME FOR AN OPEN ECONOMY

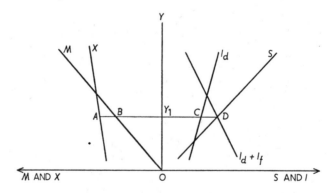

Figure 22–2 is designed to illustrate the arguments developed above. National income is shown on the vertical axis; saving, domestic investment, and foreign investment are shown on the right-hand quadrant; and the derivation of foreign investment, the difference between exports and imports, is shown in the left-hand quadrant. As in-

come grows, so do imports; exports grow to a much lesser extent; savings grow and domestic investment grows to a much lesser extent. At a position where the differenee between exports and imports is just equal to the difference between domestic investment and savings, an equilibrium level of income would exist, Y_1. This could continue only so long as the country is willing to finance an export surplus, that is, to be an international investor. Should reluctance to finance exports to other countries develop, so that the difference between A and B on Figure 22–2 becomes smaller, then the difference between C and D must become smaller. The nation would be forced to a new, lower equilibrium level of national income.

22.9. Problems of National Income and International Equilibrium

When a nation is suffering from a low-level equilibrium income with considerable unemployment, it may attempt to export its unemployment by stimulating exports or discouraging imports in order to increase the positive size of the I_f component. The techniques which it could employ would include foreign exchange rate depreciation, to make imports more expensive in national currency and exports less expensive in foreign currency, export subsidies to stimulate exports, and foreign exchange controls, quantitative restrictions, and high tariff schedules to discourage imports. The consequences for foreign trade are not likely to lead to success in achieving its objective of increasing I_f. Unless the country is willing to finance the to-be-created export surplus by means of grants, long-term loans, or increased short-term capital holdings abroad, foreign countries would lose their international monetary reserves rather quickly and would be forced into equilibrating foreign exchange depreciation of their own, or the foreign countries might simply retaliate with similar devices in a form of economic warfare. The successive waves of foreign exchange depreciation coupled with intensive restrictions on imports employed by nations during the depression of the 1930's did not bring an end to the depression but merely worsened the allocation of resources throughout the world.

The opening of internal markets via protection for import-competing industries might have the effect of improving prospects for internal capital and raising the marginal efficiency of capital at existing interest rates. The induced investment could spur a partial recovery in the rest of the economy through the operation of the multiplier principal. A price would be paid in the form of the creation of inefficient utilization of resources in order to stimulate fuller utilization of resources, a price which, in the short run, may be very worth paying, but in the long run would be a burdensome cost. It would appear that the solution for problems of the business cycle does not lie in the direction of manipulation of the international trade mechanism.

Another related problem is that of the nation which is endeavoring to correct a maladjustment in its international accounts. It may be running a continuous balance-of-payments deficit, or it may be in the relatively favorable position of building up greater and greater surpluses in its international monetary reserves at the expense of other nations. For example, the United States not only ran a deficit of $4.1 billion in 1960, in its total international accounts, but the country has also had deficits continuously for ten years (with the exception of 1957) and expects to run deficits for some time into the future. These deficits have occurred not because merchandise imports exceeded merchandise exports but because the merchandise trade balance has not been great enough to finance the other international economics commitments of the United States. In 1960, for instance, the trade surplus shown in Table 22–1 was $4.7 billion, and the surplus of goods and services exported over those imported (excluding military expenditures) was $7 billion, but the other programs included a net outflow for military expenditures of $3 billion, grants of $2.5 billion, long-term investment abroad of $3.6 billion, and finally almost a $2 billion flight of short-term capital from the country. A restoration of balance under which the gold outflow and the increase in foreign short-term debt of the United States did not occur would require either the abandonment of the international economic programs of the United States which mean so much to the country politically or the application of techniques designed to increase the goods and services surplus.

Three devices could be employed to accomplish the latter. One would be to depreciate the dollar, seeking an exchange rate at which increased exports and decreased imports would create a spread great enough to finance the balance. After all, it was pointed out in Section 22.2 that at *some* rate of foreign exchange the country's international accounts would be in balance. However, the consequences of competitive exchange rate depreciation, as mentioned above, could well result in a situation where the country gained not at all and lost immeasurably in financial stability. This would be the case almost certainly for a country which was already at virtually full employment prior to the devaluation of its currency. Chapter 19 showed how an inflationary surge could occur with no increase in real income accompanying it. This surge could originate from the reaction of both unions and employers to the consequences of exchange rate depreciation. A cost-push inflation would offset in terms of local prices any consequence of depreciation for international prices, and any adjustment in the trade balance that might have ensued.

A second device would include the pursuit of income and price level depressing tactics at home. Monetary policy of the techniques explained in Chapters 15 and 18, and fiscal policy with respect to taxes and government expenditures as indicated in Chapters 17 and 20 could so reduce imports and so cheapen exports that adjustment might occur in that fashion. However, the increase in local unemployment that would be required to bring about full adjustment would be intolerable in a modern society. For instance, the gross national product of the United States in 1960 was $504.4 billion; the exports of goods and services totaled $27.3 billion. An expansion of the trade balance by $4 billion would require so great a change in gross national output that contractionary measures must be discarded as a reasonable choice.

The third device involves the application of protective measures which impede or prevent imports. This seems popular and painless. One might think that he would be putting the burden of adjustment on the foreigners. Nevertheless, the lack of wisdom in such steps becomes apparent when one considers the loss of the advantages which derive from international trade that would ensue. The implications of protection are involved and difficult to comprehend. Consequently, they are examined in some detail in the next sections, Sections 22.10–22.16.

One remaining alternative exists. This is one where careful economizing in international military, assistance, and investment programs prevents these expenditures from expanding unreasonably while promotion of free trade and economic growth helps the favorable balance of trade in goods and services to increase as total international trade expands. In this fashion a forward-looking, expansionary economy might reasonably hope that its deficit problem would disappear in the near future.

The sympathetic treatment of the balance of payments problem of the United States just rendered might seem wholly reasonable to students who are citizens of that country. The similar problems of other countries may not have originated from the same sources and may not respond in so slow and tiny a manner to the attempts made to correct for the maladjustments which brought them forth. Nevertheless, the measures which are available to remedy deficit situations are the same measures just described, and, from the point of view of the citizens of the deficit countries, the remedies may seem just as unpalatable as did the same remedies when examined for the United States. This is one of the reasons why international trade problems are so vexing. They are, as we said at the start of this chapter, bound up with nationalism.

22.10. Impediments to International Trade: To Correct the Balance of Payments

Nations impose impediments on free international trade for four reasons: to protect their international monetary reserves and the balance of payments, to collect revenue, to affect the course of the development of national industry and the internal allocation of resources, and for political reasons. The devices employed are tariffs, exchange controls, quantitative restrictions, and administrative regulations. When any one of these devices is employed, it is frequently difficult to separate out the purposes listed above. Sometimes one purpose is the avowed one, but another purpose is the latent and perhaps the more important one. A brief analysis of the several reasons for restricting international exchange will be given, followed by a short description of each of the devices or techniques which might be employed.

The desire to protect a nation's international monetary reserves and maintain balance in her international payments is, from a short-run point of view, a desirable one. Temporary adverse conditions could cause a drain of reserves to occur. Fluctuating exchange rates might disturb economic relationships more than formal restraint would, or adverse speculation might worsen the extent of change in exchange rates in the absence of formal restraints. A widely fluctuating rate discourages the development of trade and finance on an international basis, and exchange rate depreciation has an impact on the prices of imports and eventually on internal price levels. In addition, depreciation might have a psychological effect leading to internal inflation and further external depreciation of a currency. However, frequently, restrictions on international exchange which seem to have had only a temporary purpose become permanent in that they prevent the correction of the disturbance or conceal the true source of disturbance and allow for neglect of causes.

Crop failure or flight of capital or investment-induced inflation might create a temporary and severe drain on the nation's reserves if the adverse balance is not formally blocked by denying right of access to the foreign exchange market. No exchange rate depreciation can call forth exports of primary products after crop failure. All adjustment would have to be accomplished through the decrease in the size of imports which would be the accompaniment of more expensive foreign currencies. However, certain debits, such as debt service, would remain constant in size and, if quoted in foreign currency, would increase in amount with depreciation. It would seem that arbitrary decreases in the volume of imports and formal refusal to release foreign exchange to finance capital flight might have less serious repercussions for the economy than the retention of exchange market freedom would.

On the other hand, if a currency is overvalued, so that the nation's exports are high priced in world trade, and imports seem very cheap, restrictions on international exchanges which prevent the establishment of an equilibrium rate of exchange (one where the nation's exports are no longer too high in price and imports become somewhat more dear) would have to be maintained permanently, as it is the exchange rate which, like any price, acts as the final rationing device and directs the allocation of resources into export, import-competing, and other domestic industries. However, a permanent deficit in the balance of payments should not be corrected by means of the employment of impediments to foreign trade. The restoration of free foreign trade designed for only temporary application should be accomplished by means of a change in internal national income policy. The relationships involved have been explained in Section 8 of this chapter.

22.11. Impediments to International Trade: For Government Revenue

Some nations think of the exchanges which cross their international borders as an important source for tax receipts. Taxes may be levied on imports, or on exports, or on all international financial transactions. Similarly, multiple foreign exchange rates might be employed, with exporters required to turn over the foreign exchange which they receive to the government at one set of prices and importers required to purchase that foreign exchange at other and higher prices. The difference would be a source of revenue for the government of the country. In underdeveloped nations, taxes on foreign exchanges may be the most satisfactory way of collecting revenue for the government. If wealthy landowners feel the burden of export duties on raw materials, and the same wealthy persons are the ones who consume imported commodities and make international financial payments, taxing such transactions may be the simplest and most equitable tax system that the country could have. On the other hand, for a wealthy country of diversified industry to attempt to justify duties on international payments as a means of acquiring revenue would be difficult on the grounds of equity. In such countries there is no especial reason why producers of exports and consumers of imports should be singled out as special supporters of the government's revenue system. This is not to say that duties on imports which are the equivalent of like taxes on import-competing locally produced products should not be levied.

22.12. *Trade Barriers and Protection of National Industry*

Impediments to imports and to foreign capital transactions which are intended to affect the course of development of national industry and the internal allocation of resources generally are imposed in the name of one of the three following purposes: protection of domestic industry, diversification of industry, and direction and stimulation of economic development.

The case in favor of international specialization and free trade has been offered in Sections 2 and 3 of this chapter. The participants in a certain industry, however, are not likely to feel that they should surrender their market to outside interests in the name of a general improvement in national well-being at the expense of their particular position. In fact, we have pointed out that free trade makes the plentiful resource relatively less plentiful, in that it will be supplying the world rather than only the national market. Similarly, the relatively scarce and expensive resources will become less scarce and expensive if their more plentiful counterparts elsewhere in the world can invade their home markets by means of the commodities which they participate in producing and which are imported into the country. The argument that unskilled and manual labor in the United States would be injured by imports of products from lower-wage countries which incorporate a large amount of the services of unskilled or manual labor abroad is no doubt correct, if that labor does not possess the mobility and the ability to be trained for employment as skilled labor or labor working with machines in capital-intensive industries. A woman who can only produce handmade lace would suffer from competition with the lace-makers of Belgium, under free trade. It appears that the argument for free trade involves the assumption that there is internal mobility of resources as well as external immobility of resources.

Special interest groups make an appeal that their own positions will be injured by free trade. The general and diffused interests of all other groups which gain by free trade for the commodities in question remain diffused and unrepresented before tariff-making bodies. The interests of spring clothespin makers in Maine in a tariff on spring clothespins is certainly genuine, and it is also well represented before the U.S. Tariff Commission. The interest of the rest of the people of the country in the continued importation of inexpensive spring clothes-pins from Norway is just as genuine but it is not well represented before the Tariff Commission.

As far as the national interest is concerned, the only gain to come from impediments imposed for the purpose of protecting domestic industry exists in the case where the local industry is still an "infant" and after attaining size will have lowered costs as a consequence of external and internal economies which might become the accompaniment of growth. Needless to say, the "infant-industry" argument is offered by protection advocates quite frequently. It should be remembered, however, that it is difficult to tell in advance what infants are ever going to achieve those economies of growth that allow for their departure from the sheltering nest of protection.

Somewhat related to the infant-industry argument in favor of protection is the argument that industry in a country should be diversified. This argument rests on the contention that an economy which is dependent upon world trade for an important part of its material requirements is exposed to the course of the international business cycle, to the full consequences of drouth if it is an agricultural economy, to the sequel to the invention of synthetics if it is a raw material exporter, and to being cut off from the world during a war in which it takes no part. As such, the argument is for an increased degree of security at the expense of some efficiency. In reality, no modern nation can become self-sufficient, not even the giants, the United States, and Soviet Russia. But a degree of diversification might be a wholly acceptable goal for a nation to seek.

A special case for the imposition of impediments to the free course of international exchange is sometimes made in the name of economic development. In this argument the infant-industry argument and the diversification-of-industry argument are involved and are reinforced by arguments that it is necessary to change the institutional structure of the country in order to force economic development to occur more swiftly than before and along chosen paths. For instance, the imposition of sumptuary taxes and absolute prohibitions on undesirable imports, such as luxuries, may be imposed in the name of the hoped-for breakdown of a two-class system that may have prevailed in the underdeveloped country since colonial times. Further reference to this case for interfering with the free course of international trade will be made in the next chapter, which is devoted to an analysis of the conditions under which economic development is fostered.

22.13. *Noneconomic Arguments for Protection*

Arguments in favor of intervention in the foreign trade market are offered on noneconomic grounds as well as on economic grounds. It is not the province of the economist to judge the merits of the non-economic goals of society. He must, however, be able to predict what the economic costs of attempting to attain various noneconomic goals may be. For example, one of the major political arguments in favor of protection is the argument that an industry needs to be protected because it would be essential in the event of war or that the type of services which are employed in that industry are the type which will be needed in the event of war. It is argued that the suppliers of these services need to be nurtured in time of peace in order that they may exist when and if war should occur. Such are the arguments under which a national merchant marine is subsidized. And such are the arguments offered by those who desire high protective tariffs against the importation of foreign-made watches and watch movements. The domestic precision instrument industry will draw upon the tools and skills of the local watchmakers in time of war. Of course, sometimes these arguments are absurd with respect to particular products and industries. If the next war is to be a devastating, nuclear war the argument is absurd for all industries, for the problem will be one of postwar recovery, with resources pouring in from the undevastated parts of the neutral world, and not one of sustaining production during a long drawn-out war.

Other nationalistic arguments include the contention that national pride requires that certain industries, particularly in the general area of "culture," exist. For instance, Alexander Hamilton, in his famous "Essay on Manufactures" used as part of his argument in favor of protection for national industry the rationalization that with industry comes cities and with cities comes culture, opera, concert music, drama, etc., which a nation must have to experience its fullest flowering. Another argument, in favor of special treatment for agricultural products in international as well as domestic trade, includes the contention that farmers are the backbone of democracy, the strength of the middle class, and as such they deserve treatment in a special manner which is not to be offered to all other persons.

22.14. *Tariffs*

Whatever the reasons for obstructing the free movement of commodities in international commerce, the techniques which have been mentioned above are designed to accomplish that obstruction or have the effect of accomplishing such obstruction. How these effects exist will be illustrated with a graph representing the consequences of a tariff, and then an interpretation of the similar consequences of other trade-restricting devices will be discussed briefly.

A *tariff* is a tax imposed on a commodity or service when it crosses an international boundary. It is referred to as a *customs duty* when it is imposed on imports. An *ad valorem* duty is levied as a percentage of value, and a *specific* duty is specific in amount, regardless of any change that may take place in value. Figure 22–3 illustrates the consequences

FIGURE 22–3

REVENUE, PROTECTIVE AND REDISTRIBUTION OF INCOME EFFECTS
OF AN IMPORT DUTY

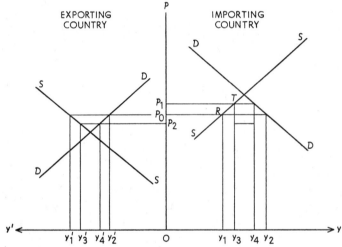

of the imposition of such a tax. Let the right-hand quadrant represent demand and supply conditions for the commodity in the importing country, and let the left-hand quadrant represent demand and supply conditions in the exporting country. It will be assumed that there are no transportation costs between the two countries. In the absence of a duty, the international price of the commodity would be p_0. The exporting country would produce the quantity y_1' and consume the quantity y_2'. The quantity $y_1' - y_2'$ would be exported. The importing country would produce the quantity y_1 and consume the quantity y_2. The quantity $y_2 - y_1$ would be imported and would be precisely the same as $y_1' - y_2'$. The excess supply of the exporting country is equal to the excess demand of the importing country at the equilibrium price.

The levying of a tariff by the importing country is illustrated by the imposition of a charge, $p_1 - p_2$, levied on units of the commodity being imported into the importing country. The consequence would be that price in the exporting country would fall to p_2, production would become y_3' and exports would be $y_3' - y_4'$. In the importing country the price would rise to p_1. Internal production would become y_3 and imports would become $y_4 - y_3$, precisely the same as $y_3' - y_4'$, with internal consumption reduced to y_4. The revenue effect of the tariff would become the amount indicated by the area given by: $(p_1 - p_2) \times (y_4 - y_3)$, but only the amount of the duty $p_0 - p_2$ would be extracted from the exporting country in the form of the lower price which exporters would receive. The remainder of the revenue for the government would be collected from the consumers of the imported commodity. The protective effect of the duty would be demonstrated by the increase in internal production from y_1 to y_3. The redistribution-of-income effect would be in the form of the larger incomes received by internal producers of the commodity in the importing country, indicated by the trapezoid $p_1 p_0 R T$, an increased income which is transferred to producers from consumers of the commodity in the importing country. The remainder of the added revenue, the trapezoid $R T y_3 y_1$, represents the opportunity cost of resources transferred from other employment to the protected industry.

It should be noted here that the figure represents a situation in which a nation both produces and imports the same commodity. This would be the case if the article is produced in an industry of increasing costs, which would have the effect of making the supply curve for the commodity slope upward to the right in the fashion of a normal supply curve. The examples used to illustrate comparative advantage in Sections 2 and 3 of this chapter were based on the assumption of constant costs. That assumption made the development of the model more simple, but it departed from the probable reality of the situation. In another respect, the model illustrated by Figure 22.3 departs from realization of the necessary conditions for international exchange that a decrease in spending on imports by one country means that other countries will be less able to purchase the first country's exports. A loss in productivity because of the reduction in trading potential and because of the uneconomic utilization of resources that would result is not clearly demonstrated in the figure employed to illustrate the effects of a tariff *on a single commodity*.

22.15. Import Quotas

An import quota would have a somewhat similar impact. If the government of the importing country orders imports of the commodity to be cut to an amount illustrated as $y_4 - y_3$ from the larger volume of imports $y_2 - y_1$, which would take place in the absence of the quota, the consequences for international trade are the same, in the first instance, as are the consequences of a tariff. However, although the protective effect and the redistribution-of-income effect would be the same as for a tariff, the revenue effect might not be. If the permits to import the allowed quota were granted without charge, the importers would get the profits, indicated by $(p_1 - p_2) \times (y_4 - y_3)$. If, on the other hand, the government auctioned off the permits to import to the highest bidders, it could, if competition for the permits existed, capture the quota profits for itself in the price it charged for the permits.

In two other respects the import quota operates differently from a tariff. Since price is not the rationer of imports but a quota is, the quota system almost certainly must lead to discrimination in favor of certain countries as sources of the imports and against others. As a consequence, import quotas tend to lead to bilateral trading arrangements, with countries which are important markets for the quota country's exports being able to make a strong case in favor of special discriminatory advantage for themselves in the assignment of shares of the quota. This, in turn, may lead to a situation where the exporters, rather than the importers, control the quota and gather in the profits from the quota privilege for themselves. In this case the price to the importing country of the imports rises to p_1 rather than drops to p_2. The other difference between an import quota and a tariff duty lies in the consequences over time. A change in the general level of prices might make a duty become relatively less burdensome and allow for imports to continue in large volume over the tariff wall. An import quota is specific as to quantity, so that there can become considerable divergence between domestic and foreign prices of quota commodities without there being any effect on the amount traded internationally.

22.16. Foreign Exchange Control

Foreign exchange controls usually operate in one of two ways. One way is to ration foreign exchange among users according to purpose for which the exchange will be used. The consequences, when a mandatory reduction in the amount of imports of a commodity is required by the exchange control authority, are the same as the consequences of an import quota in all major respects. The other way by which foreign exchange control is restrictive as to imports is the employment of a series of rates of exchange for different imports and exports. If importers of a particular commodity are required to pay, in local currency, a specially high price for the foreign exchange with which the import is paid for, the consequences are similar to the consequences of a tariff. The government gains the difference between the price it pays for foreign exchange and the price for which it sells the foreign exchange to importers. With foreign exchange control the potentialities of discrimination among countries are also great. Either one cannot have foreign exchange to import from a country with which there is an unfavorable balance of trade or he may have to pay a price for it which would not be comparable to the cross rate of foreign exchange from some other currency. Countries which do not allow their citizens to buy foreign exchange for some purposes are called inconvertible currency countries, and the currencies are called "soft" currencies. "Hard" currencies are the currencies of countries which do not practice foreign exchange control but instead allow their currencies to be converted into any other currency at the will of the holder. The U.S. dollar is a hard currency. The Turkish lira is a soft currency.

Finally, it might be added, foreign exchange controls may be employed to regulate the flow of funds for other purposes than the payment for imports. Tourist expenditures may be deliberately cut in size, debt servicing prevented, flight of capital or long-term capital investment be regulated, shipment in vessels flying the nation's own flag be encouraged, and private payments for services or grants be controlled. Foreign exchange control may, in effect, create a rate of foreign exchange which is different from the one which the free market would establish. Since the control system implies rationing, it generally means that a nation's money is overvalued by it in terms of other currencies.

Administrative regulations may be deliberately intended to influence the volume of international trade, or they may have another intended purpose. Examples are sanitary regulations which prohibit the importation of food and fiber from other parts of the world with the intention of keeping out plant and animal pests and human diseases. Complicated importing formalities and customs declarations may have the purpose of making for easy enforcement of import regulations, such as mark-of-origin requirements, specification that consular invoices be attached to shipping documents, and involved systems of customs classifications. With respect to the international mobility of resources, immigration laws and requirements concerning the ways in which capital may be employed in a country may have the intention of reducing the inflow of these resources. In addition, all of these types of impediments may be employed to control the export of commodities, labor, and capital. In fact, to an important extent it may be said that international exchange exists in spite of the efforts of governments to impede it.

QUESTIONS AND EXERCISES

1. Assume that in the U.S. a small electronic computer costs $65,000 to make and a roll of barbed wire costs $200 to make. In the German Federal Republic the computer costs Dm.325,000 and the barbed wire Dm.600 to make. If these were the only countries and the only commodities, which country would produce which commodity and why?

2. A production alternatives matrix is as follows:

Alternative Production from One Unit of Resources

	Typewriters (each)	Men's Shirts (gross)
U.S.	40	10
E.A.	20	20
S.A.	4	10

Show under what conditions E.A. will produce only typewriters. Only men's shirts.

3. For the following price matrix, show under what conditions each nation will export wheat. Assume constant production costs and no transportation costs.

Alternative Production Costs for One Unit

	Typewriters (each)	Men's Shirts (gross)	Wheat (ton)
U.S.	$ 50	$200	$ 60
E.A.	Kr.500	Kr.400	Kr.250

4. Indicate the effects on the terms of trade of the United States of:
   a) An increase in tariff levels.
   b) Rapid productivity increases in American manufacturing industry.
   c) Virtual exhaustion of domestic sources of raw material.
   d) A considerably greater expansion in U.S. national income than in the national incomes of other countries.

5. Criticize the implications of the argument used in the advertising slogan for overalls: "Kansas made by Kansas maids for Kansas men and boys."

6. Suppose that in country M, the demand and supply functions for a certain commodity, in the absence of international trade, are:

$$y_d = 56 - p, \text{ and}$$
$$y_s = 2p - 40, \text{ respectively.}$$

In country X, these functions, without international trade are:

$$y_d = 20 - 2/3\, p, \text{ and}$$
$$y_s = 4/3\, p - 4, \text{ respectively.}$$

   a) What would be the equilibrium price if international trade took place, with no transport costs.
   b) If a duty of 5 were levied, what would be the revenue effects of the tariff. How much of this would be "paid" by the importing country? The ex-

porting country? What would be the protective effect of the duty? The redistribution of income effect?

c) Suppose that an import quota of 18 units were established by the importing country. What would be the size of quota profits?

d) Suppose that under a system of foreign exchange control the importing country's currency, the dollar, equaled four units of the exporting country's currency, the krown. Also suppose that exactly Kr.1512 was allocated to pay for imports of the scarce product. What quantity would be imported? What would the import cost be? The importer's selling price?

e) What foreign exchange rate between the dollar and the krown, under a multiple rate structure, would accomplish exactly the same results as the duty?

Chapter 23

FACTORS IN ECONOMIC DEVELOPMENT

In the previous chapter it was pointed out that different nations possess different combinations of productive resources, both in quantity and quality, and consequently, the various countries of the world have attained different levels of productivity. One of the most important areas of inquiry in economics today lies in examination of the reasons for the existence of these differences among nations. As a matter of fact, the outstanding concern of economics as a broad field of inquiry over the years has been with the bases for productivity and economic growth. For example, Adam Smith's famous work, published in the year 1776, was entitled *An Inquiry into the Nature and Causes of the Wealth of Nations.*

Today our concern with economic growth is twofold. On the one hand, we are desirous of knowing what factors are responsible for economic development within our own country, in order that we may recommend policies which lead to continued growth, and perhaps so that our way of life, based as it is on the recognition of the dignity of the individual, will be attractive to others in its promise for material progress to countries which adopt it. On the other hand, we need to know what conditions promote economic development the most surely and swiftly so that we may extend this knowledge and proffer programs and assistance to the underdeveloped nations of the world. In addition, knowledge of the factors which lead to economic growth gives us a basis for analyzing the economic potential of nondemocratic areas of the world.

That there is no single body of economic theory associated with growth is evident. Instead, all of economic analysis is directed toward the goals of maximizing current material welfare and expanding future welfare.

23.1. The Underdeveloped Countries

Perhaps no country has achieved a maximum of material welfare, but, in comparison with one another, countries may be ranked according to the economic level which each has attained. Table 23–1 will

TABLE 23–1

PER CAPITA PRODUCTIVITY, SELECTED COUNTRIES
(In U.S. Dollars; 1955 Except Where Noted)

United States	2,000	Taiwan	162
Mexico	159*	Burma	49*
Guatemala	168	India	54*
Panama	241*	Turkey	211*
Ecuador	147*	Ethiopia	50*
Peru	101*	Kenya	60*
Colombia	197*	Rhodesia	122
Argentina	228*	Union of South Africa	334*
Venezuela	450*	Egypt	110*
Paraguay	96*	Jordan under	$50
Uruguay	297*	Israel	569
Brazil	273	Lebanon	255*
Dominican Republic	191	Angola under	$50
Philippines	181	Ghana	141*
Korea	81*	Cuba	300†

* 1954.
† 1953.
Source: Committee for Economic Development, *Economic Assistance Abroad*, New York, April, 1957, from United Nations figures.

give the reader some idea of the disparity in income between the richest country, the United States, and all of the other countries in the world. The countries cited are merely examples of the relatively low level of income received in many other countries. The figures should be considered to be only generalizations, of course. Inadequacies in the collection of statistics in many countries, the fact that a considerable amount of income in underdeveloped countries is received in kind (that is, goods) rather than in money in a subsistence or barter community, and other difficulties of interpretation exist. Nevertheless, the differences are so great that an examination of their causes should be made. From knowledge of reasons for such disparity in income, we can interpret the factors which are influential in raising income levels, and hence we are able to weigh somewhat more competently the alternative economic programs offered for our own economy.

It is quite clear that differing productive resource endowment is a major cause for differences in per capita productivity and income. If an area of the world lacks such resources in an absolute sense, there is little that can be done to raise its productivity. For example, the Sahara desert, low in product, may be fully developed economically in terms of known technology and known resources existing there. It is where there is a presumption that the quantity and quality of resources can be improved that a problem for economic development exists. The reasons that greater improvement has not occurred in the past must then be associated with the social institutions which exist for the area. As these institutions affect production, they create "social conditions for production."

23.2. The Social Conditions for Production

The most important condition which must be met before growth is to occur is that there be a desire in the people for improvement. The very stirring of the people of the world's great underdeveloped areas is an indicator of the awareness of the possibilities for a higher productive level which had not existed earlier. This vague desire for betterment must be accompanied by willingness to achieve by means of conscious effort and genuine sacrifice of old ways, old leisure, and old ranks before growth can occur. It is one thing for a young man to daydream of the wealth and power he would like to have; it is another thing for him to pursue wealth as a goal. This is an old homily, but it is valid for nations awaking from the past as well as for individuals awaking from childhood. In a country of a high degree of social stratification, the many serfs and poor laborers may not be aware of, or able to acquire, a better economic existence. The lords may be quite content as they are. There may, in this country, be towns where the elite do not want to invite new industry into the community for fear that problems of an unpleasant nature will accompany industrialization and for fear that their positions of power will be challenged. Similarly, the ruling group in a country may have no desire to improve an existence where they are currently on top. The two-class structure of society in many of the colonial economies is by itself alone as much responsible for the low level of average productivity as is anything.

A second essential for growth is the prospect that energy directed toward improvement will yield rewards which can be retained. Since the main devices for increasing productivity are associated with improving the quality of labor and adding to the quantity and quality of capital, there would need to be a combination of opportunity and the right to retain the rewards of effort, thrift, and enterprise before much progress could occur. This requires, then, social mobility and governmental stability, with assurance of the protection of the rights of private property.

Greater impetus towards seeking out the maximum of self-improvement might be expected to come from the carrot, not the stick.

An additional requirement would be that the governmental and administrative machinery of the country be geared to the creation of opportunity and not to the protection of existing vested interests. A corrupt bureaucracy in many countries acts to retard advance since it can be influenced for the preservation of old position rather than the forwarding of the welfare of the total society.

23.3. Human Resources

Several factors may be considered briefly with respect to the contribution which people, of themselves, may make to progress. The factors involved include health, mobility, educational advancement, and enterprise.

An important contribution to progress in many areas lies in improvements in health. A vigorous people can add more to production than an undernourished, sickly people. The elimination of disease, the improvement of sanitation, the bettering of diet have all contributed in bringing about a rapid expansion in population. Thomas Malthus, writing at the beginning of the Industrial Revolution in Europe in the year 1798, contended that population tends to outrun subsistence. He suggested that positive checks to population growth included disease, starvation, and war. Preventive checks would involve late marriage and birth control. For him, the growth of population in the face of limited natural resources made the future of man dismal, indeed—so much so that Carlyle, reading Malthus, called economics the "dismal science." Nevertheless, the very explosion of population growth that was taking place in Europe and the British Isles at that time was accompanied by the great increases in productivity, which have raised that area of the world above all of the rest (with the current exception of North America). The explanation lies in the technological revolution which was the accompaniment of the population upsurge. The improvement in ways of doing things meant that per capita productivity increased, rather than decreased, as the resistance of nature was overcome. Similarly, in the underdeveloped countries, one may despair that population increase will wipe out any potential productivity gain which originates from improved health measures. Nevertheless, if the productivity of a healthy people increases sufficiently rapidly, then improved welfare is the outcome.

In order that people may enjoy the fullest production, it is essential that there be mobility, so that each may seek out the opportunities under which he can gain the most. This requires, in turn, freeing of people from serfdom or from the bondage imposed by caste. Just as both parties benefit from an exchange, there would be gain to all of society from the right of each to seek betterment for himself.

Probably the most pressing need in many of the underdeveloped countries is for skilled labor. Capital expansion may take place but use of the capital may be limited by the absence of persons who are capable of working machines. A form of social capital that would need to precede and accompany private capital formation would be schools and the investment of manpower in the receiving of education. Therefore, one of the ways in which government can specifically speed economic growth is through the fostering of a broad system of education on all levels. Apprenticeship training programs, trade and vocational schools, standard primary and secondary schools, and colleges and universities which train engineers and agriculturists, as well as doctors and lawyers, would be needed. In fact, an index of the eagerness for economic growth in some of the Latin American countries can be constructed from the expansion of the educational system, from the provision of classical education for the sons of the gentry of early days to the offering of technical training of all sorts today. There is a certain cost involved, cost in the sense that labor is temporarily unavailable for direct employment while it is being trained, cost in the staffs of scarce experts who man the schools instead of working in industry and government, and cost in the school buildings and equipment used in the training program. It is relatively easy for the United States to have many good schools. We take it for granted that educational opportunity is available to us. In the poor countries it is difficult and involves assigning scarce resources very specifically to future productivity, to social investment, rather than production of present income, when educational programs are expanded.

An essential element in progress of any sort has been the existence of people who might be called innovators. Brilliant mechanical inventions, great improvements in management techniques, advances in methods of government, the development of military strategy—all come from the genius of the innovators. They are people who depart from the ordinary and traditional in ways of thinking and doing things. If 1 per cent of a population are people who would be innovators, but 95 per cent of the people are submerged in serfdom or are otherwise denied, then only $\frac{1}{20}$ of 1 per cent will be innovators in fact. Similarly, only a small percentage of the people may have the necessary qualities of boldness and imagination to be enterprisers, the persons who put new

ideas to work. Again, if all but a very few of them are unavailable because of the social conditions of production in a country, that country
will be that much delayed in achieving progress. It appears that mobility and opportunity must exist in a society before the advances that
these special people can contribute to the country can really take place.

The discussion of the social conditions of production and of the
human resources in production has been rather general in nature. Some
reflection on the extent to which each of the listed requirements has
been met in the more advanced nations as compared with the backward
countries should, however, allow each reader to supply examples of his
own of the operation of these factors. Similarly, the reduction or expansion of these elements in this country would affect the future productivity of our nation. During World War II, for instance, trained labor
was so scarce that apprenticeship training programs and training-in-
industry programs were instituted on a broad scale for upgrading our
labor supply and for making possible the high production levels of that
period. The stirring up of the people, the enforced creation of mobility,
and the respect for knowledge and skill that we reacquired at that time
after the decade of decay during the depression of the 1930's, have
carried over until the present and helped to make for the dynamic
growth in this country during the period ever since that war. The
movement away from the preservation of the *status quo* of the prewar
years, from the search for security above all else, has been continuing
ever since that time.

23.4. Local Capital and Savings

The other major category of resource, other than natural resources,
is capital. In the underdeveloped countries the amount of local capital
is always very small. There may be little or no surplus above the
production necessary to support the population at minimum levels of
existence. In this event, the acquisition of capital by means of voluntary
self-denial on the part of the population is very unlikely to be of any
volume. Some of the other means of increasing capital, by a richer
society, would operate to a degree, however. The slow growth of capital,
financed out of low-level savings, may continue for generations before
the accumulation of capital is sufficiently great for the explosive increase in productivity for which the people yearn to take place. The
rapid advances in European productivity during the last one hundred
years were the consequence of a slow build-up prior to that coupled with
the exploitation of the possibilities which the technological revolution
allowed for.

Nevertheless, the existence of savings and the channeling of those savings into appropriate investment channels is a precondition for economic development. In Chapter 16, Equation (16.6), $T + S \equiv G + I$, stated a truism that taxation plus savings equals government spending plus investment. And Equation (16.5), $Y \equiv C + T + S \equiv C + G + I$, indicated that only the part of net national product that was not consumed was available for government spending and investment. The need, then, is that consumption be small enough, relative to net national product, for government spending and investment to take place on the scale necessary for development to reach desired levels. Furthermore, government spending in a wasteful fashion would detract from the capacity of the nation to invest and expand. Many underdeveloped countries maintain military forces of a size that is incompatible with growth, even though these forces may be needed to keep the peace where a poor people is restless and inclined to revolt.

The marginal propensity to consume for a poor people (see Table 17–2, page 260) may be so high that little will be saved, and any attempt at increasing investment will only result in price inflation. The country would already be close to capacity production, devoted mainly to consumers' goods, so that few resources would be available for use in investment. The rising incomes engendered by attempts at increase in investment, given a high multiplier $\left(k = \dfrac{1}{1 - MPC} \right)$ would cause an expansion in money income and rising prices without bringing about adequate savings to finance the desired investment at stable prices.

In democratic countries, some means would be needed to increase saving and from that, investment. It is from saving that the financing of investment is made possible. There would also be needed a means to channel the savings into investment uses, by means of the creation of a local money market for funds, so that savings would not be dissipated in outflow of funds or in wasteful expenditures on nonproductive assets. In totalitarian countries the same desired expansion could be brought about by increasing taxes, with government spending becoming investment spending, virtually all capital being publicly owned. In both cases, a potential surplus for investment could exist only if needed consumption did not exhaust the available resources of the country.

The major need in the very poor countries, then, is for an increase in productivity with the existing resources. This is the primary requirement before growth can occur. To a certain extent this increase can be accomplished by the means suggested for changes in the social conditions of production: mobility of peoples, improved health, some education, creation of aspirations which lead to better workmanship. Another source of gain comes from the opening up of international trade. As we observed in the discussion of international economics in the preceding chapter, each area of the world possesses a comparative advantage at some things, depending upon resource availability in the country. The gains which result from specialization and exchange could result for them. Modern Argentina, for example, emerged after the invention of refrigerated shipping made it possible for that country to trade her pastoral products for the manufactures of Europe. It would appear that a raw-material-producing country does not raise its productivity and increase capital accumulation by blindly moving toward national self-sufficiency.

There is generally a class of high-income-receiving lords and landowners, small in number but great in wealth, in the poor countries. Frequently the savings which these people are capable of making do not contribute to capital formation for one of several reasons. The absence of a local money market, of corporations and the securities they issue for mobilizing savings, of stability in government such that property in the form of buildings and machinery will be protected from destruction, and of a sense of local enterprise—all result in a situation where the wealthy invest their savings in foreign countries, causing an outflow of capital from the poor country. Or it may result in a situation where the savings of the rich go into the acquisition of more and more land, a large amount of which may be kept idle, or into the purchase of precious stones and precious metals. In any event, the saving which these people undertake does not result in capital accumulation for the country. In addition, there may be rather rich living by the upper-class people: costly mansions, conspicuous consumption, and maintenance of a standard of life which they themselves can afford but which the nation cannot afford if it is to develop economically. This lavish expenditure often takes place because the motive for saving has never been developed; it is outside the experience and beyond the imagination of the landlord. One of the necessary elements of successful private enterprise society is missing: a democratic spirit under which each of the parties recognizes that duties accompany the rights of individual freedom.

Often social capital, that capital which provides basic requirements for serving other capital, is not adequate for supporting growing productivity. Such capital includes railroads and highways, water and sewer systems for the cities, harbors and docks, schools and hospitals, and power projects and communication systems. Although some of this capital may be provided by private companies, in general, the treatment of public utilities in the underdeveloped countries is such that modern-day expansion of these institutions can only be done with public money; and there is little of that. As a matter of fact, so important is social capital to economic development that there is an observable tendency, which could almost be generalized into a rule, for development to take place around one central city or region of a country, leaving the rest of it in primitive rural existence not much different from that of one hundred or three hundred years ago.

The mobilization of local savings might be accomplished by planned altering of the background for private capital development. Economic planning by the governmental agencies of poor countries could correctly direct growth of a stable legal and monetary structure and the provision of social capital and utility services. Out of such change there might be triggered a rapid growth of local savings directed toward capital formation as well as the attraction of foreign capital into the country. The governments would need financial strength to accomplish much in this direction. This strength might be thought of as coming from formal regimentation of the people in a planned society, from taxation, and from inflation.

Formal regimentation in a ruthless dictatorship can achieve goals of increasing productivity far above what would exist if nothing were done. The cream possessed by the landowners can be skimmed off, the common people can be depressed to a bare subsistence income, and the reward in the form of early higher standards of living which result from self-denial that has continued only a short while might be denied in favor of more rapid capital accumulation. This is what has been done by the U.S.S.R. We reject it for two reasons. It takes away the liberty and dignity of individuals, which is a greater possession than economic riches. And it results in all of the mistakes of interpretation of what is "satisfaction" which autarchical societies make; mistakes which are immeasurable but by their nature must be greater than the mistakes in assigning rewards which the price system might make.

23.5. *Taxation and inflation*

Taxation can accomplish all of the things which ruthless planning can accomplish. It can take the high incomes of the rich from them; it can deprive the poor of part of their low incomes. Taxation, as we observed in Chapters 16 and 20, can be designed for the purpose of reducing consumption and providing the government with income to use for government expenditures. High taxes may block incentives for saving and for growth and improvement, but if a people lacked such incentives prior to the levying of the taxes, nothing additional would be lost from the repressive effects of taxation. However, not as much would be gained as would come from a program which stimulated private effort toward capital accumulation and progress.

Because of the uneven distribution of income, taxation in the underdeveloped countries tends to have its major incidence on the low-income people of the cities. This stems from the fact that taxes are levied on purchases. In rural areas economic organization is so close to self-sufficiency that purchase taxes do not touch the farm dwellers. In addition, taxation may fall on exports and imports. In this fashion it takes from the ones who acquire income from foreign trade, the wealthy owners of the natural resources of the country and the spenders on luxuries purchased abroad. This may have the effect of discouraging international specialization and slowing up the progress which might come from such a source. Finally, there is not much possibility that the ruling class will be willing to tax itself very heavily for an economic development program which, if successful, will alter the distribution of power in the country.

The printing of paper money and the expansion of bank credit to finance governmental deficits, with resulting inflation, is often considered a painless method of raising production levels. Of course this is not so. The real productivity of the country has not been altered, at least in the first instance. However, it may be that the real purchasing power captured by the holders of the new money will be directed toward capital accumulation, while those who have lost the ability to buy goods because of inflationary high prices would only have been spenders had they retained their full spending power. In such a case, *forced saving* is said to result. This seems, on the face of it, to be an excellent method to employ for depriving the people of spending power which can then be directed toward development purposes.

The other consequences of inflation make this course of action less desirable. Inflation results in speculative direction of activity to take advantage of rising prices. There may be more investment in land; there would be the expenditure of capital on the erection of buildings; there would be speculative hoarding of inventories. In the event that foreign exchange rate depreciation did not match the internal inflation, the nation would lose its export markets because of high prices and would want to increase imports. Hence foreign exchange reserves would be dissipated, and uneconomic production would result from the loss of export markets and the inability to import. Inflation would eventually result in a situation where further expansion of money supply would be necessary to pay the wages of people who became organized to resist the losses in real income which inflation was designed to create. In that event, all of the disadvantages of inflation would remain, and none of the advantages. One thing might be said of inflation. To the extent that it does spur capital formation, it indicates that there is a possible surplus, of larger size than the inflation creates, which could be available if savings were mobilized in an orderly way.

The rejection of ruthless planning, of incentive-destroying taxation, and of monetary inflation as means for fostering economic development leaves only the possible creation of social conditions of production which spur growth as a feasible alternative. However, it has been said that creation of social conditions for economic growth is very difficult to achieve and takes a long time to establish. Help for stimulating economic growth that could be important in amount could come from the exterior, from foreign loans and grants.

23.6. The Meaning of Capital Accumulation

Capital may be received into a country from abroad. As a matter of fact, foreign investment has been a principal means of starting a nation off onto a self-sustaining program of economic growth. We shall not, in this chapter, examine the various problems associated with the transfer of capital and technique to less-developed countries of the world. Suffice it to say that the United States has made substantial contributions to economic development in this fashion, as has been indicated for one year in the balance of payments statement in the previous chapter. Other industrial countries take part in this process, as do certain international organizations which are financed by the independent countries of the world.

An idea of the contribution capital makes to economic growth may be redetermined if we repeat certain equations and interpret them for economic growth. Equations (10.1) and (19.13) convey the same information.

$$(10.1) \quad y = f(x_1, x_2)$$

$$(19.13) \quad Q = Q(N, K)$$

Both suggest that output for a commodity is a function of a combination of inputs. Furthermore, the text material which accompanies those equations indicates that the form of the function is one in which diminishing returns appear as production is extended beyond a certain point, if only one of the inputs is varied. Nevertheless, for certain purposes of measuring potential output and for stressing the importance of the employment of capital in achieving desired output levels, the statement is sometimes rendered as a linear equation which can be written:

$$(23.1) \quad Q = sK,$$

or

$$(23.2) \quad K/Q = a \text{ ,where } a = 1/s .$$

Equation (23.1) implies that an expansion in capital gives an expansion in output, where the expansion factor is the parameter s. It would follow that the more capital a nation has the greater would be its output. A similar expression is the expression of "capital-output ratio," which appears as Equation (23.2). The implication associated with this equation is somewhat different. It suggests that there might be different capital-output ratios for different industries and for different economies. As such, this form of the expression is much more useful for the analysis of economic activity than is the former equation. However, even this relationship can be misused. The planners for economic development in a country may desire to employ scarce capital at the point where its contribution to output is the greatest. However, there is no expression of the time period involved in producing output. A dam for a hydroelectric project might produce its output only over a great many years. A factory involving simple machinery for manufacturing clothing might produce its output for just as long a period, or, if the capital is thought of as being the cloth put into the production process, it uses up that capital almost at once.

The fact that the dam may be an essential for the provision of power to the textile mill must be considered. As we indicated above in connection with the notion of social overhead capital, certain capital investments may seed economic enterprise, but which those are cannot be determined by means of capital-output ratio measurements.

The creation of capital, however, would be spurred on by the acceptance of the importance of capital which is implied in the two equations just listed. Since the creation of capital in turn has been related to the savings process, by the equations of Chapter 16, attention to saving may result.

$$(16.9) \quad dK/dt = I \equiv I' - CCA$$

$$(16.12) \quad GNP \equiv NNP + CCA \equiv C + T + S' \equiv C + G + I'$$

It follows that capital formation will be greatest under conditions where the capacity of the country is directed toward investment rather than toward personal consumption or government spending. This is true not only of the less-developed nations of the world; it is true of the great industrial powers as well which have recently seemed to measure rates of economic growth as indicators of the success of their economic and political systems. Sight should not be lost of the other factors associated with growth which have appeared in this chapter. One of these is the labor supply and its utilization. Investment in the improvement of labor skills may be thought of as being the provision of human capital or it may be treated merely as an upgraded labor quantity, of larger absolute value in the equations. Additionally, the social conditions for production, the employed technology, and the over-all acceptance of capitalistic goals (not in comparison to communistic but in comparison to traditional society forms) are a part of the production process. Hence Equations (10.1) and (19.13) could be rewritten in the form:

$$(23.3) \quad Y = A\,(KNT),$$

or even

$$(23.4) \quad Y \equiv AK^n N^m T,$$

where A and T are parameters associated with the state of society and the state of technology, K is capital, N is employed labor, and n and m are exponents which by their value indicate whether the society is experiencing increasing returns, constant returns, or diminishing returns as it increases its employed resources.

Finally, attention should be turned to Equation (8.A.1):

$$(8.A.1) \quad V_t = v_0 e^{rt}.$$

This equation gives the value that a sum V_0 will become after t years at a continuous rate of growth expressed by the interest rate r. Regardless of what reasonable expansions in capital take place, what rate of training of the labor force occurs, and what adaptation of technologies developed over the years in the advanced countries there may be, it will be a long time before the countries listed in Table 23–1 reach the output levels already attained by the United States and reach the levels of political power which stems from industrial strength now enjoyed by only a few countries of the world. Rich productive economic life is not something that has occurred as a matter of luck for the fortunate few nations. It has come as a consequence of plentiful basic resources, productive economic organization, and years of application of effort.

FIGURE 23-1

A SCALE FOR MEASURING GROWTH

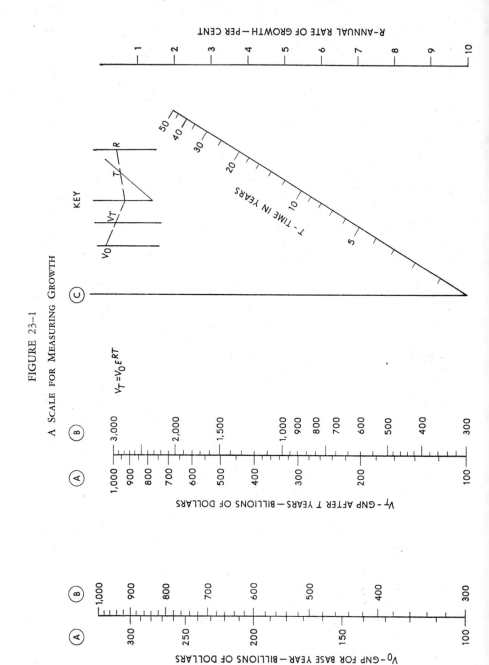

APPENDIX

The accompanying figure,[1] Figure 23–1, is a useful device for demonstrating quickly the relationship between growth rates and the absolute amount of national product of an area. Lay straight edge across the points indicating annual rate of growth as a per cent and the number of years for which this rate is expected to continue to the line C. Another straight line connecting the point on line C thus determined with the given value V_0 will pass through the point V_t showing what that value would become after the passage of T years. For instance, a 3 per cent growth rate for 10 years would cause GNP of 500 in the base year to swell to about 675. An 8 per cent growth rate for the same period would cause the 500 base period GNP to swell to over 1100. The reader may wish to test the possibilities of growth associated with relatively slight changes in growth rates. The U.S. GNP of $504 billion for 1960, if growing at 4 per cent a year, would become $1,000 billion in less than 18 years.

QUESTIONS AND EXERCISES

1. Consider the "social conditions of production" listed in the text and relate them to the development of legal, political, and social institutions in this country. To what extent can you suggest a causal connection between U.S. income and U.S. legal structure?
2. Develop the argument that "a little inflation will stimulate production." Who pays for this stimulation to production? Why do some persons contend that a slight inflation is like a slight drug addiction in its consequences?
3. Look up the current quotations on U.S. and foreign government bonds and draw up an explanation for the differences which exist in their earning rates.
4. "The existence of savings and the channeling of these savings into appropriate investment channels is a precondition for economic development." Why? (What are the appropriate investment channels?)
5. Would a lipstick factory be an appropriate investment for an underdeveloped country?
6. Determine for a country with a current per capita output of $500 the length of time that would be required for per capita output to reach $1,500, if growth is at the rate of 4 per cent per year and population increase is at the rate of 1.5 per cent per year.

[1] Figure 23–1 was drawn by J. Norman Arnold, Professor of Engineering Graphics, Purdue University, for illustrating economic growth patterns. It is reproduced here with his permission

INDEX

I

This book has been set on the Linotype in 12 and 10 point Garamond No. 3, leaded 1 point. Chapter numbers are in 18 point Spartan Medium italics and chapter titles in 18 point Spartan Medium caps. The size of the type page is 27 by 46½ picas.